When Bad Things Happen
to Privileged People

To Jill + Stacy,
with love +
gratitude.
xO
Dara

When Bad Things Happen to Privileged People

Race, Gender, and What Makes
a Crisis in America

DARA Z. STROLOVITCH

THE UNIVERSITY OF CHICAGO PRESS   CHICAGO AND LONDON

The University of Chicago Press, Chicago 60637
The University of Chicago Press, Ltd., London
© 2023 by The University of Chicago
Published 2023
Printed in the United States of America

32 31 30 29 28 27 26 25 24 23   1 2 3 4 5

ISBN-13: 978-0-226-70033-5 (cloth)
ISBN-13: 978-0-226-79881-3 (paper)
ISBN-13: 978-0-226-79895-0 (e-book)
DOI: https://doi.org/10.7208/chicago/9780226798950.001.0001

Library of Congress Cataloging-in-Publication Data

Names: Strolovitch, Dara Z., author.
Title: When bad things happen to privileged people : race, gender, and what
    makes a crisis in America / Dara Z. Strolovitch.
Other titles: Race, gender, and what makes a crisis in America
Description: Chicago ; London : The University of Chicago Press, 2023. |
    Includes bibliographical references and index.
Identifiers: LCCN 2022047040 | ISBN 9780226700335 (cloth) |
    ISBN 9780226798813 (paperback) | ISBN 9780226798950 (ebook)
Subjects: LCSH: Crises—Political aspects—United States. | Equality—United States. |
    Global Financial Crisis, 2008–2009. | United States—Politics and government. |
    BISAC: POLITICAL SCIENCE / American Government / General |
    SOCIAL SCIENCE / Gender Studies
Classification: LCC JK31 .S76 2023 | DDC 320.973—dc23/eng/20221107
LC record available at https://lccn.loc.gov/2022047040

♾ This paper meets the requirements of ANSI/NISO Z39.48-1992 (Permanence of Paper).

FOR MY GRANDPARENTS, HARRY AND ESTHER, WHO MADE IT POSSIBLE.
זיכרונם לברכה.

Contents

Figures

Tables

Abbreviations and Acronyms

ACORN	Association of Community Organizations for Reform Now
AMTPA	Alternative Mortgage Transaction Parity Act
APR	Annual Percentage Rate
ARM	Adjustable-Rate Mortgage
BLS	Bureau of Labor Statistics
CFPB	Consumer Financial Protection Bureau
COC	Office of Comptroller of the Currency
CRA	Community Reinvestment Act
CWPS	Center for Women Policy Studies
DIDMCA	Depository Institutions Deregulation and Monetary Control Act
ECOA	Equal Credit Opportunity Act
Fannie Mae	Federal National Mortgage Association
FHA	Fair Housing Act
FHA	Federal Housing Administration
FIRREA	Financial Institutions Reform, Recovery, and Enforcement Act
Freddie Mac	Federal Home Loan Mortgage Corporation
GPO	Government Printing Office
HAMP	Home Affordable Modification Program
HMDA	Home Mortgage Disclosure Act
HOEPA	Home Ownership and Equity Protection Act

HOLC	Home Owners' Loan Corporation
HUD	Department of Housing and Urban Development
LGBTQ	Lesbian, Gay, Bisexual, Transgender, and Queer
LIWC	Linguistic Inquiry and Word Count
MBA	Mortgage Bankers Association
NAACP	National Association for the Advancement of Colored People
NAREB	National Association of Real Estate Boards
NBER	National Bureau of Economic Research
NCCF	National Commission on Consumer Finance
NCCRC	National Consumer Credit Reporting Corporation
NCLC	National Consumer Law Center
NHA	National Housing Act
NOW	National Organization for Women
OPEC	Organization of Petroleum Exporting Countries
OTS	Office of Thrift Supervision
SFDR	Standardized Factual Data Report
SMMEA	Secondary Mortgage Market Enhancement Act
TARP	Troubled Asset Relief Program
TRA	Tax Reform Act
UCSB APP	University of California, Santa Barbara, American Presidency Project
USPAP	US Policy Agendas Project
VA	Department of Veterans' Affairs

Acknowledgments

When a book takes as long to write as this one has taken me, its author's debts are typically wide and deep. This is particularly likely to be true when that book addresses the politics of crisis and non-crisis and when both its author and the world have experienced several of both in the course of its writing. Writing these acknowledgments consequently fills me with both immense appreciation and also with not a small amount of wistfulness, and at the risk of trafficking in platitudes, it is just true that the last several years have made me extra-grateful to the people, institutions, and resources that have sustained me and my work on this book over the many years of work on it.

As many readers will no doubt have recognized, the title of this book is borrowed and adapted from that of Rabbi Harold Kushner's 1981 best-selling book, *When Bad Things Happen to Good People*. That title—and the book's boldly striped orange, yellow, and black cover—had been seared into my mind's eye after years of seeing it on the shelf of my childhood home in Montreal. In most ways, our two books could not be more different: Kushner's is a theologian's exploration about how to make sense of "G-d's role in an unfair and pain-filled world," while this one is a social scientist's empirical examination of crisis politics and their implications for power and marginalization in the United States. And I confess that the title for this book came to me long before I had ever read Kushner's monograph. When I did finally read it, however, I was struck by the fact that our two books converge, in some ways, around questions about what Kushner characterizes as "the unfair distribution of suffering in the world." While that is pretty much where the similarity ends, I extend my first debt of gratitude (and also my first apology) to Rabbi Kushner.

I owe particular thanks to friends and colleagues with whom I had foundational conversations about the project, several of whom read early versions of one or more chapters. I cannot overstate my gratitude to Paul Frymer, Regina Kunzel, Leslie McCall, and Naomi Murakawa, each of whom read the whole thing and each of whom provided invaluable feedback and encouragement. Naomi also listened to many (many!) iterations of the ideas animating this project over the last many (many!) years. She read early drafts of several chapters (including a few that, on her wise counsel, ended up on the cutting room floor, at least for now) and provided timely and crucial encouragement and feedback on a close-to-final version of the entire thing. Her imprint is evident in so many of the ideas in this book, as it is on my life more generally. I began this project in close conversation with Elizabeth Cohen, and it is as indelibly marked by her ideas and insights as it is by her care and support. Lynn Hudson, Lisa Park, David Pellow, and Jane Rhodes provided support, inspiration, and incredibly helpful and engaged feedback, some of it lakeside, much of it over soup. Writing retreats with Janelle Wong came at crucial junctures, even if (or perhaps especially because) they involved more retreating than writing. I can hardly imagine my work or my life without Janelle's friendship, solidarity, and generosity.

Also foundational were early conversations with Leah Bassel, Akwugo Emejulu, Antonio Vázquez-Arroyo, Yves Winter, and Chris Parker, and I have been as grateful for their ongoing interest in it as I have for their challenging questions about it. Conversations with my University of Minnesota colleagues Karen Ho, Ron Krebs, August Nimtz, Rachel Schurman, Kathryn Sikkink, and Anne Waltner were also particularly formative in the project's early stages. I have also benefitted over the years from the engagement and support of Daniel Aldrich, Lisa García Bedolla, Jonathon Catlin, Cathy Cohen, Kristin Goss, Desmond Jagmohan, Jane Junn, Claire Kim, Desmond King, Suzanne Mettler, Melynda Price, and Susan Sterett. Ben Bagozzi, Amber Boydstun, Emily Gade, Mary Kroeger, Anne Washington, John Wilkerson, and Frannie Zlotnick provided extremely helpful guidance about several data and methodological issues. I am particularly grateful to Laurel Mei-Singh for her close reading and detailed comments on an early draft of the introduction, and to Paul Frymer who, along with Tera Hunter, Stacy Wolf, and Keith Wailoo, also provided support and guidance at a particularly crucial moment. Dan Immergluck and Debbie Gruenstein Bocian were generous with their time during conversations that helped me to understand crucial things about housing foreclosures, mortgage lending, and subprime mortgages, as was Anne Hile, who helped me to understand why it was that lenders were offering me adjustable-rate mortgages to finance the purchase of my first apartment. Jeff Isaac played an important role in the initial re-framing of the project as one focused on the construction of rather than the effects of crises. So did Scott Wong, whose question, "Why is 9/11 the crisis? Why isn't the Bush Presidency the crisis?" was transformative.

I was fortunate to begin my thinking and work on this book in the company of engaged and supportive friends, colleagues, and students in the Twin Cities and at the University of Minnesota, many of whom came through in ways large and small over a period that encompassed some particularly challenging times—crises, non-crises, and often both at once. In addition to many of the people I have already mentioned, I remain grateful beyond words for the support of Kevin Murphy, Kathryn Pearson, and Libby Sharrow, as well as to Bob Burns, Steven Cutri, Chad Reichwald, David Chang, Tracy Deutch, Jigna Desai, Susan Craddock, Anna Clark, Anne Carter, Lisa Disch, Andreas Gailus, Amy Kaminsky, Sally Kenney, Elaine Tyler May, and the members of the Kunzel family. I could not have made it through much of that period without them, nor without the long-distance support (and occasional visits) from Janelle Wong, Naomi Murakawa, Devon Strolovitch, and Drea Barton-Elson. Craig Luedemann, Mary Robechon, and Tim Schwartz merit special mention for their support and general menschlichkeit. I finished the substance of this book in Princeton, NJ, where I benefitted from being in wonderful (and, in my last year there, socially distant and mostly outdoor) company and community with many of those I've already mentioned, as well as with Betsy Armstrong, Anne Cheng, Catherine Clune-Taylor, Jill Dolan, Brian Herrera, Tera Hunter, Allison Isenberg, Amaney Jamal, Tala Kanmalek, Gayle Salamon, Sarah Stazack, LaFleur Stephens-Dougan, Donna Tatro, Wendy Warren, and Stacy Wolf. Princeton also had the tremendous bonus of being Elizabeth Cohen's hometown, and the chance to spend time with her there during her visits home was a gift. I put the finishing touches on the book soon after moving (back) to New Haven. The challenges of relocating during a pandemic were eased considerably by help and accommodations from Katie Lofton, Libby Wood, Jacob Hacker, Alan Gerber, Margaret Homans, Ellen Cupo, and Rod Ferguson, as well as by the generosity and warm welcome of old friends but new colleagues Greta LaFleur, Issa Kohler-Haussman, Allison Harris, and Joanne Meirowitz. I will never be able to thank Vlad Medenica and Olivia Jonynas enough for going not just one but 134 extra miles on the eve of a predicted hurricane to help with our move.

I am also grateful for valuable feedback from participants in many workshops, colloquia, and conferences, including ones at the University at Albany—State University of New York, the University of California, Berkeley, the University of California, Santa Barbara, the University of California, Santa Cruz, the University of Chicago, the City University of New York Graduate Center, Emory University, Georgetown University, Humboldt-Universität zu Berlin, Menlo College, the University of Minnesota's Institute for Advanced Study, Ohio University's Race, Gender, and Sexuality in Law and Political Development workshop, Princeton University's Center for the Study of Democratic Politics, Purdue University, New York University's Gallatin School Critical Disaster Studies conference, the Wayne Morse Center for Law and Politics at the University of Oregon, Oxford University, the Russell Sage Foundation, Stanford University, Tulane University, Vassar College, the University of Virginia, the University of Washington, Western Washington University, and Yale University. I benefitted tremendously from questions, comments, and exchanges during and after all of those talks and panels, particularly those with and from Lisa García-Bedolla, Eva Bertram, Nadia Brown, Geoff Dancy, Michele Dauber, Shirin Deylami, Kent Eaton, Michael Fortner, Andra Gillespie, Colleen Grogan, Ange-Marie Hancock, Matt Jacobson, Alethea Jones, Sally Kenney, Taeku Lee, Michael Leo-Owens, Pei-te Lien, Ian Haney López, Joe Lowndes, Dean Mathiowetz, Michael McCann, Joanne Meirowitz, Melissa Michelson, Jamila Michener, John Mollonkopf, Julie Novkov, Menaka Phillips, Beth Reingold, Gretchen Ritter, Bertrall Ross, Lynn Sanders, Vanita Seth, Sarah Song, Patricia Strach, Megan Thomas, Daniel Tichenor, Khursheed Wadia, Denise Walsh, Vesla Weaver, Meredith Weiss, Patricia Yamin, and Elahe Haschemi Yekani. I am also grateful to Anne Washington for inviting me to participate in the the 2014 PoliInformatics Research Coordination Network Workshop, which she organized with John Wilkerson. I also benefited a huge amount from Jacob Remes's and Andy Horowitz's vision in organizing the 2018 Critical Disaster Studies conference at New York University's Gallatin School, and also from their comments and those of Kerry Smith, Claire Payton, and other conference participants. I am likewise grateful to Serena Laws for her inspired work in organizing the 2020 workshop on the Politics of Credit and Debt, where she, along with Mallory SoRelle, Chloe Thurston, Tess Wise, Patricia Posey, and Emily Zackin, provided helpful feedback at a pivotal moment. I owe special thanks to Rhea Myerscough for her close reading of and extremely helpful suggestions about my workshop paper.

In addition to being a supportive and generative space, the Credit and Debt workshop also brought this project full circle in some particularly meaningful ways, as Serena was one of the first of what would become an inter-generational and nearly trans-continental tag-team of graduate and undergraduate research assistants who helped in many and crucial ways on the project. This fabulous group includes Sophia Cherayil, Chaya Crowder, Maraam Dwidar, Ashley English, Micah English, David Forrest, Emily Gade, Matt Hindman, Jamaal Johnson, Mary Kroeger, Sheryl Lightfoot, Emma McGlennon, Zein Murib, Andrew Proctor, Tanika Raychaudhuri, Adrienne Scott, Libby Sharrow, Marie Siliciano, and Adriano Udani. Libby Sharrow gets special mention for serving as "head RA" for some of the early research and also for their support, wisdom, and generosity at some particularly important stages of the project. Libby, along with Chaya Crowder, Monica Schneider, and Zein Murib, also did as much as anyone to coax me to the finish line, while Zein's and Micah English's coding were invaluable in helping me to cross it. And I simply could not have made it over that finish line without Maraam Dwidar, who provided invaluable advice about and assistance with the US Political Agendas Project data. Likewise Andrew Proctor, whose willingness to help with everything from data analysis to citation conversion, sometimes at the eleventh hour and often when he had too much on his own plate, was invaluable and an absolute gift. Princeton librarians Sara Howard, Jeremy Darrington, David Hollander, and Steven Knowlton were indefatigable in their help as I tried—often in vain—to track down data and sources. Yale Librarians Jennifer Snow and Kenya Flash (may her memory be a blessing) came through with crucial help as the clock was running out. The students in my undergraduate and graduate seminars on Gender and Sexuality in American Politics and Policy (especially those who took those classes in the fall of 2018 and spring of 2019) provided helpful feedback and perspectives, as did many of the students with whom I have been so lucky to work at the University of Minnesota, Princeton University, and Yale University. Cheryl Rackner Olson, Judith Mitchell, Alexis Cuttance, Karen Kinoshita, Susannah Smith, and Angie Hoffman-Walter at the University of Minnesota, Maria Papadakis, Michele Epstein, Jackie Wasneski, Jennifer Bolton, Sandy Voelker, Helene Wood, Greg Blaha, and Jeremiah LaMontagne at Princeton, and Pam Greene, Ellen Cupo, Moe Gardner, and Linda Relyea at Yale all provided much-needed support of various material and other kinds, in some cases far beyond the call of duty.

My graduate school advisors Cathy Cohen, Rogers Smith, and Donald Green remain important influences, as do several undergraduate mentors, particularly Luke Harris, Beth Kelly, Molly Shanley, Peter Stillman, and Uma Narayan, whose classes introduced me to so many of the ideas and questions that have formed the basis for much of my work. The chance to spend time with Luke and Molly as a grown-up colleague has been one of the highlights of my professional life.

Several people and institutions provided the gifts of time, space, and intellectual community. I am grateful for a sabbatical supplement from the University of Minnesota, which—along with support from an American Political Science Association (APSA) Rita Mae Kelly Endowment Fellowship and Centennial Center Operating Fund Grant—allowed me to spend most of a year of leave at the APSA's Centennial Center as I was beginning this project. The University of Minnesota provided other important support as well, including a Grant-in-Aid of Research, Artistry, and Scholarship that helped to support some of the early research for the project. Particularly important were the two semesters I spent at UMN's Institute for Advanced Study (IAS), where Anne Waltner created a unique, supportive, and inspiring environment for interdisciplinary engagement. IAS also gave me the opportunity to co-teach a class on the politics of the global financial crisis with Rachel Sherman, and both she and the course helped me to formulate and explore some of the questions at the core of this project. I am similarly grateful to Princeton University for its generous research and leave support, which (with the help and support of Gary Segura) allowed me to spend a year as a Visiting Scholar at Stanford University's Center for Comparative Studies in Race and Ethnicity and the Stanford Institute on the Politics of Inequality, Race and Ethnicity, where I was also lucky to be neighbours with Carolyn Chen, Dylan Penningroth, and Melissa Michaelson. Support from Princeton's Center for the Study of Democratic Politics was crucial as well. I also thank the Russell Sage Foundation, where I spent a year as a Visiting Scholar, and where Sheldon Danziger, along with Aixa Cintrón-Vélez, David Haproff, Suzanne Nichols, Ivan Ramos, Bethzaida Rivera, Claire Gabriel, Katie Winograd, Eric Bias, Nora Mitnick, and James Wilson, worked to create a welcoming, supportive, and productive environment, and where Jimmy Beglan and Mitch Dorfman extended help and kindness far beyond the call of duty. I was extremely fortunate to spend that year in the company of an amazing group of scholars, and I am particularly grateful to the members of my lively and generative writing group, Yarimar Bonilla, Lynne Haney, Jana Morgan, and Richard Wilson, and to equally generative conversations with and comments from Deirdre Bloome, Katharine Donato, Nikole Hanna-Jones, Jen Jennings, Phil Kasinitz, Nate Kelly, Michal Kurlander, Brian Powell, and Andrea Voyer. The year at RSF also gave me the gift of friendship with Dina Okomoto, Chris Pelton, Issa Kohler-Haussman, and Katie White, who have continued to provide not only feedback and inspiration but laughter and adventures as well. It is also likely that I would not have finished this book without the sustenance and perspective provided by the Chain of Lakes, the towpath, East Rock Park, and so many other outdoor spaces.

In the midst of working on the revisions for this book, I began a term as co-editor of the American Political Science Review (APSR), where Managing Editor Dragana Svraka and Editorial Assistants Jack Greenberg and Nick Ottone have made it (almost!) possible to balance my editorial work with the work to finish this book. And working with the incredible collective of APSR co-editors Sharon Wright Austin, Michelle Dion, Clarissa Hayward, Kelly Kadera, Celeste Montoya, Julie Novkov, Valeria Sinclair-Chapman, Aili Mari Tripp, Denise Walsh, Laurel Weldon, and Libby Wood has been nothing short of inspiring.

Portions of several chapters appeared earlier in "Of Mancessions and Hecoveries: Race, Gender, and the Political Construction of Economic Crises and Recoveries." *Perspectives on Politics* 13 (2013): 167–76. My thanks to *Perspectives on Politics*, the American Political Science Association, Cambridge University Press for permission to reprint them here. Portions of chapters 4 and 5 were published as "When Does a Crisis Begin? Race, Gender, and the Foreclosure Non-Crisis of the 1990s," in *Critical Disaster Studies*, ed. Jacob A. C. Remes and Andy Horowitz, © 2021 University of Pennsylvania Press. I am grateful to the University of Pennsylvania Press for permission to make use of those materials as well. Images from The *New York Times* and *The Crisis* magazine are used with permission.

I would likely not have completed this book without the encouragement, support, and periodic gentle and not-so-gentle nudges from John Tryneski and Chuck Meyers at the University of Chicago Press. I am especially grateful for Chuck's ability to balance reassurance, patience, and prodding during the last stages of the publication process. I am also so incredibly grateful to Sara Doskow, whose compassion and ongoing enthusiasm and support for the project buoyed my work on it at crucial moments when my own energy for it flagged. Thanks, too, to Alicia Sparrow, Joel Score, and Lisa Wehrle for help with copyediting, for their patience, and for shepherding the book through its production, as well to the anonymous reviewers for their engaged reading, for their enthusiasm for the project, and for their enormously valuable comments, critiques, and suggestions.

I don't think my parents, Sheva and Ernie, have ever quite under-stood what I do much less their imprint on why and how I do it. In many ways, however, the origins of this project can be traced to them and their influence, and also to that strikingly striped copy of *When Bad Things Happen to Good People* that lived for so many years on their living room shelf. And thank you, Auntie Susie, for all your help and caring kindness. And while I hope I have caught any evidence of their actual imprints, there is no way I would have finished this book without the help of Jack and Lucas and Henry and Finnegan.

I am always grateful to and for my inimitable and brilliant (and inimi-tably brilliant) brother Devon Strolovitch, and I have been particularly thankful that he has (mostly) avoided calling me an armchair linguist and has instead helped me to understand language and words and so many other things. And because of Devon, I also am so lucky to have Andrea Barton-Elson in my life. Drea's embrace of life is infectious and like al-most nobody else's, except perhaps Ira's, with whom Regina and I still hope very much to one day go to Coney Island—on the F or the Q, which-ever comes first.

And how to acknowledge and thank Regina Kunzel? I have benefited far more than I deserve from her wisdom, humor, and patience, from her close reading and careful copyediting, and from her generosity and loving support. But I am grateful most of all just to have her in my life and that she has been willing to share hers with me for the last almost-two decades. Our next adventure(s) await (kaneinahora)!

Finally, of course, as the song goes, if in spite of all the aforementioned generosity and assistance, any errors have found their way into the pages of this book, they are the sole responsibility of the author.

Crisis Politics

Soon after Barack Obama won the 2008 presidential election, and in the depths of what was at that time the most severe economic downturn since the Great Depression, his then chief of staff, Rahm Emanuel, told a group of CEOs:

> You never want a serious crisis to go to waste.... Things that we had postponed for too long, that were long-term, are now immediate and must be dealt with. This crisis provides the opportunity for us to do things that you could not do before.[1]

Emanuel's remarks received what seemed like endless media play, much of which focused on what many observers regarded as its pithy encapsulation of his opportunistic, Machiavellian, take-no-prisoners style of politics. But his comments were equally striking for what they implied about the political significance of—and about the political work done by—crisis. First, Emanuel's statement reflected the zeitgeist of that first decade of the twenty-first century, a moment at which American politics, economics, and culture seemed increasingly and indelibly marked by an ever-expanding array of calamitous events and phenomena, from Hurricane Katrina, to the BP oil spill, to health pandemics such as H1N1 flu, to the attacks on the World Trade Center and the Pentagon, to the wars in Iraq and Afghanistan, to the economic and financial meltdowns of the Great Recession. Similarly, his suggestion that such phenomena presented opportunities "to do things that you could not do before" reflected the widely held idea that crises are particularly generative moments for political and policy change. Many observers have noted, for example, that the exceptional circumstances of the Great Depression of the first half of the twentieth century had created the opportunities for state intervention that made possible the redistributive and regulatory programs of the New Deal.

At the same time, however, Emanuel's remark that crises bring "long-term" problems to the fore also highlights something more subtle about the political implications of crisis. It reminds us that many of the issues brought into relief by phenomena such as wars, recessions, and health pandemics are not new problems, unanticipated upheavals, discrete incidents, or isolated ruptures. Rather, they are often new or particular manifestations of long-standing problems and conditions that have come to be *understood* as "serious crises," often because they have become newly salient to new—and, as I will show, often dominant and relatively privileged—populations.[2]

Among the circumstances that characterized the period during which Emanuel made this statement, for example, were high rates of unemployment and sharply rising rates of home foreclosures. Neither of these conditions was truly new, however. Instead, both issues had long confronted low-income people, people of color, and women of all races (particularly women who were sole borrowers).[3] Foreclosure rates had been higher, in fact, among African Americans, Indigenous people, Latinos, and women who were sole borrowers during what was widely regarded as the housing boom of the mid-1990s than they would be among white borrowers and male-breadwinner-headed households during what would come to be labeled a foreclosure crisis a decade later.[4] Similarly, rates of unemployment among women and within Black, Indigenous, and Latino communities had been as high during the economically booming 1990s as they would be among white men during the Great Recession of the early twenty-first century.[5] But although high rates of unemployment and foreclosure had long affected members of these and other marginalized and minoritized groups, dominant political actors and institutions had rarely used the language of crisis to characterize these problems during the previous decades, nor had they typically treated them as exceptional circumstances that created opportunities for state intervention or the chance "to do things that you could not do before."[6]

Considering Emanuel's quip in this light reminds us that it is not inevitable that a "bad thing" will be defined and treated as bad, much less that it will be widely regarded as a policy problem or as an exceptional crisis worthy of and remediable through state intervention and resources.[7] That is, his assertion alerts us to the fact that neither the recognition nor the generativity of a crisis is foreordained. More specifically, it reminds us about what Leah Bassel and Akwugo Emejulu call "the banality of every-day inequalities" and that the persistent difficulties that affect marginal-ized, oppressed, and subjugated groups are more typically normalized by dominant political actors than they are labeled and treated as crises.[8]

In this context, Emanuel's words raise questions about the selective application of the language of crisis and about the relationships among this selectivity, the likelihood that a problem will stimulate state action, and the reproduction of hierarchies, subjugation, and oppression. This context also calls into question the causal direction implied by his asser-tion that crises are things "that we had postponed for too long, that were long-term" but that have become "immediate and must be dealt with." In particular, it suggests that rather than reflecting the severity or urgency of a problem, as he claims, the act of pronouncing that a problem is a crisis is part of what *creates* the twinned perceptions that it is, in fact, severe and urgent as well as the optimistic idea that it therefore should—and, importantly, can—be "dealt with." As I will show, increased urgency is not necessarily what makes political actors treat a problem as a crisis. Instead, whether or not a bad thing comes to be labeled and treated as a crisis is of-ten itself a political outcome, the result of problem-definition and agenda-setting processes that make it one as political actors "organize it into" politics and transform it from an ongoing, taken-for-granted, and natural-ized *condition* into an intervention- and resource-worthy policy problem.[9] Emanuel's formulation thus makes visible the backdrop of persistent problems—what Bassel and Emejulu call "routinised crises"—that *do* "go to waste."[10] It also invites us to examine *crisis* as a major force in the poli-tics of marginalization, first by considering the use of that term to describe some bad things alongside its absence as designator for others, and sec-ond, to assess the rhetorical, political, and distributional conditions for and implications of these variations in its application.[11] Most centrally, it invites us to interrogate the selective application of crisis as well as the implications of that selectivity for the justification of state intervention and material resources and for the ways in which these elements work to-gether to distort, mask, and mystify the political and ideological work that crisis does. In other words, it invites us to denaturalize and analyze the effects of what is arguably one of the most naturalized forms of politics today: the politics of crisis.

This book takes up these invitations by attempting to conceptualize, operationalize, and assess the implications of *crisis politics*, the term I use to refer to the processes that structure the relationship between episodic

hard times and the kinds of ongoing and quotidian hard times that routinely affect and structure the lived experiences of marginalized groups.
Such an analysis, I argue, is critical to making sense of a historical moment
at which the seemingly constant invocation of crisis can seem to render
that word both profoundly consequential as well as vacuous and hollow.
In a political context in which labeling bad things as crises can seem both
ubiquitous and so unevenly distributed, are marginalized groups always
and inevitably the victims of crisis? Or can crises throw the status quo
into disequilibrium in ways that open opportunities for these groups to
improve their lived conditions? Faced with calamities that may detract
attention from ongoing inequities at the same time as they subject the
general population to the kinds of bad things that marginalized groups
face quite regularly, can advocates and movements harness crisis politics
to advance long-standing goals? What, in other words, are the political implications of hard times for groups for whom times are, in different ways
and to varying degrees, always hard?[12]

I answer these questions by systematically exploring the political construction, deployment, and consequences of crisis politics, a concept that
encompasses both those "bad things" that come to be treated as crises by
dominant political actors as well as those that are not afforded this treatment, which I call *non-crises*. Whereas I define *crises* as bad things that are
framed and treated as critical junctures deemed worthy of and remediable through government intervention and resources, I define *non-crises* as
similar or analogous bad things that instead are treated as natural, inevitable, immune to—and therefore as not warranting—state intervention.

Stated most boldly, I argue that understanding crisis politics is key to
understanding the political landscape of the early twenty-first century.
The twinned lenses of crisis and non-crisis, I argue further, are particularly
generative ones through which to understand the persistence and perpetuation of processes that disenfranchise, disempower, and immiserate members of marginalized, oppressed, and subjugated groups—the kinds of "endemics" and processes of "slow violence" that, as Ruth Wilson Gilmore
argues with regard to racism, produce and exploit "group-differentiated
vulnerability to premature death."[13] Engaging insights about the social
construction of disaster and arguments about the discursive power of political language for problem definition and agenda setting, I bring the vast
body of scholarship that treats crises such as wars, disasters, and recessions
as drivers of political and policy change into conversation with work by
scholars such as anthropologist Janet Roitman, who argue that "crisis is

not a condition to be observed" but rather "an observation that produces meaning."[14] Considered alongside the work of scholars like Gilmore who have offered lenses through which to understand the less spectacular but enduring conditions that structure the lives of marginalized groups, I show that whether or not something is treated as a crisis is itself a political outcome that must be explained, and one that produces its own empirical realities and lived conditions.

If Crisis is Ubiquitous, Is Crisis Meaningless?

In a 2014 review of three books about "crisis narratives," political theorist Sascha Engel writes that "numerous recent events have either been identified as crises when they unfolded, or are retroactively identified as crises." One might be tempted, he continues (quoting Michel Serres's 2014 book *Times of Crisis: What the Financial Crisis Revealed and How to Reinvent our Lives and Future*), "to consider all these at once and to diagnose that the first decades of the twenty-first century 'have seen the radical transformation of our relations to the world and nature,' culminating in a 'global crisis.' "[15]

In this environment of seemingly pervasive rhetorical invocations of crisis, one might be forgiven for wondering whether crisis is a concept in urgent need of scrutiny, whether it has become so deeply naturalized that it evades critique, or whether it has become so overdetermined as to prohibit analysis. Historian Reinhart Koselleck, for example, indicts the media for their profligate use of the term, employing it, he argues, "interchangeably with 'unrest,' 'conflict,' 'revolution,' and to describe vaguely disturbing moods or situations."[16] The concept of crisis, he contends, "which once had the power to pose unavoidable, harsh and nonnegotiable alternatives, has been transformed to fit the uncertainties of whatever might be favored at a given moment."[17] Legal scholar Peter Schuck argues similarly that terms like *crisis* and *catastrophe* have come to be used "so casually and promiscuously that their meanings have lost whatever precision they may have once possessed, and have acquired that familiar fuzziness that marks so much of our popular discourse."[18] "Crisis in Afghanistan, crisis in Darfur, crisis in Iran, crisis in Iraq, crisis in the Congo, crisis in Cairo, crisis in the Middle East, crisis in Main Street," writes Roitman.[19] Crisis, she argues, has become "an omnipresent sign in almost all forms of narrative today," mobilized as "the defining category of our contemporary situation" and "the most common and most pervasive qualifier of contemporary historical conditions." Surveying the "bibliography in the social sciences and popular press" of the preceding decade, Roitman concludes that "crisis texts are a veritable industry."[20]

Although invocations of crisis and their deployment to explain or justify political action might seem to have increased at an alarming pace over the last few decades, neither they nor concerns about their overuse are new, nor are they unique to the early twenty-first century.[21] Randolph Starn declared in the opening sentences of his 1971 article, "Historians and Crisis," for example, "that this is an 'age of crisis' seems the least controversial of statements. Old enemies, theology and science, Right and Left, swear by it; all the evidence is said to prove it."[22] French sociologist Edgar Morin lamented in his provocatively titled 1976 essay, "Pour une crisologie," that "the notion of crisis" had spread in the twentieth century "to every horizon of contemporary consciousness," leaving "no area or issue that is not haunted by the idea of crisis: capitalism, society, the couple, the family, values, youth, science, law, civilization, humanity."[23] And in 1999, two years before 9/11 and during a period more commonly recalled as "crisis-free," British scholar Colin Hay noted that "the concept of 'crisis' is ubiquitous within eighteenth, nineteenth and twentieth-century social and political thought. Despite, or perhaps because of, this pervasiveness, it remains one of the most illusive, imprecise and generally unspecified concepts within the theoreticians' armoury." In fact, he concluded, "the more one ponders this, the more it seems likely that the term's ubiquity derives precisely from this notorious imprecision."[24]

Conceptually fuzzy, imprecise, and overdeployed though the term *crisis* might be, bad things to which that designation is applied have long been considered defining elements of global and national politics. Frustrated as he was by its ubiquity, for example, Morin argued that crises reveal gaps in our knowledge as well as "in the very social reality where the 'crisis' appears."[25] Austin Sarat and Javier Lezaun claim that this "revelatory quality" offers "powerful reminders of the fragility of our social and institutional architectures" that lay bare "the conditions that make our sense of normalcy possible."[26]

Indeed, the idea that crises are turning points and precipitating forces in politics, economics, and society has been central in many domains, including medicine, religion, science, culture, and politics. On the left, the allegedly transformative potential of economic crisis was fundamental, for example, to Karl Marx and Friedrich Engel's early ideas about the ways in which capitalism's contradictions would precipitate socialist revolution.[27]

Although, as Bruce Norton explains, Marx himself came to doubt the transformative effects of crises, arguments that "capitalist development inevitably produces ever-deepening crisis tendencies" have continued to influence Marxist thought.[28] Kevin Rozario notes that David Harvey, Marshall Berman, Edward Soja, Frederic Jameson, and Michel Foucault are only a few of the many scholars and critics on the left "who have grasped the peculiar prominence and resonance of disasters in the world that capitalism has made."[29] On the right, Milton Friedman argued in the preface to the 1982 edition of his 1962 book *Capitalism and Freedom* that "only a crisis—actual or perceived—produces real change."[30] As such, crisis remains a potent frame, both as a lens through which to understand events and as a justification for political action.

This potency is particularly resonant in the United States, where what are often taken for granted to be crises have long been thought to play significant roles in political and policy change.[31] Journalist Naomi Klein argues, for example, that corporations and political actors exploit the "shock" of crises to privatize public goods, services, and rights for their own profit, with devastating consequences for low-income people and dire consequences for democracy more generally.[32] Echoing these arguments about what Klein labels the "shock doctrine" of neoliberal "disaster capitalism," Rozario goes as far as to argue that in the United States, crisis's close cousin, disasters, "have made history," playing a long and influential role in "the construction of American identities, power relations, economic systems, and environmental practices."[33] More recently, Ian Bremmer has highlighted what he argues is the unique "power of crises" to command policymakers' attention when it comes to issues such as pandemics and climate change.[34] The belief that crises are generative forces in American politics and policy is likewise evident in the scholarship across many disciplines that has addressed important and widely ranging topics and questions about their consequences: How far-reaching are the effects of crises?[35] How do crises affect civic participation, political campaigns, trust in government, and attitudes toward out-groups?[36] How does crisis rhetoric affect policy outcomes?[37] Do crises increase public tolerance for austerity measures, autocratic power, and contractions in civil liberties?[38] How do governments create crises, how well do they manage them, and what do they learn from them?[39]

Crisis and Marginalized Groups

Scholars have also explored and debated the particular implications of crises for marginalized, subjugated, and stigmatized groups such as women,

Indigenous people, people of color, low-income people, immigrants, and lesbian, gay, bisexual, transgender, and queer (LGBTQ) people in the United States. Many have argued that crises exacerbate preexisting inequities and detract attention and resources from issues affecting marginalized groups. Others such as Gwen Prowse have noted that exogenous shocks have long collided with structural inequalities "to produce catastrophes for members of race-class subjugated communities."[40] Almost by definition, for example, low-income people are likely to suffer more acutely than are more affluent people during economic and financial crises.[41] Because of racial and gender disparities in income and wealth, economic crises disproportionately disadvantage Black and Indigenous people, Latinos, and women of all races and ethnicities.[42] At the height of the Great Depression, for example, one-quarter of American workers were unemployed, but the rate was double that—approaching 50 percent—among African Americans.[43]

Analogous disparities were evident during the Great Recession in the early twenty-first century. In 2009, rates of unemployment among African Americans in the fifteen largest US metropolitan areas were, on average, seven percentage points higher than rates among whites, with differences as high as 13.8 percent in Minneapolis-St. Paul (where white unemployment was 6.6 percent and Black unemployment 20.4 percent) and 10.6 percent in Memphis (where white unemployment was 5.1 percent and Black unemployment 15.7 percent).[44] More recently, both the health and economic effects of what would come to be called the "COVID-19 crisis" took a disproportionate toll on marginalized and intersectionally marginalized groups, as Black and Indigenous people, Pacific Islanders, and Latinos experienced exponentially higher rates of infection and mortality.[45] Members of these same groups also faced higher rates of unemployment, as did women, who were also overrepresented in occupations that faced increased exposure to the virus.[46] This multi-edged and gendered disaster was particularly pronounced among Black women and Latinas, who are disproportionally employed in sectors that were especially hard-hit by the pandemic shutdowns (such as retail, hotels, restaurants, and education) as well as in sectors that left them exposed to the virus (such as healthcare). Women also bore the brunt of the care-related challenges exacerbated by the pandemic, including those related to school closures and to the rapid spread of the virus in elder care facilities, a situation that led many to try to care for their elderly parents at home.[47]

A related body of work has emphasized the crisis-born political constraints, challenges, and setbacks for groups and movements struggling to achieve social, economic, and political change. Jeffrey Berry argues, for example, that events like wars and depressions often lead advocacy groups to prioritize issues like basic economic and physical security, pulling back from their work on what he calls "post-material" issues like civil rights.[48] Calls for national unity during the Civil and First World Wars led to attacks on women's suffrage organizations as unpatriotic, for example, and unions have been similarly attacked for threatening to strike during wars and in the wake of 9/11.[49]

Similarly, a large body of scholarship documents the many ways in which so-called states of exception accompanying wars, natural disasters, economic shocks, and health pandemics have long led to increased public tolerance for—and have long been used to justify—economic austerity and other neoliberal reforms, the consolidation of executive (and often autocratic) power, and contractions in civil liberties, particularly for marginalized and minoritized groups.[50] Kyle Whyte argues, for example, that "people who perpetrate colonialism often imagine that their wrongful actions are defensible because they are responding to some crisis." This "crisis epistemology," he argues further, assumes "that to respond to a crisis, it is possible to suspend certain concerns about justice and morality," with "devastating impacts on Indigenous peoples across ancestral, living, and emerging generations."[51] In an interview with journalist David Sanger, historian Robert Caro went as far as to argue that a central lesson of the effects of the Vietnam War on the Johnson administration's ability to achieve its goals was that "wars kill movements for domestic reform."[52]

And while much of this work takes as given that bad things labeled crises indeed warrant this designation, scholars also show that political institutions and elites create crises, often ones from which they ultimately benefit either politically or materially, and often at the expense of members of marginalized groups. Whyte explains, for example, that in the first half of the twentieth century, the American government flooded the lands of Seneca and Lakota peoples to create dams, actions it justified with the assertion that "the United States needed energy and irrigation to lessen the perceived threat of the Soviet Union in the Cold War."[53] Stuart Hall and his colleagues argue that constructing crime as a "mugging crisis" in the 1970s allowed British elites to shift public attention and blame away from their repressive assaults on and declining conditions of working people and onto Black and Asian people.[54] As sociologist David Pellow summarizes Hall's argument, "some of the very institutions that helped produce and construct this crisis, benefited from it." More generally, he argues, "one person's catastrophe is another person's day at the beach," and "a crisis for one group can be an opportunity for another." Modern market economies "are supposed to produce social inequalities and environmental inequalities," Pellow continues. "Is this a crisis? That depends on whom you ask."[55]

This last point reminds us that crises can cut in multiple directions, and scholars and political observers note that elites may not be their sole beneficiaries. Thomas Birkland and others argue, for example, that "focusing events" such as wars and economic crises can have silver linings for marginalized groups—what philosopher Thomas Homer-Dixon calls "the upside of down."[56] On this view, while material conditions might worsen, crises can also open what John Kingdon calls "policy windows," broadening the "scope of the conflict" and improving conditions within what social movement scholars label the "political opportunity structure" by giving advocates and activists opportunities to push for changes that address the ongoing "bad things" that affect their constituents.[57]

A large body of scholarship presents evidence, for example, that rights and resources for groups including women, low-income people, and people of color have advanced significantly during times of or as a consequence of wars and other crises.[58] Both the welfare state and labor rights expanded dramatically in the context of the Great Depression, and scholars have argued that the same has been true of civil rights during the Revolutionary War, Civil War, the First and Second World Wars, and the Cold War.[59] Scholars attribute the creation of mothers' pensions to the Civil War, for example, and while the wartime patriotism of women's suffrage activists was attacked, some argue that the participation of women in that war and WWI ultimately eased the way for women's suffrage as well.[60] Others have argued that war can stimulate civic engagement, that public sympathy for the poor often increases during hard economic times, and that this sympathy, in turn, can open the door not only for redistributive policies that proved elusive in more prosperous times but also, perhaps, for the kinds of utopian possibilities that Rebecca Solnit characterizes as "a paradise built in hell."[61] More recently, scholars have documented the ways in which the devastation of the HIV/AIDS crisis served as an important mobilizer for LGBTQ people and movements.[62] From this perspective, even if members of a marginalized group suffer materially and disproportionately as a consequence of a recession, a disaster, or a pandemic, the movements and organizations that advocate on their behalf might "benefit" from crises through increased visibility, sympathy, media attention, or donations.

So powerful is the sense that crises are important engines of progressive change in the United States, Michele Dauber argues, that the origins and expansion of the American welfare state were based not in the claims to citizenship that were central to the development of its European counterparts but instead on "precedents drawn from the previous 150 years of federal disaster relief"—relief intended not to alleviate long-standing conditions of poverty but to provide temporary aid to deserving victims of events understood to be outside of their control.[63] "I have come to wonder," Rozario writes, "whether dominant American ideas of progress would even be imaginable without disasters."[64]

In light of both the seeming causal centrality but also the conceptual ambiguity of crisis in ideas about political and policy change, and in the midst of what can appear to be a never-ending onslaught of catastrophes, emergencies, and disasters, there is renewed urgency to interrogate and track the political construction, meanings, deployment, and effects of crisis—to, as Morin implores, "put the concept of crisis in crisis."[65]

Conceptualizing Crisis Politics as an Object of Study

This book attempts to heed that plea. My approach to doing so draws on and is indebted to the insights and interventions of the foregoing important bodies of work, but I ask a somewhat different set of questions about the ways in which crises—and ideas about crises—are implicated in American politics and public policy. First, much of the work in the vast bodies of scholarship in history, political science, and public policy that examine phenomena such as wars, natural disasters, and recessions treats these "crises" as independent variables that drive agenda setting and of political and policy change. In contrast, drawing on ideas from the sociology of disaster and critical disaster studies and on the arguments of scholars who underscore the constructed nature of disasters and crises more generally, I emphasize the development, deployment, and consequences of crisis as a political term, concept, and construct. That is, I treat the definition of *crisis* as endogenous to politics—as a dependent variable that needs to be explained rather than an independent variable that, as Leslie McCall writes, "should be doing the explaining."[66]

Second, while my approach entails examining crisis politics at a general level, my central and more proximate aim is to adjudicate some of the tensions and competing claims about their implications for marginalized

groups. These tensions and claims are thrown into relief by putting con-
structivist understandings of crises into conversation with work that treats
crises as independent variables in the ways I began to do above: On the
one hand, the bad things that shape the everyday lived experiences of marginalized groups are not considered crises unless and until they affect dominant groups.[67] On the other hand, however, once a crisis is "hailed into
being," it can have real and far-reaching political and material reverbera-
tions, both for the lived conditions of marginalized groups as well as for
the possibility of opening windows of opportunity to address long-standing
inequities.[68]

To these ends, the book is animated by and structured around three
central empirical questions about crisis politics: First, how did crisis enter
and come to so structure, even dominate, American political and policy
discourse and processes? Second, are some bad things more likely than
others to be constructed as crises, and if so, what are the political processes
through which this happens? Finally, once a bad thing has been constituted as a crisis, what are the implications of such constructions for the
political opportunities facing marginalized groups, particularly for those
whose marginality is constituted by the intersections of multiple axes of
inequality, including race, class, gender, and sexuality?

These questions contain both an ontological facet—what is a crisis?—
and an epistemological one—how do we/political actors/the state know
what a crisis is? Through my analyses, I show that when it comes to crisis
politics, these two facets are inextricably bound up with one another. In
particular, through inductive examinations of a wide array of evidence, I
begin by showing empirically that crisis neither is a neutral descriptor of
empirically bad things nor has it been a constant in mainstream political
discourse. Instead, crisis politics have a genesis and a distinct historical trajectory, and both their origins and their arc have significant implications
for the politics of marginalization and marginalized groups. We might assume, for example, that bad things are more prone to being labeled crises
the more people they affect, the more they rupture with the past, and the
more amenable they are to government intervention, but this is not the
case. Instead, I show that crisis is endogenous to and recursive within politics. That is, I show that crisis politics are not only *productive of* but also
the *products of* political battles and decisions, and that having a bad thing
"societalized" and recognized as a crisis within dominant institutions is
itself a political goal and victory that often has very real material and
policy consequences, ones that often have feedback effects of their own.[69]

As Iain White and Gauri Nandedkar put it, "crises are truth claims: they are invoked, they define, and, in doing so, they privilege certain ideologies or policy 'solutions' over others" in ways that may lead to different policy interventions and different attributions of political responsibility.[70]

In other words, it does not suffice to ask whether a particular crisis is "real" or "constructed," as the designation of any bad thing as a crisis is always, to some degree, the product of political contestation.[71] As Hannah Arendt argues, "In politics, more than anywhere else, we have no possibility of distinguishing between being and appearance. In the realm of human affairs, being and appearance are indeed one and the same."[72] "We all play language games," Murray Edelman explains in his discussion of Arendt. The goal, in his view, is therefore to understand these "multiple realities," not to try to determine "which position is real or realistic."[73] That is, understanding crisis politics entails stepping back from crisis discourse to recognize and interrogate the "contested truths" the language of crisis smuggles in under the guise of received wisdom.[74] Is it true, as many of us intuit, that the political use of crisis language has risen dramatically? If so, what are we to make of this increase, how can we understand the subtexts and assumptions that underlie it, and what, if anything, can laying them bare help us to understand about the political work that crisis politics make possible or that they frustrate? My analyses shed some light on these issues by mapping the changing political meanings of the word *crisis*, reconstructing the key historical shifts in its political uses, and exploring the implications of these meanings and uses for structuring the politics of power and marginalization.

Studying Crisis Politics Empirically

To operationalize and examine crisis politics empirically, the research for this book combines inductive and deductive approaches and draws on evidence from a range of sources, including content analyses of textual and archival evidence from print media, party platforms, congressional bills and hearings, presidential addresses, and advocacy organizations' publications and congressional testimony. Analyzed in light of insights based in theories of intersectionality, critical disaster studies, and the large body of theoretical and empirical work about crisis and related concepts such as disaster, catastrophe, and states of emergency, this evidence allows for the first examination of the genesis and evolution of American crisis politics and of their implications for the politics of marginalization and injustice in the United States.

Crisis *as a Political Keyword*

I begin with a very literal approach to identifying when and the processes through which crisis politics are constructed and are at work. In particular, I propose that we can start to appreciate their significance and their relationship to the politics of marginalization and oppression by analyzing the evolution of *crisis* as a political keyword. Here I borrow from British cultural theorist and materialist critic Raymond Williams, who uses the concept of "keywords" to capture a phenomenon that he encountered when returning home after serving in the Second World War.[75] As he describes it, the meanings of words like *culture* had multiplied and "shifted" while he was away, "forcing themselves" on his attention "because the problems of [their] meaning" were "inextricably bound up with the problems [they were] being used to discuss."[76]

Although cultural theorists originated the keyword approach, scholars across many disciplines have adopted it to explore the constitutive role of language and discourse in politics and to understand the ways in which "the terms that are used to describe social life are also active forces shaping it."[77] Daniel Rodgers uses a keyword approach, for example, to examine the role of words like *rights, freedom*, and *interests* in American political history and development.[78] Nancy Fraser and Linda Gordon examine *dependency* as a keyword, while Stuart Hall and his coauthors analyze the cultural and political work of the term *mugging*.[79] Patricia Strach draws on this method to examine the use of *family* in politics and policy, and Sarah Churchwell takes a similar approach in examining the origins, history, and significance of the phrases *American Dream* and *America First*.[80] Given its centrality in contemporary American political discourse, it is hard to think of a keyword more ripe for such an analysis than *crisis*.[81]

I bring these ideas into conversation with the insights of scholars such as Stuart Hall, Murray Edelman, Deborah Stone, Joseph Gusfield, Ange-Marie Hancock, and George Lakoff, who argue that language shapes politics and material conditions by constructing beliefs about political causes and effects.[82] To do so, I begin to chart the development and evolution of crisis politics by exploiting the availability of digitized sources including newspapers, government publications, and political documents to track the actual use of the word *crisis* in political discourse and to compare its use on the part of dominant actors with the ways in which is it used by representatives of and political actors from marginalized communities.

Using this blunt but—as I hope readers will agree—powerfully illuminating instrument, I follow the lead of scholars who denaturalize *crisis* by treating it as a political construct rather than as an empirical reality. That is, I show that *crisis* has no inherent political meaning, but instead has achieved its significance through social and political processes.[83] More specifically, the term itself entered the English lexicon as a medical term used to describe "the turning point for better or worse in an acute disease" (according to *Merriam-Webster's Dictionary*). I show that when it first traveled from its scientific origins to politics, it described a relatively narrow set of political and economic turning points, most of which had to do with wars, recessions, and conflicts in or with other countries. I show further that its expanded application to domestic phenomena in the US context seems to have originated among abolitionists and racial justice advocates in the late nineteenth and early twentieth centuries. They repurposed it as part of an effort to change the way in which ongoing and endemic racial oppression was understood: not as an inevitable and eternal fact of nature but rather as an urgent issue facing a critical juncture, one at which concerted state intervention was necessary, justified, and would make a decisive and desirable difference. In the 1960s, dominant political actors took up this meaning as well. But whereas civil rights leaders had pioneered the use of *crisis* in an effort to justify state intervention and resources to address the ongoing struggles of marginalized, oppressed, and subjugated groups, dominant political actors were far more likely to use it to signal that the status quo was under threat and to argue either that state intervention was necessary to address bad things affecting privileged people or to advance neoliberal agendas of state retrenchment.

As *crisis* made this journey from medicine to politics and economics and then to social life, its use as a political term increased markedly and took on four broad clusters of different but overlapping and politically revealing meanings. First among these is what I call *clear-cut crises*—seemingly self-evident shocks and disasters that are understood to be relatively quick, discrete, and episodic. Second, *crisis* came to be used to designate *conditions*—that is, political actors came to use the concept of crisis as a turning point as a way to raise the urgency of long-term domestic problems that had previously been viewed as intractable, shifting the timeframe within which we understand them to stimulate and justify political and policy responses.[84] Political actors also try to stimulate crises through confrontations and disruptions, a meaning that I label *crisis-as-creation*. Finally, *crisis* came to be used as a synonym for a "very bad thing," a meaning that I label *calamity-as-crisis*. Equally significant, however, is that for every bad thing that is constituted as a universalized crisis, myriad others are never so labeled. I show that the constitution of crisis as a way to understand some kinds of bad things therefore also came to constitute its inverse, *non-crisis*—bad things that are not treated as crises by dominant political actors but that have analogues that are.

The idea of non-crisis builds on and is indebted to concepts that scholars have offered as lenses through which to understand the implications of marginalization and oppression. Like "endemics," "slow or premature death," "routinized crisis," "uneventful catastrophe," "everyday state of emergency," "slow disaster," "slow violence," and "withheld violence," for example, "non-crisis" is intended to describe and encompass a range of naturalized, non-spectacular, but enduring conditions such as long-term unemployment, poverty, homelessness, mass incarceration, and racialized and gendered wage disparities and violence that structure the lives and lived experiences of members of marginalized groups.[85] It is also indebted to Rachel Luft's conceptualization of "racialized disaster patriarchy," which she describes as the "political, institutional, organizational, and cultural practices that converge before, during, and after disaster to produce injustice."[86] And like concepts such as "non-issues," "suppressed issues," "un-politics," and "semantically masked crises" that political scientists and policy scholars have developed to describe and understand the political power and powerlessness of these same groups, non-crisis also aims to provide a lens through which to understand the reasons why and mechanisms via which some issues are "organized into" politics, while others are "organized out."[87] Non-crisis brings these bodies of ideas into conversation and specifies that what are often assumed to be long-term *non*-crises often have (usually episodic and shorter-term) counterparts that are treated as aberrant and temporary crises that must—and, as importantly, can—be resolved in order to avoid some disastrous or catastrophic outcome. In these ways, the framework of crisis and non-crisis provides analytic purchase on crisis politics—the processes through which long-term and enduring problems that so often are taken for granted as unalterable parts of the normal political and economic landscape when they are related to naturalized conditions of vulnerability affecting marginalized populations become de-particularized and regarded as universalized and intervention-worthy crises when they affect dominant groups or broader publics.[88]

Crisis and Non-Crisis

Tracing the use, prevalence, and evolving meanings of *crisis* as a keyword inductively illuminates much about the construction of crisis politics but reveals only one facet of this process. So, after establishing in part 1 what *crisis politics* are and that the political meanings of *crisis* have evolved in particular ways in the American context, I move in part 2 to a more deductive examination of the construction and implications of particular crises and non-crises. The analyses in this part of the book place less emphasis on the presence and absence of the word *crisis* and focus instead on examining the processes through which bad times for some groups come to be treated as crises while the bad times endured by others do not.

To do so, I use a set of matched cases through which I explore the particular framings of one "bad thing" that became defined as a crisis, comparing it alongside an analogous "bad thing" that was treated as a non-crisis. Specifically, I compare the ways in which economic reporters and dominant political actors addressed subprime mortgages and foreclosures during what came to be widely known as the early twenty-first-century's foreclosure crisis, comparing this attention with that devoted to these issues during what I label the *foreclosure non-crisis* of the late 1990s. Subprime lending was proliferating and foreclosure rates were, by some measures, higher among people of color and sole-borrower women in the late 1990s than they would be among white and male-breadwinner households during what would come to be labeled a crisis a decade later. I show, however, that economic reporters and dominant political actors neither described nor treated these issues as problems worthy of and remediable through federal intervention during this earlier period. Instead, in a context marked by federal policymakers' efforts to replace redistribution with expanded access to credit, they accepted lenders' "zombie facts" that—in spite of a wealth of evidence to the contrary—women and people of color were "risky" borrowers who did not qualify for better loan terms. They also treated privatized subprime mortgages, rather than government spending or regulation, as the appropriate state action to increase rates of homeownership among women and people of color and to resolve distributional problems more generally.[89] In so doing, they naturalized and particularized the extractive and often predatory terms of subprime loans and the attendant high rates of foreclosure among these two groups, all but precluding the possibility of robust state intervention to address them.

Even after the crisis was "declared," economic reporters and dominant political actors continued to naturalize and particularize these race- and

gender-related inequalities as non-crises, treating the disproportionately
high rates of subprime mortgages and foreclosure among women and people of color as outside of what was understood to be the crisis and beyond
the power of the federal government to remedy. Moreover, while the "foreclosure crisis" elicited a more robust federal response, this intervention
came too late to help members of groups who had been losing their homes
at high rates in the decade before the crisis was declared. These policy interventions consequently did little to narrow disparities in rates of homeownership or to address inequitable and discriminatory access to mortgage
loans. Instead, the kinds of intersecting racial and gender disparities in rates
of high-cost mortgages and foreclosures that were evident in the 1990s have
persisted. The end of the crisis meant, in other words, a return to "normal"
pre-crisis conditions of deeply entrenched and intersectionally constituted
inequalities and injustice. This is the essence of crisis politics.

When Bad Things Happen to Privileged People?

By exposing some of the ways in which the term *crisis* has come to do the
political work that it does, the keyword analysis and the examinations of
the foreclosure crisis and non-crisis reveal some of the processes that fuel
both crisis politics and their role in processes that reinforce and perpetuate inequality and marginalization. First, by denaturalizing crisis, the analyses underscore its malleability and constructedness and remind us that,
contrary to dominant assumptions, crisis is not a material and self-evident
thing, the contours of which we can identify, measure, and distinguish from
bad times or bad things that are not crises.[90] Instead, the history of crisis politics underscores that it is conventions about what is normal and
about whose pain is tolerable that have come to serve as indicators that we
have entered or exited a crisis. The implications of these conventions are
far more than rhetorical: Because these conventions underlie arguments
about when and what kind of state intervention is and is not acceptable
and because they rely on assumptions and practices that reflect, reproduce,
and reconstitute prevailing attitudes and normative expectations about racialized and gendered inequalities, they also justify policies that preserve
and often reinforce the real material effects of both crises and non-crises.

Bringing this understanding of crisis politics to bear on the paired analyses of the subprime mortgage crisis and its non-crisis analogue helps to
understand the ways in which the power and privilege of those perceived

to be affected by hard times serve (1) to construct some troubles as "normal" and others as aberrant and temporary crises that can and must be resolved; (2) to frame problems related to structural inequalities as natural, inevitable, immune to, and therefore not warranting state intervention; and (3) to shape ideas about policy solutions to hard times that are universalized and treated as crises. As such, the cases underscore that the very notions of crisis and recovery are political and ideological constructs, and that conditions of vulnerability, typically naturalized, particularized, and simply taken for granted as part of the normal landscape when they affect marginalized populations, often become universalized as crises worthy of and remediable through state intervention and resources when they affect dominant or relatively privileged groups.[91]

This story is not at odds with arguments that crisis language is overdeployed and imprecise, nor does it contradict the scholarship showing that crises intersect with broader political conditions to present a unique mix of constraints and opportunities to raise the salience of long-standing problems and to exploit policy windows to achieve long-standing goals. But the analyses do suggest that although bad things that come to be constructed as crises can present marginalized groups and their advocates with opportunities to achieve long-standing goals, such opportunities are tenuous and contingent, and they can come with significant costs, particularly for intersectionally marginalized groups. Dauber reminds us, for example, that there was much speculation that national attention to the ways in which poverty left Black residents of New Orleans disproportionately vulnerable to Hurricane Katrina "would cure Americans of their acceptance of racial inequality." In the end, however, she argues that the lesson was "nearly the opposite: that a disaster can temporarily enable even a disadvantaged group to successfully claim large-scale resources while leaving undisturbed their inability to receive help for their chronic condition."[92] Similarly, as Luft writes with regard to disaster patriarchy, crises often "reanimate" the "most regressive elements of gender" and other axes of marginalization and exclusion "that are still embedded in social life." Rather than revealing "the radically new," Luft argues, crises reveal the ways in which "racialized patriarchy has been the underlying logic all along." "Disaster," she concludes, "simply unleashes, concentrates, and justifies its more prominent resurgence."[93] Whyte similarly emphasizes the ways in which treating climate change as an "unprecedented" and "urgent" crisis justifies the extraction of material and moral sacrifices from Indigenous peoples in ways that entrench settler colonial power.[94]

That is, even if it is true that it "takes a crisis" to expand rights and resources for some members of marginalized groups, the dynamics of crisis politics mean that such crisis-born expansions can also normalize and reinforce other axes of marginalization because they often particularize them while also privileging and reinforcing normative constructions of deservingness, citizenship, and belonging.[95] The implication is not simply that some members of some marginalized groups are excluded from the policy changes made possible by crises. Rather, the dynamics of crisis politics mean that inequalities are often rearticulated and exacerbated by precisely those policies that some group members welcome as redistributive and emancipatory. Attaching redistributive and liberatory agendas to crises can therefore frustrate efforts to address inequality and injustice by constraining which issues are addressed, delimiting who gets helped and harmed by the resulting policy changes, and reconstituting racial, gender, and economic orders and identities along new lines. A robust account of crisis politics must therefore pay particular attention to marginalized groups in general and intersectional disadvantage in particular.

Looking Ahead

I hope to provide one such account in the chapters that follow, using evidence from textual analyses to explore the evolution of crisis politics and their implications for marginalized groups. Chapter 1 develops the idea of crisis as a political keyword, exploring the ways in which it has been treated by scholars and introducing a typology of its meanings through which to understand their political constructions and their relationships to the questions about marginalization in which I am most interested. Chapter 2 brings this typology to an analysis of the evolution in the political uses and meanings of crisis on the part of both dominant political actors and political outsiders. I continue this analysis in chapter 3, but whereas the data in the analyses in chapter 2 make possible a bird's-eye view of the evolution of crisis politics, chapter 3 uses some particularly illustrative in-depth examples of the regressions, reversals, and red herrings to which dominant political actors subjected crisis as they appropriated it from advocates for marginalized groups, often deploying it in service of neoliberal attacks on the welfare state by using alleged crises as justifications for the retrenchment or privatization of state resources alongside augmented policing and punishment. Chapters 4 and 5 juxtapose a crisis against an analogous non-crisis, comparing the mortgage foreclosure crisis of the early twenty-first century with what I call the foreclosure non-crisis of the 1990s, using these matched cases to explore in greater depth both the processes and consequences of the crisis constructions illuminated by the keyword analyses.

The book concludes with brief examinations of more recent crises, with particular attention to the coronavirus pandemic, the recession, and the 2020 uprisings against anti-Black racism and police violence. Reflecting over email about the challenges of trying to write about these events as they were developing, political theorist Antonio Vázquez-Arroyo noted that it is difficult to "think through something as it unfolds and to calibrate how much to say at the closing of a book written independently of it," and scholars will no doubt say much more about many aspects of these events in the coming years. Even as I acknowledge that these issues and their consequences are still unfolding, and though my claims are admittedly speculative, I also try to heed Paula Treichler's urging that we "think carefully about ideas in the midst of" crises at the same time that we acknowledge their urgent and "relentless demand for immediate action."[96] To that end, I bring some of the frameworks and lessons of the book to bear on these more recent events to try to shed some light on their political dynamics and to suggest questions they raise about crisis politics and about the implications of hard times for marginalized groups. In addition to illustrating several ways in which crises are simultaneously endogenous to and productive of politics and policy, these more recent crises underscore the durability of a related but somewhat different phenomenon related to crisis politics: the *optimistic belief in* the productive potential of "major crises." In these ways, these events bring us full circle, returning us to newly urgent questions about the relationships between episodic hard times and the ongoing and quotidian hard times that structure the lives of marginalized groups.

PART I

Crisis and Non-Crisis in American Politics

CHAPTER ONE

Crisis as a Political Keyword

"The epidemic of gun violence in our country is a crisis," declared the opening line of an 8 January 2016 opinion piece in the *New York Times*. As a genre intended to draw attention to and mobilize public and elite opinion around issues and events, the use of dramatic language like *crisis* in an op-ed is, by some measures, unremarkable. In the week preceding the publication of this piece, in fact, that word had appeared in thirteen separate editorials and op-eds (eighteen, if we include commentary in other sections of the paper). Of the four pieces that appeared on the *Times*' op-ed page that very day, three made explicit references to a crisis of some kind.[1]

But this was no ordinary op-ed; its author was President Barack Obama, and it was published a month after the December 2015 mass shooting in San Bernadino, California.[2] That shooting was the twenty-fifth documented event of its kind since President Obama had taken office in 2009, and the fifteenth one for which he had offered public remarks up to that point (see figure 1.1).[3]

In the wake of the events in San Bernadino, political observers had noted that with every public address President Obama gave to respond to an incident of gun violence, his frustration and anger seemed to rise ever closer to the surface.[4] With its designation of gun violence as a *crisis* in the opening line (the first of four times that word would appear in the 852-word piece), the op-ed seemed to reflect that frustration and anger, as well as President Obama's growing despair over the unwillingness of congressional Republicans to work with him to address this issue. The president continued by outlining the contours of the tragic situation, telling readers that gun deaths and injuries "constitute one of the greatest threats to public health and to the safety of the American people." "Every year,"

Our Shared Responsibility

By Barack Obama

THE epidemic of gun violence in our country is a crisis. Gun deaths and injuries constitute one of the greatest threats to public health and to the safety of the American people. Every year, more than 30,000 Americans have their lives cut short by guns. Suicides. Domestic violence. Gang shootouts. Accidents. Hundreds of thousands of Americans have lost brothers and sisters, or buried their own children. We're the only advanced nation on earth that sees this kind of mass violence with this frequency.

A national crisis like this demands a national response. Reducing gun violence will be hard. It's clear that common-sense gun reform won't happen during this Congress. It won't happen during my presidency. Still, there are steps we can take now to save lives. And all of us — at every level of government, in the private sector and as citizens — have to do our part.

We all have a responsibility.

On Tuesday, I announced new steps I am taking within my legal authority to protect the American people and keep guns out of the hands of criminals and dangerous people. They include making sure that anybody engaged in the business of selling firearms conducts background checks, expanding access to mental health treatment and improving gun safety technology. These actions won't prevent every act of violence, or save every life — but if even one life is spared, they will be well worth the effort.

Even as I continue to take every action possible as president, I will also take every action I can as a citizen. I will not campaign for, vote for or support any candidate, even in my own party, who does not support common-sense gun re-

Barack Obama is president of the United States.

form. And if the 90 percent of Americans who do support common-sense gun reforms join me, we will elect the leadership we deserve.

All of us have a role to play — including gun owners. We need the vast majority of responsible gun owners who grieve with us after every mass shooting, who support common-sense gun safety and who feel that their views are not being properly represented, to stand with us and demand that leaders heed the voices of the people they are supposed to represent.

The gun industry also needs to do its part. And that starts with manufacturers.

As Americans, we hold consumer goods to high standards to keep our families and communities safe. Cars have to

---

We must do something about guns.

---

meet safety and emissions requirements. Food has to be clean and safe. We will not end the cycle of gun violence until we demand that the gun industry take simple actions to make its products safer as well. If a child can't open a bottle of aspirin, we should also make sure she can't pull the trigger of a gun.

Yet today, the gun industry is almost entirely unaccountable. Thanks to the gun lobby's decades of efforts, Congress has blocked our consumer products safety experts from being able to require that firearms have even the most basic safety measures. They've made it harder for the government's public health experts to conduct research on gun violence. They've guaranteed that manufacturers enjoy virtual immunity from lawsuits, which means that they can sell lethal products and rarely face consequences. As parents, we wouldn't

put up with this if we were talking about faulty car seats. Why should we tolerate it for products — guns — that kill so many children each year?

At a time when manufacturers are enjoying soaring profits, they should invest in research to make guns smarter and safer, like developing microstamping for ammunition, which can help trace bullets found at crime scenes to specific guns. And like all industries, gun manufacturers owe it to their customers to be better corporate citizens by selling weapons only to responsible actors.

Ultimately, this is about all of us. We are not asked to perform the heroism of 15-year-old Zaevion Dobson from Tennessee, who was killed before Christmas while shielding his friends from gunfire. We are not asked to display the grace of the countless victims' families who have dedicated themselves to ending this senseless violence. But we must find the courage and the will to mobilize, organize and do what a strong, sensible country does in response to a crisis like this one.

All of us need to demand leaders brave enough to stand up to the gun lobby's lies. All of us need to stand up and protect our fellow citizens. All of us need to demand that governors, mayors and our representatives in Congress do their part.

Change will be hard. It won't happen overnight. But securing a woman's right to vote didn't happen overnight. The liberation of African-Americans didn't happen overnight. Advancing the rights of lesbian, gay, bisexual and transgender Americans has taken decades' worth of work.

Those moments represent American democracy, and the American people, at our best. Meeting this crisis of gun violence will require the same relentless focus, over many years, at every level. If we can meet this moment with that same audacity, we will achieve the change we seek. And we will leave a stronger, safer country to our children. □

FIGURE 1.1. President Barack Obama's 8 January 2016 *New York Times* op-ed.

he explained, "more than 30,000 Americans have their lives cut short by guns. Suicides. Domestic violence. Gang shootouts. Accidents. Hundreds of thousands of Americans have lost brothers and sisters, or buried their own children." The first paragraph concludes by reminding readers that "we're the only advanced nation on earth that sees this kind of mass violence with this frequency."

Once he had laid out the contours of the problem, he pivoted in the second paragraph to a call for and justification of state intervention and action to address it, stating that "a national crisis like this demands a national response." Conceding that "common-sense gun reform won't happen during this Congress" or even "during my presidency," President Obama insisted nonetheless that "all of us—at every level of government, in the private sector and as citizens—have to do our part." To these ends, he described some of the ways in which he would use his executive power to try to stem the violence: "On Tuesday," he began, "I announced new steps I am taking within my legal authority to protect the American people and keep guns out of the hands of criminals and dangerous people." These steps included background checks, expanding access to mental health treatment, and improving gun safety technology. Although he acknowledged that "these actions won't prevent every act of violence, or save every life," he insisted that they were warranted and would make a difference in addressing this problem. If "even one life is spared," he averred, "they will be well worth the effort."

After castigating the gun industry, its lobbyists, and their congressional enablers for their stubborn opposition to any and all reforms and for their commitment to stymying federally funded research about gun violence, President Obama argued that in spite of this intransigence, "we must find the courage and the will to mobilize, organize and do what a strong, sensible country does in response to a crisis like this one." Readers who wondered what kind of crisis "this one" was "like" soon got their answer when he compared the fight for gun safety to some of the country's major battles for social justice: "Change will be hard," he wrote, and it "won't happen overnight." But "securing a woman's right to vote didn't happen overnight," either, he continued, and neither did the "liberation of African-Americans." Advancing the rights of lesbian, gay, bisexual, and transgender Americans, he reminded readers, "has taken decades' worth of work." "Meeting this crisis of gun violence," the piece concludes, "will require the same relentless focus, over many years, at every level." Underscoring the optimism embedded in the idea that crises can be resolved, he asserted that "if we can meet this moment with that same audacity, we will achieve the change we seek. And we will leave a stronger, safer country to our children."

* * *

These invocations of crisis in Barack Obama's op-ed are suggestive, raising as they do questions about what we mean when we say that something is a crisis, about how we know when or decide that we are in the midst of one, and about how we determine what we can and will do to resolve it. I take up the latter questions in chapters 4 and 5, in which I examine the official and unofficial indicators that policymakers and other political actors use to identify crises, juxtaposing those against the indicators of what I call non-crises, and exploring their political and policy outcomes. This chapter and the next two focus on the first question, examining what these same actors mean when they say that something *is* a crisis.

To do so, I start, as historian Daniel Rodgers has put it, "with the words themselves," analyzing *crisis* as what I call a political keyword by bringing ideas about the constitutive role of language in politics into conversation with scholarship that explains the constructedness of political concepts such as crisis.[5] As Rodgers characterizes his own keyword method, while we often ask "what our political tradition means," a keyword method flips this approach, asking instead "how certain of central words in our putative political creed [are] used: how they [are] employed and for what ends, how they rose in power, withered, and collapsed, how they were invented, stolen for other ends, remade, abandoned."[6] Nancy Fraser and Linda Gordon explain that keywords "typically carry unspoken assumptions and connotations that can powerfully influence the discourses they permeate." They do so, in part, by constituting what Pierre Bourdieu calls a "doxa" — "a body of taken-for-granted commonsense belief that escapes critical scrutiny."[7]

In this way, Fraser and Gordon explain, a keyword analysis extends Michel Foucault's genealogical method by "excavating broad historical shifts in linguistic usage" to unearth, reconstruct, and name what is taken for granted in the use of particular words.[8] Contextualizing "discursive shifts in relation to broad institutional and social-structural shifts" and contrasting "present and past meanings of socially and politically significant words," a keyword approach defamiliarizes taken-for-granted beliefs, critiques them, and illuminates "present-day conflicts."[9] *Crisis* is a word that,

I argue, has become so central to American politics and culture that both are unimaginable without it. But it has not always been the case that crisis has been used in the ways that President Obama deploys it in his op-ed, to signal the need for political and policy change. It is therefore revealing to cut against the naturalized sense of crisis as an empirically meaningful "thing" by unsettling its doxa and subjecting it to scrutiny so that we might understand the work that it does in politics and policy.

From this perspective, President Obama's op-ed is not merely a rallying cry, a *cri-de-coeur*, a desperate plea from a political leader to their constituents to work together to end this particular form of lethal horror. It is also, I argue, an object lesson in what is illuminated by unsettling and denaturalizing the political use of the term *crisis* by understanding and examining it as a political keyword. First, doing so encourages us to ask about historical shifts in the extent to which and the ways in which this now politically charged term has been used in public discourses. As a tip-of-the-iceberg example of what this kind of lens can reveal, we can compare the instances of *crisis* that appear in the *New York Times* during that first week of 2016, when Obama's op-ed was published, to those in the same paper a century earlier. This comparison reveals that the terms *crisis* and *crises* were used 129 times in seventy-seven *New York Times* articles during the first week of 2016 but only 35 times in twenty-nine articles over the course of that week in 1916 (a difference of 73 percent), and that only one of these former instances was in an editorial or commentary piece. It is true that the scale of this difference shrinks when we take account of the fact that the 8 January 2016 *New York Times* contained 187 articles and a word count of just over 140,000 while the 8 January 1916 issue contained only 117 articles and a word count just shy of 60,000. However, as I will show below, even accounting for the significantly smaller size of the newspaper in the early twentieth century, the ways in which *crisis* is used in each of these two eras diverges in substantively significant ways.

This first observation dovetails with a second feature that becomes apparent by denaturalizing the use of the term *crisis* and contrasting its "present and past meanings": Defamiliarizing the word in this way allows us to see that it is not only the frequency with which it is used that has expanded over the past century but that the range of topics with which it is associated has multiplied as well. For example, in early 1916, the United States and the world were in the midst of several significant events including the "grip [flu] epidemic" of 1915–16 and the war in Europe (most immediately at that point the withdrawal of Allied troops from Gallipoli in late December 1915).[10] In this context, it might not strike us as surprising that twenty of the articles using these terms during the first week of 1916 (69 percent) were about issues related to the war, a proportion that increases to 83 percent (twenty-four of twenty-nine) if we include the four references to a political standoff in Britain over conscription to that war. Two additional articles address the "grip epidemic." Of the remaining three instances, one refers to a "personal crisis" that a reporter argued was impeding negotiations between two railroad executives, and a second appears in an article about prison reform advocate George Kirchway, who had recently been appointed warden at Sing Sing prison in Ossining, New York (and who, the reporter speculates, "will face his first crisis" when the anti-reform superintendent of New York Prisons visited the prison that week). The final instance is in a review of *Clemencia's Crisis*, a recently published romance novel by Edith Ogden Harrison.

The limited range of topics with which crisis was associated during that week in 1916 stands in stark contrast to what we find a century later. Whereas in the early twentieth century, crisis was attached mainly to the kinds of issues that, as I elaborate below, I label clear-cut crisis—ostensibly punctuated and discrete events, disasters, and problems such as wars, depressions, and epidemics—by 2016, it was used with reference to a far wider range of topics. This is not to say that it was never used to describe clear-cut crises in 2016: In columns published the same day as President Obama's, for example, op-ed writer David Brooks referred to the recent "financial crisis," while Paul Krugman speculated that China's recent financial problems might cause "a global crisis." However, Krugman also refers later in his column to the recent "subprime [mortgage] crisis." Other topics labeled crises in editorials or op-eds that week included the "coming retirement crisis," New York City's "homelessness crisis," Bill Clinton's 1992 "crisis in momentum" (because he had failed to win his party's caucus and primary in Iowa and New Hampshire), the drought in California, an averted "sectarian crisis" in Saudi Arabia, the "Syria crisis," the "European debt crisis," and police violence in Chicago ("Mayor Rahm Emanuel of Chicago built his career on the claim that he is at his best in times of crisis"; but, it continues, "it will take more than political showmanship to calm the discontent that has roiled the city since November"). The only piece published in the opinion section that day that did *not* use the term *crisis* was a column about North Korea's "nuclear threat."

The foregoing inventory includes only instances of the word *crisis* appearing in the newspaper's designated opinion pages that week. Widening the lens to include columns in its arts, business, and sports sections adds several more instances, including the review of a television series in which the writer takes issue with the show's "endless sense of crisis," a crisis faced by the Seattle Mariners in the 1990s over the possible loss of Ken Griffey Jr. to the New York Mets, speculation about the possible repercussions of a financial crisis in the *Star Wars* galaxy, an "identity crisis" being suffered by the television show *American Idol* in the wake of the departure of its longtime judge Simon Cowell, and an article in the Men's Style section describing an "existential crisis" in the luxury watch industry. Among the issues covered in the *New York Times* during the corresponding week in 1916 that might have been called crises if that word was being deployed in similar ways at that time are an article about a passenger rate increase approved by the Interstate Commerce Commission; a report about a record number of bankruptcy filings in 1915; a piece about a threatened strike by metal workers at Navy Yard; news of investigations by the Department of Justice and the Federal Trade Commission into increasing gas prices; and several articles detailing incidents related to New Years' Eve revelers, including police intervention into street congestion in Times Square, a murder and two stabbings at a bar, and a story about a package that had been delivered to a man in midtown Manhattan that turned out to be a bomb (the title of which was, "Liked New Year Gift, but the Thing Blew Up"). None of these incidents, events, or developments, however, was characterized as a crisis.

Analyzing *crisis* as a political keyword also underscores the extent to which the increasing use of this term and the widening array of topics to which it has come to be attached have made and remade its political meanings. Several such makings and remakings are evident even within the single example of President Obama's op-ed. For example, in labeling gun violence a crisis in the opening sentence, he uses *crisis* as a synonym for and to designate a terrible thing. This designation is an example of the meaning that I call calamity-as-crisis, and it is one that, I will show, came into wide circulation relatively recently.

The meaning of *crisis* and the purposes to which it is put are quite different the subsequent three times he uses it, however. Implicit in his comparison between gun violence and movements for racial justice, women's suffrage, and LGBTQ rights, for example, is an argument that the prevalence of gun violence is an indicator that the country is facing extraordinary times that justify and even demand extraordinary measures, including "the courage and the will to mobilize, organize and do what a strong, sensible country does in response to a crisis like this one." By framing racial justice, women's suffrage, and LGBTQ rights as problems that have been resolved by the "extraordinary measures of the past" and by asserting that a "national crisis like this demands a national response," President Obama is also trying to change the timeframe within which readers understand gun violence. More specifically, he is trying to harness what Kyle Whyte calls the "presentism" of crisis epistemology in an effort to transform readers' understanding of gun violence from an ongoing, intractable, and perhaps even natural "condition" into an imminent, urgent, and discrete problem, one facing a critical juncture at which federal intervention is necessary, justified, and likely to provide a decisive and desirable remedy.[11] And alongside his reference to the thousands of Americans who lose their lives to "suicides," "domestic violence," and "gang shootouts," this reframing—what I call condition-as-crisis—highlights as well President Obama's effort to harness this dramatic and seemingly discrete event as a point of departure from which to argue that readers should be equally concerned about more quotidian forms of gun violence, particularly ones that affect members of stigmatized and marginalized groups.

Keywords and the Constitutive Power of Language

This preliminary excavation of some of the ways in which crisis has been used in dominant public and political discourses and of how this use changed over the course of the twentieth and early twenty-first centuries illustrates some of what can be illuminated by unpacking this increasingly, in Rodgers's terms, "central word" in our "political creed."[12] Originating in cultural studies and long the province of constructivists, keyword approaches have been adopted and adapted by scholars across the humanities and social sciences, and recent developments in the digitization of text have created converts out of many skeptics about the value of the kinds of textual analyses of which a keyword approach is one example. Echoing Rodgers's argument that "political talk is political action of a particular, often powerful, sort," political methodologists Justin Grimmer and Brandon Stewart write, for example, that "scholars of politics have long recognized that much of politics is expressed in words."[13] Because language "is the medium for politics and political conflict," they argue, "to understand what politics is about we need to know what political actors are saying and writing."[14] As Rodgers writes, such political language goes on to "create those pictures in our heads which make the structures of authority tolerable and understandable" and superimpose "some believable sense and durable legitimacy on top of the chaotic motions of day-to-day power."[15]

Keyword and related approaches such as critical discourse analysis do not claim that words such as *crisis* are themselves "causes" or that changes in their use are themselves attributable to specific causal mechanisms. Rather, these approaches emphasize the constitutive power of language as one of several factors that help to shape political reality, including our *ideas about* causes and our attributions of responsibility for outcomes.[16] In this way, keywords are like frames in that, as Robert Entman explains, they work to define problems, diagnose causes, make moral judgments, and suggest remedies.[17] Language, Murray Edelman argues, evokes beliefs about "causes and discontents and satisfactions, about policies that will bring about a future closer to the heart's desire."[18] Ange-Marie Hancock, Deborah Stone, Helen Ingram, and Anne Larason Schneider have argued similarly that language shapes politics by constructing beliefs about political causes and effects, about who or what is to blame for problems, and about the worthiness of particular policy targets.[19] Lisa Wedeen makes the related claim that paying attention to the ways in which certain meanings become authoritative while others do not provides a lens into changing beliefs and assumptions about the world.[20] It is therefore important to understand what salient political terms mean to the political actors "who invoke or consume them and how these perceptions might affect political outcomes."[21] As Fraser and Gordon explain, keyword analyses "assume that the terms that are used to describe social life are also active forces shaping it.[22] "A crucial element of politics," they continue, "is the struggle to define social reality and to interpret people's inchoate aspirations and needs."[23] Particular words and expressions, they argue, "often become focal in such struggles, functioning as keywords, sites at which the meaning of social experience is negotiated and contested."[24]

Cultural theorist Raymond Williams coined the term *keyword* to describe a phenomenon that he encountered when he returned to Britain after serving in the Second World War.[25] Upon his return, he found that the meanings of certain words had "shifted" while he was away. For Williams, "culture" was the "original difficult word," having taken on, as Tony Bennett, Lawrence Grossberg, and Meaghan Morris explain, new and specific meanings in academic disciplines such as literary studies and anthropology, while also gaining importance "in the area of art on the one hand, and society on the other."[26] As this shift took place, Williams argued, "culture" took on "very different significances," "posed new questions, and suggested new connections," thereby, as Bruce Burgett and Glenn Hendler argue, anchoring "new clusters of meaning through its interactions in popular discourse with neighboring terms such as 'art,' 'industry,' 'class,' and 'democracy.' "[27] "I call these words Keywords," Williams wrote, "in two connected senses."[28] First, he argued, "they are significant, binding words in certain activities and their interpretation [and] certain forms of thought."[29] In addition, he continued, "certain uses bound together certain ways of seeing culture and society" while other uses seemed to him "to open up issues and problems, in the same general area, of which we all needed to be very much more conscious."[30]

Keywords do more than shift and add meanings; these meanings also change "in relationship to changing political, social, and economic situations and needs," giving "expression to new experiences of reality."[31] Bennett, Grossberg, and Morris note that "whatever the origins of a word and however erratic the paths it took to enter common usage," for Williams "it was the fact that it mattered in 'two areas . . . often thought of as separate' that drew Williams to trace its travels."[32] Williams understood, they explain, that the sharing of a word across differing domains of thought and experience "was often imperfect, but this very roughness and partiality indicated that the word brought something significant to discussions of 'the central processes of our common life' " through a "shared desire to articulate something of general importance."[33] Through these discursive processes, ordinary words such as "culture" became invested "with a strangeness that unsettled their seemingly transparent meaning," while words such as "alienation" that had once been technical and forbidding were endowed "with a new and mysterious popularity," in some cases through the ways people "group or 'bond' them together, making explicit or often implicit connections that help to initiate new ways of seeing their world."[34]

Crisis as a Keyword

Crisis, I argue, is precisely such a word. It is a word that has come to figure so prominently in American politics and culture that both are all but unimaginable without it. But *crisis* also has become so common that its use hardly registers as remarkable when we hear it. Denaturalizing its doxa and tracing the ways in which its taken-for-granted meanings have been constructed by and through political and public policy processes therefore "unsettles its transparent meaning" to open a new and generative lens through which to understand the politics of marginalization and oppression. Doing so reveals in particular that crisis is neither a political constant nor a neutral descriptor of empirically bad things. Rather, the designation of bad things as crises has been uneven and selective, structured as much by ideology, partisanship, and power as by the actual "badness" of problems, developments, and events. The analysis suggests that although the evolution and applications of crisis politics have not themselves *caused* marginalization, through their feedback effects in politics, policy, and public attitudes they are one of many factors that have helped to *constitute* it. More specifically, the political history of crisis suggests that crisis designations are not merely rhetorical flourishes or efforts to draw attention to an issue. Instead, over time, calling a bad thing a crisis became an indicator of the perceived worthiness of those affected by it, a tactic intended to signal quite specifically that an issue was facing a critical juncture that warranted and could be resolved through state intervention, and a key component of the politics of problem definition and agenda setting.

To examine the relationship between crisis and marginalization in greater depth, chapters 2 and 3 explore the evolving use of *crisis* on the part of both dominant political actors and representatives of marginalized groups. Before turning to these empirical examinations, I first explore the idea of *crisis* as a political keyword and introduce the typology of its meanings through which, I argue, we can understand the political construction of crisis and the relationships of these constructions and crisis politics more generally to political processes that have helped to constitute uneven trajectories of progress for marginalized groups.

The Implications of Crisis Politics for Marginalization

Crisis has so permeated early twenty-first century politics that it can be surprising to learn that this term has not been a constant of mainstream political discourse. But as I will demonstrate through the content analyses of popular and political documents in chapters 2 and 3, crisis politics is a relatively recent construct, one that has a distinct genesis, history, and evolving trajectory. The word itself was borrowed from Greek, and its initial use in English was, as Williams argued was often true of keywords, "technical and forbidding," applied first in science and medicine, where it

TABLE 1.1. **The political meanings of** *crisis*

Term	Definition
Clear-cut crisis	A seemingly self-evident shock that is understood to constitute a turning point triggered by a purportedly quick, episodic, and seemingly discrete and exogenous cause.
Condition-as-crisis	An ongoing (domestic) issue that had been treated by dominant political actors as an intractable, inevitable, and even natural "condition" that is reframed as a discrete and solvable problem facing a critical juncture at which state intervention is necessary, justified, and likely to provide a decisive and desirable remedy.
Calamity-as-crisis	Used interchangeably with terms such as tragedy, catastrophe, and "very bad thing."
Crisis-as-creation	Attempt to draw attention to a problem and stimulate political and policy responses by creating crises through disruption.
Non-crisis	Problems that are not treated as crises by dominant political actors but that have analogues that are, have been, or could be.

was used to describe "the point in the progress of a disease when an important development or change takes place which is decisive of recovery or death" and "any marked or sudden variation occurring in the progress of a disease and to the phenomena accompanying it."[35] According to the 1989 edition of the *Oxford English Dictionary*, the term *crisis* was accepted in the early seventeenth century (1624) as a more general descriptor for "a vitally important or decisive stage in the progress of anything; a turning point" or "a state of affairs in which a decisive change for better or worse is imminent" particularly "times of difficulty, insecurity, and suspense in politics or commerce."[36] Although this latter meaning had become common in American political discourse by the late 1960s, I show in chapter 2 that it was used only rarely in that way by dominant political actors before that decade. Until that point, when those actors used the word *crisis*, it was typically to characterize a very limited set of issues. In particular, echoing the examples from the 1916 *New York Times*, it was most commonly attached to what I call clear-cut crises—wars, economic depressions, and conflicts in other countries—phenomena that were typically understood to constitute clear and discrete events, disasters, or turning points (see table 1.1).

Activists and advocates for marginalized, oppressed, and subjugated groups, however, did not so constrain their application of the term *crisis*. They had long invoked crisis as part of their efforts to reorient the time frame for understanding ongoing and domestic problems such as political exclusion, structural racism, and economic marginalization as urgent issues facing critical junctures and therefore warranting and worthy of government resources and attention. In the 1960s, dominant political actors began to adopt their language, increasingly invoking *crisis* as a way to characterize domestic issues in political rhetoric and in the law, thereby making crisis a stock framing for social, economic, and policy problems.

This application of crisis to domestic problems—the meaning I label condition-as-crisis—originated among advocates and activists for marginalized groups. But as I show in chapter 2, when dominant political actors adopted this meaning, they subjected it to a set of reversals that served to reinforce rather than to alleviate marginalization. First, although racial justice activists and advocates tried to use the framing of condition-as-crisis to shift the ways in which structural and persistent inequalities and marginalization were understood and addressed, dominant political actors rarely applied the language of crisis to characterize such issues. When they did characterize such issues as crises, they were more likely to do so in ways that treated marginalized groups as the perpetrators rather than as the victims of the crisis in question, using the language of crisis to blame, even to punish, them for the problems they faced. In addition, rather than framing such issues as crises that can be resolved through state intervention, they often argued that the appropriate solution involved withholding or withdrawing state resources. This reversal was further exacerbated by the fact that efforts to address crises typically have as their goal getting things back to their "normal" pre-crisis conditions. Because these normal conditions are often characterized by various forms of inequality, marginalization, and oppression, however, the underlying problems that maintain these conditions are preserved and renaturalized. In other words, while racial justice activists and advocates tried to use the idea of condition-as-crisis to frame structural inequalities and marginalization as remediable through state intervention, crisis politics came more typically to reinforce inequalities within and among marginalized groups.

As it traveled from the "technical and forbidding" realm of science to the domain of everyday social, economic, and political life, crisis took on "a new and mysterious popularity," as Bennett, Grossberg, and Morris characterize such transformations.[37] It came to matter, in Williams's words, "in two areas . . . often thought of as separate."[38] As it did, it experienced major shifts and added new and widely varying meanings so that by 1970, the word *crisis* had "bonded," to borrow Williams's formulation, to more than one hundred different terms in the realm of politics and policy. Through these journeys and their attendant "interactions in popular discourse with

neighboring terms," crisis also came to anchor "new clusters of meaning."
Most centrally, although the political terms to which *crisis* bonded vary
widely—applied to issues from "abortion" to "Middle-East" to "youth"—
its connotations came to converge around four principal clusters of meanings that both "initiate and reveal new ways of seeing the world."[39]

I label the first such cluster of meanings *clear-cut crises*, by which I mean
the kinds of bad things that, as I began to explain above, are popularly
recognized as paradigmatic crises—wars, depressions, disasters, and the
like, often occurring in other countries or having to do with foreign affairs.
Ostensibly self-evident and episodic, they are understood to constitute
turning points triggered by seemingly discrete or exogenous causes.[40] The
second cluster I call *condition-as-crisis*, in which political actors use the
concept of crisis as a turning point to shape ideas about the nature, causes,
and consequences of ongoing and enduring bad things—particularly domestic ones—as well as ideas about how they might be resolved and their
potentially disastrous or catastrophic effects avoided.[41] Eventually, *crisis*
came also to be used synonymously with terms such as *tragedy*, *catastrophe*, and *very bad thing*. This cluster of synonyms represents the third
meaning, which I refer to as *calamity-as-crisis*. Finally, *crisis-as-creation*
refers to the kinds of disruptions that scholars such as Frances Fox Piven
and Richard Cloward and Desmond King argue are often "created" by
political actors to draw attention to a problem.[42] These include acts of civil
disobedience or actions such as sit-down strikes that halt production. For
example, as Martin Luther King Jr. wrote in his "Letter from Birmingham
Jail," the goal of civil disobedience is "to create such a crisis and foster
such a tension that a community which has constantly refused to negotiate
is forced to confront the issue . . . to create a situation so crisis packed that
it will inevitably open the door to negotiation."[43]

But for every bad thing to which the word *crisis* came to be attached,
there have always been countless, often analogous, bad things to which the
term has not been applied. As a consequence, the constitution of crisis as a
way to understand some kinds of bad things also came to constitute its inverse. As important as these four meanings are, therefore, also important
are non-crises: bad things that are not treated as crises by dominant political actors but that have analogues that are (see table 1.2). Examples of
non-crises include those that I juxtapose against crises in the case studies
I explore in chapters 4 and 5, such as the high rates of foreclosure among
low-income people, African Americans, Latinos, and Indigenous people,
and among women who were sole borrowers in the mid-1990s, a time

TABLE 1.2. *Crisis* and *non-crisis*

	Crisis	Non-crisis
General definition	"Bad thing" framed and treated as a critical juncture/ turning point worthy of and remediable through government intervention and resources	"Bad thing" framed and treated as natural, inevitable, immune to, outside the scope of, unlikely to be remedied by, and not warranting government intervention and resources
Typically affects	Dominant or privileged groups	Marginalized groups
Impact framed as	Universal	Exceptional; particular; as affecting a narrow group or a "special" interest
Appropriate solution framed as	Government intervention and/ or expenditure of public or collective resources; might warrant "state of exception"	Private sector and/or affected group
Causes framed as	Quick, discrete, episodic, or exogenous	Long-term, enduring, intractable, inevitable, and perhaps even natural
Effects framed as	Aberrant and temporary	Normal conditions

more typically associated with a real estate boom. Non-crises also include many of the ongoing forms of racialized and gendered inequalities, marginalization, oppression, and violence to which President Obama referred in his op-ed. As these examples suggest, among the features that typically characterize non-crises is that their effects are felt disproportionately by members of marginalized and oppressed groups. So while crises are likely to be universalized (even when their effects are unevenly distributed), non-crises are consequently more likely to be exceptionalized and particularized, treated as affecting a narrow group of "special" interests.

As the meaning of *crisis* expanded beyond its initial connotation and came to encompass ever more ongoing domestic problems and conditions, calling a bad thing a crisis became a shorthand for arguments about turning points and tractability, about which problems are particular and which are universal, about what political actors think the state can and should do to address whose problems, and about what the possible outcomes of state action and inaction will and will not be. That is, as I show in chapter 2, when dominant political actors began to argue that cities—or civil rights, transportation, education, "the family," and, eventually gun violence—were "in crisis," they were not merely trying to sound the alarm, get attention, drum up support, or assert that these things were in bad shape. As illustrated by the example of President Obama's characterization of gun violence, calling a problem a crisis became a tactic used to try to transform an ongoing condition into an actionable problem—to claim that it was at a *critical juncture* and that it was facing a decisive crossroads that would determine whether it would be resolved or whether it would worsen and become a disaster or a catastrophe. Invoking crisis, therefore, was intended to signal quite specifically the *need* for state intervention; the belief that such intervention is *justified*; the optimism that such intervention will *make a difference* in resolving a problem, righting a wrong, or changing the course of events to avert potentially disastrous or catastrophic outcomes; and the hopeful conviction that the resulting change would be desirable. Embedded in the construction of a bad thing as a crisis, therefore, are often implicit or explicit claims that it is "universal" and that addressing it warrants a "state of exception" and the suspension of the rules that typically govern social, economic, and political processes and relationships.[44]

By constructing an ever-increasing array of domestic issues as turning points worthy of government attention and resources and as broad problems that warrant state intervention and for which such intervention will make a desirable difference, crisis politics became a key component not just of the politics of war, recessions, and disaster relief, but of the everyday politics of problem definition and agenda setting. The processes through which crises and non-crises are constructed have become integral to the construction of policy problems and the determination of policy solutions more generally. Scholars have long argued that the kinds of bad things that I call clear-cut crises play an important role in agenda setting by opening policy windows through which long-standing ideas about interventions and solutions can be pushed.[45] Building on the ideas of scholars who maintain that we must examine the processes through which issues are constructed as problems in the first place, I put the needle on the record earlier in the process and examine the agenda-setting role of *crisis politics*—the processes through which some problems are constructed as crises and others as non-crises.[46] That is, I treat crisis as at least partly endogenous *to* politics and policy, not merely productive *of* them. I show that in the 1960s, these processes came to both constitute and reflect different assessments about which (and whose) problems do and do not warrant government intervention and resources, about what kind of intervention and resources are justified, about whether such intervention is likely to make a difference, and to what end. More specifically, in a political order in which battles over agenda setting came to be waged increasingly through conflicts about the appropriate size of government, the correct scope of state intervention, and ideas about who is worthy of what kind of state resources, having a bad thing constituted and recognized as a crisis became a political victory in which relevant political actors were persuaded that its resolution was possible, desirable, and worthy of state action and resources.

These changing meanings of *crisis* also created feedback effects that served (as Fraser and Gordon argue in the case of *dependency*) "to constitute and reconstitute" its political significance and, ultimately, to signify that the bad things that happen to some people and groups are solvable problems worthy of state attention and resources while the bad things that happen to other, usually already marginalized groups, are normal, inevitable, and not worthy of or amenable to state intervention or resources. Crisis and non-crisis became, in other words (and borrowing once again from Fraser and Gordon), "vehicles for elaborating meanings of worthiness and belonging that were deeply inflected by gender, race, and class."[47]

Put simply, one consequence of the mainstreaming of crisis politics has been to create a language and a conduit for putting issues on the mainstream policy agenda and for arguing that they require, deserve, and can be addressed through state intervention and resources. From this perspective, calling a problem a crisis is an act of optimism on the part of dominant political actors, reflecting both their ability to, in Janet Roitman's words, "think otherwise" about it as well as their faith that it can be fixed.[48] Another consequence of crisis politics, however, has been to construct other problems as non-crises, ones about which dominant political actors do not conjure alternative futures but instead treat as natural and inevitable, as outside the scope of state intervention, and as unlikely to be remedied by such resources.[49] Taken together, these consequences suggest that one of the ways in which crisis politics work to maintain conditions of marginality is through dominant political actors' assumptions that, at best, there is no turning point for these conditions but only slow, incremental, and gradual change, and, at worst, that these conditions have always been and will always be thus. Instead of summoning hopefulness that conditions of marginalization can be fixed, crisis politics presume that the non-crises of enduring conditions function as metrics for gauging whether *dominant* groups might be in crisis. Crisis politics, therefore, also reinforce marginalization by justifying state intervention so that dominant groups will not have to experience the disastrous and catastrophic lived conditions endured by members of marginalized groups.

In this way, non-crises function as a version of Lani Guinier and Gerald Torres's "miner's canary," but as seen through a funhouse mirror in which difficult conditions for marginalized and minoritized groups are viewed not as the "first sign of danger that threatens us all" but instead as a sign that things are or have returned to "normal."[50] For these issues there are no critical junctures and no turning points, so there are no crises and there is nothing to be done. They are treated as facts of nature, and to try is to resolve them is to throw good money after bad.

Keywords, Meanings, and Typologies: Some Notes and Caveats

A few caveats about some of the foregoing assertions about crises and non-crises bear mention, as do some distinctions between a keyword analysis and related approaches such as frames and rhetoric, along with a few words about the relationship between crisis and related concepts such as disaster, catastrophe, and emergency.

First, the four "political meanings" of *crisis* that I describe above are not meant to be exhaustive, the significance of each one is not necessarily parallel or commensurate, and I do not mean to suggest that political actors self-consciously conceive of crises in these ways or using these terms. I also recognize that classifying the meanings and constitutive elements of crisis typologically assumes to some degree that the categories within the typology are politically meaningful, but any classification scheme or typology is itself, of course, a construction.[51] As such, I acknowledge that both the concepts of interest here and the categories that I propose are malleable, contingent, and debatable.

I similarly acknowledge that the categories in the crisis typology are unavoidably plastic, and also that there are many other schemas through which we might analyze crises and related concepts. Scholars have indeed proposed compelling alternatives that illuminate other political processes. Desmond King, for example, conceptualizes crisis dichotomously, distinguishing between an "objective" crisis—brought about by "an exogenous event, the consequences of which cannot be disregarded politically"— and a "designated" crisis—"an endogenous event or continuing problem deemed a crisis for political and electoral reasons."[52] Edgar Morin identifies three systems within which we should understand crises (systemic, cybernetic, and bio-negentropic), as well as ten components of crises.[53] Both Peter Schuck and Richard Posner offer classification schemes through which to understand the related concept of catastrophe.[54] Focusing on the status of crisis in social science theory and writing, Roitman explores "the kinds of work the term 'crisis' is or is not doing in the construction of narrative forms" and how it is "constituted as an object of knowledge."[55] Kyle Whyte distinguishes between "epistemologies of crisis" and "epistemologies of coordination." The former, he argues, are associated with presentist logics of settler colonialism that justify the suspension of concerns about justice and morality, while the latter draw on Indigenous ways of knowing that "emphasise the importance of moral bonds" and respond to "constant change in the world . . . without validating harm or violence."[56] No single classification scheme or approach needs to be the definitive or correct one: All are useful, each teaches us something important about crisis and crisis politics, and no one alternative need undermine what is illuminated through any other, including the typology that I offer here. I see my effort as being in conversation rather than in conflict with these and other schemas, all of which have influenced the typology that I develop here.[57]

Similarly, many of the questions and arguments at the center of this book overlap with scholarship that analyzes and addresses terms and concepts that intersect with and are closely related to crisis. Among the most germane are the bodies of theoretical, conceptual, and empirical work that focus on the politics, political construction, and policy implications of catastrophe and disaster. In addition to Schuck's and Posner's treatments of catastrophe, for example, Antonio Vázquez-Arroyo explores the ways in which "the intersections between contemporary narratives of catastrophe and political life . . . mediate discursive and objective processes of catastrophization."[58] Scholars including E. L. Quarantelli have engaged in similar explorations of disaster, some of which have been taken up and elaborated by Arjen Boin, Paul 't Hart, and Sanneke Kuipers in their discussions about both the connections among and distinctions between crisis and disaster.[59] While I am in conversation with, draw on, and am indebted to these and other careful analyses and distinctions, I show in chapter 2 that these other terms do not function as political keywords in the way that *crisis* does. As such, although I reference these other terms and concepts and use them as points of comparison, I keep my focus on the particular political work of crisis.

Second, my goal is not to derive a working definition of the word *crisis*, even though my purpose overlaps with work that parses the etymological genealogy and semantic history of crisis and some related concepts and even as I am interested in tracing the evolving meanings and political significance of the word *crisis* over time.[60] Similarly, while I draw on ideas from widely ranging bodies of scholarship that address and engage crisis from several angles, my aim is not to survey or critique this literature. And like Roitman, I do not attempt to provide a conceptual history or an etymological or semantic analysis of crisis, to provide a definitive definition of it, or to determine who has used it "correctly" and who has not.[61] As Dauber argues with regard to the "fluidity" around what constitutes a disaster, we would "do better to observe these contests over the meaning and content of the concept of" crisis "than to enroll ourselves as partisans on one side or the other of the question of what constitutes a true" crisis.[62] Likewise, although the analyses in chapter 2 begin chronologically and unfold over time and in a somewhat periodized manner, the periods are not discrete, and the relevance of the developments in each one is not evenly distributed. As such, my account does not proceed blow-by-blow through the decades and up to the present, but is instead syncopated, emphasizing periods that are significant for the particular questions about the relationship between crisis politics and the politics of marginalization that are the focus of the book. And although the analyses track rises and falls in the rates at which the word *crisis* is used, it is also true that like almost all words (including words like *it, about,* and *around*), even at its most frequent, *crisis* never comprises even 1 percent of the words used in any context at any given moment. Some of my arguments are consequently based on analyses of a small number of observations and would not reach conventional levels of statistical significance, even as I argue that they are substantively meaningful.

My approach to understanding crisis as a construct also overlaps with but is different from approaches that examine the frames that the media or political actors apply to particular events that a scholar has identified a priori as crises (see, for example, Amber Boydstun and Rebecca Glazier's argument about the "crisis framing cycle").[63] I take up a version of the latter approach in chapters 4 and 5 when I examine the framing and treatment of foreclosures in one era as a crisis and in another era as a non-crisis. But I begin by first shifting the focus from questions about how bad things that we come to understand as crises are thusly framed to emphasize a somewhat different question: In what context and to what ends do political actors use the word *crisis*, and what political work is the word *crisis* doing in such contexts? In this approach, we might say that language matters less for its obliqueness than for its obviousness; that rather than looking for "hidden transcripts" or engaging in what historians term "reading against the grain" of the archive, I instead tease out the meanings from the transcripts that we might characterize as hiding in plain sight.[64] And while I do not intend to ascribe too much intentionality to any particular writer, speaker, or actor, a keyword approach provides a lens through which to examine *patterns* of use across many writers, speakers, and actors and to consider what their collective use and non-use of language signals politically about the issues and groups they are engaging.

My goal is also not to articulate a comprehensive typology of crises or even of the meanings of crisis, and those that I chart are consequently not exhaustive but instead focus almost exclusively on its political uses and meanings. So, for example, while some of my searches turned up references to "identity crises," the typology I offer does not attempt to conceptualize these and other similarly psychological or individual-level applications of crisis. Instead, I offer a more constrained and question-driven framework that puts into relief the political and ideological work that crisis has come to perform in American politics and political culture, particularly when it comes to structuring the politics of power and marginalization. To do so, I contend that we must understand how *crisis* found its way into the American political lexicon, how differently located political actors have deployed the word and developed the concept of crisis, under what circumstances they have done so, and what they have been trying to do when they have characterized something as a crisis. How has this usage evolved, what can we make of this evolution, and how should we understand the clashes among its meanings?[65] As Roitman asks, how is it that *crisis*, a term that was "once a signifier for a critical, decisive moment," came to be "construed as a protracted historical and experiential condition" and a way to describe an "ongoing state of affairs?"[66] My objective, in other words, is to examine the particular ways in which crisis has been used, constructed, understood, and deployed by dominant and marginalized political actors and policymakers; to appreciate the kinds of politics and policies that crisis consequently facilitates or forecloses when it comes to issues of inequality and marginalization; and, ultimately, to understand the implications of these uses, constructions, understandings, and deployments for the ways in which the issues facing marginalized groups are—and are not—addressed in dominant politics.

In addition, although I locate the origins of the use of *crisis* as a way to describe domestic phenomena among abolitionists and racial justice advocates, the twinned lenses of crisis and non-crises that together produce what I call crisis politics are constituted primarily through dominant political actors and institutions. And while I continue to attend to both their deployment on the part of advocates for marginalized groups and to battles between dominant and marginalized political actors over crisis definition throughout the book, their deployment on the part of dominant political actors and in dominant institutions figures more centrally in my sources and therefore in my analyses. For similar reasons, Marxist conceptualizations of crisis do not figure as prominently in the analyses that follow, even though, as I note in the introductory chapter, they have significant implications for the politics of marginalized groups and speak in important ways to and are clearly an important component of the politics of resistance. I also do not devote equal time to each kind of crisis in the typology. For example, although what I call crisis-as-creation has significant implications for social movements and marginalized groups, this meaning is not evident in the sources I analyze in chapters 2 and 3, and so I devote only a very abbreviated treatment to this meaning there and discuss this meaning only in passing in the rest of the book.

Most broadly, although I hope that readers will agree that examining the use and evolution of *crisis* as a keyword is revealing, I am not arguing that a keyword approach is the only way to explore the political construction of crisis or crisis politics more generally. I also do not contend that the presence (or absence) of the word *crisis* constitutes necessary or sufficient evidence that crisis politics are (or are not) taking place: Words are important, but political language involves more than words, and the presence or absence of the word *crisis* is not the only way to tell that one is being constructed or that we are observing or not observing crisis politics any more than the presence or absence of the word *poverty*, *gender*, or *race* is necessary for those issues to be at stake in political discourse or policy language. Ian Haney-Lopez's arguments about the ways in which white political actors use "dog whistles" to send implicit messages about race to their white constituents is one example of the ways in which political actors use coded language to send signals to constituencies about issues of race, gender, and sexuality, particularly in contexts in which overtly discriminatory appeals might not be tolerated (see also, inter alia, work by Eduardo Bonilla-Silva and LaFleur Stephens-Dougan).[67] Consequently, as significant as the deployment (or lack of deployment) of crisis language alongside words like *poverty*, *gender*, or *race* is, such interactions "with neighboring terms," as Burgett and Hendler describe it, are far from the only indicator that those issues are being framed as crises.[68]

The corollary to this point is that political language is often so blustery and overblown that we cannot necessarily trust the meanings of the words that are being used. "Political language," George Orwell writes in *Politics and the English Language*, "is designed to make lies sound truthful and murder respectable, and to give an appearance of solidity to pure wind."[69] From this perspective, some readers may question the value and reliability of using a keyword approach as the basis for a political analysis. Perhaps *crisis* is simply puffed-up or alarmist rhetoric intended to scare and persuade a pliable public but that ultimately has little impact on politics and policy?[70] Rodgers notes, for example, the temptation to "dismiss the verbal guff of politics as 'mere rhetoric,' a veil drawn over the hidden games of politics." He concedes that political words are intended to mystify; to conceal the "interests at stake," the "covert agendas," and the "hands in the till"; to "hide the policy of the day behind the popular slogans of the moment"; to "screen political acts, obscure them behind a cloud of rhetoric so dense that most of us are left to play fools' parts, trying to guess what is really going on."[71] However, he insists as well that "political words do more than mystify"; they also "inspire, persuade, enrage, mobilize." With words, he writes, "minds are changed, votes acquired, enemies labeled, alliances secured, unpopular programs made palatable," and, crucially for my purposes, "the status quo suddenly unveiled as unjust and intolerable. . . . Words make mass actions possible. . . . Through words some of the most potent forces of modern politics are wheeled into motion." "Mystify as they may," he concludes, words "are the stuff that holds political coalitions and political movements together."[72]

From this perspective, even if the term *crisis* is uttered in the course of political hyperventilation, even when it is used as a rhetorical flourish, and even though it might seem at times to be thrown around as a histrionic embellishment invoked to garner attention and inflame passions, we must understand it as more than melodramatic language or empty rhetoric. As I began to argue above and as I elaborate in what follows, whether a bad thing is constituted as a crisis has become an indicator of the perceived worthiness of those affected by it, of whether political actors want it to change, of whether they believe it is amenable to change and are willing to devote state resources to do so, and of what they believe it would mean for the status quo if it were resolved. So even if the use of the term *crisis* is alarmist, understanding who is alarmed, about which issues they try to sound the alarm to others, and to what political and policy effect they are able to do so reveals much about the unevenness of the opportunities and trajectories of progress available to marginalized groups. If *crisis* is invoked to mystify, then it is important to understand what is being distorted and masked in that mystification and what is at stake in trying to do so. I also acknowledge that some of the unevenness and selectiveness in the issues to which *crisis* becomes bonded is undoubtedly aesthetic: *mortgage crisis* rolls off the tongue more easily than, for example, *housing discrimination crisis*. And there are probably similar aesthetic reasons that bondings such as *Cuban missile crisis* take on a kind of proper name or brand quality that then might seem to develop lives of their own.

Finally, in pointing to the constructedness of bad things that come to be understood as crises, and in arguing that we cannot simply identify, measure, and distinguish crises from times or bad things that are not crises, I do not mean to suggest that those to which the label crisis ultimately "sticks" are without real or material effects. Rather, following historian Barbara Melosh's characterization of the constructedness of categories such as gender, race, and sexuality, I mean that crisis is "simultaneously arbitrary and deeply embedded."[73] That is, although crisis is mutable and historically constructed, crisis politics are nonetheless a central and powerful force in social, political, and economic life (as the examination of the politics of foreclosure crisis and non-crisis in chapters 4 and 5 makes clear and as my brief discussions about the opioid and COVID-19 crises in the concluding chapter suggest).[74] As Andy Horowitz and Jacob Remes explain with regard to understanding disaster as an "analytical construct," doing so does not mean "that how disaster is constructed or defined does not matter." To the contrary, they continue: The "consequences of 'disaster' as a belief are made real in the distribution of sympathy, material resources, and state power."[75]

Similarly, in arguing that it is important to understand that bad things understood as crises are more likely to be ones that affect relatively privileged groups, I do not intend to suggest that any of those things are not truly awful, that we ought not have sympathy for those affected by them, or that the state intervention and resources devoted to them are unwarranted. For example (and as I explain at greater length in chapters 4 and 5), in showing that rates of foreclosure during a period we came to view as a "foreclosure crisis" were, by some measures, similar to the rates during what continues to be framed as a time of booming rates of homeownership, my argument is not that the time of crisis was not a "bad" one. I certainly do not mean to suggest that the state intervention that was proposed and deployed was unwarranted nor that those who were helped by the government programs intended to stem its tide were unworthy of such assistance. And because political and economic resources are rarely unlimited, it may at times be necessary to prioritize issues that seem to affect "broad" populations. In using the term "privileged" to describe the groups affected by the issues most likely to be treated as crises, I also do not mean that members of these groups face no social, political, or economic challenges or disadvantages. From an intersectional perspective, privilege is not dichotomous, and those who are privileged along one axis may be disadvantaged along another one or relative to the broader population. Rather than questioning whether foreclosure rates warranted the use of state resources, I argue that these cases illuminate the ways in which dominant assumptions and expectations about what is normal both construct and are constructed by what are identified as problems and crisis, what demands an explanation and a solution, and what is naturalized.

Conclusion

The issue of gun violence that President Obama addressed in his column was among the grimmest ones taken up in *New York Times* op-eds that first week of 2016. But it was far from the only issue to be labeled a crisis by columnists and other opinion writers that week, and it was not even the only issue that was labeled a crisis on the op-ed page that day. This relatively indiscriminate use of *crisis* as a way to characterize issues and problems was not the practice a century earlier, however. I suggested at the outset of this chapter that an op-ed framed around crisis might seem unremarkable to contemporary readers. As evidence of its typicality, I showed that *crisis* appeared frequently in op-eds and in articles published in the newspaper more generally that week. But treating *crisis* as a political keyword by paying attention to its evolution, to its meanings, and to the work that it is doing suggests that both the contexts in which President Obama used this word in his column and its frequent deployment in the *New York Times* that week might well be considered quite remarkable after all. In these ways, a keyword approach begins to provide some clues about the relationship among crisis politics, the politics of agenda setting, and the politics of marginalization. I explore these clues in greater depth in the next chapter, examining the use of crisis language on the part of both dominant political actors and political outsiders and assessing the significance of this use for the development of crisis politics.

CHAPTER TWO

What We Talk about When We Talk about Crisis

Against the backdrop of the contemporary political moment, when everything from wars to budgetary issues to climate change to racial injustice, health care, and child care is described as being in a state of crisis or as a crisis itself, it can be hard to imagine that there was a time when the word was not part of the lingua franca of mainstream American political discourse. But the brief comparison in chapter 1 between the use of *crisis* in the *New York Times* in 1916 and in 2016 suggests that it was not always thus, and considering some key founding documents of American politics reinforces this impression. The revolutionary period, for example, would surely be considered a time of crisis in our current and conventional understanding of the term, a time when, through conquest, murder, expulsion, enslavement, and expropriation of land, the colonists created what were certainly crises for Black and Indigenous people. It was also a period during which the colonists faced war and British aggression, and a period during which political leaders wanted to convince as many Americans as possible that they faced several critical junctures that demanded decisive action. The word *crisis*, however, is never used in such signal documents as the Declaration of Independence, the Articles of Confederation, or the US Constitution. This absence is not complete, however: Thomas Paine's Revolutionary War pamphlet series, for example, was titled *The American Crisis*, and the term appears eleven times in the *Federalist Papers*.[1] As such, its infrequency cannot simply be attributed to the word's lack of availability for such purposes.

A Prehistory of Crisis Politics in Dominant
American Discourses: 1840s–1960s

Content analyses and other systematic examinations of evidence from books, newspapers, party platforms, bills, and congressional hearings confirm that this relatively infrequent use of crisis language was the norm in dominant American political and cultural discourse for well over a century. Figure 2.1 depicts the use of the word *crisis* alongside the incidence of two comparison words—*poverty* and *accident*—in English-language American books from the 1810s through the 2000s (see endnote and appendices for details about sources, search parameters, and coding decisions and for descriptions of the methods used to compile and analyze the data described and depicted in this chapter, including considerations about the reliability and validity of Google Ngram and Google Books data).[2] The data summarized in the figure are intended to provide only an initial and rough measure of language usage, but they nonetheless serve as a preliminary and general indicator that this word that has so infiltrated and been so naturalized

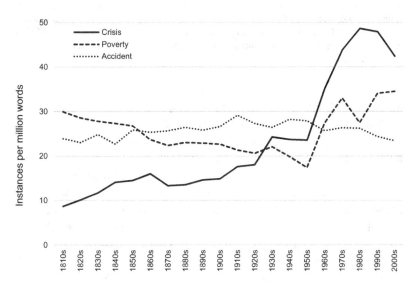

FIGURE 2.1. Instances of the terms *crisis/es, poverty,* and *accident* (per million words) in English-language American books, by decade, 1810s–2000s. *Note:* Search was for "crisis", "poverty", and "accident". 1810 is year of first observation. For additional information, see appendices A and C, and note 2 in chapter 2. *Source:* Mark Davies, 2011–. *Google Books Corpus* (based on Google Books Ngrams).

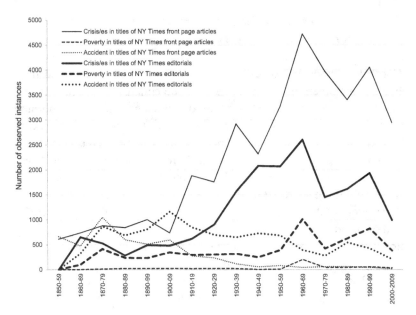

FIGURE 2.2. Instances of the terms *crisis/es, poverty*, and *accident* in *New York Times* editorials and front-page articles, by decade, 1851–2009. *Note:* Search was for "crisis OR crises", "poverty", and "accident". For additional information, see appendices A and C, and note 3 in chapter 2. Unlike the data depicted in other figures, figure 2.2 depicts only the number of observations of the terms in these pieces, not the proportion of the total that they comprise. *Source:* ProQuest Historical Newspapers Database.

in the American political vocabulary did so quite recently, in the 1930s during the Great Depression. Its use then ebbed somewhat, before climbing steeply in the 1960s and 1970s. It continued to be used regularly after that point before receding slightly in the 1990s (a decline that continues, somewhat counterintuitively, even after the events of 11 September 2001).

Examining the trajectory of *crisis*'s use alongside the patterns for the comparison words confirms that its net increase over time is not simply a function of more general increases in the use of all words. More specifically, *crisis* initially appears far less frequently than *poverty* and *accident* but then substantially outpaces both of those words. Analogous data from editorials and the titles of front-page articles in the *New York Times* reveal similar patterns (see figure 2.2; see endnote and appendices for details about how these data were collected, coded, and analyzed, including information about variations in the periodization of and periods covered by the different sources).[3] These patterns suggest that the escalation evident in the 1960s and 1970s represents a new and, I argue, consequential development.

The patterns in the use of the word *crisis* in books and newspapers are also mirrored in its political usage. Figures 2.3 to 2.6 track instances of its use in the titles of congressional hearings, party platforms, the titles of congressional bills, and State of the Union addresses (see endnote and appendices for details about sources, search parameters, units of analysis, and coding).[4] The evidence in these important parts of what I call the "transcript of dominant politics" further confirms that although the catastrophizing language of crisis might seem both inevitable and omnipresent from our contemporary vantage point, it has not always been a staple of American political communication. Rather, it was not until the second decade of the twentieth century that the word *crisis* began to appear regularly in the transcript of dominant politics in the United States.

Crisis made its first appearance in a major party's platform in 1848, for example, when the Whigs wrote that the "heart" of their presidential nominee, General Zachary Taylor, was "with us at the crisis of our political destiny" (see table 2.1). It did not appear again until 1872, when the Republicans used it to praise President Ulysses S. Grant for reducing the debt and allowing the country to avoid "financial crises."[5] After these few

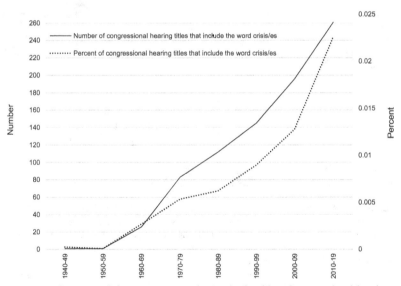

FIGURE 2.3. Instances of the terms *crisis* and *crises* in the titles of congressional hearings, 1940s–2010s (number and as percent of all hearings). *Notes:* Search was for "crisis OR crises". ProQuest Congressional makes hearings searchable beginning in 1824, but figure begins in 1940 because there are no observations prior to 1947. For additional information, see appendices A, B, and C, and note 4 in chapter 2. *Source:* ProQuest Congressional.

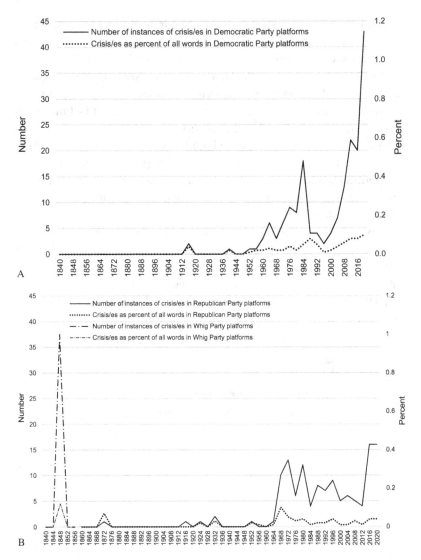

FIGURE 2.4A–B. Instances of the terms *crisis* and *crises* in Democratic, Republican, and Whig Party platforms (number and as percent of all words), 1840–2020. *Note:* Data were compiled using LIWC to search the full text of all platforms for "crisis" or "crises". For additional information, see appendices A, B, and C, and note 4 in chapter 2. *Source:* Gerhard Peters and John T. Woolley, The American Presidency Project.

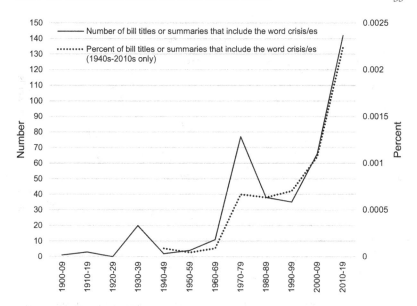

FIGURE 2.5. Instances of the terms *crisis* and *crises* in congressional bill titles and summaries, 1910s–2010s (number and as percent of all bills beginning in 1947). For additional information, see appendices A, B, and C, and note 4 in chapter 2. *Notes:* Search was for "crisis OR crises". ProQuest Congressional makes bills searchable beginning in 1776, but figure begins in 1908 because there are no observations prior to 1908. *Source:* ProQuest Congressional.

and sporadic deployments, however, *crisis* vanished from the text of major party platforms for nearly a half century, until 1916, when the Democrats used it twice: first at the outset of their platform, to credit the 1913 Federal Reserve Act with having saved the country from the previous "archaic banking and currency system, prolific of panic and disaster under Republican administrations, long the refuge of the money trust." The platform's writers argued that the law, which was signed by President Woodrow Wilson, "proved a financial bulwark in a world crisis" by "mobilizing our resources, placing abundant credit at the disposal of legitimate industry and making a currency panic impossible." The second instance was in a section of the platform addressing international relations (titled "Americanism" in the platform itself), in which the writers argued that it is patriotic rather than partisan to assert that "the indivisibility and coherent strength of the nation" is "the supreme issue of this day in which the whole world faces the crisis of manifold change." Put simply, of the sixty platforms written by major parties over the course of the 116-year period between 1840 and 1956,

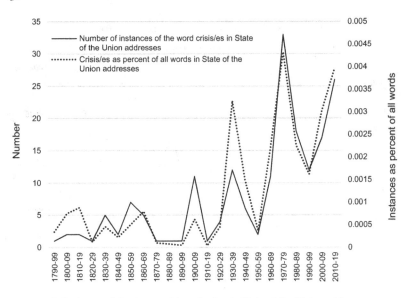

FIGURE 2.6. Instances of the terms *crisis* and *crises* in State of the Union addresses, 1790s–2010s (number and as percent of all words). For additional information, see appendices A, B, and C, and note 4 in chapter 2. *Note:* Search was for "crisis" or "crises". *Source:* Brad Borevitz, *State of the Union.*

the Whigs used the term *crisis* once and the Democrats and the Republicans each used it only five times in only four of their respective platforms (see table 2.2). It did not appear at all in the platforms of the Constitutional Union or Southern Democratic Parties (1860), the Populist Party platform (1892), the Progressive Party platform (1912), or the States' Rights Party platform (1948)—all parties that might be described as having been born of some form of crisis.

Similar trajectories are evident in the titles of congressional hearings and bills. The word *crisis* was not used in a bill title or summary until 1908, when it appeared in the title of one introduced in the House: "To create a Currency Commission to frame a suitable measure for diminishing the intensity of financial crises." Not until 1947 did it appear in the title of a congressional hearing, when it was used in one addressing the "Italian Crisis and Interim Aid," after which it disappeared again until 1962. (Congressional hearings are available in a searchable format beginning only in 1824, so it is possible that I might have observed instances of it before this date if those data were available. However, since it takes more than a century for the term to be used in the title of a hearing after that point, what is clear

TABLE 2.1. *Crisis* and *crises* in the text of major party platforms, 1840–1956

Year	Whig platform	Democratic platform	Republican platform
1840			
1844			
1848	Crisis as existential: "Resolved, That General Taylor, in saying that, had he voted in 1844, he would have voted the Whig ticket, gives us the assurance and no better is needed from a consistent and truth-speaking man that his heart was with us at the **crisis** of our political destiny, when Henry Clay was our candidate and when not only Whig principles were well defined and clearly asserted, but Whig measures depended on success. The heart that was with us then is with us now, and we have a soldier's word of honor, and a life of public and private virtue, as the security."		
1852			
1856			
1860			
1864			
1868			
1872			"Despite large annual reductions of the rates of taxation, the public debt has been reduced during General Grant's Presidency at the rate of a hundred millions a year, great **financial crises** have been avoided, and peace and plenty prevail throughout the land."
1876			
1880			
1884			
1888			
1892			
1896			
1900			
1904			
1908			

continues

TABLE 2.1. (*continued*)

Year	Whig platform	Democratic platform	Republican platform
1912			
1916		World crisis: "Our archaic banking and currency system, prolific of panic and disaster under Republican administrations, long the refuge of the money trust, has been supplanted by the Federal Reserve Act, a true democracy of credit under government control, already proved a financial bulwark in a **world crisis**, mobilizing our resources, placing abundant credit at the disposal of legitimate industry and making a currency panic impossible."	
1916		"The part that the United States will play in the new day of international relationships that is now upon us will depend upon our preparation and our character. The Democratic party, therefore, recognizes the assertion and triumphant demonstration of the indivisibility and coherent strength of the nation as the supreme issue of this day in which the whole world faces the **crisis of manifold change**. It summons all men of whatever origin or creed who would count themselves Americans, to join in making clear to all the world the unity and consequent power of America. This is an issue of patriotism. To taint it with partisanship would be to defile it...."	

TABLE 2.1. (*continued*)

Year	Whig platform	Democratic platform	Republican platform
1920			
1924			"Railroads: We believe that the demand of the American people for improved railroad service at cheaper rates is justified and that it can be fulfilled by the consolidation of the railroads into a lesser number of connecting systems with the resultant operating economy. The labor board provision should be amended to meet the requirements made evident by experience gained from its actual creation. Collective bargaining, voluntary mediation and arbitration are the most important steps in maintaining peaceful labor relations. We do not believe in compulsory action at any time. Public opinion must be the final arbiter in any **crisis** which so vitally affects public welfare as the suspension of transportation. Therefore, the interests of the public require the maintenance of an impartial tribunal which can in any emergency make an investigation of the fact and publish its conclusions. This is accepted as a basis of popular judgment."
1928			
1932			Economic recession: "Leadership: For nearly three years the world has endured an economic depression of unparalleled extent and severity. The patience and courage of our people have been severely tested, but their

continues

TABLE 2.1. (*continued*)

Year	Whig platform	Democratic platform	Republican platform
			faith in themselves, in their institutions and in their future remains unshaken. When victory comes, as it will, this generation will hand on to the next a great heritage unimpaired. This will be due in large measure to the quality of the leadership that this country has had during this **crisis**. We have had in the White House a leader— wise, courageous, patient, understanding, resourceful, ever present at his post of duty, tireless in his efforts and unswervingly faithful to American principles and ideals. At the outset of the depression, when no man could foresee its depth and extent, the President succeeded in averting much distress by securing agreement between industry and labor to maintain wages and by stimulating programs of private and governmental construction."
1932			"Democratic Failure: The vagaries of the present Democratic House of Representatives offer characteristic and appalling proof of the existing incapacity of that party for leadership in a **national crisis**. Individualism running amuck has displaced party discipline and has trampled under foot party leadership. A bewildered electorate has viewed the spectacle with profound dismay and deep misgivings.

TABLE 2.1. (*continued*)

Year	Whig platform	Democratic platform	Republican platform
			Goaded to desperation by their confessed failure, the party leaders have resorted to "pork barrel" legislation to obtain a unity of action which could not otherwise be achieved. A Republican President stands resolutely between the helpless citizen and the disaster threatened by such measures; and the people, regardless of party, will demand his continued service. Many times during his useful life has Herbert Hoover responded to such a call, and his response has never disappointed. He will not disappoint us now."
1936			
1940		"To this generation of Americans it is given to defend this democratic faith as it is challenged by social maladjustment within and totalitarian greed without. The world revolution against which we prepare our defense is so threatening that not until it has burned itself out in the last corner of the earth will our democracy be able to relax its guard. In this **world crisis**, the purpose of the Democratic Party is to defend against external attack and justify by internal progress the system of government and way of life from which the Democratic Party takes its name."	
1944			

continues

TABLE 2.1. (*continued*)

Year	Whig platform	Democratic platform	Republican platform
1948 1952		"The Democratic Party has demonstrated its belief in the Constitution as a charter of individual freedom and an effective instrument for human progress. Democratic Administrations have placed upon the statute books during the last twenty years a multitude of measures which testify to our belief in the Jeffersonian principle of local control, even in general legislation involving nation-wide programs. Selective service, Social Security, Agricultural Adjustment, Low Rent Housing, Hospital, and many other legislative programs have placed major responsibilities in States and counties and provide fine examples of how benefits can be extended through Federal-State cooperation. In the present **world crisis** with new requirements of Federal action for national security, and accompanying provision for public services and individual rights related to defense, constitutional principles must and will be closely followed. Our record and our clear commitments, in this platform, measure our strong faith in the ability of constitutional government to meet the needs of our times."	"They claim prosperity but the appearance of economic health is created by war expenditures, waste and extravagance, planned emergencies, and **war crises**. They have debauched our money by cutting in half the purchasing power of our dollar."

TABLE 2.1. (*continued*)

Year	Whig platform	Democratic platform	Republican platform
1956		"The Failure Abroad. Blustering without dynamic action will not alter the fact that the unity and strength of the free world have been drastically impaired. Witness the decline of NATO, the bitter tragedy of Cyprus, the withdrawal of French forces to North Africa, the uncertainty and dangers in the Middle East, an uncertain and insecure Germany, and resentment rising against United States leadership everywhere. In Asia, in Burma, Ceylon, Indonesia, India, anti-Americanism grows apace, aggravated by the clumsy actions of our Government, and fanned by the inept utterances of our 'statesmen.' In the Middle East, the Eisenhower Administration has dawdled and drifted. The results have been disastrous, and worse threatens. Only the good offices of the United Nations in maintaining peace between Israel and her neighbors conceal the diplomatic incapacities of the Republican Administration. The current **crisis over Suez** is a consequence of inept and vacillating Republican policy. Our Government's mistakes have placed us in a position in the Middle East which threatens the free world with a loss of power and prestige, potentially more dangerous than any we have suffered in the past decade."	

Note: Data were compiled using LIWC to search the full text of all major party platforms from 1840–1956 for "crisis" or "crises". Data were coded using Nvivo. Emphases added by author. For additional information, see appendices A and C, and note 4 in chapter 2. *Source:* Gerhard Peters and John T. Woolley, The American Presidency Project.

TABLE 2.2. **Summary of uses of** *crisis* **or** *crises* **in major party platforms, 1840–1956**

Domestic	
"crisis of our political destiny"	1 (Whig 1848)
"financial crises"	1 (Republican 1872)
railroad crisis[a]	1 (Republican 1924)
economic recession[b]	1 (Republican 1932)
"national crisis"	1 (Republican 1932)

International	
"world crisis"	3 (Democratic 1916 1940, 1952)
"crisis of manifold change"	1 (Democratic 1916)
"war crises"	1 (Republican 1952)
"Crisis over Suez"	1 (Democratic 1956)

Note: Data were compiled using LIWC to search the full text of all major party platforms from 1840–1956 for "crisis" or "crises". Data were coded using Nvivo. For additional information, see appendices A and C, and note 4 in chapter 2. *Source:* Gerhard Peters and John T. Woolley, The American Presidency Project.
[a] Not in quotes because in this instance, the plank was titled "Railroads," and the term "crisis" was used to refer to it later in the section. See table 2.1.
[b] Not in quotes because in this instance, the plank was titled "Economic recession," and the term "crisis" was used to refer to it later in the section. See table 2.1.

and most significant is that the 1947 instance is the first and only observation in these data for well over one hundred years.) It appears earlier and somewhat more consistently in State of the Union addresses, but here, too, the spike in its use does not come until the late twentieth century.

The rareness of crisis language in these early political documents is not a function of an unusually polite and serene political climate, nor is it for want of rhetorical bluster during the periods in which they were written. Although some scholars argue that the particular genre of heightened acrimony that many believe now characterizes American political discourse is a relatively recent development, both parties made ample use of coarse and dramatic language to describe their goals, their accomplishments, and their opponents' failures during this period.[6] Susan Herbst demonstrates, for example, that harsh language has long been a mainstay of American politics, while linguist Zoltan Kovecses argues that hyperbolic "tall talk" became characteristic of American political speech in the 1830s and 1840s.[7] Kenneth Cmiel writes that political oratory "has always had its share of invective. Demosthenes's 'On the Crown' and Cicero against Catiline contain violent personal abuse." "Certainly Federalist and Republican debates of the 1790s, he continues, "were not short of the same."[8] Andrew Jackson, Stephen Douglas, Benjamin Butler, and Andrew Johnson, he argues, were only a few of the nineteenth-century politicians who "built their careers around bitter personal harangues," while politicians, ministers, and journalists regularly deployed "inflated speech," bombast, and "pompous and often meaningless images" that "exalted words over meaning" and replaced "content with sound to impress their audiences with the importance of the occasion and the learnedness of the speaker."[9]

Nor can the limited political use of crisis language before the late nineteenth century be understood as a manifestation of a shortage of significant problems or meaningful critical junctures in American politics during this period. Had either of the two major parties been using *crisis* in their platforms in the ways their contemporaries do now, either of them might well have referenced any number of the issues they took up during this era — from the struggle over slavery and the Civil War that are arguably among the most definitive of national American crises, to women's suffrage and child labor, to periodic economic depressions. But they did not. President Lincoln might seem to have been describing slavery as a crisis when he argued in his House Divided speech at the 1858 Illinois Republican state convention that anti-slavery agitation would "not cease, until a crisis shall have been reached, and passed." But although abolitionists used the language of crisis to describe the violence and inhumanity of enslaving Black Americans, Lincoln did not label slavery itself a crisis in this passage. He also was not suggesting that the decision about whether to abolish slavery constituted a critical juncture with regard to this issue. Instead, he used the term *crisis* to refer to the turmoil that would be generated by abolitionist *agitation*, a use that is more in line with the meaning I call crisis-as-creation.

Rather than using the term *crisis* to make the case that slavery faced "a vitally important or decisive stage," "a turning point," or "a state of affairs in which a decisive change for better or worse is imminent," dominant political actors more typically used terms such as "evil" to describe it. The 1864 Republican platform included a resolution, for example, characterizing slavery as a "gigantic evil." *Evil* is certainly an appropriate word to describe slavery, but it carries a very different meaning than *crisis* when it comes to problem definition and ideas about state intervention. *Merriam-Webster's Dictionary* defines *evil* as something that is "morally reprehensible," "sinful, wicked," "arising from actual or imputed bad character or conduct, a person of evil reputation," "causing harm," or "marked by misfortune."[10] *Evil* therefore has an ethical or religious connotation that, while perhaps intended to stimulate state action, suggests a moral failure or an enemy to be vanquished rather than a problem facing a critical juncture that can be solved through government intervention.[11] In addition, although figures 2.5 and 2.6 make clear that *crisis* appeared more frequently in books, newspapers, bill titles and summaries, and State of the Union addresses around the time of the Great Depression, there is no concomitant uptick in its use in hearing titles during this period. (As I will discuss at greater length below, the crisis being referenced in the bill titles and summaries in the 1930s had to do with financing for public education, while the uptick in the word's use in State of the Union addresses during this period is due almost entirely to references to economic crises in the United States and Europe.)

Finally, comparing the incidence of *crisis* with that of several other words and expressions that might be considered synonyms suggests that its rela-

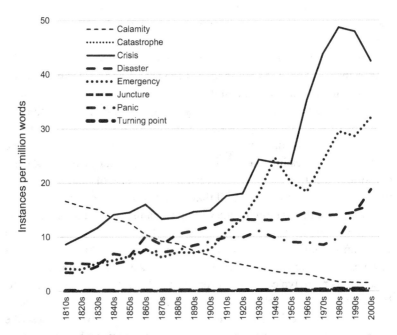

FIGURE 2.7. Instances of the terms *calamity, catastrophe, crisis, disaster, emergency, juncture, panic,* and *turning point* in English-language American books (per million words), 1810s–2000s. *Note:* Search was for "calamity", "catastrophe", "crisis", "disaster", "emergency", "juncture", "panic", and "turning point". Because the lines *catastrophe, juncture,* and *turning point* hug the x-axis, supplemental figure A.6 shows only the values for those words to make it easier to see them. For additional information, see appendices A and C, and notes 2 and 13 in chapter 2. *Source:* Mark Davies, 2011–. *Google Books Corpus* (based on Google Books n-grams).

tive paucity is not a function of the fact that some other term was being used in its stead during this period. Although it is difficult to rule out all synonyms, figure 2.7 compares instances of *crisis* in English-language American books to instances of several possible alternative expressions: *calamity*, *catastrophe*, *disaster*, *emergency*, *juncture* (as in *critical juncture*), *panic*, and *turning point*.[12] Of these possibilities, only *calamity* (and, fleetingly, *emergency*) appears to ever have been used more frequently than *crisis*, and this was true only during the first half of the nineteenth century.[13] The relatively rare use of the word *crisis* during this period is therefore not an artefact of the fact that these alternative terms were being used in its place, nor is it because the term was simply not being used at all. Instead, it suggests that neither the word *crisis* nor the concept of crisis politics was typical in the political rhetoric of this period and that its subsequent proliferation warrants scrutiny and explanation. In addition, although disaster declarations and states of emergency can carry legal and administrative force, the comparatively *in*frequent use of the terms *disaster* and *emergency* suggests that neither comes to function as a keyword in the way that *crisis* comes eventually to do.[14] (Note as well that *catastrophe*, *juncture*, and *turning point* are used so infrequently that the lines for them hug the x-axis in figure 2.7. To make them more legible, supplemental figure A.6 presents only the values for those words.)

Meaning I. Clear-Cut Crises

Taken together, the evidence suggests that from at least the early nineteenth century until the second half of the twentieth, *crisis* scarcely appeared in the transcript of dominant politics. Reinforcing the example of the January 1916 issue of the *New York Times* that I discuss in chapter 1, the evidence suggests further that when *crisis* was invoked by dominant political actors during this period, its meaning hewed closely to its origins in medicine and science, used mainly to indicate a decisive development or sudden variation. For example, the evidence summarized in table 2.2 makes clear that of the eleven instances of the word *crisis* in major party platforms from 1840 through 1956, six (54.5 percent) refer to wars, foreign policy and international tensions, or issues in countries other than the United States; an additional three (27.3 percent) refer to economic depressions or financial crisis (such as the "financial crisis" in 1872 that I note above; see table 2.2). The remaining two instances are a mix: *Crisis* is used in the 1924 Republican Party platform as part of its argument that passenger rail systems should be consolidated. The final instance, the foregoing reference to a "crisis of our political destiny," might be characterized as a metaphor for national malaise.[15]

Crisis is applied to an even narrower range of topics in the titles and summaries of bills before 1960. It is used twice to refer to financial crises, twice to the First World War, twice to the "global depression," once to a "famine crisis" in Pakistan, once to the "Suez crisis," and twice to the "Berlin crisis."[16] In a seeming departure from the more general pattern of references to wars, bad things in other countries, and domestic economic issues, Democrats in the House and Senate introduced a series of bills in 1934 and 1935, the goal of which was "to provide for the cooperation by the Federal Government with the several States and Territories and the District of Columbia in meeting the crisis in public education" (it is this issue, rather than the Great Depression, that accounts for the increase in the use of *crisis* in bill titles and summaries during the 1930s in figure 2.5). This application of *crisis* might seem precocious in foreshadowing its eventual application to a much broader range of domestic issues. However, the "education crisis" in question concerned the implications of the Great Depression for public education financing. As the text of the bill states, "the present economic depression has created a crisis in public education." As such, although the issue to which *crisis* was being applied in this case was somewhat unusual for that time, contextualizing its meaning makes clear that it was being used to describe an economic issue, a use that is in line with the *clear-cut crisis* meaning that was typical during this era.

To investigate the use and evolution of crisis language on the part of dominant political actors in finer detail, in figures 2.8 to 2.11 I use data from the University of Texas's US Policy Agendas Project (USPAP) to depict the topics with which *crisis* is associated in bill and hearing titles, State of the Union addresses, and party platforms. USPAP collects data from archived sources to trace changes in the national policy agenda and public policy outcomes, classifying policy activities into 20 major topics and over 200 subtopics and allowing scholars to track and compare them over time.[17] These data therefore allow me to identify the topics addressed by each hearing and bill with *crisis* or *crises* in its title as well as the topic with which each instance of these words is associated in the full text of party platforms and State of the Union addresses.[18] The figures aggregate these data to track the range and number of topics with which *crisis* is associated, to trace how *crisis*'s use with regard to these topics has changed over time, and to gauge

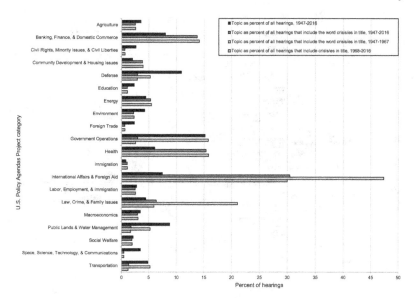

FIGURE 2.8. Proportion of congressional hearings that include the term *crisis* or *crises* in their titles, by US Policy Agendas Project category, 1947–2016. *Notes: Crisis* is used in the titles of hearings falling under seven of twenty USPAP categories before 1967 and in hearings falling under all twenty categories from 1968–2010. Search was for "crisis" or "crises". Blank spaces indicate that there were no observations of *crisis* or *crises* in hearing titles on that topic during the period that would be represented by the missing bar. From 1947–2016, Congress held 99,973 hearings, 676 of which used the term *crisis* or *crises* in their titles. For additional information, see appendices A and C, and notes 18, 19, and 22 in chapter 2. *Source:* US Policy Agendas Project.

the relative incidence of the topics with which *crisis* is associated as a proportion of all bills (excluding private bills), hearings, and State of the Union speech and party platform "quasi-sentences" (see endnote and appendices for further details about the search parameters, periods covered, coding, and compilation of the data in figures 2.8–2.11).[19]

The distributions of topics in these four components of the transcript of dominant politics confirm what the examples in the previous section suggest: That until the 1960s, dominant political actors used the term *crisis* only rarely. When they did use it, it was to describe a very narrow range of issues, most of which were episodic and sudden events such as wars, economic depressions, and (echoing Carmen Reinhardt and Kenneth Rogoff's argument that crises are things that "can't happen here") to conflicts in other countries.[20]

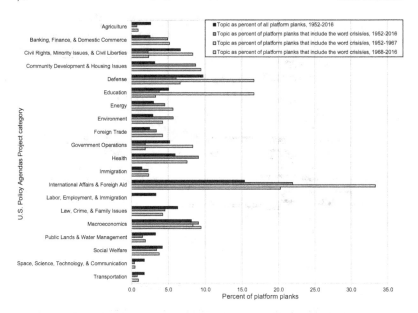

FIGURE 2.9. Proportion of party platform quasi-sentences that include the term *crisis* or *crises*, by US Policy Agendas Project category, 1952–2016. *Notes: Crisis* is used in platform planks falling under six of twenty USPAP categories before 1967 and in hearings falling under nineteen categories from 1968–2016. Search was for "crisis" or "crises". Blank spaces indicate that there were no observations of *crisis* or *crises* in quasi-sentences on that topic during the period that would be represented by the missing bar. The US Policy Agendas Project identified 15,953 separate quasi-sentences in Democratic Party platforms and 19,836 in Republican Party platforms (total N=35,789) from 1952 through 2016. Of these, 265 use the terms *crisis* or *crises*. For additional information, see appendices A and C, and notes 14, 15, and 19 in chapter 2. *Source:* US Policy Agendas Project.

These patterns are evident in figure 2.8, for example, which summarizes the distributions of USPAP topics in hearing titles. The black bars depict the proportion of all hearings (of which there were just over 99,000) held from 1947 through 2016 on each of the twenty US Policy Agendas Project categories (recall that the first time *crisis* is used in a hearing title is 1947). The striped bars indicate the proportion of the titles of the 600 hearings held during this entire period that contain the words *crisis* or *crises* that fall under the designated USPAP category. The speckled bars break this proportion out for the period that ends in 1967, and the gray bars break it out for 1968 to 2016. For this figure as well as figures 2.9 to 2.11, topics for which the striped, speckled, and gray bars are *longer* than the black bar are those for which *crisis* is used at a disproportionately *high* rate during the period in question, and those for which this same bar is *shorter* (or absent) indicate that *crisis* is observed *less frequently* than would be strictly proportional during each period (blank spaces indicate that there were no observations of *crisis* or *crises* in hearing titles, bill titles, platform planks, or State of the Union quasi-sentences on that topic during the period that would be represented by the missing bar). Hearings about International Affairs and Foreign Aid, for example, accounted for 7.4 percent of all hearings held from 1947 through 2016, and for 30.5 percent of all hearings during this same period that had the word *crisis* in their titles. In keeping with the broader pattern I have described, however, hearings on these topics accounted for 47.4 percent of all those with *crisis* in their titles from

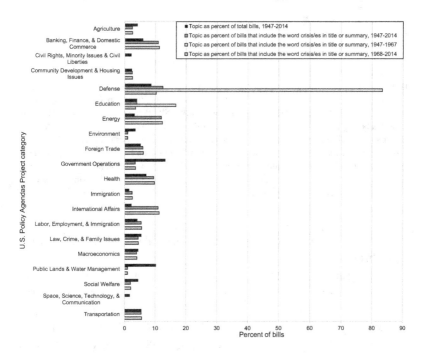

FIGURE 2.10. Proportion of congressional bill titles and summaries that include the term *crisis*, by US Policy Agendas Project category, 1947–2014. *Notes: Crisis* is used in the titles of bills falling under two of twenty USPAP categories before 1967 and in hearings falling under eighteen categories from 1968–2014. Search was for "crisis" or "crises". Blank spaces indicate that there were no observations of *crisis* or *crises* in bill titles on that topic during the period that would be represented by the missing bar. From 1947 through 2014, 376,488 bills were introduced in the House and Senate (excluding private bills), 201 of which used the term *crisis* or *crises* in their titles or summaries. For additional information, see appendices A and C, and notes 14, 15, and 19 in chapter 2. *Source:* US Policy Agendas Project.

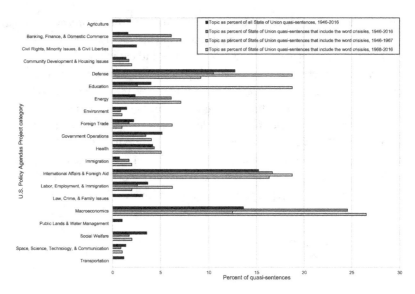

FIGURE 2.11. Proportion of State of the Union quasi-sentences that include the term *crisis* or *crises*, by US Policy Agendas Project category, 1946–2016. *Notes: Crisis* is used in State of the Union quasi-sentences falling under six of twenty USPAP categories before 1967 and in hearings falling under fourteen categories from 1968–2060. Search was for "crisis" or "crises". Blank spaces indicate that there were no observations of *crisis* or *crises* in hearing titles on that topic during the period that would be represented by the missing bar. The US Policy Agendas Project identified 21,604 separate quasi-sentences in State of the Union addresses from 1946 through 2016. Of these, 110 use the terms *crisis* or *crises*. For additional information, see appendices A and C, and notes 14, 15, and 19 in chapter 2. *Source:* US Policy Agendas Project.

1947 through 1967, but for only 30 percent of similarly titled hearings from 1968 through 2016.

Looking at the striped bars more generally (which disaggregate the hearing topics for the period ending in 1967) makes clear that *crisis* was used in the titles of hearings addressing only six of the twenty possible topics (30 percent) before 1968 (from 1947 through 1965, *crisis* appeared in the titles of hearings on even fewer—only five—USPAP topics).[21] Of these, hearings addressing "International Affairs and Foreign Aid" account for just under half (47.3 percent) of all observations. Hearings classified as having to do with "Law, Crime, and Family Issues" and "Government Operations" are a distant second and third (at 21.1 and 15.8 percent respectively). Each of the other three issue areas—"Defense," "Public Lands and Water Management," and "Transportation"—accounts for just 5.3 percent of hearings with *crisis* in their titles during this period. Of particular note is that *crisis* is never used in the title of any hearings categorized as "Civil Rights, Minority Issues, and Civil Liberties," "Community Development and Housing Issues," or "Social Welfare" during this period. Similar patterns are evident in the cases of party platforms, State of the Union addresses, and bill titles and summaries in figures 2.9–2.11.[22]

But regardless of whether *crisis* was being invoked to reference issues at home or abroad, and irrespective of the particular issues in question, its near-exclusive connotation during this period was to describe discrete and relatively episodic bad things that were understood by dominant political actors as turning points in the trajectories of the problems in question. This meaning is nearly the only way in which the word was used in dominant politics over the course of this entire period and across both of the two major parties. The 1932 Republican platform praises Herbert Hoover, for example, for his leadership during the crisis of the economic depression, and castigates the Democratic House for its "characteristic and appalling proof of the existing incapacity of that party for leadership in a national crisis." Eight years later, the 1940 Democratic platform refers to the looming war in Europe as a "world crisis." This near-exclusive use of *crisis* to describe wars, depressions, and bad things happening in other countries continued through the 1950s, with, for example, the Republicans arguing in their 1952 platform that the "appearance of economic health" claimed by the Democrats had been "created" by them through expenditures for the "war crisis." That same year, the Democrats blamed the "current crisis over Suez" on "inept and vacillating Republican policy," while simultaneously praising President Truman for preserving individual rights in the face of the *crisis* of the Cold War.

Clear-Cut Crises *Defined*

This cluster of uses, I argue, constituted the first meaning of *crisis* as a political keyword—what I call clear-cut crises. Clear-cut crises are ostensibly self-evident, objective, and seemingly unambiguously urgent problems. They are thought to be universal, easily recognizable, and brought about by relatively discrete, quick, and episodic shocks that are triggered by seemingly exogenous causes and arrive suddenly or otherwise unexpectedly. In this meaning, crisis connotes a development that is, on its face, "unique and threatening," and it encompasses the kinds of "bad things" that have come to be familiarly labeled crises—wars, terrorist attacks, depressions, health pandemics, so-called natural disasters, and the like.[23] We might think of these as "Justice Potter Stewart" crises, ones that we alleg-edly "know when we see."

It is difficult to argue that such paradigmatic examples of crises are not horrible things, that they do not represent crossroads that require swift responses, or that they do not warrant large-scale interventions and re-sources that might mitigate catastrophic or disastrous outcomes. Bad things such as these seem so obviously to be crises that Desmond King labels them "objective crises" and argues that their distinguishing feature is that they "cannot be disregarded politically."[24] In addition, as Michele Dauber ar-gues in the case of disasters, the victims of clear-cut crises are typically understood to be blameless. It was to leverage this perceived innocence, she shows, that Democrats went to great lengths to frame the Great De-pression as a disaster, comparing its damage to that caused by floods and calling it an "economic earthquake."[25] And like the tornados that Paul Pierson uses to illustrate the role of time in different kinds of political change, the causes and effects of such events are understood to be rela-tively "short."[26] As a result, clear-cut crises also invite arguments that gov-ernment action or resources are mandated and will make or have made a positive difference in addressing them.

Meaning II. Condition-as-Crisis

The evidence from party platforms, State of the Union addresses, con-gressional hearings, and bills makes clear that from the 1840s through the early 1960s, *crisis* was used rarely among dominant political actors. When it was used during this period, it was reserved primarily for "clear-cut" bad things. And it may seem unsurprising, particularly in retrospect, that po-litical actors would borrow the word *crisis* from medicine and apply it to events like military conflicts. It may seem similarly unremarkable that one political party would use this term as a partisan brickbat or in the course of blaming its opponents for a bad thing while throwing bouquets at its own leaders for saving the day. But although bad things like wars and de-pressions would seem to be easily identifiable and their political salience similarly self-evident, their "clear-cut" legibility as crises and the nature and scale of intervention deemed appropriate and warranted to address them are not necessarily correlated with the actual magnitude of their severity.[27] Rather, as Colin Hay maintains (and echoing Dauber's arguments about "disaster narratives"), crises are constituted "in and through narrative."[28] It is how the magnitude of a bad thing is framed, perceived, and constructed by the actors with the power to respond to it and to shape these narratives about it that determines whether a particular one will be constituted as a crisis. King, for example, argues that the kinds of crises I label clear-cut are "objectively" understood as crises and that political actors therefore cannot ignore them.[29] This un-ignorability is anything but inevitable, however. Instead, as scholars of agenda setting and problem definition have long argued (and as I demonstrate in what follows), ignorability and un-ignorability are themselves products of processes of political contestation and construction.[30]

This point is well illustrated by the fact that over the course of the period during which dominant actors confined their use of *crisis* to the clear-cut variety, non-dominant political actors introduced and constituted a second keyword meaning of *crisis*—what I call condition-as-crisis.[31] Drawing on language, ideas, and imagery originating in the movement to abolish slavery, racial justice and other progressive activists and advocates began to use the word *crisis* as a way to argue that the enduring and quotidian *domestic* problems and injustices faced by marginalized groups, particularly African Americans, should be understood as being at *critical junctures* in their trajectories, and therefore as warranting of a political response.[32] That is, they used crisis language to frame these persistent injustices as dynamic problems facing crossroads at which the presence or absence of government intervention and resources would determine whether conditions would improve or worsen. In so doing, they tried to harness the agenda-setting and constitutive power of language to shape ideas about the causes of and solutions to forms of "slow violence," particularly ideas about the causes of and solutions to the ongoing horrors, "premature death," "slow death," "routinised crisis," and "attritional devastation" of racial oppression.[33] Through their efforts to change public understandings of bad things that have causes and effects that play out, as scholars including Ariella Azoulay and Adi Ophir, Leah Bassel and Akwugo Emejulu, Annie Menzel, Paul Pierson, Shannon Sullivan, and Antonio Vázquez-Arroyo have described, over long periods and that are consequently often obscured, racial justice advocates transformed *crisis* from a descriptor attached to some clear-cut bad things into an *argument* about how other kinds of bad things ought to be understood as well as how they might be resolved.[34]

The NAACP and The Crisis *Magazine*

This innovation in the political deployment of the word *crisis* on the part of advocates for marginalized groups and its attendant refiguring of crisis

FIGURE 2.12. Cover of the inaugural issue of *The Crisis* magazine, 1910.

as a political concept are exemplified by the National Association for the Advancement of Colored People's (NAACP) magazine *The Crisis* (see figure 2.12). NAACP cofounder Mary White Ovington recalled the story of the magazine's naming in a piece that she contributed to its August 1914 issue, which marked its fourth anniversary. According to her account, she and some of the other founders had been "having an informal talk regarding the new magazine" and "touched the subject of poetry." Ovington recalled that she had mentioned somewhat offhandedly that there is "a poem of [nineteenth-century white abolitionist James Russell] Lowell's . . . that means more to me today than any other poem in the world." Upon hearing that the title of the poem was "The Present Crisis," Ovington recounts, William English Walling, another NAACP cofounder "looked up and said, " 'The Crisis' . . . There's the name for your magazine, 'The Crisis.' "[35]

Lowell's 1845 poem addressed the national conflict over slavery in the years leading up to the Civil War. In recalling the poem's significance for that foundational moment in the history of what would become the mouthpiece of one of the most important and longest-surviving racial justice organizations in the United States, Ovington wrote that "if we had a creed to which our members, black and white, our branches North and South and East and West, our college societies, our children circles, should all subscribe, it should be these lines of Lowell's noble verse," several of which she included in her essay (see figure 2.13):

Once to every man and nation comes the moment to decide,
In the strife of Truth with Falsehood, for the good or evil side;
Some great cause, G-d's new Messiah, offering each the bloom or blight,
Parts the goats upon the left hand, and the sheep upon the right,
And the choice goes by forever 'twixt that darkness and that light. . . .

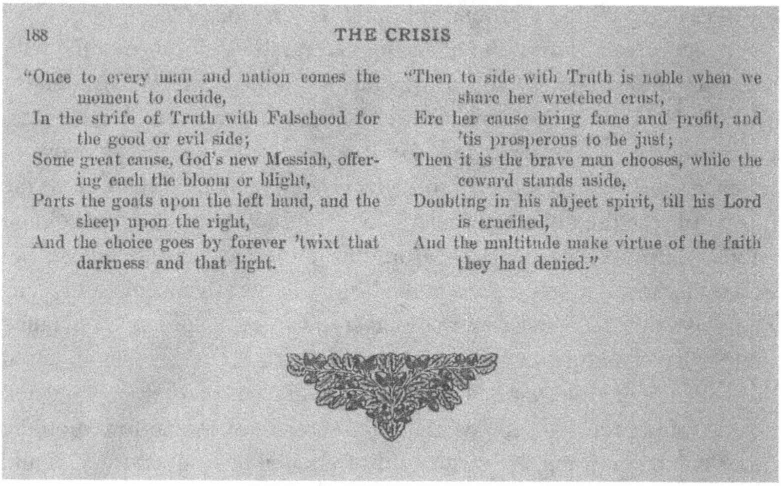

188   THE CRISIS

"Once to every man and nation comes the   "Then to side with Truth is noble when we
    moment to decide,   share her wretched crust,
In the strife of Truth with Falsehood for   Ere her cause bring fame and profit, and
    the good or evil side;   'tis prosperous to be just;
Some great cause, God's new Messiah, offer-   Then it is the brave man chooses, while the
    ing each the bloom or blight,   coward stands aside,
Parts the goats upon the left hand, and the   Doubting in his abject spirit, till his Lord
    sheep upon the right,   is crucified,
And the choice goes by forever 'twixt that   And the multitude make virtue of the faith
    darkness and that light.   they had denied."

FIGURE 2.13. Passages from James Russell Lowell, "The Present Crisis," 1845, quoted in "How the National Association for the Advancement of Colored People Began," by Mary White Ovington in the August 1914 issue of *The Crisis* magazine.

Then to side with Truth is noble when we share her wretched crust,
Ere her cause bring fame and profit, and 'tis prosperous to be just;
Then it is the brave man chooses, while the coward stands aside,
Doubting in his abject spirit, till his Lord is crucified,
And the multitude make virtue of the faith they had denied.

The sentiments expressed in these lines, Ovington noted in her article, "are as true to-day as when they were written seventy years ago."[36]

Of significance here is not simply that the NAACP cofounders chose to use the word *crisis* as the title for their organization's new magazine at a time when the word was not in much use. Equally significant are the ways in which the poem title that served as the magazine's namesake juxtaposes imagery and language that figure the "race crisis" not as an inevitable and intractable fact of nature but as a set of critical junctures at which alternately good or evil trajectories result from human decisions and actions.[37] From the assertion that "once" comes a moment of decision; to the argument that the moment of decision represents a crossroads at which either "truth" or "falsehood," "good" or "evil," and "bravery" or "cowardice" would triumph; to the understanding that these crossroads would lead to outcomes of either "bloom" or "blight" and "darkness" or "light," the quoted passages suggest that the cofounders were trying to use crisis as an "active force" in shaping political reality, particularly in shaping the ways in which racial injustice and possible solutions to it were understood.

Ovington's account of the title's origins and its significance to the publication's mission reinforced a previous account given by *Crisis* editor W. E. B. Du Bois in the November 1910 editorial he wrote for the inaugural issue of the magazine. In it, Du Bois explained that the objective of the magazine was "to set forth those facts and arguments which show the danger of race prejudice, particularly as manifested to-day toward colored people."[38] It takes its name, he wrote, "from the fact that the editors believed that this is a *critical time* in the history of the advancement of men" (emphasis added).[39] Echoing the imagery in Lowell's poem, he detailed the particular nature of this "critical time" as a set of choices between "Catholicity and tolerance, reason and forbearance" on the one hand and "bigotry and prejudice, emphasized race consciousness and force" on the other hand. Choosing the former set of possibilities, he asserted, would lead the country down a path that would "make the world-old dream of human brotherhood approach realization." Electing the latter set, however, would "repeat the awful history of the contact of nations and groups in the past." "We strive," he concluded hopefully, "for this higher and broader vision of Peace and Good Will."[40] In sharp contrast to dominant political actors during this period who used *crisis* sparingly and mainly to describe wars, recessions, and conflicts in or with other countries, Du Bois invoked and repurposed this term in an effort to denaturalize and transform the way in which ongoing and endemic racial oppression was understood: not as a fact of nature or as the historically inevitable (and therefore unchangeable) result of "the contact of nations and groups" but as the contingent outcomes of human decisions and agentic behavior. He hoped especially, Megan Ming Francis explains, that broadcasting the "terror of lynching" to a broader white audience would shatter what Francis labels the "normalized attitudes" toward it—attitudes that were characterized by "acceptability in the South and indifference in the North."[41] The NAACP hoped further, Francis explains, that "familiarity with and careless disregard for lynching could be transformed into critique and protest."[42]

This meaning of *crisis* is one of the central concepts framing and informing the magazine's mission, its politics, and its attempt to frame a broader understanding of race and racial inequality. The term was used sparingly in article titles and text during the magazine's early years; excluding eponymous references to the title of the publication itself, it appeared a mere 234 times in only 138 of the 371 issues published from 1910 through 1959 (see endnote and appendices for information about working with and content-coding *The Crisis*).[43] *Crisis* writers occasionally used the word to describe the kinds of clear-cut crises the term was being used to designate in dominant discourses during this period, but they did so only infrequently. For example, from 1910 through 1959, the magazine contained five references each to the First World War and the Civil War as crises, thirteen to the Second World War, four to the Cold War, ten to economic depressions and financial crises, and several to crises in other countries (including three to race-related crises in India, Haiti, and the Philippines). Such references to clear-cut crises were the exceptions, however; the vast majority (62 percent) of substantive invocations of the term *crisis* by authors of nonfiction articles or columns in *The Crisis* during this period were to domestic issues such as housing and segregation, and 54 percent used it in a way that reframed a long-term problem of racial injustice into a critical juncture.[44] That is, most *Crisis* authors used the word as it was used in the magazine's title: as part of an argument that the conditions being endured by African Americans were not inevitable, that the United States faced a crossroads regarding racial injustice, and that choosing the correct path required concerted state action and resources. This meaning framed the NAACP's approach to understanding racial injustice and distinguished it from its use on the part of dominant political actors during that period.

"The Crisis of His Career"

The first time that the word *crisis* was used substantively in a *Crisis* magazine article illustrates its use to frame racial inequality as a problem facing a crossroads that warranted state action and resources. The piece in question, an editorial titled "The Truth," was published in the April 1911 issue and addressed Supreme Court decisions in two cases: *Franklin v. State of South Carolina* and *Bailey v. Alabama. Bailey* overturned the peonage (unfree labor) laws of Alabama.[45] *Franklin* was the first Supreme Court case argued by the NAACP and is typically referred to as the "Pink Franklin Case." The case involved Pink Franklin, a Black sharecropper in South Carolina who had been sentenced to death for killing a white police officer who burst into his home unannounced before dawn with a warrant for his arrest because he had allegedly not shown up for work one day after receiving an advance on his pay. After several failed appeals to have the conviction overturned, the NAACP—with the help of Thomas E. Miller (a lawyer and then-president of South Carolina State College) and NAACP executive secretary Frances Blascoer—took up the case and persuaded South Carolina governor Martin Ansel to commute Franklin's sentence to life in prison.[46]

"There are friends of black folk in this land," the editorial asserts, alluding to the white supporters and allies who had played a part in achieving these important but qualified victories.[47] It continues:

> There is continual advance in human sympathy. There is an awakening in the white South on the race problem. All that is true. It is also true that the Negro American today faces the crisis of his career; race prejudice is rampant and is successfully overcoming humanitarianism in many lines, and the determination of the dominant South to beat the black man to his knees, to make him a docile ignorant beast of burden, was never stronger than to-day. This is the truth. Let us tell the truth, unpleasant though it be, and through the truth seek freedom. There is no other way.[48]

Like the explanations about the decision to name the magazine *The Crisis*, the crisis that this editorial describes is not the "bad thing" of racism itself, nor is it the particular episodic events involved in the Supreme

Court cases or their decisions. The crisis referenced here is instead the critical juncture in the long and ongoing battle between "race prejudice" and "humanitarianism," a battle in which the outcome is unknown and anything but inevitable. In this case, it is not the inevitability of ongoing racism that was being denaturalized. In arguing that the significance of these two positive outcomes and the role of sympathetic white allies in them should not be overstated, it is instead the Whiggish view that racism is on an inevitable decline that is being challenged. The editorial acknowledges that the developments it discusses imply that the status quo is not inescapable, that white racism is not natural, and that things can consequently get better. But it insists as well that conditions could also go on as they had been and that they could also get worse. Any continued improvements therefore entail more than the inertial goodwill of sympathetic and liberal whites or individual legal and political actors. Instead, they demand the political equivalent of medical intervention into the body politic—intentional action and the force of the state.

I cannot demonstrate definitively, of course, that the idea of condition-as-crisis was introduced into the lexicon of domestic politics and policy by racial justice activists in the early twentieth century, much less that its introduction there is responsible for or that it "caused" the broader shift in its meaning. But while there is no "smoking gun," what Patricia Strach has described as the "chain of evidence" suggests at the very least that racial justice advocates and activists were early adopters and disseminators of this innovative meaning, which they deployed in an explicit and concerted attempt to reframe and reconstitute the ongoing and domestic injustices affecting them and their marginalized constituents as well as the timeframe within which the causes of, solutions to, and the injustices themselves were understood.[49] In doing so, they took a word that had been used mainly to describe wars and economic hard times and turned it into an *argument* about how racial injustice should be understood, addressed, and resolved: Not as an inevitable, intractable, and eternal fact of nature, but rather as a problem facing a critical juncture with alternative trajectories and outcomes—a problem that was created by, and therefore could be resolved by, human decisions and agency and state intervention and resources. The evidence also suggests that these advocates and activists used this meaning of *crisis* precociously, well before dominant political actors were doing so. Even if we cannot know for certain that they were its originators, it seems clear that racial justice advocates are a central part of the story about how the term *crisis* evolved from "a signifier for a critical, decisive moment" to one that was, as Janet Roitman argues, applied to protracted conditions in ways that, as I show, would come to be reflected in and to constitute dominant political discourses of crisis politics down the road.[50]

Condition-as-Crisis in Dominant Politics: The 1960s and 1970s

While racial justice advocates increased their use of *crisis* in the very early twentieth century and shifted its meaning as part of their effort to reframe the ways in which ongoing conditions and domestic issues were understood and addressed, dominant political actors continued to apply the term sparingly and mainly as a designation for clear-cut bad things and bad things happening abroad through the early 1960s. The mid- and late 1960s witnessed a significant increase in the word's deployment on the part of dominant political actors, however, as well as substantive changes in its meanings brought about by a substantial expansion in the issues to which it was applied. More specifically, although dominant political actors had once reserved *crisis* primarily to characterize wars, recessions, and problems abroad, in the 1960s they began to adopt the meaning that had been initiated by civil rights advocates, applying it to an ever-widening array of bad things that they sought to frame as turning points worthy of state intervention and resources. As it was disseminated and attached to an increasingly broad range of domestic issues beyond recessions, *crisis* became, as Fraser and Gordon put it in the case of *dependency*, fair game, thereby consolidating—but also significantly altering—the meaning of *condition-as-crisis* within dominant political discourses.[51]

Increased Use

The increasing use of the term *crisis* on the part of dominant political actors becomes evident in books, newspapers, party platforms, State of the Union addresses, hearing titles, and bill titles and summaries in the early 1960s (see figures 2.1–2.6). Its rate of use in party platforms, for example, began to steepen in 1964, at which point each party invoked it at least once in every platform from that year forward. Although its concentration declined somewhat in the 1970s, it was never again absent from the platforms of either of the two major parties. This escalation remains substantial even after taking into account the exponential increase in the word counts of the platforms over this same period, and even in comparison to other politically salient words such as *poverty*, *accident*, and *tax*. The use of *crisis* in the titles of hearings and bills also began to escalate during this period (accompanied by changes in its substance and meanings), with sharp escalations in the proportions of titles containing the word *crisis* becoming evident in both of these sources beginning in the 1970s.

Proliferation of Applications and Meanings

This explosion in the use of the term *crisis* on the part of dominant political actors in the late 1960s and early 1970s was accompanied by striking substantive changes in its meanings, as political actors, observers, and policymakers applied it not only to more issues but to different kinds of issues as well (see table 2.3; see endnote and appendices for details about how these "first observations" were identified).[52] This ever-increasing range of issues labeled crises included everything from "housing" (in the 1968 Republican platform), "cities" and "transportation" (in the 1972 Democratic platform), to "environmental" and "air pollution" (in the 1972 Republican platform), to "urban" and "juvenile delinquency" (in the 1976 Democratic platform). As dominant political actors used *crisis* in these new ways, they transformed it from a word that they had attached primarily to wars, problems in other countries, and economic bad times to one that was

TABLE 2.3. **First observations of *crisis* or *crises* in State of the Union addresses and major party platforms, 1960–2016**

Year	State of the Union addresses	Democratic Party platforms	Republican Party platforms
1960	Crises with Soviet Union	National crisis Education financial crisis	
1961	Gold crisis		
1962	Communist crisis		
1963	Military crisis Cuban crisis		
1964		Crucible of crisis Cuban crisis Crises in Caribbean and Gulf of Tonkin	Crises of confidence
1965			
1966			
1967			
1968	World crises Cyprus crisis Urban crisis	Farm crisis International monetary crisis	Housing crisis Payments crisis Cuban missile crisis
1969	Middle East crisis		

continues

TABLE 2.3. (*continued*)

Year	State of the Union addresses	Democratic Party platforms	Republican Party platforms
1970			
1971	State and city financial crisis		
1972		Cities in crisis Rural mobility crisis Transportation crisis	Middle East crisis Periodic crises Berlin crises Crisis with USSR Government fiscal crises Environmental crisis Air pollution crisis
1973			
1974	Energy crisis		
1975			
1976		Economic crisis Crisis in education costs (tuition) Urban crisis Fiscal crises Environmental crises Crises in Africa Juvenile delinquency crisis	Physical crisis Energy crisis
1977	Regional crises		
1978	Crisis management		
1979			
1980	Crises in Iran and Afghanistan	Refugee crisis Welfare crisis Family crisis Family Crisis Center Program (Domestic Violence)	Time of crisis Minority youth unemployment crisis Crisis of overregulation Water crisis Social crises Inflation crisis Nuclear crisis
1981	Refugee crisis (Haiti and Cuba)		
1982			
1983	Economic crises		
1984	Government crisis	Energy crisis Debt crisis in Mexico Third World debt crisis Deficit crisis Children in crisis Drug crisis Crisis in Central America Nuclear crisis	Social Security crisis Crisis management
1985			
1986	Family welfare crisis		
1987			
1988		Crisis of underinvestment (in children) Housing crisis	Drought crisis Youth crisis

TABLE 2.3. (*continued*)

Year	State of the Union addresses	Democratic Party platforms	Republican Party platforms
		Trash crisis	Terrorist crises
			Domestic crisis
1989	Government by crisis		
1990			
1991			
1992		Families in crisis	Medical liability crisis
			AIDS crisis
			Savings and loan crisis
1993	Health care crisis		
1994			
1995	Financial crisis in Mexico		
1996		Family health crisis	Lumber crisis
			Drug crisis
			Illegal immigration crisis
1997			
1998	Global warming crisis		
1999	Y2K crisis		
2000	Domestic crisis	Asian financial crisis	Debt crisis
	Crisis between Indian and Pakistan	Tobacco health crisis	East Timor crisis
2001			
2002	9/11 crisis		
2003	AIDS crisis in Africa		
2004		Jobs crisis	Venezuelan political crisis
			California energy crisis
			Crisis pregnancy programs
2005			
2006			
2007			
2008		Dropout crisis	
		Social Security crisis	
		Humanitarian crisis	
		National security crisis	
2009	Housing crisis		
2010			
2011			
2012		Mortgage crisis	
2013			
2014			
2015			
2016			Constitution in crisis
			Judiciary crisis
			Manufactured fiscal crises
			Pornography crisis
			Opioid crisis
			National security crisis

Note: Search was for "crisis" or "crises". Data were compiled using the "kwic" command (key words in context) in the R quanteda package. Doing so produces an output file that identifies the year, row in data, context before the word, and context after the word, from which bi-gram and tri-grams were identified. This list was then sorted alphabetically and by source and year to identify the earliest observation for each bi-gram and tri-gram. For additional information, see appendices A, B, and C, and note 4 in chapter 2. *Sources:* Brad Borevitz, State of the Union; Gerhard Peters and John T. Woolley, The American Presidency Project.

increasingly associated with domestic conflicts and policy problems. These new "bindings" reflected, communicated, and played a part in constructing broader social, economic, and political developments and anxieties, in part by transforming what had been understood as protracted and intransigent conditions into urgent problems facing critical junctures that warranted and could be resolved through government attention and resources.[53]

Some of the manifestations and implications of this shift are illustrated by revisiting figures 2.8 to 2.11, which depict the changing issues referred to as crises in hearing titles, bill titles and summaries, State of the Union addresses, and party platforms. In stark contrast to the limited range of issues labeled crises in previous eras, beginning in 1968, *crisis* was used in titles of congressional hearings on all twenty USPAP topics (compared to six categories up to that point), in bill titles or summaries on eighteen topics (compared with two during the earlier period), on fourteen of twenty categories in State of the Union addresses (compared to five during the earlier period), and on nineteen topics in party platforms (compared to six during the earlier period). And whereas the predominant application of *crisis* prior to the 1960s had been to wars, problems in other countries, and economic distress, beginning in that decade, domestic issues began to comprise an increasing share of its applications.

For example, among the USPAP congressional hearing categories in which *crisis* had not appeared in titles before 1968 but did after this date are Agriculture; Banking, Finance, and Domestic Commerce; Civil Rights, Minority Issues, and Civil Liberties; "Community Development and Housing Issues;" Education; Energy; Environment; Health; Immigration; Labor, Employment, and Immigration; Macroeconomics; Social Welfare; and Space, Science, Technology, and Communications. Conversely, the proportion of hearings on the more "traditional" crisis categories of Defense and International Affairs and Foreign Aid declined (in the latter case, precipitously). The use of the word declined as well in the titles of hearings on several domestic categories (including Government Operations; Law, Crime, and Family Issues; Public Lands and Water Management; and Transportation). But most striking and germane here is the juxtapositioning of the overall broadening of the kinds of issues to which the term *crisis* came to be applied alongside the increases in its application to domestic issues alongside declines in its use within typical pre-1960 categories. Similar patterns are evident in the other political documents as well. In the case of bill titles and summaries, for example, *crisis* is used in two of twenty possible categories through 1967 but in seventeen out of twenty from 1968 to

2015. When it comes to party platforms, the increase is from six of twenty categories before 1967 to nineteen of twenty from 1968 to 2016. The word is used in six of twenty categories in State of the Union addresses in the first period and in fourteen out of twenty in the second.

The period that witnessed the expanded use of the term *crisis* to characterize domestic problems coincides with what Frank Baumgartner and Bryan Jones show was a dramatic broadening of issues addressed by the federal government in the 1960s and 1970s.[54] They label this broadening of the policy agenda the "Great Issues Expansion," with more issues begetting more committees, subcommittees, staff, and policy institutions to manage these new issues. And to some degree, the increasing tendency of dominant political actors to characterize domestic issues as crises may be due, at least in part, to the fact that this expansion meant that there were simply more opportunities—and, perhaps, more incentives—to do so, as political actors battled to raise the profile of issues on a newly crowded policy agenda. But if this were all that was driving the increasing frequency with which dominant political actors used the term *crisis*, we should observe parallel increases in other words that signal urgency, and the data presented earlier in this chapter demonstrate that this is not the case. Regardless, the proliferation of crisis politics alongside the more general "issues expansion" suggests that the two phenomena are importantly and deeply imbricated in ways that, as I establish in subsequent chapters, have significant implications for understanding the relationship between episodic hard times and the kinds of ongoing and quotidian hard times that routinely affect and structure the lived experiences of marginalized groups.

To be sure, dominant political actors and policymakers continued to use the term *crisis* to characterize clear-cut bad things such as wars and recessions. They also continued to use the word as a metaphor for national malaise and to describe difficult situations in and troubled relationships with other countries. In 1964, for example, the Democratic Party platform referred three times to the Cuban missile crisis, twice to other security crises, and twice to general national crises, including the statement, "The leadership we offer has already been tested in the crucible of crisis and challenge." The 1968 GOP platform similarly used the language of crisis to discuss national defense and trade policy ("the Cuban missile crisis" and "the balance of payments crisis") and to argue that the National Security Council should be reinvigorated (to "enable our nation once again to anticipate and prevent crises rather than hastily contriving counter-measures after they arise").

Clear-cut crisis also experienced a revival in the years following the events of 11 September 2001, when the term *crisis* was attached to the wars in Iraq and Afghanistan and the "war on terror" more generally. In their 2008 platform, for example, the Republicans invoked *crisis* to demand further military intervention, to justify intervention and resource allocation, and to castigate opponents for alleged intransigence on these issues:

> The waging of war—and the achieving of peace—should never be micromanaged in a party platform, or on the floor of the Senate and House of Representatives for that matter. In dealing with present conflicts and future crises, our next president must preserve all options. It would be presumptuous to specify them in advance and foolhardy to rule out any action deemed necessary for our security. . . .

For its part, the Democratic Party used the language of crisis to argue in its 2004 platform that too many resources were being devoted to the post-9/11 response:

> The war in Iraq has overextended our armed services. The vast majority of the Army's active duty combat divisions are committed to Iraq—currently there, preparing to go, or recently returned. That is a dangerous and potentially disastrous strain that limits our capacity to respond to other crises.

But whereas applications such as these had previously dominated the use of crisis language on the part of dominant political actors, by the mid-1970s, they constituted an ever-smaller portion of the bad things labeled crises in the transcript of dominant politics. In 1972, for example, the Democratic platform invoked *crisis* twice with reference to cities and urban issues, twice regarding transportation issues, and once with reference to higher education. The only reference that year to the kinds of issues that had been characterized as crises before the 1960s, however, was to "13 years of boycott, crisis and hostility" in Cuba. While that instance referred to the clear-cut-crisis-type issue of national defense, by using it with regard to an issue that had endured for "13 years," this invocation, too, reflected the newly popular meaning of crisis as an ongoing condition. So although dominant political actors and media have continued to use *crisis* to characterize international and global problems (for example, today's "global refugee crisis"), the shift in which the word came to be used as way to designate and characterize ongoing and domestic bad things was new.[55]

And so, after decades of relatively stable and uncontested use as a designation for clear-cut crises, dominant political actors borrowed the idea of condition-as-crisis from racial justice activists and brought it into mainstream political discourse. As they did, they shifted *crisis* from a mainly descriptive term that they had applied almost exclusively to presumptively episodic and foreign phenomena to one that became a common characterization for a broad range of ongoing domestic problems and an argument that aimed to justify state intervention and resources as the way to address them. It was also then that *crisis* made its way into the vernacular of dominant American political discourse and that its status as a political keyword was consolidated.

Meaning III. Calamity-as-Crisis

After the idea of condition-as-crisis took root within dominant political discourses, the domestic issues to which *crisis* was attached continued to expand and evolve. The 1984 Democratic Party platform, for example, referred to teen suicide, drug trafficking, and drug abuse as crises, while the 1996 Republican platform was the first major party platform to include the term *immigration crisis*. This application of *crisis* to an ever-broader array of domestic issues eventually generated a third and broader meaning that I call *calamity-as-crisis*. Calamity-as-crisis is the now common and relatively generic meaning that has become familiar, and which Reinhart Koselleck protested has come to be used "interchangeably with 'unrest,' 'conflict,' 'revolution,' and to describe vaguely disturbing moods or situations."[56] As illustrated by President Obama's declaration that the "epidemic of gun violence in our country is a crisis" in the opening line of his 2016 *New York Times* op-ed, in this more general usage, political actors began to use *crisis* as a synonym for *terrible thing*, *tragedy*, and *emergency*.[57] But as the data that I have presented in this chapter make clear, the expansion of the issues to which dominant political actors applied the term *crisis* rarely extended to ones affecting marginalized groups, and when they did apply it to such issues, they rarely did so in ways that reframed them as longer-term problems facing critical junctures that could be resolved through state intervention. As a consequence, the proliferation of *calamity-as-crisis* reinforced the unevenness and selectivity of the kinds of bad things that were designated as crises. This unevenness, in turn, signaled that the bad things that happen to some people and groups are real problems worthy of state attention and resources while the longer-term structures and patterns of marginalization are natural, inevitable, and not worthy of or amenable to such intervention.

Conclusion

The expansion and evolution of the issues to which dominant political actors applied the term *crisis* are among the processes through which American politics witnessed the genesis and proliferation of *crisis* as a common way to characterize ongoing and quotidian domestic problems. It was also through these processes that *crisis* came to be used to reframe the time horizons through which such problems were understood. That is, as with the medical meaning of crisis as "the point in the progress of a disease" at which medical intervention is "decisive of recovery or death," conditions deemed crises were treated not as eternal and inevitable but as problems facing crossroads at which they will either get better or deteriorate and to argue that state intervention and resources were warranted and would make a difference in resolving them.

The political deployment of *crisis* was not, of course, the only strategy— and not even the only discursive strategy—through which dominant political actors and policymakers made the case for state intervention and resources when it came to domestic issues. Dauber, as I have discussed, has documented the ways in which Democrats strategically deployed the term *disaster* to justify welfare state expansion.[58] Scholars including Marc Bacharach, Mary Dudziak, and Peter Andreas and Richard Price have described the ways in which political actors use the formulation of "wars on" problems such as poverty, crime, and drugs to justify state intervention and resources.[59] And even though its use increased significantly, even at its most frequent, *crisis* never accounted for even 1 percent of all words used in any context at any given moment.

Nonetheless, the shift that I have documented was a key component of the process through which the term *crisis* evolved, as Roitman notes, from "a signifier for a critical, decisive moment" to a word that was applied to describe any number of protracted conditions.[60] That is, part of how *crisis* became the political keyword that we have come to know and part of the process through which crisis politics were constituted more generally is that, whether unconsciously or by design, dominant political actors took a page from civil rights activists: They began to use *crisis* in ways that denaturalized domestic problems and issues that had been taken as given and unchangeable, that shifted the time frame in which they are understood to take place, and that did so in ways that demanded and made them amenable to state intervention. However, they did so unevenly, and, as I show in the next chapter, it is through this uneven application of the term *crisis* to domestic issues that the implications of crisis politics for the politics of marginalization and marginalized groups are manifest.

Regressions, Reversals, and Red Herrings

With the benefit of hindsight, it may seem unremarkable that dominant political actors adopted, extended, and proliferated the uses and new meanings of *crisis*, helping to transform it from a technical term that they had applied only rarely and almost exclusively to characterize relatively episodic events (particularly wars, recessions, and conflicts in other countries) to one used frequently and to discuss a broad range of ongoing domestic problems. And it might seem similarly intuitive from a contemporary vantage point that this development would unfold over the course of the 1960s and 1970s, an era during which political actors wrestled with an ever-expanding array of issues, many of which seemed to connect ongoing problems at home with various forms of turmoil in which the nation was enmeshed (and was instigating) abroad.[1]

But as unsurprising as it might appear in retrospect that dominant political actors would come to characterize an ever-wider array of domestic political and policy problems as crises, a keyword approach reminds us that such shifts in political language are rarely neutral.[2] In particular, although civil rights leaders had pioneered condition-as-crisis as a way to change the understandings of ongoing domestic issues and to justify state intervention and resources for marginalized groups, dominant political actors who adopted this meaning rarely applied it in this way. From 1965 through 1979, for example, ninety-seven congressional hearings included the word *crisis* in their titles, and sixty-eight of these (70.1 percent) addressed issues that are classified in US Policy Agendas Project (USPAP) categories that focus on domestic issues (see table 3.1; see endnote and appendices for details about data collection and coding).[3] Among these

TABLE 3.1. **Topics of congressional hearing titles containing** *crisis* **or** *crises*, **1965–1979**

US Policy Agendas Project category	N	% of titles containing *crisis/crises*	N domestic
Agriculture	2	2.1	2
Banking, Finance, and Domestic Commerce	4	4.1	2
Civil Rights, Minority Issues, and Civil Liberties	0	0	
Community Development and Housing Issues	7	7.2	7
Defense	1	1.0	0
Education	2	2.1	2
Energy	17	17.5	14
Environment	0	0	
Foreign Trade	0	0	
Government Operations	4	4.1	1
Health	16	16.5	16
Immigration	0	0	
International Affairs and Foreign Aid	22	22.7	5
Labor, Employment, and Immigration	3	3.1	3
Law, Crime, and Family Issues	5	5.2	2
Macroeconomics	3	3.1	3
Public Lands and Water Management	1	1.0	1
Social Welfare	2	2.1	2
Space, Science, Technology, and Communication	0	0	
Transportation	8	8.2	8
Total	97	100	68

Note: Search was for "crisis" or "crises". These data are a subset of those depicted in figure 2.8. The hearings data were compiled by using the Legacy CIS numbers to match each result of each search with its coded US Policy Agendas Project entry. For additional information, see appendix B, appendix C, and notes 4, 18, and 19 in chapter 2.
Sources: ProQuest Congressional and US Policy Agendas Project.

were sixteen hearings addressing domestic issues classified by the USPAP as having to do with "Health," two that addressed issues classified as having to do with "Education," and two that addressed issues categorized under "Social Welfare." A few of these hearings—including ones titled "Fuel Crisis Impact on Low-Income and Elderly," "Youth Crisis Services," and "Crisis in the National School Lunch Program"—took up issues that might seem to focus on marginalized groups. None of these almost one hundred hearings, however, was concerned primarily with issues classified in the USPAP as having to do with "Civil Rights, Minority Issues, and Civil Liberties," a category that includes voting rights, fair housing, and discrimination based on race, sex, sexual orientation, disability, or age. The pattern is similar for party platforms, bill titles and summaries, and State of the

Union addresses (see table A.5). In all of these cases, the increase in the range of domestic issues that are characterized as crises does not extend (or extends far less expansively) to those Agendas Project topics most likely to encompass issues related to inequality and marginalization.

The relative scarcity of crisis language in these sources cannot be explained by a more general absence of attention to such issues in hearings, bills, platforms, or State of the Union addresses during the 1960s and 1970s. As I showed in chapter 2, these same decades during which condition-as-crisis took root in dominant politics were ones in which issues related to racial inequality, economic justice, and gender discrimination were hotly contested, and the salience of these and related topics is reflected in all of these dominant political "transcripts." The platforms of both major parties from this era, for example, paid increasing attention to issues ranging from voting rights and equal pay to housing discrimination, poverty, and reproductive rights. Presidents also devoted increasing attention to these issues in their State of the Union addresses during this period, and the number of hearings held and bills introduced on all of these topics in Congress increased as well.

But with a few exceptions (several representative and illustrative examples of which I explore below), dominant political actors did not invoke crisis politics to justify state action and resources when such issues were addressed in these fora during this era. When they did apply the language of crisis to such issues, it was more typically the status quo rather than the status of marginalized groups that was treated as the crisis for which the deployment of state action and resources was being justified. And when crisis language was used to characterize issues affecting marginalized groups, it was rarely invoked in ways that signaled optimism or faith that a problem could be solved. Instead, it was more typically used in regressive ways, often to blame and punish marginalized groups for the problems they faced.[4]

Through such elisions and appropriations, the meaning of condition-as-crisis was subjected to several reversals that served to structure crisis politics in ways that typically reinforced rather than alleviated ongoing structural inequalities and marginalization. In other words, even as crisis language increased, and although the meaning of condition-as-crisis was imported into the dominant political lexicon from the language of social movement struggles, dominant political actors seldom used crisis politics to justify the use of state action and resources to address the ongoing structural inequalities for which activists had originally introduced it. Rather, initially foreshadowing and eventually reflecting what would come to be understood as neoliberal attacks on the welfare state, dominant political actors more typically argued that such crises demanded the retrenchment or privatization of such resources to regain lost ground.[5] Arguments such as these would eventually play a key role, for example, in justifying the creation and proliferation of subprime mortgages as the appropriate state action to increase homeownership among women and people of color.

Crisis and Ongoing Structural Inequalities and Marginalization

That dominant political actors did not use crisis politics to justify state intervention aimed at addressing structural inequalities is well illustrated in platform planks and congressional hearings addressing education and "population control" during the early and mid-1960s. In both of these cases, dominant political actors used the language of crisis to frame these issues as problems that faced critical junctures and that demanded and were ameliorable though state intervention and resources. But while both education and ideas about "population control" were bound up then as now with questions about racial and gender inequality, it was the threats they posed to status quo arrangements and their implications for dominant groups that were treated as the crises that demanded attention and resources.

Education

In their 1960 platform, for example, the Democrats wrote about the "financial crisis" facing "America's education." They noted that the "tremendous increase in the number of children of school and college age has far outrun the available supply of educational facilities and qualified teachers." "The classroom shortage alone," they explained, "is interfering with the education of 10 million students."[6]

This application of crisis language to education reflected, in part, newly urgent challenges associated with educating the large number of "baby boom" children entering school age around that time. But the strain these students were putting on the supply of classrooms and teachers was far from the only public education issue in 1960 that qualified as an urgent one in need of intervention and resources. Rather, 1960 was also the first year in which presidential nominating conventions were held following President Eisenhower's 1957 decision to send federal troops to Little

Rock in response to Governor Orval Faubus's deployment of the Arkansas National Guard under the guise of "states' rights" to prevent nine Black students from entering and enrolling in that city's Central High School. It was also only the second such convention and presidential election following the Supreme Court's 1954 and 1955 decisions in the *Brown v. Board of Education* cases.

Given Governor Faubus's appeal to the segregationist idea of states' rights in opposing school desegregation, Democrats' failure to use their discussion about a "crisis" in public education to draw attention to issues of racial inequality, marginalization, and subjugation is significant. Even more significant is that their proposed solutions to this alleged crisis included language that affirmed their support for states' rights. In particular, they argued in their 1960 platform that "America can meet its educational obligations only with generous Federal financial support, within the traditional framework of *local control*" (emphasis added), "local control" serving as coded language meant to indicate that they would not use federal resources and power to force schools to integrate.[7]

In other words, not only did the Democrats fail to connect racial inequity and segregation in education to the crises in education for which they urged increased federal resources and intervention, but they actually used the language of crisis to *oppose* intervention that would address and alleviate these inequalities.[8]

"Population Crises"

Two hearings held in the summer of 1965 about what was labeled a domestic "population crisis" further illustrate the failure of dominant political actors to frame structural inequalities as crises worthy of or remediable through state intervention, even as they applied this frame to an ever-broader array of domestic issues.[9] The hearings in question were held by the Subcommittee on Foreign Aid Expenditures of the Senate Committee on Government Operations, and were part of a series of discussions about S. 1676, a bill to "reorganize the Department of State and the Department of Health, Education, and Welfare." The bill's generic-sounding description obscured the substantive concern of these hearings, which was to address federal funding for "population control." Several of the hearings in this series were concerned with foreign aid programs that funded birth control in other countries, but these two hearings about the "population crisis" addressed funding for programs within the United States itself.

The hearings were held five years after the Food and Drug Administration had approved the birth control pill for use as oral contraception and almost immediately on the heels of the Supreme Court's June 1965 ruling in *Griswold v. Connecticut*, which overturned that state's "Comstock" law prohibiting contraception. These sessions took place in this context and in the midst of increasing feminist activism around reproductive rights and justice. Of the forty-two invited witnesses who testified at the hearings, however, only four were representatives from women's organizations while sixteen were physicians.[10] All were white, and only seven were women.

Among these witnesses were some who delivered testimony in which they highlighted the importance of access to contraception for women's well-being and autonomy, and some of them argued that access to contraception was a component of equality and justice for women more generally. But the alleged crisis that had prompted the hearings did not have to do with gendered injustices or with inequalities related to access to contraception. It also had nothing to do with how significant it would have been to increase access to contraception during an era in which many states (including the District of Columbia, where the hearings took place) prohibited abortion except when "necessary for the preservation of the mother's life or health."[11] Instead, the crisis referenced in the hearing title had to do with concerns about "overpopulation," a concept that has long been and was at the time associated with eugenicist efforts to drive down birth rates among low-income women—particularly low-income immigrant women and women of color—quickly and inexpensively, and often in coercive ways.[12] Most of the witnesses at this hearing consequently focused on what they argued was the need to address "land scarcity" and "rapid population growth," particularly in the District of Columbia.[13] Several witnesses, for example, quoted President Lyndon Johnson's State of the Union address from earlier that year, in which he had expressed concern about the "explosion of world population and the growing scarcity of world resources." In his testimony, Marriner Eccles, who had served as chair of the Federal Reserve's Board of Governors under presidents Franklin Roosevelt and Harry Truman, quoted Secretary of the Interior Stewart Udall, who stated that the "present population is in a headlong collision course with our resources."[14] Unless we "master this problem," Udall explained, "it will increasingly sit in all parliaments and at all council tables as the silent master of all decisions that concern life, liberty, and the pursuit of happiness."[15]

In other words, although the "population crisis" in question was a domestic one, and while the language of crisis was being used to shift the way in which this gendered issue would be understood, the crisis addressed at the hearings was not related to gender inequality, nor was the state intervention being promoted as warranted, necessary, and likely to make a difference aimed at improving women's health or at giving women the right to make choices about their bodies. Rather than arguing that gender-related injustices were crises that could and should be addressed or ended through state intervention, witnesses instead naturalized these injustices and promoted what Angela Davis has characterized as "the racist strategy of *population control*."[16] And although the suggested state intervention (more funding for information about contraception) was directed at women, witnesses made few attempts to challenge the framing of the "population explosion" as a crisis in ways that encompassed issues related to women's equality.[17]

Regressive and Repressive Uses

In the foregoing cases, dominant political actors used crisis politics to justify state intervention that protected the status quo and failed to address racial and gender inequalities. If these cases were ones of malign neglect, the hearings, federal government reports, and platform planks that I describe below illustrate a related but more proactive version of this phenomenon. In these examples, dominant political actors used crisis politics to advance more explicitly regressive and repressive domestic agendas. In particular, these cases demonstrate some of the ways in which these actors framed issues having to with energy shortages, drugs, crime, and problems facing cities as crises that faced critical junctures and that demanded and were ameliorable through state intervention and resources. Once again, however, although all of these issues have implications for inequality and marginalization, the ends to which dominant political actors put crisis politics did not address the inequalities in question, but were instead used to justify measures that exacerbated them.

Red Herrings: Energy Crises

In December 1973, Representative Robert Huber (R-MI) introduced H.R. 11862, a bill "to amend the Elementary and Secondary Education Act of 1965 to prohibit nonessential educational transportation in recognition of the current energy crisis." The use of *crisis* in the title of this bill has some obvious but important implications. First, the title references the "energy crisis," a binding of crisis to a problem that was helping to shape the word's political meaning at the time. In addition, as historian Meg Jacobs has shown, the energy crisis was being framed during the 1970s as a dramatic critical juncture precipitated by the confluence of an ongoing decline in domestic oil production and the external shock of the Organization of Petroleum Exporting Countries (OPEC) imposition of an oil embargo against the United States.[18] Less obvious but no less significant, however, is that Huber fiercely opposed school desegregation, and this bill, which he introduced under the guise of energy saving, was, in reality, an anti-busing bill. Far from addressing energy conservation, Huber used the bill to make the cynical argument that busing children to schools far from the neighborhoods in which they lived was undesirable because it wasted fuel.

H.R. 11862 never made it out of the House, but it nonetheless illustrates the kind of reversal that often characterized dominant political actors' use of condition-as-crisis and exemplifies the deleterious implications of such reversals for marginalized groups. In this case, civil rights were at stake, but crisis was not invoked to argue that increased state intervention was warranted and necessary to advance racial justice. Instead, it was deployed in an effort to undermine state attempts to advance racial equality.

Missed Opportunities: DC's "Narcotics-Crime" Crisis

Two hearings held in 1970 by the Senate Committee on the District of Columbia to address the "Narcotics-Crime Crisis in the Washington Area" provide another example in which dominant political actors invoked crisis in ways that undermined rather than advanced racial equality and justice.[19] The hearings were part of a series of hearings on the broader topic of "Crime in the National Capital" and were intended, their chair Senator Joseph Tydings (D-MD) explained, to "explore the progress which Federal and local officials have made during the past year toward combating the narcotics problem in the National Capital."[20] "At our hearings last spring," he continued, "we discovered that the Federal and District Governments had failed to meet the narcotics crime crisis which had invaded the entire National Capital regional area. . . . We learned that, as of the time of our hearings last year, a major narcotics ring had not been smashed in 17 years." Moreover, he recalled, "at the close of those hearings last year," he had called "the narcotics-crime crisis in the National Capital a tragic and intolerable picture of government inertia and inaction."[21]

With the hearing title's link between two long-standing issues and Tydings's own reference to seventeen years of ineffectiveness, the use of the language of crisis here seems to mirror its deployment on the part of advocates for marginalized groups. That is, it might seem that dominant political actors were using crisis language to denaturalize the inevitability of the long-standing problems of and connections between substance abuse and crime, and it might seem as well that they were doing so in a way that framed this problem as one that faced a crossroads, one at which state intervention was warranted and would make a difference. What becomes clear in the transcript, however, is that the crisis with which the hearings were centrally concerned was not one produced by the effects of "narcotics-crime" on low-income and Black residents of the District of Columbia. Rather, it was the implications of "narcotics-crime" for the more affluent and predominantly white residents of the broader capital region that had prompted these hearings.

In his opening statement on the third day of the hearings, for example, Tydings said, "when we began this investigation of the drug-abuse problem in the Washington area, we found a *narcotics-crime crisis* which was literally ripping apart our social and economic fabric" (emphasis added). Tydings's concerns about the lives of people struggling with addiction proved fleeting, however. Instead, it soon became clear that his real concern was that "heroin addicts alone were costing the law-abiding citizens of this region between a quarter and a half billion dollars a year in crime to support their hard-drug habits." Most important, he continued, "these dollars are stolen from the *homes and businesses of law-abiding citizens in the Washington-Maryland-Virginia region*" (emphasis added).[22]

In fact, of the thirty-five witnesses who delivered a total of 315 pages of testimony and prepared statements at these hearings, only one — Col. Jeru-Ahmed Hassan, Director of the Black Man's Development Center — spoke explicitly about the toll of drugs and crime on the city's Black communities. Hassan was also the only witness who spoke about the relationship between these problems and broader issues of racial discrimination, poverty, and unemployment. This is not to say that other witnesses did not speak in sympathetic terms about addiction, about the effects of narcotics on those who used them, or about the effects of crime on community members. To the contrary: A central concern of the hearings was the "failure to create facilities to treat narcotics addicts so they don't return to crime" and "to document the rather harsh and tragic realities of the failure of not having any significant effective treatment program in the National Capital of the United States." As such, many of the invited witnesses and participating members of Congress expressed sadness about the rise in deaths attributed to heroin, about the inadequate number of beds in treatment and mental health facilities, and about the increasing number of "juvenile drug addicts."[23] But these witnesses were far more likely to characterize these issues as unfortunate tragedies than they were to treat them as part of what constituted the crisis that warranted state resources. In addressing concerns about "juvenile addicts," for example, the focus was on their increased propensity to commit crime. Senator Tydings asked Deputy District of Columbia Mayor Graham Watt, for example,

> Doesn't the District Government realize how serious juvenile crime is and how many dangerous crimes are committed by juveniles who are heroin addicts. We brought this failure out last and yet even today, all you can say is "We are going to do something about it in the future." Does the Mayor realize how tragic it is when a Juvenile, 15, 16, 17, gets hooked on heroin and turns to stealing, robbing, and violence?[24]

Tydings was not unconcerned about the young people to whom he was referring. But the crisis to which he referred in this statement was not the conditions of the young people's lives, of which addiction was merely one aspect. Rather, the crisis was the alleged criminality of these young people. This reversal was made clearest in his opening comments on the second day of the hearings: "The only way to break that narcotics-crime crisis is to have effective law enforcement against major narcotics traffickers and effective treatment programs to cure crimes to buy drugs."[25] In other words, in his view, the solution to DC's "narcotics-crime crisis" was not to harness state resources to improve conditions for these "juveniles." Instead, the state interventions being justified to address the crisis were mainly ones that would punish their alleged criminality.

Crisis Reversals: The "Urban Crisis," the Moynihan Report, and Early Shock Doctrines

In other cases in which dominant political actors characterized domestic issues affecting marginalized groups as crises during this period, they proposed privatized or individualized solutions to these problems rather than ones that justified state intervention and resources. In 1968, for example, the Senate held hearings on "Financial Institutions and the Urban Crisis."[26] These hearings took place several months after the Kerner Commission had published its final report, "The Report of the National Advisory Commission on Civil Disorders."[27] The Kerner Commission report did not use the term *crisis* to describe racial injustice. It did, however, depict this problem *as* a crisis, arguing as it did that "deepening racial division is not inevitable. The movement apart can be reversed. Choice is still possible. Our principal task is to define that choice and to press for a national resolution."[28] That is, it characterized racial division as a dire situation that was neither natural nor inevitable, as one that faced a crossroads, and one at which conditions would either be resolved or worsen. Most of the forty-four committee members and witnesses at these hearings took seriously the problems laid out in the report, with over half of them making clear in their statements and testimony that they understood either or both structural racism (twelve) and poverty (seventeen) as central to the "disorders" that had prompted President Johnson to create the commission (four witnesses explicitly denied the role of discrimination and one dismissed poverty as an explanation).[29] Four committee members and witnesses even referenced or read from the Kerner Commission report in framing their comments and testimony. Senator Walter Mondale (D-MN), for example, quoted the report's avowal that "our nation is moving toward two societies, one black, one white—separate and unequal."

But although the authors of the Kerner report had argued forcefully that state intervention and resources were warranted and would make a difference in addressing the racial divisions with which the report was concerned, almost none of the witnesses at this hearing about "the urban crisis" argued for direct state intervention as necessary or even desirable to resolve it. Instead, as scholars including Sidney Milkis and Keeanga-Yamahtta Taylor have shown, witnesses and members of Congress echoed President Johnson's determination to harness private industry in constructing the Great Society and emphasized the central role of private investment in urban centers.[30] In opening the hearings, for example, Senator William Proxmire (D-WI) explained that their purpose was to determine what "financial institutions are doing now to help meet the investment and credit needs of the ghetto, and to explore what additional steps *can be taken to channel more private investment into the inner city*" (emphasis added).[31]

Also reflecting Johnson's commitment to centering private industry in Great Society programs, witnesses who did advocate for policy proposals that entailed government action and resources typically proposed that such action be effected through public-private partnerships that involved the infusion of cash into private banks, government guarantees of loans, regulations encouraging more robust credit unions, or the development of entities like a Domestic Development Bank or a US Community Development Bank.[32] John E. Jacob, Acting Executive Director of the Washington Urban League, began his testimony with a forceful statement in which he blamed racial discrimination for the lack of credit "extended to ghetto residents."[33] But he went on to note approvingly that these hearings indicate "that America has finally decided that it might be appropriate to begin to extend capitalism to black Americans," if only, he continued, because "official, white America" has discovered "that putting capital in the hands of Negro citizens might be part of the answer to easing urban unrest."[34] Along with "recent pushes by the Small Business Administration and other government agencies, with investments from private industries" and "coupled with the recent precedent-setting announcement by the Ford Foundation of its new investment policy," he argued, the hearing "heralds a new day for black business, industry and finance in this country."[35]

While Jacob praised capitalism and said nothing that directly supported state intervention, several witnesses went further, suggesting that it would be foolish to use state resources to address the "urban crisis." After noting that redistribution "has been a central feature of Federal policy since President Roosevelt, and that such policies had worked reasonably well," for example, Senator Mondale pivoted and declared, "Yet, there are limits to public action."[36] Rather than taxation and government investment, he explained, the "consensus of today is that we must shift still farther toward a true partnership of the public with the private sector." Foreshadowing the advent and proliferation of what would come to be known as neoliberalism, Mondale argued that rather than intervening directly to address the crisis, the appropriate role of public policy would be to "develop new methods for inducing the private sector of the economy to bring their resources and funds into the inner city and into areas of rural blight as well.[37]

The point here is not that members of Congress should have eschewed attempts to extend credit to low-income people and people of color. Nor do I mean to suggest that they should have discouraged private investment in urban areas. Demands for such access and investment have long been central to movements for gender, racial, and economic justice.[38] But while it is true that what Monica Prasad calls "the democratization of credit" has figured prominently in the goals of these and other movements, the idea of "credit as justice" has come at a cost. In particular, scholars including Prasad, Greta Krippner, and Abbye Atkinson have demonstrated that treating credit expansion as a substitute for public spending and redistribution has come at the expense of more robust measures to advance racial and gender equality.[39] From this perspective (and as I discuss at greater length in chapters 4 and 5), the neoliberal ideas advanced by Mondale and other witnesses at this hearing laid the foundation for the idea that it was privatized subprime mortgages rather than government spending or regulation that were the appropriate state action to increase rates of homeownership among women and people of color. In so doing, they also helped to lay the foundation for the proliferation of such mortgages and for the attendant high rates of foreclosure among members of these two groups as well.[40]

I also do not mean to suggest that these hearings were the only ones to address "urban issues" during this period, an era in which activists and political actors mobilized for improvements in areas such as housing, transportation, and education.[41] This hearing was, however, the only one addressing these issues that was explicitly titled "The Urban Crisis." As scholars such as Stuart Hall, Thomas Sugrue, and Taylor have shown, "urban crisis" is a presumptively race-neutral shorthand that has long been deployed to pathologize low-income marginalized populations of color and to blame members of these communities for their problems and for their effects on dominant groups.[42] As such, the way in which the conveners of and participants in this hearing framed what that crisis was and how it might be resolved is revealing, particularly since their frame partly reversed the racial justice goals for which advocates had introduced the meaning of *condition-as-crisis*. That is, rather than arguing for increased state resources and intervention, most of the witnesses at this hearing argued that state resources should be scaled back, withdrawn, or privatized.

Unemployment Crisis

The 1980 Republican Party platform plank titled "Training and skills" provides another example of a reversal in which dominant political actors used crisis politics to justify privatized solutions rather than state intervention. The section appears about a third of the way into the platform, and begins by framing racial disparities in employment rates as a crisis, stating:

Unemployment is a growing problem for millions of Americans, but it is an un-
paralleled disaster for minority Americans. As this country's economic growth
has slowed over the past decade, unemployment has become more intractable.
The gravity of the crisis is so severe that as we entered the present recession,
unemployment was over six percent for the entire labor force but it was 33 percent for minority youth. In addition, the black unemployment rate was 10.8 percent and youth between the ages of 16 and 24 continued to account for about
one-half of the total unemployed.[43]

Once again, this passage might seem to suggest that the Republican Party
was using crisis in the spirit in which it had been invoked by racial justice
advocates. A reader might even assume that that the platform's writers
were trying to draw attention to the disproportionate impact of broader
economic problems on marginalized groups. But this passage was not
a call for state intervention and resources to resolve this crisis. Rather,
as was true in the case of the proposed solutions to the "urban crisis,"
the platform instead went on to criticize such interventions, stating that
"the structural unemployment problem continues to fester among minorities and young people" despite "the almost $100 billion spent on well-
intended public sector employment and training programs." "Throughout
America," it declared, "the private and independent sectors have repeatedly helped in the creation of minority business through donated counseling and consulting services. They have encouraged equal opportunity
hiring practices within their own industries and have built nonprofit, self-
supporting training centers where the products produced during training
are sold to support the programs."
    As Taylor argues, among the key goals of neoliberal attacks on the so-
cial welfare state has been to restore "the profitability of business and
capital by undermining the social obstacles that had destabilized its pri-
macy," including through "rollbacks of aspects of the welfare state but also
by attacks on unions, especially public sector unions made up of Black and
Brown workers."[44] In keeping with such attacks, the solution embraced
by the platform writers was not to increase the use of state resources but
rather to insist that the private sector is "the ultimate location for unsub-
sidized jobs, as the provider of means to attain this end, and as an active
participant in the formulation of employment and training policies on the
local and national level." As such, the platform's writers explained, efforts
to address "minority unemployment" should offer "adequate incentives
to the private sector," should focus "on both large and small business,"

and should minimize "red tape" by abolishing laws that "create additional barriers for unemployed youth." Echoing Mondale's argument in the 1968 "urban crisis" hearings that there are "limits to state action," the platform insisted that government policy made it "too expensive for employers to hire unskilled youths" and urged "a reduction of payroll tax rates, a youth differential for the minimum wage, and alleviation of other costs of employment until a young person can be a productive employee." That is, it called not for more robust state resources and intervention but for what, in its writers' view, was less of both, at least insofar as these were seen to hinder rather than to enable the restoration of "social order on the terms of business."[45]

The Moynihan Report and the "Crisis" in Race Relations

Another variation on the foregoing reversal is evident in cases in which dominant political actors characterized domestic issues with implications for marginalized groups as crises but cast members of those groups as themselves to blame for the crisis in question. The 1965 Department of Labor report *The Negro Family: The Case for National Action* (known colloquially as the "Moynihan Report") provides a particularly illustrative example of this reversal, one that has served for decades to justify individualized and punitive policy solutions that entailed withdrawing rather than augmenting state resources.[46]

The lead author of this controversial but influential report was Daniel Patrick Moynihan. Moynihan would eventually become a US senator from the state of New York, but at the time, he was serving as assistant secretary of labor in the Democratic administration of President Lyndon B. Johnson. Moynihan had been appointed, in part, to help develop policies to implement and administer Johnson's War on Poverty. The report was originally intended as an internal document that would be read only by Johnson and some of his close advisers, but it was leaked to newspaper columnists a few days after the uprising in the predominantly African American Watts neighborhood in Los Angeles.[47]

The report opened with a one-sentence declaration: "The United States is approaching a new crisis in race relations."[48] The crisis, the next few lines explained, had been produced by a tension between the recent political and legal victories through which "the demand of Negro Americans for full recognition of their civil rights was finally met."[49] But, the report argued, the crisis had also raised the expectation among African Americans "that in the near future equal opportunities for them as a group will produce roughly equal results."[50]

The report's writers acknowledged that among the barriers to these "equal results" was the persistence of "the racist virus in the American blood stream." But they insisted as well that "the fundamental problem ... is that of family structure." "The evidence," the report continued, is that "the Negro family in the urban ghettos is crumbling."[51] The writers then shifted the main locus of blame from white racism to what they characterized as the "pathological" behavior of low-income Black people, particularly that of Black women. The report blamed the "matriarchal structure" for a "tangle of pathology" that, it argued, was indexed by "divorce, separation and desertion, female family head, children in broken homes, and illegitimacy."[52] The writers also blamed the Black "middle class," which, they insisted, had selfishly "managed to save itself." This salvation, the report's writers averred, had meant that "the fabric of conventional social relationships has all but disintegrated ... [for] vast numbers of the unskilled, poorly educated city working class." "So long as this situation persists," they maintained, "the cycle of poverty and disadvantage will continue to repeat itself."[53]

In keeping with the qualities that characterize condition-as-crisis, Moynihan and his coauthors deployed crisis to recast a long-standing issue as a solvable problem facing a crossroads and to assert that the developments that they recounted presented the nation with "a new kind of problem." As such (and like the aforementioned Kerner Commission report, which would not be published until approximately two years after this one), their formulation might seem to mirror the logic behind the naming of *The Crisis* magazine, in which the term was used to denaturalize racial oppression and make the case for federal interventions to eradicate it. Here, however, the contemporary racial inequalities to which the authors referred were decoupled from the injustices of the past. Moynihan and his coauthors also detached these inequalities from the anti-discrimination and redistributive policies for which activists and advocates called to remedy them.

The report's call for a "national effort ... that will give a unity of purpose to the many activities of the Federal government in this area" might similarly seem to be in line with the use of condition-as-crisis on the part of advocates for marginalized groups. That is, it might seem that the idea that "race relations" were in crisis was being introduced to justify state intervention and resources that would alleviate discrimination, reduce poverty, and help Black people, and many have argued that Moynihan intended the report to make just this case.[54] Continuing to read, however, reveals that the report does just the opposite, insisting that "measures that have worked in the past, or would work for most groups in the present, will not work here."[55] Moreover, the critical juncture the authors posit is one that mandates that resources and efforts be "directed to a new kind of national goal: the establishment of a stable Negro family structure."[56] This goal, they conceded, "would be a new departure for Federal policy," and would be "a difficult one." But, they insisted, "it almost certainly offers the only possibility of resolving in our time what is, after all, the nation's oldest, and most intransigent, and now its most dangerous social problem."[57]

In other words, the report's writers deployed condition-as-crisis to argue that the country was facing a critical juncture regarding "race relations," one that required and could be remedied through, as its title stated, "national action." But while they did so as part of their attempt to denaturalize the status quo regarding racial inequality, they hoped as well to disrupt the idea that these inequalities could be remedied through the state action of redistributive and anti-discrimination policies. Echoing Mondale's 1968 statements about the "urban crisis" and the Republican Party's 1980 "unemployment crisis" platform plank, the authors of this report insisted that redistribution and anti-discrimination might have worked in the past and for other groups and that readers might assume that such measures would provide the solution to the crisis they describe here. But, they warned, the crisis in question was not related to inequities in resources or political power but one of reproduction and family structure. In so doing—and as scholars, activists, and advocates argued at the time of the report's publication and as many have continued to argue since then—the report framed the cause of the "race crisis" not as white racism or as a lack of resources but rather as the product of African Americans' own values and behaviors.[58]

Having framed the crisis in this way, the report's authors claimed that the appropriate recourse was not the redistribution of resources that would alleviate and perhaps even destabilize the intersecting systems of racism, capitalism, and misogyny that produce poverty, but rather disciplinary measures that would strengthen and reinforce heteropatriarchal family structures.[59] The ideas the report popularized continue to have what historian Susan Greenbaum characterizes as "regrettably durable impact" and "undeserved influence" in a range of policy areas.[60] Roderick Ferguson argues, for example, that the report "authorize[d] a hegemonic discourse about black matriarchy" that "facilitated a conservative block-ade of social welfare policy in the United States" and "provided the dis-cursive origins for the dismantling of welfare."[61]

* * *

The rhetorical moves in the Moynihan Report illustrate and are emblem-atic of a more general reversal in the deployment of condition-as-crisis on the part of dominant political actors: The political deployment of condition-as-crisis originated among racial justice advocates as part of an effort to shift the frameworks within which marginalization and oppres-sion were understood and addressed. Its assimilation into dominant po-litical discourse might consequently have been used by dominant politi-cal actors in these same ways. Instead, something more like the opposite took place, a dynamic in which dominant political actors either detached the alleged crisis in question from the inequalities facing marginalized groups or framed the crisis as a problem for which marginalized groups themselves were to blame. Moreover, they often did so in ways that were subsequently used to justify new forms of discipline, surveillance, and punishment as well as to provide the rationale for the disinvestment and withdrawal—rather than the augmentation or redistribution—of state power and resources.

That is, dominant political actors did not use crisis politics as part of a strategy to denaturalize ongoing forms of oppression and to argue that they face turning points, could be resolved, and conditions improved. In-stead, echoing what Stuart Hall and his colleagues argued in the case of the "mugging crisis" in 1970s Britain, they framed the foregoing crises as ones for which marginalized and minoritized groups themselves were to blame.[62] So although in the 1960s and 1970s *crisis* became a more common way in which dominant political actors described and defined ongoing do-mestic political and policy problems and justified the use of state resources to address them, its meaning as a frame for ongoing problems associated with structural marginalization did not. Instead, it came increasingly to signal that the well-being of relatively privileged groups was under threat or in decline and that state intervention was necessary to address these bad things that were happening (or could happen) to members of these groups. Through this process, crisis politics began to both reflect and to construct some domestic problems as worthy of and amenable to state intervention while contributing to the normalization and entrenchment of others. That is, crisis politics became one mechanism justifying both the use of state power and resources to protect privileged groups and also the withdrawal or privatization of resources when it came to marginalized ones. The results of this reversal are evident in areas ranging from anti-poverty and housing policy, to employment, to policing and the carceral state.[63]

The appropriation and reversal of condition-as-crisis and the development of crisis politics are certainly not the first or only cases in which political actors borrowed an evocative political image or metaphor for purposes that would seem to be at odds with the intentions of its originators. Scholars have documented, for example, the ways in which conservatives have appropriated Supreme Court Justice John Marshall Harlan's dissent to the decision in *Plessy v. Ferguson* arguing that the US Constitution is "color-blind and neither knows nor tolerates class among citizens," reversing it in service to claims that ameliorative efforts in areas such as affirmative action and voting rights are, themselves, the vehicles of racism about which we ought to be concerned.[64]

The appropriation of condition-as-crisis is also by no means the only circumstance under which the bad things that affect more privileged people are treated as worse than those that affect members of marginalized groups. Scholars have shown, for example, that many people's perceptions of the gravity of an issue often varies depending on whether they think it hurts or helps people they consider to be "like them."[65] Moreover, as widespread as it was, dominant political actors' disinclination to treat structural inequalities as crises during this period was not ubiquitous, and there were certainly exceptions in which they—mostly Democrats— invoked crises in at least ostensibly progressive ways. The 1976 Democratic platform, for example, argued that solving the "urban crisis" would entail policies that promoted "full employment, incentives for urban and rural economic development, welfare reform, adequate health care, equalization of education expenditures, energy conservation and environmental quality." The party's 1980 platform referenced not only a "fiscal crisis" facing states and cities "as federal contributions have declined" but also the deepening "fiscal crisis of welfare recipients" themselves, which they attributed to the unwillingness of states and localities "to adjust benefits to prevent inflation from robbing them of their worth." That is, they framed these long-term conditions as problems that faced turning points that could and should be resolved through robust federal action and infusions of resources.

These are noteworthy exceptions, but the particular transmogrification of condition-as-crisis from an "outsider's word" to an "insider's word" is nonetheless striking and significant.[66] Specifically, dominant political actors did not merely come to use crisis to characterize bad things that happen to relatively privileged people. Rather, in borrowing this new meaning and reversing its implications, they were also far more likely to treat state action and resources as justified and necessary and understood to make a positive difference for privileged people than they were when the issues in question affected marginalized groups. These developments made crisis both an indicator and a symptom of the very problems that its originators and early adopters had been trying to use it to signify. Through this trajectory, the "problems of crisis's meaning" became, in Raymond Williams's terms, "inextricably bound up with the problems it was being used to discuss," and the application of condition-as-crisis came simultaneously to reflect, constitute, and perpetuate the very situations that advocates and activists for marginalized and minoritized groups had hoped to use it to highlight: that the issues affecting them and their constituents were taken to be natural, inevitable, and immune to state intervention.

Conclusion: Crisis and Non-Crisis

In his description of the political uses of national crises, Murray Edelman writes that what "events mean for policy formation" depends on "whether they are defined as exceptional or, alternatively, as one more set of incidents in a world that is chronically in crisis."[67] Crisis, he continues, is therefore a "form of problematic categorization" when applied to a set of events because "the development it highlights can also be perceived as recurring rather than singular and as an instance of arbitrary labeling."[68] But although patterns in crisis labeling may be arbitrary in that not every bad thing with a given set of characteristics is thusly named, the evidence that I have presented suggests quite strongly that crisis *politics* are not random. Instead, they are correlated with—and co-constituted with and by—patterns of marginalization and power. Racial justice advocates forged a new meaning for the term *crisis* as a way to denaturalize and shift political understandings of ongoing oppression and to justify state intervention and resources to address them. Dominant political actors borrowed this meaning and applied it to a wide range of ongoing issues. But only rarely did these same actors describe the kinds of ongoing and quotidian "bad things" endured by marginalized populations as crises. When they did, it was often in ways that were either at odds with or at least not congruent with the goals of civil rights activists and advocates. As I discuss briefly in the concluding chapter, it was not only dominant political actors who adopted crisis language from civil rights activists; this terminological tactic was adopted by advocates and activists associated with other movements as well, most notably feminists (evident in, for example, the rise of the term *rape crisis center*), AIDS activists (exemplified by the HIV/AIDS organization "Gay Men's Health Crisis"), civil rights activists (illustrated by calls to address a "crisis of the Black male)," and, on the right, the anti-abortion movement's "crisis pregnancy centers." And as activists from these and other movements tried to harness the power of crisis politics to make the case for resources and intervention in a range of areas, the political meanings of crisis continued to evolve.

Understanding these patterns in the trajectory of crisis politics and the developments that have fueled them therefore provides a partial answer to Roitman's provocation asking whether it is an oxymoron to "speak of a state of enduring crisis" or to use the term *crisis* to describe an "ongoing state of affairs."[69] The evidence in this chapter suggests that the shifting meanings of the term *crisis* represent neither a contradiction nor a misuse or distortion of its original and "true" meaning. Instead, what might appear to be a contradiction or distortion seems less paradoxical once we understand that dominant political actors appropriated this meaning from advocates and activists, who had invoked the concept of crisis to shift the way in which long-standing issues of structural marginalization and oppression are understood. In this light, although it is true, as Reinhart Koselleck puts it, that crisis came to be used "interchangeably with 'unrest,' 'conflict,' 'revolution,' and to describe vaguely disturbing moods or situations," the origins of its application to ongoing and domestic problems is truer to its "legacy meaning" as a turning point than might be first apparent.[70]

That is, when nondominant political actors initially began to label more problems crises, they were not just saying that they were urgent issues nor were they simply trying to draw attention to them. Instead, their attempts to designate ongoing bad things as crises began as efforts to transform them from what were understood as "protracted historical and experiential conditions" into "critical, decisive moments."[71] In so doing, they were invoking crisis in a way that parallels the invocation of wars— on crime, on drugs, on poverty—to define problems and justify federal action. That is, they were using crisis as a way to make arguments that what had previously been construed as unchangeable conditions were, in fact, problems that were remediable through state intervention and resources (even if, at times, this has meant withdrawing or reallocating resources).[72]

This last point underscores the fact that the increased invocation of crisis to describe some bad things also underscores its *absence* as a designator for other ones.[73] And just as crises are constituted, as Colin Hay has written, "in and through narrative," narratives that construct some bad things as crises also help to constitute other ones as *non-crises*: bad things that are not treated as crises by dominant political actors but that might well be were they to afflict dominant, powerful, privileged, or normative groups.[74] Among members of marginalized, oppressed, and subjugated groups, bad things are often ongoing and continuous, and times can be perennially hard in precisely the ways that they are temporarily difficult for members of dominant groups under conditions deemed crises. Rather than being treated as aberrant and temporary crises that can and must be resolved, however, conditions related to these persistent problems are more likely to be naturalized. For they are, indeed, part of the fabric of "ordinary life."[75]

Put differently, for every bad thing that is constituted as a crisis by dominant political actors, there are myriad others that are never so labeled or that never achieve this status. Thus, the constitution of crisis as a way to understand some bad things also constitutes its inverse, non-crisis. Among the signature features of non-crises are therefore the inverses of those that signify crises: they are perceived as natural, inevitable, and immune to—and therefore not warranting—state intervention. The concept of non-crisis, in other words, provides analytic purchase on *crisis politics*, the term I use to describe the processes through which problems that become regarded as crises when they affect dominant groups or broader publics are often taken for granted as part of the normal political and economic landscape when they are related to the normalized conditions of vulnerability that affect marginalized populations. Juxtaposing crises and non-crises also underscores that part of what defines and constitutes marginalization in the contemporary United States is that many of the persistent bad things associated with it—problems such as unemployment, poverty, discrimination, and illness—are not deemed worthy of or remediable through state intervention by dominant political actors because the status quo is regarded as natural and inevitable and the resulting changes are viewed as more disruptive than desirable.

As I demonstrate in part 2, many of the defining features of the melt-down in the mortgage market in the early twenty-first century resembled conditions in the mid-1990s, a period during which rates of subprime loans and foreclosures were rising among low-income people, people of color, and sole-borrower women of all races. But while the former came to be labeled and treated as a mortgage foreclosure crisis by economic report-ers and dominant political actors, the latter did not. In fact, there were red flags in the 1990s that should have alerted policymakers that meltdowns in the mortgage and housing markets were imminent. Instead, that era was widely regarded as a very good one for the housing market, in part be-cause the problems were concentrated among members of groups whose suffering has long been simultaneously normalized, exceptionalized, and treated as outside the power of the state to remedy.

PART II

Foreclosure Crises and Non-Crises

CHAPTER FOUR

When Does a Crisis Begin?

On 19 September 2010, the Business Cycle Dating Committee of the National Bureau of Economic Research (NBER) met by conference call and determined that the "Great Recession" that had begun in December 2007 was over. The committee was careful to note that its members "did not conclude that economic conditions since that month" had been "favorable" or that the economy had "returned to operating at normal capacity." But they nonetheless expressed confidence that the recession had ended in June 2009 and that the American economy was recovering from what was, at the time, the longest recession since the Second World War.[1]

Several months later, a March 2011 report from the Bureau of Labor Statistics (BLS) found that approximately 90 percent of the jobs that had been created in the preceding year, during the NBER-declared recovery, had gone to men.[2] In other words, what the NBER had labeled a recovery had been, up to that point, what some journalists and observers called a "*he*covery," with benefits going primarily to male workers. Moreover, because cuts in public sector jobs—held disproportionately by women and African Americans—continued well after the recovery was said to have begun, by some indicators both women and people of color had been faring *worse* since the economic crisis of the Great Recession had "officially" ended.[3]

Read in tandem, the NBER and BLS reports underscore three clusters of issues revealed by considering the relationships among power, normativity, and the political construction of crises. Most broadly, juxtaposing the reports raises questions about the official and unofficial indicators that political elites use to identify crises, defined here as bad things that are framed as critical junctures deemed worthy of and remediable through government intervention and resources. Comparing the reports also illustrates the ways in which raced and gendered inequalities are implicated in these definitions. More specifically, this comparison illustrates in greater depth how this imbrication works to define *some* "bad things" as "crises" even as analogous others—particularly ones related to ongoing and quotidian inequalities endured by marginalized populations—are treated instead as what I call *non-crises*. Finally, considering the two reports together draws our attention not only to the framings and constructions of bad things as crises, but also to the ways in which racialized and gendered norms and expectations—in this case, regarding employment—shape ideas about solutions to problems, assumptions about how we can tell that crises and bad times are over, and the criteria based on which we determine that things are back to normal and that times are once again "good."

This part of the book takes the three constellations of issues highlighted by this juxtapositioning as a point of departure from which to explore in greater depth the processes and implications of the crisis constructions that are revealed in chapters 2 and 3. Whereas tracking and assessing the presence and absence of the word *crisis* inductively as I did in those previous chapters demonstrates the ways in which its uses and meanings have evolved, the chapters in this section adopt a more deductive approach to understanding crisis politics. Turning from the emphasis on the presence, absence, and evolving meanings of the word *crisis* itself, I expand the focus here to examine the *processes through which* some bad things come to be treated as crises while other seemingly similar bad things do not.

To do so, I use a set of matched cases through which I compare dominant media and political attention to and framings of one "bad thing" that came to be treated as a crisis alongside an analogous but "semantically masked" bad thing that was treated as a non-crisis, contrasting the mortgage foreclosure crisis of the early twenty-first century with what I call the foreclosure non-crisis of the 1990s.[4] I begin in this chapter by tracing the history of the key political and policy developments that laid the foundations for, created, and provided the rationale for subprime mortgages, and that stoked the attendant rising rates of foreclosures in each era. This history begins with the discriminatory housing and lending policies of the New Deal era, continues with the subsequent attempts to "democratize" access to credit during the 1960s and 1970s, and culminates in the wave of deregulatory legislation that was passed over the course of the 1980s. I then turn, in chapter 5, to an examination of dominant political and media attention to the non-crises of subprime mortgages and rising foreclosure rates during what was widely regarded as the housing boom of the late 1990s, comparing this coverage with levels of attention to and framings of these issues during what came to be called a "foreclosure crisis" in 2007.

Juxtaposing these two cases demonstrates empirically two of the central implications of the analyses in part 1: First, doing so illustrates the ways in which manifestations of conditions of vulnerability and harm, so often naturalized and treated as inevitable products of the normal social, economic, and political landscape when they affect marginalized populations, are likely to become regarded as problems that can and must be resolved through state action—that is, as crises—when they affect dominant groups or disrupt dominant institutions and processes. The implication is not simply that such conditions are more likely to be labeled or to be perceived as crises, however. Instead, the matched cases also demonstrate a second key point about crisis politics: That whether a problem is labeled a crisis has significant consequences for whether policymakers frame and treat it is as a critical juncture worthy of and remediable through government intervention and resources as well as for the kinds of solutions deemed appropriate to address it. In the cases I examine, among these consequences is that the policy response to the foreclosure "crisis" came too late to help those who had lost their homes before the crisis was "hailed into being."[5] The response consequently did little to address—and in some ways exacerbated—long-standing and intersecting racial and gender disparities in rates of homeownership, foreclosures, and access to conventional mortgage loans, all of which continued to be treated as natural, inevitable, and outside the power of the state to remedy.

The Seeds of the Non-Crisis, and of the Crisis

There is no official starting date for what would come to be regarded as the American foreclosure crisis of the first decade of the twenty-first century. Housing policy scholar Daniel Immergluck explains, however, that it was in late 2006 and early 2007 that rates of foreclosure began to increase rapidly and markedly, particularly in Arizona, California, Florida, and Nevada where they had previously been quite low.[6] In early December 2006, two major subprime mortgage lenders, Sebring Capital and Ownit Solutions, failed, sending what the *Wall Street Journal* described as "shock waves" through the market.[7] Then, in the spring of 2007, New Century, one of the largest subprime lenders in the United States, went bankrupt. Around that same time, Federal Reserve Board Chair Ben Bernanke and

TABLE 4.1. **Percent of home mortgages in default and/or foreclosure, 1996 and 2007**

	1996*	2007[†]
White	2.9	4.5
Asian American	3.7	4.6
African American	4.8	7.9
Latino	5.4	7.7
Indigenous/American Indian	4.4	NA
Houses with conventional mortgages		2.4[‡]
Houses with subprime mortgages		17

Notes: *Rates of default. *Source:* Department of Housing and Urban Development, 2002.
[†]Rates of completed foreclosures. *Source:* Gruenstein-Bocian, Li, & Ernst 2010.
[‡]*Source:* Immergluck 2011, 136.

Housing and Urban Development (HUD) Secretary Alphonso Jackson endorsed a call from Senator Charles Schumer (D-NY) to provide "federal funding for foreclosure prevention counseling."[8] In August of that year, the Federal Housing Administration (FHA) announced its FHA Secure program, the stated goal of which was to "refinance delinquent homeowners into more affordable loans to reduce foreclosures."[9]

By the fourth quarter of 2007, a foreclosure crisis was widely understood to be underway. The Mortgage Bankers Association (MBA) issued a report early the following year estimating that 3.6 percent of all loans had been seriously delinquent (that is, more than 90 days late) or in foreclosure by the end of 2007, and that an additional 0.9 percent were entering foreclosure, for a total of 4.5 percent.[10] As Jeff Crump and his colleagues noted in a paper published soon after the MBA report was released, the comparable figures in 2005 had been that 2.1 percent of loans were seriously delinquent and 0.4 percent were entering foreclosure, for a total of 2.5 percent.[11] By 2009, an estimated 2.5 million foreclosures had been completed.[12]

Much of this increase reflected high rates of default and foreclosure on houses financed through what came to be known as *subprime mortgages.* The designation "subprime" typically refers to mortgages that carry higher interest rates and more restrictive terms than those of so-called prime mortgages. Such loans are also ostensibly designed for prospective borrowers who have what lenders claim are impaired credit records (see endnote, however, for an overview of scholarship that has addressed the evolution of "subprime" from its origins as an ostensibly "racially neutral" description of African American neighborhoods, to a definition of financial products, and to a designation for a category of people).[13] The high interest rates are, in theory, intended to "compensate the lender for accepting the greater risk in lending to such borrowers."[14] Many subprime mortgages are financed as adjustable-rate mortgages (ARMs), with interest rates that can vary significantly over time. Among the reasons for high rates of default and foreclosure on such loans in 2007–9 was that many of them had been taken out a few years earlier at low "teaser" rates that adjusted upward when rates reset at the end of their first three- to five-year period, leading to payments that were often far higher than they had been when borrowers had originally bought their houses. As a consequence, while 2.4 percent of homes financed through conventional mortgages were in foreclosure at the height of the crisis, this was the case for 17 percent of homes financed by subprime loans (see table 4.1). Because, as I explain below, women and people of color were disproportionately likely to be targeted for and to hold subprime mortgages, rates of both subprime mortgages and foreclosures were especially high among sole-borrower women and Black sole-borrower women in particular.

The Codification of Raced and Gendered "Risk"

The kinds of exclusionary, extractive, and usurious housing and lending policies and practices of which subprime mortgages are one example have a long and well-documented history in the United States.[15] Understanding the particular policies and practices that converged to produce subprime mortgages as well as their racialized and gendered implications requires reviewing in some detail several developments in housing and lending policies and practices that began with the state-building policies of the New Deal. Particularly important for understanding the logics that justified and lay the foundations for the non-crisis of high rates of subprime mortgages among women and people of color are exclusions that can be traced to New Deal–era model credit reports and home loan underwriting guidelines.

Federal administrators developed these reports and guidelines in close consultation with experts from the real estate, credit rating, and lending professions, who promised that they would bring scientific methods to assessments of home values and borrower "risk." But the measures based on which they made such assessments reflected the explicitly segregationist and more implicitly heteropatriarchal agendas to which professionals in these fields were committed. Rather than using federal power to oppose these practices and agendas, federal agencies embraced and codified them. In so doing, they excluded African Americans as well as many women from the benefits of the FHA-insured mortgages that, with their 20 percent down payments, long terms, fixed interest rates, and self-amortizing contracts, came to be considered the "gold standard" of home loans, credited with laying the foundations for housing stability and wealth creation for generations of Americans.[16] They also, however, lay another foundation, this one for the race- and gender-related patterns in subprime mortgage lending and home foreclosures that would come to mark the late twentieth and early twenty-first centuries.[17]

New Deal Roots

A defining feature of the Great Depression of the 1930s was a near halt in home building and repair alongside a massive increase in foreclosures and evictions. As Chloe Thurston explains, residential construction plummeted by almost 95 percent between 1925 and 1933, while foreclosure rates tripled over this same period.[18] Among the sources of these foreclosures were the mortgage lending practices typical at the time, which were characterized by high down payment requirements (often as high as 40 to 50 percent of the cost of the house) and short repayment periods (as few as two years and rarely longer than fifteen). Mortgage agreements also typically required that borrowers repay the entire value of the loan at the end of the term, which led to high rates of second and third mortgages. Lenders claimed that this system protected them against the risks associated with housing finance, but the potential perils it posed both to them and to borrowers came to a head as unemployment rates skyrocketed and millions of Americans were unable to repay their mortgages at the same time as cash-starved banks called back the full value of the loans. Because lenders would not allow borrowers to refinance their mortgages, even those borrowers who might have been able to continue to pay their monthly loan costs found themselves facing foreclosure.[19] Bank foreclosures, in turn, drove down house values, and many borrowers consequently found themselves "underwater," owing more on their mortgages than the value of their house.[20]

To help homeowners at risk of imminent foreclosure, in 1933 the Roosevelt administration created the Home Owners' Loan Corporation (HOLC).

HOLC purchased at-risk mortgages and refinanced them on more favorable terms that included lower interest rates, longer repayment periods, and self-amortization. To determine whether borrowers would be able to make the required regular payments, HOLC deployed examiners who worked with local bank loan officers, city officials, appraisers, and realtors to classify neighborhoods "by their perceived level of lending risk."[21] At the time, however, the professional associations to which many of these officials belonged were committed to preserving and reinforcing racial segregation. The National Association of Real Estate Boards' (NAREB) code of ethics, for example, warned its members that "a realtor should never be instrumental in introducing into a neighborhood ... members of any race or nationality ... whose presence will clearly be detrimental to property values in that neighborhood."[22]

Rather than use its power to oppose such white supremacist ideas and practices, HOLC instead codified them. In particular, HOLC used a neighborhood's racial composition as a central component of its risk assessment, treating racial demographics as more determinative than criteria such as residents' economic class and employment status, the age and condition of housing, or its proximity to transportation, to amenities such as parks, or to hazards like polluting industries.[23] Based on these assessments, HOLC created color-coded "Residential Security" maps of American cities, in which "'the safest' neighborhoods were colored in green and the 'riskiest' ones in red." As Richard Rothstein explains, a neighborhood "earned a red color if African Americans lived in it," regardless of its residents' income or the kind of homes in it. While the white middle-class St. Louis suburb of Ladue, for example, "was colored green because, according to an HOLC appraiser in 1940, it had 'not a single foreigner or negro,'" the similarly middle-class suburban area of Lincoln Terrace "was colored red because it had 'little or no value today ... due to the colored element now controlling the district.'"[24]

HOLC was relatively short-lived and ended its operations in 1951.[25] But the white supremacist and segregationist commitments underlying its security maps lived on and were amplified by the more enduring 1934 National Housing Act (NHA), which was intended to make stable and safe home mortgages affordable to more Americans on a longer-term basis. Among the law's key components was the creation of the FHA, which insured lenders such as banks and mortgage companies in exchange for borrower-friendly mortgage terms.[26] These measures were intended to promote "the construction of new homes and the repair of existing" ones. They were also intended to encourage lenders to extend loans to would-be home-buyers by protecting lenders against some of the risks associated with mort-gage lending.

While government-backed mortgage insurance promised to reduce the risks to private lenders, however, many legislators raised concerns that it did so by transferring these risks to borrowers and to the federal govern-ment itself.[27] To win over skeptics, Thurston explains, proponents promised "that only high-quality lenders, borrowers who met strict credit standards, properties sure to hold their value, and a mortgage contract itself that con-tained all of the latest safeguards would be eligible for insurance under the new program."[28] This promise proved reassuring enough to allow the legislation to pass, but Congress left it to FHA officials to specify "just what kinds of borrowers, what kinds of lenders, and what kinds of prop-erties would be of the quality that the government deemed insurable."[29]

As FHA administrators worked to write rules that would allow the agency to function on terms "enticing enough to lure private providers" without exposing the federal government to excessive risk, they sought guidance from experts in the real estate and financial industries in search of what they claimed would be "the most advanced and technically correct methods of mortgage analysis available."[30] By making it easier to "deter-mine maximum safe loan values, and to predict fairly accurately the safety of the investment and probability of repayment," Thurston explains, FHA officials were confident that "this new data-driven approach to real estate valuation and risk determination" represented "an advancement on ear-lier subjective approaches to mortgage risk assessment."[31]

As in the case of the HOLC security maps, however, subjective judg-ments reflecting troubling assumptions and agendas were baked into the FHA risk ratings. To assess borrower creditworthiness, for example, the FHA drew heavily on advice from organizations in the growing credit rat-ing industry. Like their colleagues in the real estate industry, Thurston ex-plains, the credit rating field based many of its theories and practices on racist ideas and segregationist agendas, as well as on heteropatriarchal and misogynist ones. Basing lending policies on the guidance of "experts" in this field consequently meant that, once again, rather than using their authority to combat the exclusionary and discriminatory practices of the private sector, the FHA and other government lending agencies (such as the Department of Veterans' Affairs) instead reflected and reinforced the racism and misogyny of private industry practices (as well as its hetero-sexism, as the VA denied loans to soldiers with undesirable discharges "issued because of homosexual acts or tendencies").[32]

Working with the National Consumer Credit Reporting Corporation (NCCRC), for example, the FHA constructed a model credit report called the "Standardized Factual Data Report" (SFDR), based on which agents from "character and credit reporting agencies" collected information about prospective borrowers.[33] As this designation suggests, agents were instructed to determine not only criteria such as a borrower's age, employment, and income, but also data about their "character." To do so, the SFDR included subjective questions about a potential borrower such as "Is he regarded as steady and dependable?", "Is his reputation as to character, habits and morals good? (IF not, state nature of unfavorable reports)," and "Is his personal reputation as to honesty good?" Agents were also told to indicate the applicant's "racial descent" ("answer whether Anglo-Saxon, Greek, Hebrew, Italian, Negro etc."), whether the agent "learn[ed] of any domestic difficulties," and whether "his wife lend[s] encouragement to him?"[34] Making clear that the use of male pronouns in these questions reflected a default presumption that borrowers would be men, the very last item on the list instructed the agent, "If [applicant is] a woman, cover husband's or Father's reputation, business history, worth and income."[35]

The SFDR was designed to assess a prospective borrower's creditworthiness and risk. In order to determine whether a proposed *transaction* "was of insurable risk," the FHA's Underwriting Manual included "Risk Rating Instructions" that applied analogous questions and criteria to the property being financed and to the neighborhood in which it was located.[36] As in the case of the HOLC ratings, these criteria meant that majority Black and "mixed" neighborhoods were typically designated as risky and unfit. Houses in those neighborhoods were therefore deemed ineligible for FHA-insured mortgages, regardless of the financial capacity of the would-be borrower. The manual's "Risk Rating Instructions" also linked assessments of "neighborhood stability" to racial homogeneity and asserted that changing the "ethnic mix" in a neighborhood—generally interpreted to mean an increase in the number of Black, and in some cases, Jewish, homeowners—would destabilize and lead to risk in home prices. Mortgages were consequently also denied to African Americans trying to buy houses in predominantly white neighborhoods, also regardless of their individual financial profiles. (The FHA's commitment to maintaining racial segregation meant that it also refused to insure loans to white borrowers hoping to finance houses in majority Black neighborhoods.) Until the Supreme Court ruled in 1948 that restrictive covenants were unconstitutional, the FHA promoted the use of—and sometimes even made assistance contingent on—owners establishing deeds stipulating that properties could not be transferred to people of color or to Jewish buyers, claiming that such restrictions were necessary to preserve neighborhood demographics and protect property values.[37]

Together, the redlining of Black neighborhoods and the refusal to insure mortgages for African Americans attempting to buy houses in majority white neighborhoods excluded both Black people and Black neighborhoods from the benefits of FHA-insured mortgages. By articulating "racism and exclusion as risk," as Keeanga-Yamahtta Taylor has described it, the federal government used its power to endorse, enforce, and entrench racial segregation and to increase the racial wealth gap even as, as scholars have noted, the civil rights movement was dismantling some of the legal architecture of segregation.[38]

Many white women married to white men were able to benefit from FHA mortgages, but the implicitly and explicitly misogynist and heteropatriarchal logics embedded in real estate valuation and assessments of risk were also codified through FHA underwriting guidelines. These logics are evident in the questions in the SFDR that I describe above, and the FHA's 1955 Underwriting Manual added further instructions directing underwriters to consider factors such as "a working wife's 'age, size of family, length of time employed, length of time employed since marriage, nature of the employment, training for the work, and whether her employment is definitely needed or required to meet the minimum living necessities of the family'" before deciding whether to count her income in the application.[39] In practice, Thurston explains, "this tended to mean that women younger than thirty-two could expect their income to be fully ignored."[40]

Sex discrimination pervaded mortgage lending more generally as well. Banks, lenders, and other financial institutions treated women as "higher-risk" consumers than their male counterparts and typically offered them worse terms.[41] Many lenders "openly conceded that they used separate procedures to evaluate the creditworthiness of men and women," often justifying these double standards based on self-reinforcing presumptions that women who had children would leave the workforce, but that men would not.[42] In the case of (presumptively heterosexual) married couples, mortgage lenders often issued credit only in a husband's name, leaving women with no credit history of their own, a particularly significant problem if they were to divorce. Thurston recounts the experience of a woman who wrote to the National Organization for Women (NOW), explaining that although she "had supplied the majority of the down payment for

her and her fiancé's house," the deed listed only him as the owner.[43] Until
1974, a married woman needed her husband's approval to get a credit card
or mortgage and often needed a male cosigner as well.[44] During congressional hearings held by the National Commission on Consumer Finance
(NCCF) in 1972, one witness "recounted a letter from a working woman
in her forties who was forced to ask her seventy-year-old pensioner father
to cosign on a mortgage loan."[45] Women were also often required to submit
"baby letters" signed by doctors "assuring that there was little risk of pregnancy because [they'd] had a hysterectomy or [were] using birth control."[46]

The misogynist assumptions underlying risk assessments were evident
as well in the particular concerns expressed by lenders about single unmarried women, who they worried were not "fit" to "to carry out the everyday maintenance tasks of homeownership necessary to preserve the
house's value."[47] Thurston quotes an especially illustrative and revealing
1973 article in *Banking* magazine, which explained:

> *[R]eal estate lending presents a special problem for women.* Bankers, appraisers
> and others who deal with real estate know that from a practical viewpoint, "It's
> nice to have a man around the house."
>
> The reason for this is that there is often a lot of heavy labor around a
> house—labor that a male head-of-family frequently does. If there is no male,
> the work must either be left undone or be done by professionals who charge for
> their services. In the first case, the property itself declines in value. In the second
> case, the owner's cash assets will be reduced. In either case, the woman involved
> finds her creditworthiness reduced.[48]

Taylor's research demonstrates the particular toxicity of these assumptions
when it came to Black women, who were portrayed in media accounts
and congressional hearings as "unsophisticated and domestically dysfunctional" and unable to do even "simple maintenance of their homes."[49] Research conducted by the NCCF suggested that such characterizations of
women as incapable and dependent translated quite directly into discriminatory lending practices, finding that unmarried women had more trouble obtaining credit—particularly mortgage credit—than their unmarried
male counterparts.[50]

Some of the foregoing ideas and practices might seem to reflect reasonable assessments of risk in a world in which women and African Americans typically had (and continue to have) lower incomes than their white
male counterparts. But there was very little empirical evidence to support

claims that lower average incomes meant that women were worse credit risks than men, that race was associated with repayment risks that warranted excluding African Americans or charging them higher interest rates, or that increasing racial diversity in a neighborhood led to declining home values.[51] Links between repayment risk or declining property values and characteristics such as a borrower's sex, marital status, or "social reputation" or the homogeneity of neighborhood were based on lenders', underwriters', and federal agency officials' own assumptions.[52] Thurston's research makes clear that what evidence there was for any of these relationships suggested that it was not the characteristics of a borrower but rather those of the loans themselves (such as the terms of the financing) that predicted the risk of nonpayment or default.[53] Moreover, "to the extent that there was evidence that the sex of the borrower made a difference," Thurston explains, it more typically showed "that women posed a similar, or in some cases lower, risk than men."[54] A 1941 study found that women were better mortgage risks than men, for example, while a 1964 study found "that women were more likely than men with the same marital status to keep their credit accounts in good standing."[55] Another study found that delinquency rates for home improvement loans to "female-headed households" were half of those overall.[56]

In spite of such evidence, however, assumptions about women's dependence and weak labor force attachment were codified, and women as a group were "blocked from credit access as well as property ownership" well into the latter half of the twentieth century.[57] And both these misogynist presumptions and the white supremacist agendas that excluded Black people from the benefits of FHA programs had long tails: Well after many exclusionary and discriminatory practices had been rendered formally illegal, their racist and misogynist logics would remain available, disguised as conventional wisdom and smuggled into lending practices under the guise of the alleged "risks" they posed to home values and loan repayment.[58]

Fair Lending, Deregulation, and the "Credit-Welfare State Trade-Off"

The foregoing policies and practices made it difficult and often impossible for women and people of color to access federally insured home mortgage loans. But the particular kinds of high interest rates and inflexible terms that would come to typify subprime mortgages had previously, if briefly, been prohibited or mitigated by state and federal legislation. They were made possible, however, by a series of changes that unfolded over the course of the 1960s through the 1980s. Among these changes were three particularly important clusters of developments: a series of anti-discrimination and fair-lending laws, the shift to private credit in place of public spending, and a wave of deregulatory legislation that opened the doors to new, less regulated, and, in some cases, previously prohibited forms of lending. Together, these changes played a particularly important role in both permitting subprime mortgages and in legitimizing and entrenching the idea that such loans were a more appropriate way than other more direct forms of state action to increase rates of homeownership among women and people of color.

The first of these developments, a series of important pieces of legislation passed during the 1960s and 1970s, was intended to "democratize" access to credit and to address the long histories of racial and gender discrimination in housing and lending. Among these stage-setting anti-discrimination and fair-lending laws was the 1968 Fair Housing Act (FHA), which prohibited discrimination in the sale, rental, and financing of housing based on race, religion, and national origin, and which was extended to include gender in 1974 and to people with disabilities and families with children in 1988. (In spite of long-standing evidence of housing discrimination against LGBTQ people, it was not until February 2021 that HUD announced that it would also prohibit discrimination based on sexual orientation and gender identity.[59])

A second crucial piece of legislation that was passed during this era was the 1974 Equal Credit Opportunity Act (ECOA), which prohibited creditors from engaging in many of the discriminatory practices that I describe above. In addition to prohibiting discrimination based on race, sex, and marital status, ECOA also prohibited practices that discriminated based on age and national origin as well as those that discriminated against borrowers who receive public assistance. (As in the case of the FHA, in spite of evidence that lenders discriminated against same-sex couples and LGBTQ people, the ECOA's protections were not extended to these groups until 2021, when the Consumer Financial Protection Bureau issued a rule stating that its prohibition against sex discrimination should be understood to include sexual orientation discrimination and gender identity discrimination.[60])

The 1975 Home Mortgage Disclosure Act (HMDA) required financial institutions to provide the public with information to determine whether they are serving the housing credit needs of the neighborhoods in which they are located and to aid public officials in targeting public investments from the private sector. In the wake of the massive failure in the savings and loan sector, federal lawmakers amended HMDA in 1989 with the Financial Institutions Reform, Recovery, and Enforcement Act (FIRREA), which required additional data collection and disclosures to help identify discriminatory lending patterns and to enforce anti-discrimination statutes. Finally, the 1977 Community Reinvestment Act (CRA) encouraged banks and savings associations to lend to borrowers hoping to buy houses in low- and moderate-income neighborhoods to reduce the practice known as redlining, through which lenders denied mortgages to homeowners and would-be homeowners in neighborhoods deemed "unfit for investment."

These anti-discrimination and fair-lending laws dovetailed with a second and related development, this one associated with the recession of the 1970s and the accompanying pressure to cut federal spending. During this period, lawmakers from across the political spectrum sought to avoid difficult discussions about, conflicts over, and political responsibility for distributional decisions. Among the key strategies lawmakers adopted to accomplish this goal was what Monica Prasad has termed the "credit-welfare state trade-off," in which they tried to expand access to credit as a way to channel private resources into areas including housing, education, and social insurance.[61] Their goal, Greta Krippner argues, was to resolve distributional conflicts through mechanisms that relied on the state in less obvious ways than welfare state spending.[62] Scholars including Prasad, Krippner, and Abbye Atkinson have demonstrated, however, that shifting resources and responsibilities in these ways displaced more robust efforts to advance racial and gender equality. As such, to the extent that the democratization of credit resolved distributional conflicts over federal spending, it was on very unequal terms.[63]

Some of the resource and responsibility-shifting objectives of the credit-welfare state trade-off were advanced in the 1980s by a closely related third cluster of developments: a set of lending-related laws passed as part of that decade's wave of federal deregulatory legislation. Among the key deregulatory changes abetting the development and proliferation of subprime mortgage lending were transformations enabled by four laws: the 1980 Depository Institutions Deregulation and Monetary Control Act (DIDMCA), the 1982 Alternative Mortgage Transaction Parity Act (AMTPA, also known as the Garn–St. Germain Depository Institutions Act), 1984 Secondary Mortgage Market Enhancement Act (SMMEA), and the 1986 Tax Reform Act (TRA). The first of these, DIDMCA, overrode state usury laws and interest rate caps in mortgage lending and made it possible not only to charge high interest rates but also to charge the high fees that became signatures of many subprime loans. AMTPA enhanced the exploitative potential of the high interest rates enabled by DIDMCA by allowing the use of variable interest rates and balloon payments, easing the way for another of the subprime market's signal and exploitative features. The SMMEA allowed investment banks to buy, pool, and resell mortgages, while the TRA, for its part, created incentives for consumers to take advantage of these newly available mortgages because it allowed interest deductions on mortgages for up to two homes but prohibited the deduction of interest on consumer loans. Because the TRA made even high-cost mortgages less expensive than other kinds of debt, it fueled huge increases in second mortgages and other kinds of refinancing to pay for other loans, particularly in the context of the low and declining interest rates that characterized the late 1990s and early 2000s.[64] Also important was the 1978 Supreme Court decision in *Marquette National Bank of Minneapolis v. First of Omaha Service Corp.*, which "gave national banks the right to take their most favored lender status across state lines and preempt the usury law of the borrower's home state."[65]

By overriding state-level anti-usury laws, permitting variable interest rates and balloon payments, incentivizing mortgage loans over other kinds of debt, and allowing investment banks to buy, pool, and resell mortgages, these laws worked together to open the doors for new and less regulated forms of mortgages and other loans and credit. They also reinforced the centrality of what Prasad calls "mortgage Keynesianism," a political economic approach that had been forged during the New Deal, in which credit-driven housing consumption enabled by mortgage finance came to be used as a primary mechanism for sustaining economic growth at the macro level and wealth accumulation at the individual level.[66]

The Credit-Welfare State Trade-Off as Predatory Inclusion

From one perspective, the convergence of these three clusters of developments extended the logic of mortgage Keynesianism to members of groups who had previously been excluded from housing ownership and its wealth-building benefits. On this view, the expanded access to credit enabled by the wave of deregulatory laws might be understood to have overlapped with and advanced feminist and civil rights activists' fights for "equal access to conventional loans and [home] purchase money."[67]

Activists in these movements had, as Atkinson explains, pursued credit democratization as one part of "their broader quest for equality and first-class citizenship." Lawmakers, however, treated increased access to credit for women and African Americans as a substitute for—rather than as a supplement to—the kinds of public spending and redistribution that activists had understood as necessary to achieve their larger goals.[68] In addition, as Amy Castro Baker explains, the protections of the fair-lending legislation of the 1960s and 1970s that had governed mortgages purchased in the so-called prime market were not extended to cover many of the new kinds of mortgages made possible under the loosened regulations. Promoting equitable access to the mortgage market without mandating that lenders ensure that this access be to "equitable products or prime markets within the loan pool" created a regulatory gap in which shifts in the market developed in the absence of new protective legislation, leaving previously excluded borrowers vulnerable to predatory lending practices.[69]

This vulnerability was exacerbated by lenders' increasing reliance on credit scoring and other automated methods as central tools for allocating consumer credit.[70] Like their early twentieth-century predecessors who had argued that they could provide objective and scientific evaluations of borrower "risk," late twentieth-century credit raters claimed that credit scores and other algorithms would serve as objective and bias-free measures for determining credit risk, even in the absence of protective laws.[71] In practice, however, the kinds of characteristics commonly used to determine credit scores—occupation, length of time with one's current employer, history of homeownership, and income—were the same race- and gender-correlated indicators based on which women and people of color had been deemed too "risky" before the ECOA was passed.[72] And like their predecessors, lenders continued to rely on these criteria in spite of research showing that any gender differences typically favored women as lower risk and that it was the structure of a loan, not the characteristics of a borrower, that predicted repayment risk.[73] As such, the increasing reliance on credit scores to determine who deserved what kind of loan and on what terms resuscitated the same long-disproven "zombie facts" about race- and gender-related risk factors that had been codified in the SFDR and FHA underwriting guidelines during the 1930s through the 1950s. The pervasiveness of credit scores consequently renaturalized the idea that women and people of color were risky borrowers who did not qualify for better loans while also making it more difficult for them to prove discrimination.[74]

While the discriminatory effects of credit scores echoed those of previous exclusionary practices, there was a key difference this time: Before the reforms and deregulation of the 1970s and 1980s, the alleged risks associated with lending to women and people of color typically meant that they were denied access to mortgages. But in a context of loosened regulations, determinations of "risk" instead licensed lenders to offer *different kinds of loans* to those they deemed risky. And under a policy regime in which borrowing was treated as the route to equality, lenders were also able to claim that this flexibility was itself the way to advance the goals of increasing homeownership among women and people of color articulated in the FHA and the ECOA, even as they hawked products that were exempt from the anti-discrimination protections of these laws.[75] And once again, rather than use its power to combat assertions that African Americans and women were too risky for conventional mortgages, the federal government accepted, codified, and amplified those claims.

In this context, the federal deregulatory actions of the 1980s did not democratize access to credit, at least not access to the "gold standard" FHA-insured, thirty-year fixed-rate, and self-amortizing mortgages that had allowed white (and presumptively) heterosexual male heads-of-household to build wealth since the federal government intervened to stabilize the housing market during the Great Depression.[76] Instead, federal legislators and regulatory agencies ratified lenders' claims that the appropriate way to promote homeownership among groups who had been excluded from these benefits was to remove the very guardrails through which the government had helped and protected dominant groups and to replace them with and support profit-seeking private market solutions. As a consequence, Baker explains, people of color and sole-borrower women who had for decades been systematically locked out of home ownership and its wealth-building and credit-record-generating benefits were left with increased access to mortgages but on "more expensive and comparatively unequal terms." They were also, she continues, immersed in "a fractured, risky market without a legislative safety net," in which "public-private partnerships" were treated as a substitute for public spending, redistribution, and anti-discrimination protections and in which claims of discrimination were harder to prove.[77]

In other words, the system was transformed from one "based on exclusion" to one "based on exploitation," and women, African Americans, Latinos, and Indigenous people were transformed from credit outcasts into what appeared to lenders to be untapped pools of newly available, underserved, and vulnerable borrowers.[78] Where once excluded, they were now, as Baker writes, "included but unprotected" in a system that scholars including Louise Seamster, Raphaël Charron-Chénier, and Taylor call "predatory inclusion."[79]

Predatory Lending and the 1994 Home Ownership and Equity Protection Act

By 1993, concerns had begun to surface about the increasing amount of evidence of abusive lending practices enabled by this legislative and regulatory vacuum. In response, Congress held a series of hearings about what came to be labeled predatory mortgage lending, culminating in the passage of the 1994 Home Ownership and Equity Protection Act (HOEPA). HOEPA's stated goal was to prohibit "certain predatory lending practices in the costliest subprime loans" by subjecting a small subset of home equity (or refinance) loans to special disclosure requirements and restrictions on loan terms.[80] It also provided covered consumers with "enhanced remedies for violations of the law."[81] As their titles suggest—"Problems in Community Development Banking, Mortgage Lending Discrimination, Reverse Redlining, and Home Equity Lending;" "Adding Injury to Injury: Credit on the Fringe;" and "New Hope for Old Victims"—these hearings were intended to address discriminatory, deceptive, and exploitative practices that impeded access to credit among low-income people and people of color. "Adding Injury to Injury," for example, was prompted by allegations that Boston-based Fleet Finance had deceived low-income borrowers and borrowers of color in Boston and Atlanta into taking loans with excessive interest rates that often led to foreclosure on those properties.[82]

In his opening remarks at those hearings, Representative Joseph Kennedy (D-MA), Chair of the House Banking, Finance and Urban Affairs Subcommittee on Consumer Credit and Insurance, explained that he and his colleagues wished to examine "what happens to consumers who lack access to affordable credit and deposit services, particularly those who live in poor, working, and predominantly minority neighborhoods."[83] Kennedy also emphasized that borrowers who took out such loans were neither uncreditworthy nor randomly distributed. Instead, he explained, lenders "target[ed] middle-aged or elderly black men and women who have worked hard to own their own homes," visiting local deed offices to track down "people with the highest home equity in the neighborhoods least served by mainstream lending."[84] "Citizens in these communities," he argued, do not "lack any financial services. Rather . . . they have plenty of services, all of which receive a DDD rating for consumer helpfulness: Damaging, discriminatory, and destructive."[85] Kennedy also gestured toward the role of structural racism in such practices, stating that for "Americans who live in the barrio or the ghetto, the only credit they know is a trap. It does not enrich, it impoverishes." He indicted "the very mainstream lenders that long ago closed branches and stopped offering affordable services in affected areas" for creating this situation.[86]

There was some similar recognition of discrimination and exploitation at the House and Senate hearings held later that year to consider HOEPA itself. For example, at the Senate hearing about the bill, Comptroller of the Currency Eugene Ludwig acknowledged the twin problems of the "men and women who, all too often, have been forgotten or ignored by our so-called traditional banking system because they ha[ve] no credit history," on the one hand, and "reverse redlining," on the other hand.[87] Donald Riegle (D-MI; the bill's sponsor and chair of the Senate Committee on Banking, Housing, and Urban Affairs) asked Terry Drent, Housing Coordinator for the City of Ann Arbor Community Development Department, "why people are not able to connect with the normal system of credit and how they get shoved into the arms of loan-shark operators."[88] Drent replied that a key reason was the "ugly head . . . of racism." "Over 90 percent of the people I deal with," he said, "are of African-American descent. For whatever reason, they seem to be denied traditional credit, more so than other groups."[89] To illustrate his point, he explained that in his home county of Washtenaw County, Michigan, the bank with the "best record . . . of giving loans to African Americans" had sold only 16 mortgages—out of 926—to African Americans the previous year (out of a pool of 96 Black applicants).[90] Advocates like Drent also tried to make clear that the claim that these borrowers were too risky or otherwise unqualified for conventional loans was belied by the fact that when his organization sponsored borrowers "suffering from reverse redlining and facing foreclosure," they were often able to "take someone who's got a loan with an interest rate of 25 percent and give them something at 7 1/2 or 8 percent, whatever the market is, something that they can manage."[91]

This political and policymaking attention to predatory mortgage lending in the early 1990s represented a meaningful attempt to address some of the problems created by the new lending regime. Journalist Elinore Longobardi argues that the use of the term *predatory* to describe these mortgages was itself an important intervention, the force of which was lost in the shift to the use of *subprime* as the primary descriptor for such mortgages.[92] Dominant political actors might well have been committed to addressing predatory mortgage lending, and they might have tried in earnest to grapple with the ways in which it both fueled and reflected structural racial discrimination. Nonetheless, the net effect of their attention to predatory mortgages in the early 1990s was to lay the foundations for the construction of subprime lending and foreclosures as non-crises later that decade.[93] In particular, dominant political actors exceptionalized such mortgages and individualized borrowers' problems with them. They also disconnected predatory mortgages from the more general practice of subprime lending, the legitimacy and necessity of which they repeatedly affirmed and which they continued to treat as the solution to inequalities in access to credit. As Elvin Wyly and C. S. Ponder write, "the more shocking the stories" of predatory lending became, "the more likely they were to be challenged as not representative of any broader market problem" and to be "dismissed as unusual, exceptional cases—a few unfortunate consumers victimized by a few bad-apple lenders or brokers."[94] Even among members of Congress and advocates for borrowers who were concerned that some loans were exploitative, few questioned the assumption that the problem was that members of underserved groups such as women and people of color did not qualify for conventional mortgages or that they posed heightened risk to lenders. At the Senate HOEPA hearings, for example, Ludwig defined the problem thusly:

> These are men and women who, all too often, have been forgotten or ignored by our so-called traditional banking system because they don't fit a standard pattern. For example, many banks are reluctant to lend if a loan applicant has no credit history. So where does that leave the nurse at last weekend's workshop who had no credit history because she has always paid in cash? How does she qualify for a loan?"

Riegle, the Michigan Democrat who had introduced the bill, remained convinced that "where credit is available, on fair terms, there is no market for predatory lenders."[95]

Because lawmakers took lenders at their word that women and people of color were risky bets who were unworthy of conventional loans and that lenders therefore required more flexibility if they were to serve these groups, HOEPA also emphasized disclosures about—rather than prohibitions of—particular practices. Even these modest interventions applied only to "high-cost" refinance mortgages, which were defined very narrowly to include only those that exceeded either of two thresholds: (1) mortgages in which the annual percentage rate (APR) at closing exceeded the yield on comparable Treasury security plus 8 percent for first-lien loans and plus 10 percent for junior-lien loans; or (2) mortgages in which the total points and fees exceeded "the greater of eight percent of the total loan amount or $400 (indexed annually)."[96]

That the law would do little to protect consumers from extractive subprime mortgages and might, in fact, make them even more vulnerable to them than they already were was foreshadowed by testimony delivered at the House and Senate hearings on the bill, at which members of Congress and representatives from the banking sector praised the legislation for its restraint while consumer advocates and advocates for low-income people expressed concerns that it would prove ineffective.[97] Kennedy was explicit in detailing the bill's modesty and its consequent support from many major banks. "I want to just clarify that this bill, I believe, is reasonable, as Household [International Bank], Beneficial [Bank], Fleet [Bank], and others in the industry have said."[98] Because, he noted, HOEPA's disclosure requirements and its ban on practices including negative amortization and prepayment penalties kicked in under only very limited circumstances, he was confident that the law "really . . . get[s] to the bad apples and leaves the good ones alone." Underscoring just how uncontentious he believed the bill was among lenders, he concluded, "I just want to say for the record that none of these provisions even caused any kind of controversy really in passing the Senate."[99]

Lenders' enthusiasm for the bill was affirmed by the House testimony of Robert Elliott, an executive at Illinois-based Household International. "Your work is not perfect," he stated," "[we] doubt that any such effort could be." But, he continued, "you have focused upon straightforward disclosure and we applaud that. . . . In short, Mr. Chairman, we feel that your work is temperate and we support it. . . . We share your desire to see that your constituents and our customers are free of credit abuse, but also have free access to credit."[100] At the Senate hearing about the bill, Ludwig expressed similar confidence that HOEPA's disclosure requirements and restrictions would reduce discrimination by "encourag[ing] reputable lenders to enter the market" while not "prevent[ing] any lender from making mortgages that serve legitimate credit needs."[101]

These laudatory comments stand in stark contrast to those of Margot Saunders, counsel with the National Consumer Law Center (NCLC). At the Senate hearings about the legislation, Saunders argued that despite what she characterized as the committee's "excellent intentions," she was concerned that "only a fraction of the evils this legislation intends to address would in fact be stopped by this bill." As she explained, "the prohibitions included in the act and the disclosures required by the act" were simply not very onerous, and "very few legitimate lenders make loans which have terms which are prohibited by the act, such as negative amortization, balloon payments or prepayment penalties." Even if a loan fell under the bill's triggers, she noted, that would not necessarily mean that it "will not be made," just that the lender had to disclose that it was considered a "high-cost" mortgage under the law's definition.[102]

To illustrate the bill's weakness, Saunders explained that its definition of "high-cost" meant that in the 1993 market, when the average interest rate for a thirty-year fixed-rate mortgage was 7.31 percent, "a first mortgage loan at 16.75 percent would not be covered."[103] As Drent summarized the issue in his House testimony, relying on disclosures to address problems with mortgage lending "is like putting a beeper in a red flashing light on a shark. If you're in a house that's burning with needed home repair and medical expenses, you'll jump into the water and take your chances with the shark."[104] Advocates also predicted that "the lenders that are engaged in the type of lending that this bill is trying to address" are "ingenious in coming up with ways of avoiding the law" and "extremely imaginative in coming up with innovative ways to steal from borrowers."[105]

And sure enough, lenders soon found ways to evade these narrowly defined triggers, by, for example, using ARMs featuring teaser rates with low initial APRs that did not violate the terms under which high APRs were defined and prohibited.[106] As a result, HOEPA ended up covering fewer than 1 percent of all mortgages and protecting very few borrowers.[107] Immergluck argues that rather than reducing problematic lending practices, HOEPA instead paved the way for the emergence of the subprime mortgage market by "implicitly sanctioning many high-cost and high-risk loans that were not prohibited by the law and that did not reach the HOEPA pricing thresholds." "In effect," he argues, "HOEPA provided lenders with an implicit endorsement for high-risk loans that were priced under—even just under—these thresholds."[108] And so, less than two decades after it became formally illegal to redline, and within a decade of making it formally illegal to deny credit to women, the federal government had all but abandoned the key protections against usurious and extractive forms of credit that had benefited borrowers who had been, up to that point, mainly straight white men.

The Subprime and Foreclosure Non-Crises of the Late 1990s

And extract they did: The proportion of ARMs and refinance loans increased substantially after HOEPA's passage, peaking at 14.5 percent of market share in 1997, dipping to 10.3 percent in 1998, and then expanding rapidly again during the first decade of the twenty-first century.[109] The increases in the overall rate of subprime borrowing and in rates of foreclosure on such loans (described above) are alarming on their own. Also alarming is that these rates concealed equally troubling racial patterns in both subprime lending and rates of foreclosure. A 1999 study of Chicago by the National Training and Information Center (NTIC) showed, for example, that by 1998, subprime loans accounted for less than a quarter (22 percent) of mortgages in majority-white neighborhoods but for over a third (34 percent) of mortgages in neighborhoods in which people of color comprised half or more of the residents.[110] In 2000, a report issued by HUD and the US Department of Treasury examined national data for refinance mortgages and found even wider disparities, with subprime loans accounting for 51 percent of refinance loans in majority Black neighborhoods but only 9 percent of refinance mortgages in predominately white ones.[111] A 2002 analysis by the Association of Community Organizations for Reform Now (ACORN) of changes in prime and subprime mortgage loans from 1995 and 2002 likewise found that while the number of subprime home purchase loans had risen among all racial groups, these rates ranged from an increase of 415 percent in the case of white borrowers to 686 percent for Black borrowers and 882 percent for Latino borrowers.[112] In addition, while the number of prime conventional purchase loans increased 8 percent among white borrowers and 65 percent among Latino borrowers during this period, they declined by almost 6 percent among African American homebuyers.[113]

Several studies also showed that many of these disparities persisted after controlling for neighborhood income.[114] The 2000 HUD and Treasury Department analysis, for example, found that borrowers living in upper-income Black neighborhoods were six times more likely than borrowers living in upper-income white neighborhoods to refinance their houses with a subprime mortgage (39 percent in the former, 6 percent in the latter).[115] In addition, many studies showed that these disparities also increased as incomes rose. The analyses in the HUD and Treasury report showed that "borrowers in *upper-income* black neighborhoods were twice as likely as homeowners in *low-income* white neighborhoods to refinance with a subprime loan," with "18 percent of borrowers in low-income white neighborhoods and 39 percent of borrowers living in upper-income black neighborhoods relying on subprime mortgages" (italics in original).[116] Jacob Rugh, Len Albright, and Douglas Massey found evidence of these practices at both the individual and neighborhood levels in Baltimore, with the widest "racial penalty" for African Americans with annual incomes higher than $50,000.[117]

By 1999, racial justice, anti-poverty, and consumer advocates were drawing attention to and decrying a practice they called reverse redlining. Whereas the practice of redlining had excluded borrowers of color based on the neighborhoods in which they lived and regardless of their financial capacity, the practice of reverse redlining is a form of predatory inclusion that *targets* entire neighborhoods for expensive and restrictive mortgages, also without taking into account borrowers' financial capacity or creditworthiness and still often trafficking in long-standing (and long-discredited) narratives of risk.[118]

Less often noted, and naturalized to the point of invisibility even by many scholars of and advocates for fair lending, were gendered patterns in subprime mortgage loans.[119] Particularly troubling were the disproportionate shares of subprime mortgages sold to women, particularly to women who were sole borrowers, and especially particularly to sole-borrower women of color.[120] A 2006 study using data about more than 4 million home loans published by the Consumer Federation on what would come to be understood as the eve of the foreclosure crisis, for example, found that women were 32 percent more likely than men to receive subprime mortgages and 41 percent more likely to receive "high cost" subprime loans (defined by the report as "loans that were made more than 5 percentage points above comparable Treasury notes").[121] These patterns were anything but accidental; instead, lenders intentionally targeted Black, Latina, elderly, and sole-borrower women and corralled them into unconventional mortgages through "subprime steering."[122]

As a consequence, despite having higher credit scores than their sole-borrower male counterparts, sole-borrower women homeowners were overrepresented among subprime mortgage holders by 30 percent.[123] Effects were so exponentially worse for sole-borrower African American women that the Consumer Federation study found that they were 256 percent more likely to have a subprime mortgage "than white men with identical geographic and financial profiles."[124] A study published several years later by Wyly and Ponder found similarly significant, if somewhat less extreme, race-gender disparities.[125]

That much of this inequitable access to mortgage financing was rooted in gender discrimination was further evident in the fact that women were also more likely to receive subprime mortgages than men of the same race, with Black women 5.7 percent more likely to receive subprime loans than Black men and Latinas 12.7 percent more likely to receive subprime loans than Latino men. And while white women were half as likely as Latinas and three times less likely than Black women to receive subprime purchase loans, they were 25.8 percent more likely to receive them than white men.[126] Moreover, as in the case of the foregoing racial disparities, disparities between men and women not only persisted after controlling for income but also widened as women's incomes rose.[127] The Consumer Federation study found, for example, that while women earning below the median income were 3.3 percent more likely to receive subprime purchase loans than men with similar incomes, this relative disparity increased to 28.1 percent among women earning twice the median income and to 46.4 percent among those earning more than twice the median income. These disparities were even more pronounced for high-cost subprime purchase loans and for home improvement and refinance subprime loans, with the largest observed disparity, 58.3 percent, for high-cost refinance loans.[128] In other words, no amount of creditworthiness leveled the raced and gendered credit playing field. Determinations of women's risk and worthiness were essentially immune to the facts of their financial profiles, leading to what Baker characterizes as "a glass ceiling of lending" that prevented women from "accessing safer mortgages."[129]

Together, the foregoing patterns meant that at the height of the housing boom, more than one-third of borrowers who were well qualified for prime loans instead received subprime mortgages with fluctuating rates, and this proportion increased to almost 50 percent among women, African Americans, and Latinos.[130] A 2011 study conducted by researchers at the Center for Responsible Lending, for example, found that even after controlling for income and creditworthiness, Black and Latino borrowers were three times more likely to have been sold a subprime loan than their white counterparts.[131] A series of studies in the late 1990s and early 2000s—some conducted or commissioned by agencies of the federal government itself—showed further that these disparities in rates of subprime lending translated quite directly into disparities in foreclosures. A 2000 HUD study of Baltimore, for example, found that subprime mortgages comprised 21 percent of home loans in 1998 but 45 percent of foreclosures, rising to 57 percent of those in majority-Black neighborhoods.[132]

The 2007 Foreclosure Crisis in the Context
of the Non-Crisis of the Mid-1990s

It is not surprising, then, that the sharp increase in foreclosures that began
in 2007 took a disproportionate toll on African Americans and Latinos.
From 2007 through 2009, 7.9 percent of African American homeowners
and 7.7 percent of Latino homeowners experienced a completed foreclosure, compared with 4.5 percent of white homeowners and 4.6 percent of
Asian American homeowners (see table 4.1).[133] A 2010 study conducted by
the Center for Responsible Lending (CRL) estimated that 17 percent of
Latino homeowners, 11 percent of African American homeowners, and
7 percent of white homeowners lost or were at imminent risk of losing their
homes during this period.[134] The increase in foreclosure rates was particularly pronounced among borrowers who owned homes in majority-minority
neighborhoods (defined in the Joint Center for Housing Studies of Harvard University report as census tracts in which more than 50 percent of
residents are of color).[135] Foreclosure rates during that period were higher
and increased more steeply in such neighborhoods compared to "mixed"
(defined in the report as census tracts with 10–50 percent minority residents) and "white" (defined as less than 10 percent minority) tracts, a result
that held even after controlling for average income. Rates of foreclosure
in moderate-income majority-minority neighborhoods approached those in
low-income white neighborhoods, and rates in high-income minority neighborhoods *exceeded* rates in moderate-income white neighborhoods.[136]

These disparities are troubling examples of the ways in which the material effects of times recognized broadly as "hard" so often inflict disproportionate harm and suffering on members of marginalized groups.
From this perspective, the disproportionately high rates of both subprime
mortgages and foreclosure experienced by people of color, sole-borrower
women, and especially by sole-borrower Black women in the midst of the
broader meltdown is a classic story about the politics of racial, gender, and
economic inequality in the United States, a story in which the marginalized and intersectionally marginalized get pneumonia when the rest of
the country has a particularly bad cold. This narrative is not wrong, but
it obscures as much as it reveals about the constitutive relationship between crisis politics and racial and gender inequalities, particularly when
it comes to mortgage lending and foreclosure.

More specifically, considering the indicators that were regarded as the
harbingers of the early twenty-first-century crisis in the context of longer-

term trends complicates the dominant narratives about its origins and effects and brings into sharper focus the deeper implications of the startling disparities laid bare by—and that drove—the 2007 meltdown. It does so by making clear that many of the problems in the subprime market that would receive so much attention during the crisis had been well documented as early as the mid-1990s.[137] In particular, by the late 1990s, subprime lenders dominated the mortgage markets in majority-minority neighborhoods and foreclosures had reached what Baker characterizes as crisis rates in many of these communities.[138] Longer-term data also make clear that rates of foreclosure and delinquency had reached similar and even higher levels among subprime mortgage holders, sole-borrower women, and people of color by the late 1990s as those that would affect white male breadwinner households when the crisis was declared in 2007.

At 4.5 percent, the overall proportion of loans that were seriously delinquent or in foreclosure in 2007 represented a significant increase over previous years. However, rates of delinquency, default, and foreclosure among people of color, low-income people, and sole-borrower women had reached similar and even higher levels well before the crisis was said to have begun.[139] For example, a 2002 study for the Office of Policy Development and Research of the US Department of Housing and Urban Development estimated that in 1996, two years after HOEPA was passed, default rates among African American, Indigenous, and Latino homeowners were 4.8 percent, 4.4 percent, and 5.4 percent respectively, while rates were 2.9 percent for whites and 3.7 percent for Asian Americans (see table 4.1 above).[140] Another study estimated that 5.8 percent of subprime loans were in foreclosure as early as 1998.[141] Among the other features that would come to distinguish the widespread foreclosures of this era from their counterparts at the end of the following decade, however, was that the market had managed to forecast these high default rates and to contain their effects "within the fees and rates of subprime loans."[142] As a consequence, no widespread market meltdown occurred, and most lenders and investors managed to remain profitable despite high default rates, even as increasing numbers of people risked losing or were already losing their homes.[143]

Although these post-HOEPA developments did not cause a broad meltdown in the mortgage lending industry in the 1990s, neither did they go unnoticed. Advocates, activists, and state and local officials in states including Illinois, North Carolina, Georgia, and New York argued that the high foreclosure rates exposed the weaknesses of HOEPA and its inability to protect borrowers.[144] To address these gaps, in the mid-to-late 1990s and early 2000s, these and other states passed more stringent state and local regulations, most of which were intended to protect borrowers from predatory lending.[145] By 2005, thirty-one states had passed laws attempting to restrict or prohibit many of the practices associated with subprime lending, and in 2004, attorneys general in twenty-four states launched an investigation into Ameriquest Mortgage, which was, at the time, the nation's biggest subprime lender.[146] Many of the most protective aspects of their efforts were undone, however, when federal regulatory agencies yielded to the demands of financial services industry lobbyists for national lending standards.[147] Federal regulators acceded to their demands and issued new regulations that weakened, blocked, or overrode state laws.[148]

Of greatest consequence were regulations issued between 1996 and 2004 by the Office of Thrift Supervision (OTS) and the Office of the Comptroller of the Currency (OCC), which were the primary regulators of federal depository institutions.[149] These new regulations preempted states from applying their laws to the institutions these federal agencies regulated—institutions that, by that point, included the mortgage banks operating subsidiaries of these institutions. In addition to allowing national banks to ignore state anti-predatory laws, they also ruled that state agencies lacked the right to enforce states' lending anti-discrimination laws against these institutions. The regulations therefore severely limited the number of lenders covered by these state laws.[150] As a consequence, "an increasing number of mortgage loans were made by independent mortgage banking institutions subject to less federal oversight than depository institutions and their mortgage banking subsidiaries."[151] The effect, as Crump and his colleagues write, was to create "two different regulatory structures."[152] William Apgar and his coauthors call this dual system "channel specialization," a fragmented system in which prime credit flows through one set of more stringent regulatory structures, "while subprime credit flows through a different set of less well regulated" ones.[153] Through these efforts, as Baker sums it up, the federal government intervened to operationalize neoliberal ideals in one way for borrowers and in another way for lenders. "Lending institutions benefited from profit windfalls as federal legislation intervened in the market on their behalf," she argues, "while consumers lost homes and equity under the guise of maintaining a laissez-faire market economy."[154]

Conclusion

If we take at face value lenders' claims that subprime mortgages were gifts to "risky" borrowers who were not creditworthy enough for conventional loans, then separate credit channels, disparities in rates of subprime lending, and the accompanying high rates of foreclosure among some groups in the late 1990s might seem not only reasonable, but also to confirm the ostensible rationale for subprime mortgages. But as the studies and congressional hearings that I have described make clear, policymakers knew by the late 1990s that there was no basis for their claims. Instead, there was ample evidence by that time that subprime mortgages were being sold in discriminatory and predatory ways to people who were often well qualified for conventional ones. There was also ample evidence that this discrimination was the result of long-discredited racist and misogynist ideas about creditworthiness and risk—ideas that were given new life in a context of deregulation and in which credit was treated as a substitute for more direct forms of state spending and action.

Moreover, as I show in the next chapter, economic reporters and dominant political actors unquestioningly repeated and amplified lenders' assertions that the high interest rates and inflexible terms of subprime mortgages were necessary if they were to lend money to allegedly uncreditworthy but aspiring homeowners. They also failed to question the validity of "creditworthiness" and "risk" as metrics, lenders' assertions that women and people of color were particularly likely to be risky and uncreditworthy, that it was this riskiness and lack of "good credit" that posed the key barrier to homeownership among members of these groups, or that subprime mortgages were the solution to this problem. In a context in which credit was increasingly treated as the route to equality, accepting these long-discredited assertions allowed reporters and policymakers to treat the consequent racial and (on the rare occasions at which they recognized them) gender disparities in subprime borrowing as evidence that making subprime mortgages available was the correct intervention to address inequities. It also allowed them to normalize the high rates of foreclosure on subprime mortgages as a natural and inevitable outcome of taking "risks" on these borrowers. Because subprime mortgages were treated not as a policy problem to be addressed but rather as themselves the appropriate intervention to provide credit to borrowers deemed unworthy, the idea that the federal government might have a role to play beyond the prosecution of individual predatory lenders was rarely taken seriously. Together, these unquestioned assertions, zombie facts, and characterizations lay the foundations for the ways in which these issues would be understood and addressed once the situation was deemed a crisis and, more generally, for the perpetuation of the exploitation and immiseration of members of marginalized groups.

CHAPTER FIVE

How to Semantically Mask a Crisis

E ven a dedicated consumer of economic reporting in dominant news sources might have had little idea about the high rates of subprime mortgage lending and foreclosure among women, Latinos, Black and Indigenous people, and in communities of color during the 1990s. And if they had known about them, immersing themselves in these sources would still have provided them with little sense about the extent of the problems, about the role of the federal government in creating them, or about how these patterns were related to broader issues and longer histories of racism and misogyny in and beyond housing and lending. Readers would have instead likely gotten the impression that subprime mortgage lending was a gift to "risky" and "unworthy" borrowers and that such loans were the solution to, rather than a source of, racial and gender discrimination in mortgage lending. The same would likely have been true of readers committed to following policy deliberations in sources like party platforms, presidential addresses, and the *Congressional Record* during that era. In 2007, however, even a casual reader would almost certainly have had a clear sense that rates of foreclosure had risen exponentially, that subprime mortgages were partially to blame for this increase, and that dominant political actors believed that a resolution to these predicaments deserved, required, and could be achieved through federal intervention.

I show in this chapter that through these framings and patterns of attention, mainstream economic journalists and dominant political actors constituted the high rates of subprime mortgage lending and foreclosures as non-crises from 1995 through 2006 and as crises during the period that began in 2007. Drawing on data from content analyses of sources including economic reporting, party platforms, congressional hearings, and State of the Union addresses, I show further that three key components of the treatment of subprime mortgages and foreclosures as non-crises during the earlier period lay the foundation for the ways in which long-standing race and gender inequalities would be reinscribed once the crisis was "declared."

First, mainstream economic journalists and dominant political actors accepted the claims of lenders and policymakers that women and people of color were "risky," naïve, and uncreditworthy borrowers and that subprime mortgages were therefore necessary to increase homeownership among members of these groups. Failing to question the long-standing racist and misogynist beliefs underlying these assertions or the validity of "creditworthiness" and "risk" as metrics served to naturalize the extractive terms of subprime mortgages while simultaneously rendering invisible their implications for women and people of color, and for women of color in particular.

Second, these same economic journalists and political actors accepted the validity of the turn to private credit as an effective, appropriate, and preferable alternative to public spending and redistribution. Accepting such arguments about credit democratization as the route to equality led them to treat subprime mortgage lending not as a policy problem to be addressed, but rather as itself the appropriate intervention to address inequities in lending and homeownership. It also meant that mainstream economic journalists and dominant political actors rarely took seriously the possibility of more direct state action to address subprime lending and foreclosures during the non-crisis period, even as activists and advocates demanded such intervention.

Finally, and most literally, I show that, for all intents and purposes, mainstream economic reporters and dominant political actors never treated subprime mortgage lending and foreclosures as crises from 1995 through 2006. Instead of describing these issues as crises worthy of and remediable through state intervention, they treated them as natural, inevitable, immune to, and not warranting government intervention and resources.

Together, these processes, beliefs, and assumptions lay the foundation for the ways in which subprime mortgage lending and foreclosures would be understood and addressed once the situation was deemed a crisis. In particular, as evidence of the damaging effects of subprime mortgages and foreclosures spread beyond people of color and sole-borrower women, mainstream economic journalists and dominant political actors began increasingly to question lenders' assertions about subprime borrowers and rising rates of foreclosure on such loans and to argue that federal attention was necessary to address these issues. But even as they became more likely to describe the situation as a crisis that could and should be addressed using state intervention and resources, journalists and political actors continued to treat it as a non-crisis for women and people of color, naturalizing the race and gender patterns in subprime lending and foreclosures and treating them as outside of the crisis and beyond the remedial power of the federal government.

Comparing the subprime mortgage crisis to its non-crisis analogue therefore provides a window onto the ways in which ideas about the proper role of the state and the power, normativity, and privilege of those perceived to be affected by bad things work together (1) to construct some troubles as "normal" and others as aberrant and temporary crises that can and must resolved; (2) to frame problems related to structural inequalities as natural, inevitable, immune to, and therefore not warranting state intervention, at least not the kind deemed appropriate to address crises; and (3) to shape ideas about the ostensible solutions and ends to hard times and bad things that *are* treated as crises.[1]

Creditworthiness and Risk Are the Problems, Subprime Mortgages Are the Solution

To examine the ways in which mainstream economic reporters and dominant political actors addressed subprime mortgages and foreclosures, I combined data available through the US Policy Agendas Project (USPAP) with evidence from systematic searches and content analyses of congressional hearings, party platforms, State of the Union addresses, and two of the most important sources of mainstream economic reporting in the United States—the *New York Times* and the *Wall Street Journal*.[2] I draw on additional evidence from searches of ProQuest's Ethnic NewsWatch, Gender-Watch, and Alt-Press Watch databases, the results of which are discussed in endnotes and the appendices. The analyses that follow focus on data from two eras, periodized as: (1) the non-crisis period that begins the year after the passage of the 1994 Home Ownership and Equity Protection Act (HOEPA) in 1995 and ends in 2006; and (2) the crisis period of 2007–2008, although data in some of the tables and figures in this chapter extend as far back as 1980.[3]

The evidence from these analyses reveals that mainstream economic reporters failed to question assertions that extending credit to underserved groups demanded and justified the high interest rates and constraining terms characteristic of such loans. This was the first process through which high rates of subprime mortgages and foreclosures among people of color and sole-borrower women were naturalized. In particular, analyzing coverage of high rates of subprime mortgage lending and foreclosure in the *New York Times* and the *Wall Street Journal* during the non-crisis period demonstrates that economic reporters in these two papers instead took as given the claims of lenders and policymakers that private credit is preferable to public spending and redistribution. They similarly took as given that such loans were necessary to extend credit to "risky" borrowers who, they contended, would not otherwise qualify for mortgages and would therefore not be able to buy a house.[4] For example, one of the first *New York Times* articles to address subprime mortgages, "Lowering the Credit Fence; Big Players Are Jumping into the Risky Loan Business" (published in 1997), contrasted "those [borrowers] considered prime-lending prospects" with subprime borrowers, who, the article's writer averred, "generally include people with poor credit histories—or no credit history at all." "A large number," they continued, "appear to be low-income, inner-city minority residents. Others with more substantial incomes," the article continued, "may patronize subprime lenders and pay their higher interest rates because they have suffered a recent financial calamity."[5]

The data in table 5.1 demonstrate that characterizations such as these abounded in stories published throughout this period (see table 5.1; see endnote and appendices for details about sources, search parameters, coding decisions, and other methodological considerations).[6] Despite accumulating evidence to the contrary, reporters consistently repeated these "zombie facts" and depicted subprime mortgages as ones that made homeownership available to people whose credit they described using an ever-expanding array of damning modifiers including "weak credit," "poor credit," "dicey credit," "tarnished credit," "rocky credit," "damaged credit," "questionable credit," "scuffed credit," or, in the foregoing case, "no credit at all." Of the 68 stories about subprime mortgages published in the *New York Times* from 1995 through 2006, for example, a full 62 percent included at least one of these descriptors, as did just under half (45 percent) of the 189 stories in the *Wall Street Journal*.[7]

After describing subprime borrowers as people who lack credit histories, for example, "Lowering the Credit Fence" declared that "so rich are the profits to be mined from borrowers like Mrs. Smith that major companies are lining up to lend to them—despite the risks these borrowers

TABLE 5.1. **Characterizations of subprime mortgage lending and rising rates of foreclosure,**
New York Times **and** *Wall Street Journal,* **1995–2006, 2007, and 2008**

	New York Times			Wall Street Journal		
	1995–2006	2007	2008	1995–2006	2007	2008
Total number of stories about subprime mortgages published during period (N)[a]	68	731	663	189	1805	1156
Percent of stories about subprime mortgages suggesting that they are sold to borrowers with bad (or "weak," "poor," "dicey," "tarnished," "rocky," "damaged," "questionable," "scuffed," or "no") credit	62%	12.3%	5%	45%	18%	8%
Total number of stories about rising rates of foreclosures published during period (N)[b]	10	186	345	22	247	367
Percent of stories about rising rates of foreclosures attributing them to borrowers with bad (or "weak," "poor," "dicey," "tarnished," "rocky," "damaged," "questionable," "scuffed," or "no") credit or borrowers who took on more debt than they could afford	60%	35%	8.5%	40.1%	20%	13%

Note: Data are organized to depict the periodization of two eras: (1) the non-crisis period that begins the year after the passage of HOEPA in 1995 and ends in 2006; and (2) the crisis period of 2007–8.
[a] Search was for "subprime NEAR mortgage", which returns documents that contain the two search terms, in any order, within four words apart. After removing irrelevant observations, I then used Nvivo to identify and compile a list of all descriptors accompanying "credit" in these articles and calculated the proportion of articles that contained any of these (mostly) bi-grams.
[b] Search was for "rising NEAR foreclosure" or "increasing NEAR foreclosure", which returns documents that contain the two search terms, in any order, within four words apart. After removing irrelevant observations, I then used Nvivo to identify and compile a list of all descriptors accompanying "credit" in these articles and calculated the proportion of articles that contained any of these (mostly) bi-grams.
For additional information, see appendices A, B, and C, and notes 6 and 7 in chapter 5.
Source: ProQuest US Newsstream.

pose." The "risk" that Beatrice Smith, the woman referenced (and whose story would later be featured on an anti-predatory website called "Tell Citibank"), might lose her home is not considered. Also not considered is that the practice of "mining profits" might itself signal that these loans were problematic.[8] Instead, the article framed the risk of such loans as one that borrowers posed to lenders:

This financial frontier is already littered with the wreckage of small lenders that have been severely battered or crippled the last year by bad loans and dubious management practices. But the big players now plowing into the market say they bring sounder lending policies and a less free-wheeling approach to what has long been one of the shabbier arenas in lending. They argue that their sophistication will enable them to succeed where the small-fry lenders have failed.[9]

These frames were not new, of course. While some of the details were particular to subprime mortgages, such characterizations were, as Paula Treichler has written with regard to HIV/AIDS, "already peopled," linked to a set of "preexisting worldviews, institutional discourses, material realities, and cultural phenomena" about race and gender.[10] That is, these frames were available because they echoed, reinforced, and reinscribed the misogynist and racist tropes about women and people of color as "risky" and "unsophisticated buyers" that, as I showed in chapter 4, had long been deployed to deflect responsibility from the federal government and housing industry and to project it onto borrowers.[11]

Once economic reporters had defined the policy problem as one in which some borrowers were too risky for conventional loans and had framed subprime mortgages as a favor to these borrowers and as themselves the solution to this problem, they then depicted federal support for and encouragement of such mortgages as the government's appropriate intervention into this issue. A 1999 *New York Times* article reporting on a policy change that allowed the Federal National Mortgage Association (Fannie Mae) to begin to purchase subprime mortgages, for example, stated, "In a move that could help increase home ownership rates among minorities and low-income consumers," Fannie Mae "is easing the credit requirements on loans that it will purchase from banks and other lenders." In framing the issue as a boon to these consumers, the story reinforced the notion that such loans—and not state spending or other redistributive or anti-discrimination measures—were the correct way for the state to help aspiring but presumptively "unqualified" homeowners.

While a plurality of *New York Times* and *Wall Street Journal* stories naturalized the claims of lenders who asserted that subprime mortgages were the appropriate way in which the federal government should help people with "bad credit" become homeowners, I could identify not a single story in either newspaper during this period that questioned the notion that credit scores were valid and objective measures of a borrower's capacity to repay a loan. I similarly was unable to find even one story that questioned the assertion that borrowers who took out subprime mortgages did so because they did not qualify for conventional loans. None mentioned the growing corpus of studies and congressional hearings that, as I demonstrated in chapter 4, by that point had established that a substantial proportion of subprime mortgages were sold to people who were, in fact, well qualified for conventional ones.[12] And while subprime mortgages were treated as the solution to the problem of creditworthiness, little attention was devoted to the legislation that had paved the way for these practices.[13]

Similarly, none of the reporting during this period acknowledged that women who took out subprime mortgages had better credit, on average, than their white male counterparts who took out prime loans.[14] Some articles did note that a sizable portion of subprime loans were second mortgages or home equity loans.[15] Even those stories that recognized this fact, however, typically failed to link it to the legislative changes that had incentivized such debt, and failed as well to contextualize the need to take on such debt within the neoliberal welfare state retrenchment that treated credit expansion as a substitute for public spending and redistribution. So although many of the women and people of color who took out such loans had bought—and, in many cases, had nearly paid off—their homes long ago, few reporters allowed this fact to complicate the claim that subprime mortgages "democratized credit" and were essential to increasing rates of homeownership among members of these groups. For example, the 1997 story about Beatrice Smith noted that she had paid off her mortgage three years before she had refinanced her home through a subprime mortgage. It said nothing, however, about the changes to the home finance terrain in the years since she had originally bought her house, nor did it acknowledge that her subprime mortgage had not enabled but instead threatened her ability to own a home. The article also did not question whether borrowing against one's home was an appropriate substitution for higher wages or more robust redistribution.

Naturalizing lenders' assertions about both the propriety of private subprime credit as a substitute for public spending and about the "riskiness" of subprime borrowers themselves allowed economic reporters to similarly naturalize and individualize the rising rates of default and foreclosure among these borrowers.[16] If subprime mortgages were a gift to risky and otherwise unqualified borrowers, then it simply followed that members of this group were at greater risk of not being able to stay in their homes. The data in table 5.1, for example, demonstrate that of the twenty-two stories about rising rates of foreclosure published in the *Wall*

Street Journal from 1995 through 2006, 40.1 percent attributed them to bad credit or to borrowers who "took on more debt than they could afford" (see table 5.1; see endnote for search parameters).[17] Of the ten relevant *New York Times* stories addressing these rising rates, 60 percent contained such attributions. "Easier access to credit in the 90's has made it possible for less creditworthy purchasers to buy a house," one *New York Times* story asserted. "The ongoing problems of these borrowers," it continued, "have contributed disproportionately to the nation's growing foreclosure rate."[18] Another article published in that paper a few years later was even more explicit:

> Foreclosures among the 26.4 million families with sound enough credit to get conventional loans are rare but growing.... They are much higher among low- and moderate-income families with so-called subprime loans—higher-interest-rate loans made to borrowers with imperfect credit.... "We're seeing the implications of reduced standards that subprime lenders applied," said William Apgar, the federal housing commissioner in the Clinton administration, now a senior scholar at the Joint Center for Housing Studies at Harvard. "The expectations were that we would see more fail, and now we're seeing them fail."[19]

In other words, Apgar was saying that because subprime mortgages were a solution that enabled homeownership among members of groups who, it was assumed, would not otherwise qualify for conventional mortgages, there was little reason to be alarmed about the rising rates of foreclosure connected to these practices.

Laying the blame for foreclosures associated with subprime mortgages on "reduced standards" for borrowers rather than on federal government retrenchment or on the extractive terms of the loans themselves also left little room for contemplating the possibility that robust state intervention might be warranted and effective in addressing them.[20] This absence is evident, for example, in the fact that of the thirty-two articles about the increasing number of foreclosures appearing in each paper during this non-crisis period (ten in the *New York Times*, twenty-two in the *Wall Street Journal*), only four pieces across both papers discussed ways in which the federal government might intervene to stem them. Three of these four articles addressed legal action taken by the federal government to prosecute mortgage fraud and fraudulent appraisals. The only article that highlighted the power of the federal government to provide a more general and robust solution to this issue appeared in the *Wall Street*

Journal, and reported on a September 2002 decision by Fannie Mae to tighten standards on mortgage refinancing loans. Each newspaper also published one article about the lending industry's efforts to get the federal government to squash state anti-predatory lending laws. Even toward the end of 2006, as both papers began to pay more attention to what economists were increasingly arguing was a housing "bubble," neither one published any articles suggesting that federal policy had played any role in creating this bubble. Likewise, neither paper published any articles suggesting that the federal government might do anything to prevent the bubble from bursting or to protect homeowners should that happen. And none of the articles about increasing foreclosures published during this period questioned the use of private credit as a substitute for higher wages, more generous social welfare benefits, or other forms of redistribution or public spending.

Attention to and Elision of Racial and Gender Disparities

The naturalizing effects of the foregoing characterizations of subprime borrowers and of borrowers experiencing foreclosure were also enabled and reinforced by the ways in which mainstream economic reporters simultaneously addressed and elided the racial and gender implications of and patterns evident in subprime mortgage lending and its attendant increases in foreclosures. On the one hand, mainstream economic reporters failed to investigate the claims of lenders and legislators who argued that the relaxed lending standards associated with subprime mortgages were necessary to extend mortgage credit to previously excluded groups, and they failed as well to scrutinize their implications for these groups. On the other hand, stories that did examine the implications of subprime mortgage lending for women and people of color provided little legal or historical context about the origins of such practices. These articles also said little about the ways in which the deregulatory legislation of the 1980s had undermined state and federal fair-lending and anti-discrimination protections. Instead of providing such context, reporters more typically elided the role of the federal government and relied on racist and misogynist shorthands, assumptions, and stereotypes to explain the prevalence of subprime mortgages and home foreclosures among women and people of color.

For example, as the data in table 5.2 make clear, only 15 percent of the sixty-eight *New York Times* articles about subprime mortgages published during this period focused on the implications of such loans for people of color (an additional 4 percent addressed race in some secondary way; see table 5.2; see endnote and appendices for the criteria I used to determine and code whether a story addressed race or gender).[21] The proportion was even lower for pieces in the *Wall Street Journal*, in which only 10 percent of articles about subprime mortgage lending examined its racial implications (2.4 percent took up this question in a secondary way). Attention to race in articles about rising rates of foreclosures was even rarer: None of the twenty-two stories addressing foreclosures in the *Wall Street Journal* during this period examined their implications for people of color. The proportion is higher for coverage in the *New York Times* (20 percent), but since that paper published only ten stories about rising rates of foreclosure from 1995 through 2006, the higher proportion amounts to only two stories.[22]

And even this scant attention to the implications of subprime mortgage lending and foreclosure for borrowers of color is extensive compared to the attention devoted to the gendered implications of these issues and to their intersectionally constituted effects on women of color.[23] Although, as the *New York Times* article that featured Beatrice Smith suggests, stories about subprime mortgage lending often featured or were framed around accounts about women homebuyers, gender was almost never thematized as a factor in the ways in which these issues played out: Not a single article about subprime mortgage lending published in the *Wall Street Journal* during this period focused on its implications for women nor did any note the gendered patterns in rates of subprime mortgage lending. The same was true of stories in the *New York Times* until March 2000, when that paper finally published one story in which women and the possibility of gender discrimination in mortgage lending featured as subjects ("Home Lender Settles Suit over Fees"). Over the course of the period from 1995 to 2006, however, a mere 3.8 percent of stories about subprime mortgage lending in the *Times* focused on its gendered implications (an additional 12.2 percent addressed women or gender in some secondary way). No story about rising rates of foreclosure in either paper during this period addressed women or gender in even a cursory or incidental way.

That first *New York Times* story addressing gender and subprime mortgages also illustrates some of the ways in which mainstream economic reporting of this period served to naturalize racialized inequalities in mortgage lending and foreclosure, to invisibilize gendered ones, and to obscure the simultaneous workings of racism and sexism in structuring the

TABLE 5.2. *New York Times* and *Wall Street Journal* articles addressing race and gender (as a percent of all stories about subprime mortgages, rising rates of foreclosure, and mortgage, foreclosure, or subprime crisis), 1995–2006, 2007, and 2008

	New York Times			Wall Street Journal		
	1995–2006	2007	2008	1995–2006	2007	2008
Total number of stories about subprime mortgages during period (N)[a]	68	731	663	189	1805	1156
Percent of stories about subprime mortgages during period addressing people of color/race	15%	0.4%	0.3%	10%	0.3%	0%
Secondary way	4.0%	1.8%	12%	2.4%	0.3%	0%
Percent of stories about subprime mortgages during period addressing women/gender	3.8%	0.1%	1.8%	0%	0%	0%
Secondary way	12.2%	0%	0%	0%	0%	0%
Total number of stories about rising rates of foreclosures during period (N)[b]	10	186	345	22	247	367
Percent of stories about rising rates of foreclosures during period addressing people of color/race	20%	1.6%	0.6%	0%	1.2%	0.5%
Percent of stories about rising rates of foreclosures during period addressing women/gender	0%	0%	0%	0%	0%	0%
Total number of stories using terms *mortgage crisis*, *foreclosure crisis*, or *subprime crisis* during period (N)[c]	3	228	557	1	307	536
Percent of stories using terms *mortgage crisis*, *foreclosure crisis*, or *subprime crisis* during period addressing people of color/race	0%	1.8%	2.0%	0%	2.0%	0.9%
Percent of stories using terms *mortgage crisis*, *foreclosure crisis*, or *subprime crisis* during period addressing women/gender	0%	0.4%	0.3%	0%	0.7%	0%

Note: Data are organized to depict the periodization of two eras: (1) the non-crisis period that begins the year after the passage of HOEPA in 1995 and ends in 2006; and (2) the crisis period of 2007–8. I used Nvivo to search articles retrieved through the foregoing searches, coding them as "1" if they included (and "0" if they did not include) the following terms: *African American, American Indian, Asian American, Black, Hispanic, "inner city," Latino, minority/minorities, Native American, female, gender, lady/ladies, woman/women, discriminate,* and *discrimination.* I read each story in which these terms were observed to determine whether it did, in fact, address people of color or race and women or gender. For additional information, see appendices A, B, and C, and note 21 in chapter 5.

[a] Search was for "subprime NEAR mortgage", which returns documents that contain the two search terms, in any order, within four words apart.

[b] Search was for "rising NEAR foreclosure" or "increasing NEAR foreclosure", which returns documents that contain the two search terms, in any order, within four words apart.

[c] Search was for "'mortgage crisis' OR 'foreclosure crisis' OR 'subprime crisis'". *Source:* ProQuest US Newsstream.

mortgage-lending and home-buying terrain during the non-crisis period. The story reported on a settlement by the Delta Financial Corporation in a lawsuit filed by three federal agencies. The lawsuit alleged that Delta had engaged in a "longstanding pattern of illegal lending practices, including charging black women higher fees than other borrowers." But although the article opened with this acknowledgment that the suit emphasized the exploitation of Black *women*, the author did not sustain a gender analysis. Beginning with the title, "Home Lender Settles Suit over Fees: U.S. Says Blacks Had to Pay More," the article emphasized instead that Delta provided "high-interest mortgages to borrowers in poor neighborhoods who are unable to get help from other banks," violating "among other laws, a set of civil rights laws enacted in the 1970s when big banks were refusing to lend in troubled minority neighborhoods." A previous *New York Times* article about the suit, titled "Buyers get benefit of easier terms, but some charge deception," similarly characterized Delta's misdeeds as having "allegedly enticed minority homeowners into borrowing more money than they could repay."[24]

Most centrally, by abandoning its initial acknowledgement that it was not only African Americans but also women—and particularly Black women—who were exploited by subprime loans, the article elided the continued relevance of the ways in which the federal government itself had not only permitted, but in some cases had mandated, the exclusion of women from access to credit. It likewise elided, normalized, and invisibilized the ways in which these gendered exclusions intersected with racialized patterns of discrimination and exploitation to become a defining feature of subprime mortgage lending and foreclosures. Similar elisions of the role of gender are evident in other stories as well. Although the article about Beatrice Smith described her as a "68-year-old former cleaning woman," for example, and although, as I showed above, its author did not hesitate to draw on misogynist gender stereotypes as implicit explanations for her troubles, the Atlanta Legal Aid attorney who helped her with her suit described the situation as one of "financial apartheid" affecting "low-income, often minority borrowers." The structuring role of gender in this system was invisible even to a lawyer who specialized in addressing lending abuses that were, as Amy Castro Baker has argued, "eroding the wealth of women" during this period.[25]

The foregoing stories are notable for their thematic references to redlining and for acknowledging the possibility of ongoing discrimination against borrowers in majority-minority neighborhoods.[26] But both articles also nonetheless participated in the naturalization of subprime mortgage lending to people of color. Like the previously quoted passages from the story about Beatrice Smith, the story about Delta Financial characterized that company as one that "typically provides high-interest mortgages to borrowers in poor neighborhoods who are unable to get help from other banks." It also described the practice of "making loans based on collateral, not on the ability of the borrower to keep up with payments" as "a hallmark of unscrupulous high-interest lenders," and quoted a statement issued by the Federal Trade Commission after the settlement arguing that "Delta's practice of approving loans without regard to borrowers' ability to repay exposed borrowers to unwarranted risk of default and foreclosure."

To be clear, I am not suggesting that lenders should sell loans that borrowers have no hope of repaying, much less that they should be permitted to use deception to do so. There may even be conditions under which a home mortgage interest rate of 15 or 20 percent might be justified. But in most cases, demonstrating that a borrower could repay a loan at those rates would not constitute evidence that its terms were warranted or fair. Rather, an assessment that a borrower had the ability to repay such an expensive loan would be better understood as an indication that they had access to resources that should qualify for better terms. Moreover, as I detailed in chapter 4, decades of research make clear that the terms of financing rather than the characteristics of a borrower predict the risk of nonpayment or default and that approximately half of women, African American, and Latino borrowers who received subprime mortgages with fluctuating rates were well qualified for prime loans.[27] Framing the problem as one having to do with "borrowers' ability to repay" rather than as a question about whether the terms of the loan are reasonable and offered in good faith, however, relies on (and perpetuates) the false assumption that it is the amount of the loan rather than the terms associated with it that were the source of borrowers' problems. It also accepts the discredited assumption that borrowers were given those terms because they did not qualify for better ones.

Articles thematizing race and gender disparities during this period further reinforced these individualizing and naturalizing effects by providing little historical, legal, or legislative context for these patterns.[28] Instead of explaining the role of the federal government in their creation, these articles attributed ongoing discrimination in mortgage lending to individual bad actors, and they played into and perpetuated racist and misogynist controlling images of women and people of color as financially naïve and risky borrowers.[29] For example, only one article about subprime mortgage lending published in each of the two papers during this period mentioned the Community Reinvestment Act, and only nine mentioned the Home Mortgage Disclosure Act (two in the *Wall Street Journal* and seven in the *New York Times*, based on the search for articles about subprime mortgages that I described previously). Not one article published about subprime mortgages in either of these two papers during this period mentioned analogously relevant laws addressing sex discrimination such as the Equal Credit Opportunity Act, nor did any question whether subprime mortgages might violate this law.[30]

References to specific laws or to particular court decisions might strike some readers as an unreasonably high standard of evidence for determining whether an article contains relevant historical and legal context. As scholars such as Shanto Iyengar have shown, however, people are more likely to hold government responsible for alleviating problems when news stories provide this kind of contextualizing "thematic" information.[31] Catherine Squires explains similarly that a focus on individuals alongside the "absence of reporting on structural and historical influences on racial disparities" are parts of the process through which the media "demonize people of color in ways that buttress modern racist understandings of issues."[32] Unlike issues such as crime and welfare, the portrayals of subprime borrowers and of people experiencing foreclosure in these sources during this period did not necessarily demonize them, nor were they inevitably unsympathetic.[33] But neither did these depictions blame policy changes or argue that state intervention and reinvestment in public benefit provision might replace subprime mortgage lending or provide a remedy for people facing foreclosure.

Even if references to particular laws represent a high bar, less stringent indicators of historical and legal context do not fare much better. Few of the stories about subprime mortgage lending or rising rates of foreclosure that addressed race, for example, contained even passing references to historical or contemporary evidence of discrimination in mortgage lending. None of the 189 articles about subprime mortgages published in the *Wall Street Journal* from 1995 through 2006 referenced redlining, for example, and the *New York Times* published only one such story (out of 68) during this period. Likewise, only two stories about subprime mortgages in the *Times* (out of 10) and three in the *Wall Street Journal* (out of 22) during this period referenced racial discrimination in any way (one published in 1998, three in 2005). The very first of these stories about subprime mortgages, a 1998 article in the *Wall Street Journal*, reported on a Justice Department and Federal Trade Commission investigation into "alleged abuses in the booming businesses of home-equity and subprime-mortgage lending."[34] Although the reporter acknowledged that some lenders engaged in deceptive practices, they nonetheless described subprime lenders as ones who "serve clients with poor credit." The remaining four stories were all published in 2005. Two of these articles addressed an inquiry brought by the New York State Attorney General into racial bias in subprime mortgage lending, a third addressed a similar federal investigation, and the fourth discussed the results of a report that found evidence of such bias. The data in this sympathetic report indicted what one expert referred to as "rapacious loan providers who are able to get away with more with black borrowers than with white borrowers."[35] But the article nonetheless shifted the blame away from these lenders and the policy changes and onto the alleged naïveté of the borrowers themselves: "Because they tend to have less experience with home buying and the intricacies of mortgage-loan pricing," the expert continued, "many blacks may be less prepared than whites to shop around effectively for the best terms."[36] And by failing to contextualize these lending practices within the deregulatory legislation that permitted such previously prohibited terms, the article also deflected blame from the federal government, taking the possibility of a federal remedy for them and their discriminatory effects off the table.

As the vanishingly small number of articles paying attention to gender might suggest, reporters provided even less legal, policy, or historical context for the gendered patterns in subprime mortgage lending. The very few stories that acknowledged that women were disproportionately likely to hold a subprime mortgage and to experience foreclosure did not typically attribute these disparities to discrimination or to policy changes. Instead, they explained them using many of the same long-standing stereotypes about women's naïveté, inexperience, or lack of negotiating skills that, as Taylor details, had fueled the characterizations of Black women as "unsophisticated borrowers" and that, as I described in chapter 4, had structured HOEPA's emphasis on information and disclosures about extractive lending practices rather than prioritizing prohibitions of them.

The story about Beatrice Smith, for example, stated that "she was not aware how the home equity loans the companies arranged caused any borrowing she made against the line to increase her debt," quoting her as saying that "'I thought I could get $32,000 in my hand and my note to the bank wouldn't go up each month," but instead, she continued, "my note went up to $500, and I didn't understand why." The article was sympathetic to Smith's situation and the reporter clearly believed that the lender had deceived her. However, in framing the problem as one having to do with banks exploiting the vulnerabilities of elderly women, the story exceptionalized Smith's experience and individualized the problems she faced as ones having to do with her lack of knowledge rather than as the result of changes such as deregulation and the undermining of anti-discrimination protections. The framing also implies that men are less likely to take out subprime mortgages because they are savvier and—in spite of having lower average credit ratings than women—worthier borrowers than women, not because they do not face gender discrimination or because they do not have to contend with stereotypes about their inexperience and naïveté.[37] The article also noted, however, that Smith had bought her home in 1969, a period during which the FHA and the CRA were in force, but also a time when it was perfectly legal to deny credit to her based on gender. That she was able to buy a home in this context suggests that she was actually quite savvy, not naïve.

Together, these patterns of elision and attention naturalized the troubling relationships among race, gender, and subprime mortgage lending and foreclosure as they were taking root. This naturalization, in turn, deflected attention from federal action and inaction, reinforcing the effects of the assumptions about risk and creditworthiness and structuring understandings of and responses to the eventual "crisis." Lengthier and more comprehensive treatments of these issues intended for popular audiences typically elided their racialized and gendered implications as well. For example, nowhere in the warnings issued by Robert Shiller about the housing bubble in the second edition of *Irrational Exuberance*, published in 2005, does he address the implications of race or gender.[38] Michael Lewis's 2010 book *The Big Short*—about the ways in which investment banks and other Wall Street firms profited from the mortgage crisis—also said nothing about race or gender (see the endnote, however, for a discussion about the gender and racial tropes and stereotypes deployed in the 2015 film adaptation of the book).[39] Dean Starkman pays similarly little attention to these issues in *The Watchdog That Didn't Bark*, his 2014 book about the failure of the business press to hold banks and mortgage lenders accountable in the years leading up to the financial crisis.[40]

Language of Crisis and Non-Crisis

Perhaps the most telling indication that subprime mortgages and rising rates of foreclosure among women and people of color were constituted as non-crises by mainstream economic reporters and dominant political actors in the late 1990s and early 2000s is also the most literal: that is, the term *crisis* scarcely appears in conjunction with these issues before 2007.

Crisis and Non-Crisis in Economic Reporting

Figure 5.1 provides a bird's-eye view of this treatment in dominant economic reporting, depicting the use of the terms *mortgage crisis, foreclosure crisis*, and *subprime crisis* in the *New York Times* and the *Wall Street Journal* from 1980 to 2017 (1982 for the *Wall Street Journal*; see endnote for search parameters).[41] As the figure makes clear, during the non-crisis period of 1995 to 2006, the *Wall Street Journal* published only one article containing any of these terms (in 1996). The *New York Times*, for its part, published a mere four articles containing any of them during this period (one in 1985, two in 1996, and one in 2006).[42] The first of these *New York Times* pieces, published in 1985, reported on troubles at the financial services firm EPIC Holdings Inc. The second, published in 1996, speculated about a possible mortgage crisis in Japan after the arrest of a "property magnate" there (this arrest was also the subject of the one 1996 *Wall Street Journal* piece during this period). The third, also published in 1996, referenced an earlier "farm foreclosure crisis" in 1982. The fourth was published in December 2006 and reported on the findings of a report that had recently been issued by the Center for Responsible Lending, which warned that approximately "one in five subprime mortgages made in the last two years are likely to go into foreclosure" and "that risky lending practices could lead to the worst foreclosure crisis in the modern mortgage market."[43] This last article was also the only one to appear in either of the two newspapers during this period that referenced the potential implications of such a crisis for people of color, noting that "minority homeowners take out a disproportionate share of subprime loans," with "over half of African-Americans and 40 percent of Hispanics receiv[ing] subprime loans." The report projected that "10 percent of the African-American borrowers and 8 percent of Hispanic borrowers will be affected by foreclosure. In contrast," the article explained, "only 4 percent of recent white borrowers are expected to be affected."[44]

In stark contrast to the non-crisis period during which the lack of attention implied that these high rates were normal and unremarkable, 239 articles containing these terms appeared in the *New York Times* and 319 were published in the *Wall Street Journal* in 2007 alone. That number would more than double again in the *New York Times* in 2008, when it published 565 articles referencing a mortgage or foreclosure crisis. That

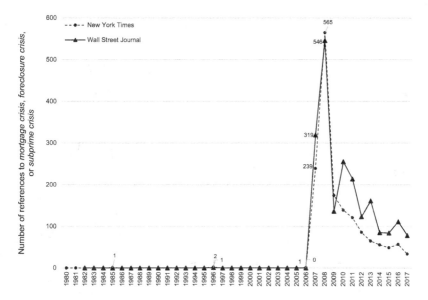

FIGURE 5.1. References to *mortgage crisis, foreclosure crisis*, and *subprime crisis* in the *New York Times*, 1980–2017, and *Wall Street Journal*, 1982–2017. *Note:* Search was for "'mortgage crisis' OR 'foreclosure crisis' OR 'subprime crisis'". ProQuest US Newsstream provides full text access to the *New York Times* beginning in 1980 and to the *Wall Street Journal* beginning in 1982. For additional information, see appendices A and C, and note 41 in chapter 5. *Source:* ProQuest US Newsstream.

same year, the *Wall Street Journal* used these terms in 546 separate stories. I noted previously that it takes more than simply labeling something a crisis for it to be constituted as one, and this part of the book places less emphasis than the previous one on the presence or absence of the term itself. However, it is nonetheless striking that the term *crisis* was never used to describe subprime mortgages and foreclosures when their calamitous rates seemed to be restricted to marginalized groups, particularly alongside the widespread use of that word to characterize these practices and rates once evidence of their damaging effects began to extend beyond people of color and sole-borrower women, as they began to threaten both homeownership among white male-breadwinner-headed households and lenders themselves.

Crisis and Non-Crisis in the Transcript of Dominant Politics

Consistent with the patterns in economic reporting, the terms *subprime crisis, mortgage crisis*, and *foreclosure crisis* appear very rarely in the transcript

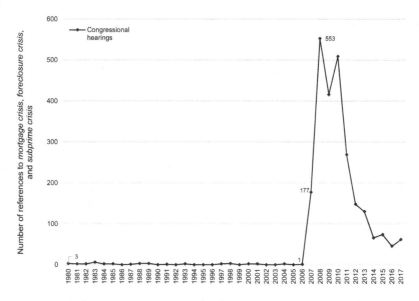

FIGURE 5.2. References to *mortgage crisis, foreclosure crisis,* and *subprime crisis* in the titles and text of congressional hearings, 1980–2017. *Note:* Search was for "'mortgage crisis' OR 'foreclosure crisis' OR 'subprime crisis'". For additional information, see appendices A and C, and note 46 in chapter 5. *Source:* ProQuest Congressional.

of dominant politics from 1995 to 2006. None of these terms is used in party platforms, executive orders, or State of the Union addresses during this period.[45] The term *subprime crisis* itself was never used by a member of Congress or witness at a hearing before 2007, while the latter two terms appeared in the transcripts of and prepared testimony for a combined total of only twelve hearings during the pre-crisis period of 1995–2006 (see figure 5.2).[46] In 2007 alone, however, these terms would appear in 177 hearings, tripling to 553 in 2008 and holding relatively steady in 2009, when they were used in 416 hearings.

Most significant is that on the rare occasions on which the terms *mortgage crisis* or *foreclosure crisis* appeared in the transcript of dominant politics from 1995 through 2006, they were almost always being invoked by advocates for marginalized groups. Of the twelve instances of the terms *mortgage crisis* or *foreclosure crisis* in the oral or written testimony at hearings during this period, all but two were spoken or written by consumer advocates or advocates for low-income people, who tried to frame the high foreclosure rates of the era as a crisis—that is, as a problem facing a critical juncture that was caused by, merited, and could be resolved through state intervention and resources.

Margot Saunders, counsel with the National Consumer Law Center (NCLC), testified several times during this period about what she and her organization repeatedly called a "mortgage crisis for low-income homeowners." Saunders not only labeled the situation a crisis, but echoing the 2006 Center for Responsible Lending (CRL) report covered by the *New York Times*, she also conceptualized it as one, describing it as a situation that was both created by and that could be remediated through state action. More specifically, she attributed this crisis directly to the legislative changes of the 1980s, including the "deregulation [that] has allowed a wide range of marginal players into the lending and loan brokering business"; to the fact that "many of the historic protections against unfair lending practices, such as state ceilings on interest rates and licensing requirements, were removed or eviscerated during the 1980's"; and to the ways in which the 1986 Tax Reform Act encouraged home equity borrowing, even among low-income homeowners who earned too little to take the mortgage interest deduction.[47] Community Legal Services attorney Irv Ackelsberg likewise described a "Mortgage Crisis for American Households" in his 2001 testimony (which he delivered on behalf of that organization as well as the National Consumer Law Center, the Consumer Federation of America, the Consumers Union, the National Association of Consumer Advocates, and the US Public Interest Research Group). Like Saunders, Ackelsberg attributed this crisis to "the deregulation of home lending laws" and to the fact that "Congress has done little to ensure that the needs of homeowners are balanced against the interests of the lending industry." He directed particular ire against the fact that "Congress has even restricted the states' abilities to set limits on the rates and terms lenders can impose on home loans."[48]

While advocates for marginalized groups tried to frame the situation in the late 1990s as a crisis, dominant political actors who used the terms *mortgage crisis* or *foreclosure crisis* during this period typically did so in service to assertions that no such crisis was imminent or in progress. In his prepared testimony at a 23 August, 2006 meeting of the House Financial Services Subcommittee on Housing and Community Opportunity addressing "Community Solutions for the Prevention of and Management of Foreclosures," for example, Michael Fratantoni, then Senior Director for Single-Family Research and Economics at the Mortgage Bankers Association (MBA), maintained that although "some argue that default and foreclosure rates are at crisis levels and that a greater percentage of borrowers are losing their homes," the MBA data, he insisted, "do not support this" characterization. "In fact," he asserted, "they tell quite a different story." Mortgage delinquencies, he declared, "are still caused by the same things that have historically caused mortgage delinquencies: 'life events,' such as job loss, illness, divorce, or some other unexpected challenge." Foreclosures following delinquencies, he continued, "may be caused by the inability to sell a house due to local market conditions after one of the above items has occurred."[49] In other words, Fratantoni was arguing that these increasing rates of foreclosure were a non-crisis: They were natural and inevitable, affected a narrow band of borrowers, and were caused by unalarming conditions that were unremediable through—and therefore were unwarranting of—federal action.

While we might have predicted that spokespeople for the mortgage banking industry would insist that there was no crisis, they were not alone. Federal policymakers, too, downplayed the problems with subprime mortgage lending and foreclosure rates and the need for federal intervention during this era, insisting that they were limited to particular groups and could be explained away as natural, normal, and therefore unwarranting of government concern or intervention.[50] Federal Reserve officials, including its chair Alan Greenspan, "repeatedly dismissed warnings about a speculative bubble in housing prices. Mr. Greenspan predicted several times—incorrectly, it turned out—that housing declines would be local but almost certainly not nationwide."[51] In December 2004, a New York Federal Reserve report declared "that market fundamentals are sufficiently strong to explain the recent path of home prices and support our view that a bubble does not exist."[52] The point here is less that policymakers "got it wrong" than that they erred in part because of controlling racialized and gendered images and narratives that allowed them to exceptionalize the experiences of women and people and color.[53] This exceptionalization, in turn, allowed policymakers to naturalize rising rates of foreclosure among members of these groups and to argue that these rates should not alarm lawmakers or the public because they affected small populations we might *expect* would face foreclosure. That is, rather than prompting policymakers to intervene, they particularized these increasing rates of foreclosure, treating them as the perhaps unfortunate but nonetheless natural and inevitable results of unremarkable conditions affecting small populations we might predict would have trouble keeping up with their mortgages and would therefore, also predictably, face foreclosure at higher rates.

Alternative Indicators?

Might mainstream economic reporters and dominant political actors have conveyed the idea that subprime mortgage lending and foreclosure were problems facing critical junctures worthy of and remediable through state intervention and resources during the earlier period in less explicit ways than those evident in the use of the term *crisis* itself? There is little evidence that this was the case. Instead, comparing the levels of attention paid to these topics during the two periods reinforces the conclusion that subprime mortgage lending and foreclosure were constructed as non-crises—that is, as natural, inevitable, immune to, and not warranting government intervention and resources—when their problematic effects were felt mainly among people of color and sole-borrower women.

Alternative Indicators in Economic Reporting

In particular, the data depicted in table 5.3 and figures 5.3 and 5.4 make clear that the patterns in the numbers of articles addressing subprime mortgages in the *New York Times* and the *Wall Street Journal* follow those in articles using the terms *mortgage crisis* or *foreclosure crisis*, with very modest levels of attention in the late 1990s through 2006 followed by steep upticks in 2007 (see table 5.3 and figures 5.3 and 5.4; see endnote for search parameters).[54] The pattern is slightly different for stories using the term *predatory mortgage*, an issue to which both newspapers paid slightly higher levels of attention in 2000 through 2003, the period during which, as I explained in chapter 4, several states and localities were passing more stringent regulations to protect borrowers from these high-cost loans. The data depicted in figure 5.5 also demonstrate that neither of the two papers used the term *nonconforming mortgage* very often in either the non-crisis or the crisis period, and show that they each began to do so much later, with a significant increase in 2013 in the *Wall Street Journal* (when it published thirty-three stories using this term) and in 2015 in the *New York Times* (when it published thirty-nine stories using it; see figure 5.5). In other words, these references to *subprime mortgage, predatory mortgage*, and *nonconforming mortgage* do not suggest "crisis level" concern about these issues on the part of economic reporters. (Searching for additional alternative terms such as *reverse redlining* does not change this story, having been used only twice in the *New York Times* and only once in the *Wall Street Journal* before 2007).

TABLE 5.3. Number of *New York Times* and *Wall Street Journal* articles addressing subprime, nonconforming, and predatory mortgages, 1995–2006, 2007, and 2008

	New York Times			Wall Street Journal		
	1995–2006	2007	2008	1995–2006	2007	2008
Subprime mortgages[a]	68	731	663	189	1805	1156
Predatory mortgages[b]	119	65	73	112	49	42
Nonconforming mortgages[c]	76	8	8	49	4	8

Note: Data are organized to depict the periodization of two eras: (1) the non-crisis period that begins the year after the passage of HOEPA in 1995 and ends in 2006; and (2) the crisis period of 2007–8. For additional information, see appendices A, B, and C, and note 54 in chapter 5.
[a] Search was for "subprime NEAR mortgage", which returns documents that contain the two search terms, in any order, within four words apart.
[b] Search was for "predatory NEAR mortgage", which returns documents that contain the two search terms, in any order, within four words apart.
[c] Search was for "nonconforming NEAR mortgage", which returns documents that contain the two search terms, in any order, within four words apart.
Source: ProQuest US Newsstream.

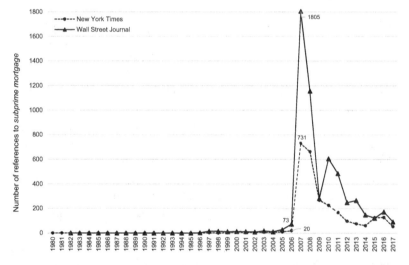

FIGURE 5.3. References to *subprime mortgage* in the *New York Times*, 1980–2017, and *Wall Street Journal*, 1982–2017. *Note:* Search was for "subprime NEAR mortgage", which returns documents that contain the two search terms, in any order, within four words apart. For additional information, see appendices A and C, and note 54 in chapter 5. *Source:* ProQuest US Newsstream.

Similarly, from 1995 through 2006, the *New York Times* published a total of only 68 articles addressing subprime mortgages.[55] The *Wall Street Journal*, for its part, published only 189 articles referring to subprime mortgages over the course of this period. This infrequency is attributable, in part, to the fact that the term *subprime* was less commonly applied to mortgage lending before 1993 than it was during the 2000s.[56] However, the low numbers during that first period are nonetheless notable given that it was during this era that consumer advocates and state officials were battling the financial services industry over their efforts to pass federal legislation that would weaken or override state and local efforts to regulate subprime mortgage lending. It was also during this period that the Office of Thrift Supervision (OTS) and the Office of the Comptroller of the Currency (COC) issued their preemptory regulations that gutted these state and local laws. Moreover, even by 2006, the year that would come to be understood as the eve of the meltdown and by which point the term *subprime* was in wide circulation, only 20 *New York Times* articles and 69 *Wall Street Journal* articles addressed subprime mortgages. In 2007 alone, however, the *Times* published 731 separate articles using this term, true of 1,805 *Wall Street Journal* articles during that year as well. Similarly, although instances of the term *predatory mortgage* appearing in articles in these

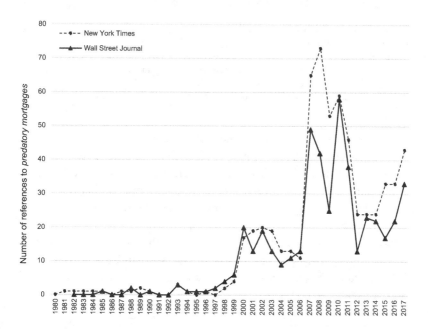

FIGURE 5.4. References to *predatory mortgage* in the *New York Times*, 1980–2017, and *Wall Street Journal*, 1982–2017. *Note:* Search was for "predatory NEAR mortgage", which returns documents that contain the two search terms, in any order, within four words apart. ProQuest US Newsstream provides full text access to the *New York Times* beginning in 1980 and to the *Wall Street Journal* beginning in 1982. For additional information, see appendices A and C, and note 54 in chapter 5. *Source:* ProQuest US Newsstream.

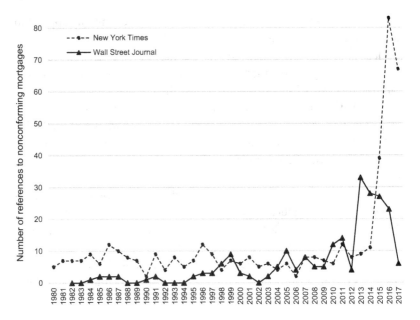

FIGURE 5.5. References to *nonconforming mortgage* in the *New York Times*, 1980–2017, and *Wall Street Journal*, 1982–2017. *Note:* Search was for "nonconforming NEAR mortgage", which returns documents that contain the two search terms, in any order, within four words apart. ProQuest US Newsstream provides full text access to the *New York Times* beginning in 1980 and to the *Wall Street Journal* beginning in 1982. For additional information, see appendices A and C, and note 54 in chapter 5. *Source:* ProQuest US Newsstream.

sources in 2006 would not by themselves have suggested that a crisis loomed, much less that one might already be in progress, these modest numbers were followed by exponential increases in attention to this issue in 2007 and 2008 (see figures 5.3–5.5).[57] The pattern is similar for articles addressing increasing rates of foreclosure: The *New York Times* published an average of only 20.1 stories on this topic each year in the eleven years between the passage of HOEPA and the eve of the crisis in 2006, a number that constitutes only a tiny fraction of the 186 such stories it would publish in 2007 and the 345 it would publish in 2008 alone (see figure 5.6; see endnote for search parameters).[58]

Alternative Indicators in the Transcript of Dominant Politics

Systematic searches and analyses of major party platforms, State of the Union addresses, hearing titles, and bill titles and summaries reveal that

dominant political actors likewise paid little attention to subprime mortgages or foreclosures during this period (see endnote for the search parameters for the evidence based on which I make this claim and the arguments that follow).[59] Even as their platforms became ever longer, for
example, at no point during this period did either major party include a
plank that directly addressed the deleterious effects of subprime mortgages, much less one that called for action to tackle them.[60] It would take
until the late 2000s for the platform of either the Democratic or Republican Party to address subprime mortgages and until the following decade
for the platforms of either one to address the attendant rising rates of
foreclosures (2008 in the case of subprime mortgages and 2012 for rising
rates foreclosures). There are references to foreclosure itself in four platforms before 2007: It appears in the platforms of both of the two major
parties in 1988 and in the Republican platform in both 1992 and 2000.

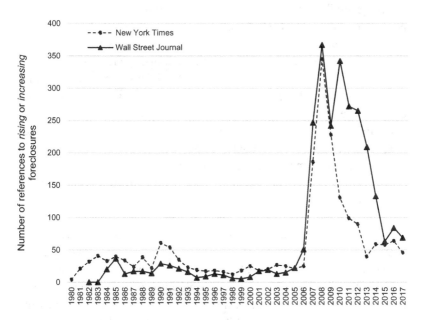

FIGURE 5.6. References to *rising foreclosures* and *increasing foreclosures* in the *New York
Times*, 1980–2017, and *Wall Street Journal*, 1982–2017. *Note:* Search was for "'rising NEAR
foreclosure' OR 'increasing NEAR foreclosure'", which returns documents that contain the
two search terms, in any order, within four words apart. ProQuest US Newsstream provides
full text access to the *New York Times* beginning in 1980 and to the *Wall Street Journal* beginning in 1982. For additional information, see appendices A and C, and note 58 in chapter 5.
Source: ProQuest US Newsstream.

In none of these cases, however, do these references address the rising rates that are the focus of this analysis. For example, the 1992 Republican plank "urge[d] federal departments and agencies to work with the private sector to bring foreclosed housing stock back into service as soon as possible." As this passage makes clear, the concern being addressed in this plank had nothing to do with government assistance for people losing their homes to foreclosure but was rather about federal help for developers to rehabilitate foreclosed properties and sell them on the private market.

These comparatively low levels of attention to subprime mortgages and foreclosures were not a function of a more general lack of attention to mortgage lending and home buying on the part of dominant political actors. Rather, both of those latter topics garnered considerable and consistent attention in party platforms and congressional hearings during this period (although no president issued an executive order addressing mortgage lending or home buying during either the non-crisis or the crisis period, and there were few references to these issues in State of the Union addresses either). From 1996 through 2004, for example, the platforms of both major parties addressed either or both mortgage lending and homeownership every year (there were no presidential nominating conventions in 1995 or 2006 and therefore no platforms in those years either; see table 5.4; see endnote and appendices for a description of the methods used to compile and code the data in tables 5.4 and 5.5).[61] The Republicans, for their part, addressed issues related to home buying and homeownership an average of six times in each of their platforms during this era.

When these issues were taken up in these fora during this period, however, dominant political actors sounded few alarms. Instead, reflecting their faith in mortgage Keynesianism and the democratization of credit as a route to equality, they emphasized issues such as rising rates of homeownership and the importance of preserving and extending mortgage interest deductibility.[62] In 1996, for example, as subprime mortgages were proliferating and foreclosure rates rising among sole-borrower women and people of color, the Democratic Party platform praised Bill Clinton's presidency for the lowest "combined rate of inflation, unemployment, and mortgage interest rates" in three decades," crediting these low rates with helping "4.4 million more Americans own their own home." The Democrats went even further in their 2004 platform, arguing that reduced government spending had been good for the economy, crediting "fiscal discipline" with helping "create 23 million new jobs in the 1990s"

TABLE 5.4. **Party platform planks addressing mortgage lending, home buying, subprime mortgages, increasing foreclosures, and predatory mortgage lending, 1980–2012**

	Democratic Party platforms											Republican Party platforms										
	Mortgage lending[a]		Home buying/ homeownership[b]		Subprime mortgages[c]		Increasing foreclosures[d]		Predatory mortgages[e]			Mortgage lending[a]		Home buying/ homeownership[b]		Subprime mortgages[c]		Increasing foreclosures[d]		Predatory mortgages[e]	
	N	% of all quasi-sentence topics	N	% of all quasi-sentence topics	N	% of all quasi-sentence topics	N	% of all quasi-sentence topics	N	% of all quasi-sentence topics		N	% of all quasi-sentence topics	N	% of all quasi-sentence topics	N	% of all quasi-sentence topics	N	% of all quasi-sentence topics	N	% of all quasi-sentence topics
1980	0	0%	0	0%	0	0%	0	0%	1	0.06%		6	0.39%	4	0.26%	0	0%	0	0%	0	0%
1984	5	0.29	3	0.17	0	0	0	0	0	0		3	0.20	3	0.20	0	0	0	0	0	0
1988	0	0	2	1.5	0	0	1	0.75	0	0		4	0.21	4	0.21	0	0	1	0.05	1	0.05
1992	1	0.24	0	0	0	0	0	0	0	0		5	0.32	5	0.32	0	0	1	0.06	0	0
1996	2	0.24	2	0.24	0	0	0	0	0	0		0	0	4	0.29	0	0	0	0	0	0
2000	1	0.09	0	0	0	0	0	0	0	0		2	0.12	4	0.25	0	0	1	0.06	0	0
2004	0	0	1	0.11	0	0	0	0	1	0.11		2	0.11	10	0.54	0	0	0	0	3	0.16
2008	1	0.09	3	0.26	1	0.09	1	0.09	2	0.17		3	0.28	3	0.28	0	0	0	0	0	0
2012	6	0.53	7	0.62	1	0.09	2	0.18	2	0.18		7	0.5	7	0.50	0	0	0	0	1	0.07

Note: Data are derived from keyword searches of housing- and lending-related categories of USPAP party platform quasi-sentences during the period of interest. Data in the "N" column represent the raw count of the number of observed quasi-sentences pertaining to each topic by year; data in the column "% of all topics" represent the percentage of observed quasi-sentences addressing each topic in a given year as a percentage of *all* platform quasi-sentences that year. For more information, including the list of USPAP categories and robustness check, see appendices A, B, and C, and notes 59 and 61 in chapter 5.

[a] Search was for "mortgage".
[b] Search was for "homeown" or "home buy".
[c] Search was for "subprime", "sub-prime", or "sub prime".
[d] Search was for "foreclos*" NEAR rising or increasing".
[e] Search was for "predator*", "reverse redlining", "abusive NEAR mortgage", "unscrupulous lenders", or "usurious NEAR mortgage".

Source: US Policy Agendas Project.

and "free[ing] up money for productive investment." And underscoring the centrality of their commitment to replacing public spending with individual access to private credit, they also celebrated the fact that "over time, fiscal discipline saves families thousands of dollars on their mortgages and credit cards." That same year, the Republican platform included a statement of support for President George W. Bush's "goal of increasing the number of minority homeowners by at least 5.5 million families by the end of the decade." Neither party, however, acknowledged—much less advocated federal action to address—the rising rates of foreclosure among women and people of color.

Similarly, as the data in table 5.5 make clear, Congress held a substantial number of hearings addressing issues related to mortgage lending and homeownership during the non-crisis period (see table 5.5). For example, from 1995 to 2006, it held an average of 4.25 hearings a year addressing mortgage lending, which constitute an average of 0.3 percent of all hearings held each year during the non-crisis period. While it held no hearings about mortgage lending in 2002, most other years during this twelve-year period witnessed many more—four, five, nine, and as many, in 2004, as ten—hearings on this topic. Only six of the fifty-one hearings about mortgage lending held during this period addressed subprime mortgages, however, and only four focused in particular on housing foreclosures. In most years, no hearings addressed either of these topics, and in no year during this period were these issues taken up in more than two such proceedings. And in keeping with the pattern in economic reporting, although in 2006 Congress held six hearings on mortgage lending (comprising 0.4 percent of all hearings that year), only one of these hearings addressed subprime mortgage lending and only one addressed rising rates of foreclosures. Attention to this topic increased exponentially after that point, however: In 2007, Congress held twenty-seven hearings addressing mortgage lending, which accounted for 1.3 percent of all hearings held that year. Of these hearings, twenty-two addressed subprime mortgage lending and seventeen addressed foreclosures. These numbers increased again in 2008, when Congress held twenty-eight hearings on mortgage lending, accounting for almost 2 percent (1.9) of all hearings held that year. Twenty of those hearings addressed foreclosure and twelve addressed subprime mortgage lending.

Together, the lack of crisis language, the emphasis on creditworthiness as the problem in need of a resolution, the idea that subprime mortgages themselves were the solution to this problem alongside the paltry, decon-

TABLE 5.5. Congressional hearings addressing mortgage lending, home buying, subprime mortgages, foreclosures, and predatory mortgage lending, 1980–2014

	Mortgage lending[a]		Home buying[b]		Subprime mortgages[c]		Foreclosures[d]		Predatory mortgages[e]	
	N	% of all hearings	N	% of all hearings	N	% of all hearings	N	% of all hearings	N	% of all hearings
1980	5	0.30%	0	0%	0	0%	0	0%	0	0%
1981	5	0.25	0	0	0	0	0	0	0	0
1982	5	0.29	0	0	0	0	0	0	0	0
1983	4	0.20	0	0	0	0	4	0.2	0	0
1984	4	0.24	0	0	0	0	0	0	0	0
1985	2	0.11	0	0	0	0	0	0	0	0
1986	1	0.07	0	0	0	0	1	0.07	0	0
1987	2	0.10	1	0.05	0	0	1	0.05	0	0
1988	1	0.06	1	0.06	0	0	0	0	0	0
1989	3	0.15	1	0.05	0	0	0	0	0	0
1990	9	0.47	1	0.05	0	0	0	0	0	0
1991	4	0.19	1	0.05	0	0	1	0.05	2	0.10
1992	4	0.25	0	0	0	0	0	0	2	0.12
1993	5	0.27	2	0.11	0	0	0	0	4	0.22
1994	6	0.34	0	0	0	0	0	0	2	0.11
1995	2	0.14	0	0	0	0	0	0	0	0
1996	1	0.09	0	0	0	0	1	0.09	2	0.19
1997	4	0.28	2	0.14	0	0	0	0	3	0.21
1998	3	0.24	0	0	0	0	0	0	4	0.32
1999	3	0.18	0	0	0	0	1	0.06	2	0.12
2000	4	0.29	1	0.07	1	0.07	1	0.07	1	0.07
2001	9	0.64	1	0.07	1	0.07	0	0	1	0.07
2002	0	0	0	0	0	0	0	0	1	0.07
2003	5	0.33	1	0.07	1	0.07	0	0	1	0.07
2004	10	0.78	1	0.08	2	0.16	0	0	4	0.32
2005	4	0.25	1	0.06	0	0	0	0	1	0.06
2006	6	0.39	0	0	1	0.06	1	0.06	1	0.06
2007	27	1.32	2	0.1	22	1.07	17	0.83	8	0.39
2008	28	1.89	4	0.27	12	0.81	20	1.35	2	0.14
2009	24	1.45	3	0.18	2	0.12	18	1.09	13	0.79
2010	25	1.88	2	0.15	1	0.08	15	1.13	7	0.53
2011	20	1.55	1	0.08	0	0	5	0.39	2	0.15
2012	10	0.84	3	0.25	0	0	6	0.51	2	0.17
2013	25	1.76	4	0.03	0	0	1	0.07	6	0.42
2014	1	0.08	1	0.09	0	0	1	0.08	2	0.16

Note: Data are derived from keyword searches of housing- and lending related categories of USPAP congressional hearings data during the period of interest. Data in the "N" column represent the raw count of the number of observed hearings pertaining to each topic by year; data in the column "% of all topics" represent the percentage of observed hearings addressing each topic in a given year as a percentage of *all* hearings that year. For more information, including the list of USPAP categories and robustness check, see appendices A, B, and C, and notes 59 and 61 in chapter 5.
[a] Search was for "mortgage".
[b] Search was for "homeown" or "home buy".
[c] Search was for "subprime", "sub-prime", or "sub prime".
[d] Search was for "'foreclos*' NEAR rising or increasing".
[e] Search was for "predator*", "reverse redlining", "abusive NEAR mortgage", "unscrupulous lenders", or "usurious NEAR mortgage".
Source: US Policy Agendas Project.

textualized, misleading, and often "colorblind" and "genderblind" stories and deliberations constituted subprime lending and foreclosures during this period as a non-crisis. These same features also, however, lay the groundwork for the ways in which "the crisis" would be understood and addressed once foreclosures began to spread.

The Crisis Begins

As rates of foreclosure began to rise in 2007—and as their effects became more conspicuous across the country, to the broader population, and especially to financial intuitions—so, too, did attention to and alarm about them. The first indication that the situation was being constructed as a crisis by mainstream economic reporters and dominant political actors is the explosive upsurge in instances of the terms *mortgage crisis, foreclosure crisis*, and *subprime crisis* to describe the situation. The headline of the lead article in the 5 March 2007 Business section of the *New York Times* declared, for example, "A Mortgage Crisis Begins to Spiral, and the Casualties Mount." "Just as the technology boom of the late 1990s turned twenty-something programmers into dot-com billionaires," it explained, "the explosive growth in subprime lending turned mortgage bankers and brokers into multimillionaires seemingly overnight." Now, however, "an escalating crisis in the market, which seemed to reach a new crescendo late last week, is threatening a wide band of people."[63] As Senator Chris Dodd (D-CT) put it in his opening remarks at a 22 March 2007 Senate Banking, Housing, and Urban Affairs hearing titled "Mortgage Market Turmoil: Causes and Consequences," "You cannot pick up a newspaper lately without seeing another story about the implosion of the subprime mortgage market."[64]

The shift from *non-crisis* to *crisis* is apparent not only in the fact that mainstream economic reporters and dominant political actors began to use the term *crisis* to describe the situation, however. It is evident as well in the uptick in the volume of news stories, congressional hearings, State of the Union addresses, and platform planks addressing these issues, as well as in the increasing number of *New York Times* and *Wall Street Journal* stories featuring the phrase "rising rates of foreclosure" beginning in 2007 (see tables 5.2 and 5.3 and figures 5.1–5.6).[65] In 2008, the first year in which the major parties wrote platforms after the crisis had been "declared," the Democratic Party platform finally contained several references to subprime mortgage lending and foreclosures. The preamble, for example, noted that "the American Dream is at risk" because "incomes are down and foreclosures are up," while a later section stated that "the sub-prime lending debacle has sent the housing market into a tailspin, and many Americans have lost their homes." Although the Republicans did not use the word *subprime*, they, too, addressed these issues in their 2008 platform, which included a plank they titled "Rebuilding Homeowner-ship," in which they referenced a "housing crisis" and wrote that "home-ownership remains key to creating an opportunity society."

Another element in the shift from *non-crisis* to *crisis* is evident in the de-individualization of blame and the move to structural explanations for rising rates of foreclosures. Although economic reporters continued to refer to *easy, bad, poor, weak*, or *damaged* credit, for example, the use of such descriptors declined, with only 12.3 percent of *New York Times* stories about subprime mortgage lending in 2007 and 5 percent in 2008 using these terms (compared with 62 percent during the non-crisis period; similar declines are evident in the use of these terms in stories about rising rates of foreclosures and for *Wall Street Journal* coverage as well; see table 5.2). Reporters continued to refer to buyers taking on more debt or buying more expensive houses than they "could afford," but they also be-gan to acknowledge that borrower behavior might be neither the primary source of the problems with subprime mortgages nor the primary reason for rising rates of foreclosure on houses financed with such loans.

Rather than blaming borrowers' greed, their naïveté, or the amount of their loans, mainstream economic reporters began to attribute some of the culpability to developments like the spike in interest rates that occurred when ARMs reset, which left borrowers paying far more than those they had been paying under the initial "teaser" rates of their loans. *New York Times* reporter Gretchen Morgenson wrote in a 10 June 2007 article, for example, "Chances are slim that even the most creditworthy borrowers can survive payment shocks like these. And so, as the reset storm hits, delinquencies will rise and foreclosures will follow."[66] Baked into the use of the term *creditworthy borrowers*, of course, is the assumption that those who had lost their homes previously were *un*creditworthy. The implica-tion, in other words, was that while those newly experiencing foreclosure did not deserve this fate, those who had lost their homes previously did.

As this last point about creditworthiness suggests, mainstream eco-nomic reporters did not mince words in their assertions that part of what made the situation a crisis was that it affected relatively privileged and "worthy" groups. A particularly revealing article in the *Wall Street Journal*, titled "Subprime Debacle Traps Even Very Credit-Worthy," stated bluntly, "One common assumption about the subprime mortgage crisis is that it revolves around borrowers with sketchy credit who couldn't have bought a home without paying punitively high interest rates. "But," the article continues, "it turns out that plenty of people with seemingly good credit are also caught in the subprime trap." In particular, the reporter explained, 55 percent of subprime loans made in 2005 and 61 percent in 2006 "went to people with credit scores high enough to often qualify for conventional loans with far better terms." The reporter noted further that this number had increased from "just" 41 percent in 2000, implying that 41 percent was not itself a proportion that should alarm readers. "Even a significant number of borrowers with top-notch credit," they found, "signed up for expensive subprime loans." Most tellingly, the article stated that fair-lending advocates had "long alleged that minority and poor borrowers are often steered into subprime loans that carry excessively high interest rates and steep prepayment penalties." The growing use of subprime loans "by people with higher credit scores," the article continues, "suggests that such problems exist among a much wider swath of borrowers than previously thought and may have little to do with the ethnicity of borrowers."[67] An article published in that paper in August 2007 quoted a frustrated—and revealingly candid—would-be borrower who complained that "the market isn't discriminating between me and every deadbeat, zero-down borrower."[68]

Mainstream economic reporters not only treated the rising rates of subprime mortgage lending and foreclosure among members of dominant groups as a crisis in ways that they had not done previously. They also, at times, defined the crisis less by its effects on the increasing number of people losing their homes than by the threats posed to lenders and to the "economy" more generally. For example, the previously referenced 5 March 2007 *New York Times* story that first referred to a *mortgage crisis* began by acknowledging that the "escalating crisis in the market . . . is threatening a wide band of people." "Foremost," it noted, are "poor and minority homeowners." It went on, however, to reinforce the idea that the most concerning crisis was not the one facing marginalized homeowners but the one in "the market," stating that "the pain is also being felt widely throughout the business world," particularly among "large companies that bought subprime lenders during the boom, like H&R Block and HSBC. . . . Many investors are also likely to suffer."

Similarly typical was a *New York Times* story from June 2007 "Pimco Foresees Widening Subprime Harm."[69] This particular story never acknowledged that the crisis involved huge and increasing numbers of people losing their homes and the money they had invested in them, nor did it acknowledge that in many cases these people found themselves with insurmountable debt. Instead, the story opened and ended with a discussion about the implications of rising numbers of foreclosures for "the economy." "Bill Gross," the piece began, "manager of the world's largest bond fund, said yesterday that the subprime mortgage crisis gripping financial markets was not an isolated event and would eventually take a toll on the economy." In other words, it was not long-term structural inequities that constituted the situation as a crisis. Rather, the crisis was that dominant groups were increasingly relegated to and affected by economic conditions previously and unceremoniously experienced by and reserved for women and people of color.

Blaming Lenders and State Actors

As economic reporters discovered this pool of "worthy" subprime borrowers facing foreclosure, and as they began to reckon with the effects of the "crisis" for the economy more generally, they were also increasingly likely to blame lenders for having "lax lending standards" than they were to blame borrowers for taking on loans they could not afford. In some cases, they went as far as to suggest—often implicitly, but at times quite overtly—that regulators and legislators were to blame for failing to intervene during the previous era. A 23 March 2007 story in the *New York Times*, for example, reported that the Senate Banking Committee had held hearings at which legislators criticized banking regulators" for "failing to respond more quickly to curb the growth in risky home loans to people with weak credit." This shift on the part of economic reporters—from previously blaming borrowers and non-state actors such as lenders to now blaming government actors such as regulators—reflects a concomitant shift among dominant political actors. During the 1993 HOEPA hearings, for example, Joseph Kennedy had blamed lenders who "closed branches and stopped offering affordable services in affected areas." Now Senator Dodd berated regulators, arguing at the Senate Banking Committee hearing featured in the foregoing report that the "checks and balances that we are told exist in the marketplace and the oversight that the regulators are supposed to exercise have been absent until recently. . . . Our

Nation's financial regulators are supposed to be the cops on the beat," his rebuke continued, "protecting working Americans from unscrupulous financial actors. Yet they appear for the most part to have been spectators for too long."[70]

This increased willingness to consider structural explanations and to blame federal action (and inaction) for the proliferation of subprime mortgage lending and foreclosures was accompanied by a related and signal component of crisis construction: increased calls for federal action to address these issues. This change is evident in the fact that the stories, hearings, and other political documents addressing these topics increasingly assumed and asserted that federal intervention and resources were warranted and that they could and would make a difference in resolving the issue. For example, from 1995 through 2006, very few stories in either the *New York Times* or the *Wall Street Journal* had discussed how the federal government might intervene to prevent or to help people affected by foreclosures. Beginning in 2007, however, a significant majority of stories about subprime mortgages in the *New York Times* (64 percent) included such discussions. A 14 March 2007 *New York Times* article reported, for example, that Senator Dodd "said the government might have to step in to provide aid to struggling homeowners." An article published in that paper the following week reported that "as problems with subprime mortgages have escalated, officials on Wall Street as well as in Washington have urged lenders and the government to step in and cushion the blow to troubled borrowers and find ways to enable them to remain in their homes." Dodd, the article explains, "suggested that the federal government may need to bail out homeowners in trouble, and some housing advocacy groups are calling for a moratorium on foreclosures."[71]

As these last few statements suggest, some of the increased willingness on the part of economic reporters to consider federal action is a function of the fact that dominant political actors were, in fact, doing more by that point, and so there was more state action on which to report than there had been previously. But it was not only the quantity of such discussion that increased; the increased volume was matched by increased calls for action, evident especially in the editorials and op-eds published in the two papers. The *New York Times*, for example, which had published only two editorials or op-eds addressing rising rates of foreclosure from 1995 through 2006, published sixteen such pieces in 2007 and 2008 alone (see table 5.6; see endnote and appendices for details about data compilation and coding).[72] Eleven (66 percent) of those pieces noted the possibility of

TABLE 5.6. *New York Times* and *Wall Street Journal* editorials and op-eds addressing rising rates of foreclosure, 1995–2006, 2007–2008

	New York Times		Wall Street Journal	
	1995–2006	2007–8	1995–2006	2007–8
Total number of editorials and op-ed pieces addressing rising or increasing rates of foreclosure during each period	2	16	1	8
Number (%) of editorials and op-ed pieces addressing rising or increasing rates of foreclosure noting the possibility of federal intervention	1 (50%)	11 (66 %)	0	7 (88)
Number (%) of those noting possibility of federal intervention that *support* federal intervention	1 (50%)	8 (80%)	NA	5 (71.4)‡
N (%) of those noting possibility federal intervention that *oppose* federal intervention	0	(1) (9%)	NA	3 (43.8)‡

Note: Search was for "rising NEAR foreclosure" or "increasing NEAR foreclosure", which returns documents that contain the two search terms, in any order, within four words apart. Each observation was coded for whether it mentioned federal, state, or local intervention or the possibility for it and, for each positive observation, for whether these mentions are supportive, unsupportive, or neutral with regard to said intervention. For additional information, see appendices A, B, and C, and note 74 in chapter 5.
‡ Column totals exceed the total N and 100 percent because three of the five supportive op-eds also opposed some forms of federal intervention.
Source: ProQuest US Newsstream.

federal intervention to address this issue. Of these, eight (80 percent) supported such action while only one opposed it. A 31 January 2008 editorial in that paper, for example, argued that

> the damage, now becoming apparent, demands that policy makers take stock of how the economy arrived at this place. The bubbles in housing and mortgages would not have been possible were it not for the progressive deterioration in regulation over the past several decades, culminating for all practical purposes in a regulatory collapse during the Bush years. The antiregulatory ethos, in turn, derived its potency from a pervasive ideology that markets are self-regulating and self-correcting and therefore best handled with incentives and voluntary best practices, rather than rules and boundaries.[73]

The *Wall Street Journal*, for its part, published eight op-eds and editorials on this issue during this period, 88 percent of which noted the possibility of federal intervention. Of these pieces, five (71 percent) supported at least some such action and three (44 percent) opposed it (these numbers exceed the total number of observations and 100 percent because three of the five supportive op-eds also opposed some forms of federal intervention). Some of these supportive editorials emphasized aid for banks and lenders, but many—even many in the free-market-oriented *Wall Street Journal*— advocated federal intervention to help homeowners, at least those deemed "deserving." On 15 November 2007, for example, that paper published an op-ed by David Wessel titled "Why Some Mortgage Bailouts Make Sense." Wessel argued that "some folks should lose property if they can't make payments: those who lied on applications or speculated by buying properties for investment (although tenants may deserve help)." Temporarily cutting mortgage payments "for those who never will be able to afford houses they bought," he continued, "is unwise and doomed to failure." But he also argued that "it's the folks in the middle who need and deserve help from the industry and, if need be, the government: those who are making payments, would have refinanced easily if not for the housing bust and dysfunction of mortgage markets and can't afford the reset payments."[74]

Evidence of support for federal intervention increased in the transcript of dominant politics as well. The 2008 Democratic platform, for example, went as far as to invoke the New Deal—widely understood as the signal and most robust federal intervention in American history—to justify federal action to address subprime mortgages and foreclosures. In particular, the platform stated:

> We will start by renewing the American Dream for a new era—with the same new hope and new ideas that propelled Franklin Delano Roosevelt towards the New Deal and John F. Kennedy to the New Frontier. We will provide immediate relief to working people who have lost their jobs, families who are in danger of losing their homes, and those who—no matter how hard they work—are seeing prices go up more than their income . . . Because we have an obligation to prevent this crisis from recurring in the future, we will crack down on fraudulent brokers and lenders and invest in financial literacy. We will pass a Homebuyers Bill of Rights, which will include establishing new lending standards to ensure that loans are affordable and fair, provide adequate remedies to make sure the standards are met, and ensure that homeowners have accurate and complete information about their mortgage options.[75]

The Democrats followed this statement with a promise to "ensure that the foreclosure prevention program enacted by Congress is implemented quickly and effectively so that at-risk homeowners can get help and hopefully stay in their homes. We will work to reform bankruptcy laws to re-store balance between lender and homeowner rights."

The Republican platform that year similarly asserted that party's sup-port for "timely and carefully targeted aid to those hurt by the housing crisis so that affected individuals can have a chance to trade a burdensome mortgage for a manageable loan that reflects their home's market value." President Bush made the case for state intervention in 2008 as well, not-ing in his State of the Union address that year—the last of his second term, but also the first one he gave after the extent of the mortgage crisis had become clear—that "we must trust Americans with the responsibil-ity of homeownership and empower them to weather turbulent times in the housing market." To do so, he reminded listeners, his "administration brought together the HOPE NOW alliance, which is helping many strug-gling homeowners avoid foreclosure."[76] He called for even more exten-sive federal intervention, arguing that "Congress can help even more" by passing "legislation to reform Fannie Mae and Freddie Mac, modernize the Federal Housing Administration, and allow state housing agencies to issue tax-free bonds to help homeowners refinance their mortgages. These are difficult times for many American families," he concluded, "and by taking these steps, we can help more of them keep their homes."

Newly elected President Barack Obama began the first substantive sec-tion of his 2009 inaugural address with the pronouncement that "that we are in the midst of crisis is now well understood." Among the constitutive elements of that crisis, he explained, were that "homes have been lost, jobs shed, businesses shuttered." "These," he averred in the last section of that paragraph, "are the indicators of crisis, subject to data and statistics. Less measurable, but no less profound," he argued, "is a sapping of confidence across our land; a nagging fear that America's decline is inevitable, that the next generation must lower its sights. . . . But our time of standing pat," he continued, "has surely passed. Starting today, we must pick ourselves up, dust ourselves off, and begin again the work of remaking America. . . . The state of our economy calls for action, bold and swift."[77]

Foreclosures were only one element of the "crisis" that President Obama described and only one of the many issues about which he spoke in that portion of his address. But his message was clear: Problems such as foreclosures are not inevitable conditions that must be endured, and those facing them need not resign themselves to their fates. Rather, such issues face a crossroads, the course of which could be righted with robust state action. Although I demonstrate in the next section that the policies that were ultimately passed and implemented diverged less than they could have from the modest ones that were codified in HOEPA, President Obama's approach is nonetheless representative of a major reversal in the treatment of subprime mortgage lending and foreclosures.

Non-Crisis in the Midst of Crisis

The foregoing differences between the ways in which subprime mortgage lending and foreclosures were framed in each period highlight a few of the key processes through which the high foreclosure rates documented among some groups as early as 1996 were constructed as non-crises while analogous issues were constructed as crises when their effects were felt more broadly and among members of more privileged groups. But even as economic reporters and dominant political actors treated the situation as a crisis—that is, as a problem facing a critical juncture that merited and could be resolved through state intervention and resources—their patterns of attention to and elisions of the racialized and gendered disparities associated with subprime mortgages and foreclosures continued to figure the situation as a non-crisis for women, people of color, and women of color in particular. This "non-crisis in the midst of crisis" is evident in the fact that these glaring disparities were, at best, peripheral to the concerns driving the attention and even more peripheral to dominant ideas about what it would mean to end it. Instead, economic reporters and dominant political actors continued to naturalize the race and gender disparities revealed by the "crisis." That is, they did not treat racialized and gendered patterns as part of the crisis and as problems that might be resolved. Instead, they continued to naturalize them as inevitable, intractable, and as the baseline "normal" conditions that would signal that—and, implicitly, to which we would return after—the crisis had ended.

Continued Low Levels of Attention

Given the particular toll of the "crisis" on women and people of color, we might expect that mainstream economic reporters would pay more attention to issues of race and gender once their centrality to the crisis came into view. However, even as advocates and activists made clear that foreclosures—particularly foreclosures on properties financed through subprime mortgages—were taking a particularly heavy toll on members of these groups, very little of the attention paid to subprime mortgage lending and foreclosures under the crisis rubric that gained traction beginning in 2007 addressed their raced, gendered, or raced-gendered facets. Mainstream economic reporters paid even less attention to the ways in which historical and ongoing discrimination and exploitation were related to subprime mortgage lending and foreclosures. To the contrary, race and gender figured almost not at all in coverage of the crisis itself (see table 5.2). Only 1.8 percent of the 228 stories that used the terms *mortgage crisis, subprime crisis,* or *foreclosure crisis* in the *New York Times* in 2007, for example, focused on the racialized patterns in foreclosures and only 0.4 percent addressed gender. The analogous numbers for the 557 pieces published in that paper in 2008 were 11 stories (2 percent) about race and 2 stories (0.3 percent) about gender. The levels of attention in the *Wall Street Journal* were similarly microscopic: Of more than 300 stories discussing the *mortgage, foreclosure,* or *subprime crisis* in that paper in 2007, six addressed race (2 percent) and two (0.7 percent) addressed gender. In 2008, these proportions dropped even further: Of the 530 stories that addressed these topics that year, only 0.9 percent discussed race and none addressed women or gender in an even incidental way.

Broadening the lens to include articles addressing subprime mortgage lending and increasing rates of foreclosure only reinforces this story, as the data presented in table 5.2 make clear that the proportions of articles about these issues that paid attention to race and gender declined from their already low rates as well. For example, the proportion of *New York Times* articles about subprime mortgages that addressed race declined from 15 percent in the non-crisis era to 0.4 percent in 2007 and 0.3 percent in 2008. Similarly, from a high of 10 percent in the non-crisis era, the proportion of *Wall Street Journal* articles about subprime mortgage lending addressing race declined to 0.3 percent in 2007 before disappearing altogether in 2008. And although stories addressing the gender implications of subprime mortgage lending and increasing rates of foreclosures were mostly nonexistent from 1995 through 2006, the very small proportion of those articles that noted the high rates of subprime mortgages among women declined from 3.8 percent during this earlier era to 0.1 percent in 2007 and 1.8 percent in 2008 (a slight increase from 2007, but still a lower proportion than the previous era). These declining levels of attention to race and gender suggest that the "crisis" did not draw attention to these issues. Instead, new alarm at what was being recognized as a crisis displaced what little interest mainstream economic reporters had evinced in race and gender during the non-crisis period. That is, not only were similar rates of subprime mortgage lending and foreclosure treated as crises when they affected white male-breadwinner-headed households and as non-crises when they affected people of color and sole-borrower women, but attention to the implications of these long-standing issues for marginalized groups declined once the crisis was declared.

As had been the case in the previous era, the implications of the paucity of attention to these issues were exacerbated by the kinds of frames and tropes that were applied when they were addressed. For example, although mainstream economic reporters and dominant political actors were increasingly likely to attribute foreclosures to structural factors after 2007, they rarely extended these new understandings to include foreclosures experienced by women and people of color. In these cases, they continued to assume that borrowers from these groups were unqualified for conventional loans and that they would be unable to own homes but for subprime mortgages. These twinned presumptions were so deeply ingrained that even in the face of disillusionment with subprime mortgage lending and under a mounting pile of evidence that, for example, women were, on average, more creditworthy than their male counterparts, few stories challenged them. The very first *New York Times* story to refer directly to a "mortgage crisis" (published on 5 March 2007), for example, stated that "poor and minority homeowners . . . used easy credit to buy houses that are turning out to be too expensive for them now that mortgage rates are going up."[78]

Even when journalists acknowledged the existence of race and gender discrimination in mortgage lending, they typically failed to question assertions that subprime mortgages alleviated rather than exacerbated such biases. One of the only *New York Times* stories to engage issues of race in mortgage lending during the *crisis* period exemplifies this tendency. The 18 December 2007 article "Fed Shrugged as Subprime Crisis Spread," quoted Edward Gramlich, a Democratic appointee to the Federal Reserve who served as the head of its Committee on Consumer and Community Affairs from 1997 to 2005 and who had spent much of his career studying problems of poverty. Gramlich "saw both great benefits and great perils in the new industry."[79] He agreed, the article explained, "that subprime lending had opened new doors to people with low incomes or poor credit histories. Home ownership," it continued, "which had hovered around 64 percent for years, climbed to almost 70 percent by 2005. The biggest gains were among blacks and Hispanics, groups that had suffered discrimina-

tion for decades." Even in this fairly long article in which the overall tone
was quite skeptical toward subprime mortgage lending and critical of the
federal government's lack of intervention, there was no follow-up to this
statement. The article did concede that African Americans and Latinos
suffered discrimination. But rather than acknowledge the evidence that
subprime loans were often sold to members of marginalized groups who
were well qualified for conventional ones, and rather than recognize that
this pattern constituted evidence of ongoing discrimination, the article
treated discrimination as a relic of a bygone era and as a problem that had
been remedied or at least mitigated through subprime mortgage lending.
That is, even in the face of evidence that subprime mortgage lending was
both a function of and a perpetuator of inequality and discrimination and
that it was consequently also a *source* of the "crisis," the article continued
to credit such loans with increasing homeownership among members of
these groups.

Once again, as inadequate and misleading as the attention to subprime
mortgage lending and rising rates of foreclosure was when it came to analyzing their racial implications, this coverage was still vastly more extensive than that afforded to the gendered aspects of the "crisis." Returning
to the data in table 5.2 makes clear that very few articles referencing a subprime, foreclosure, or mortgage "crisis" in either paper focused primarily
on women or gender. Two of the only three pieces that addressed women
or gender in even an implicit or cursory way in 2007 and 2008 were opinion pieces rather than reported stories. The first was a 20 November 2007
New York Times op-ed by columnist Bob Herbert, which recounted the
story of two older women on fixed incomes who had lost their homes. The
story he told seems clearly to be one in which the women were targeted
for extractive loans in part because of gender, but gender is never thematized as such. Similarly, although US Census and Social Security records
make clear that both women are African American, race is not thematized
as a factor either.[80] As was the case during the non-crisis, the portrayal is
not unsympathetic, but the women are described in terms that evoke gendered stereotypes of naïveté and vulnerability:

> Like vultures, the mortgage lenders began circling the single-family house with
> the tiny front lawn on Merrill Avenue. They knew that the woman who owned
> the house was old and sick and that her two aging daughters were struggling
> with illness and poverty as well. That was all to the good as far as the lenders
> were concerned. The predator's mission is to home in on the vulnerable.... One

aspect of the so-called mortgage crisis that hasn't been adequately explored is the extent to which predatory lenders have committed fraud against vulnerable homeowners. They have pushed overpriced loans and outlandish fees on hapless victims who didn't understand—and could not possibly have met—the terms of the contracts they signed. In some cases, corporate con artists have deliberately targeted and seized the equity of financially strapped and unsophisticated owners.[81]

Another of the very few *New York Times* articles about the "crisis" to discuss anything having to do with gender was a 9 December 2008 editorial titled "Mortgages and Minorities." As its title suggests, the piece focused on racial discrimination in mortgage lending, but it made one reference to "troubling gender differences" in rates of subprime mortgage lending. It reported in detail about the racial disparities, noting, for example, that "a particularly striking analysis in 2006 by the National Community Reinvestment Coalition found that nearly 55 percent of loans to African-Americans, 40 percent of loans to Hispanics and 35 percent of loans to American Indians fell into the high-cost category, as opposed to about 23 percent for whites." Regarding gender, however, it stated only that "there also were troubling gender differences. Women got less-favorable terms than men."[82]

Rather than providing an opportunity for more nuanced and expansive attention to gender or a more thorough understanding of its centrality to the "crisis," the very few stories addressing women and gender that were published at the height of the crisis instead continued to traffic in long-discredited ideas and stereotypes that naturalized women's overrepresentation among subprime borrowers and people experiencing foreclosure. So sticky were the controlling narratives underlying the construction of high rates of subprime mortgage lending and foreclosure among women as a non-crisis that even some advocates for women participated in discourses that naturalized the gender inequalities made manifest by subprime mortgages. In 2007, for example, the *New York Times* finally reported on the 2006 Consumer Federation report that had shown that women paid higher interest rates in spite of having better credit than men. The story included a quote from an interview with one of the report's authors, who stated that "the most likely reason for the disparity was that women were less familiar with the mortgage market than men and were therefore less likely to shop around for the best mortgage deal. 'There is some research indicating that women are, on the whole, less likely than men to bargain for major consumer purchases and credit transactions,' he said."[83] (Such stereotypes smack of paternalism and "old fashioned sexism." See endnote for evidence that other gendered tropes deployed during and about the crisis, though less prevalent, were more overt and no less malign.[84])

In other words, even as subprime mortgage lending and foreclosures received more coverage, and even as dominant political actors framed them as solvable problems facing critical junctures at which federal intervention would make a "decisive change" for the better, they continued to naturalize the race and gender patterns the meltdown revealed as non-crises. As a consequence, rather than understanding racial and gender inequalities as a crucial indicator and constitutive part of the crisis, these same actors continued to treat these inequalities as outside of both the crisis and the power of the federal government to remedy.

How to End a Crisis (but not a Non-Crisis)

Constructed though they are, once a crisis is "hailed into being," it can serve as a focusing event that opens policy windows that have real and far-reaching political and policy consequences.[85] Some scholars and political analysts argue that activists and advocates can exploit these policy windows to push policy solutions that benefit marginalized groups.[86] Others counter that although problems affecting broad swaths of the population may shine a light on long-standing problems faced by marginalized groups, the goal of the solutions deemed reasonable to address them is typically to return to "normal" pre-crisis conditions.[87] Since these pre-crisis conditions usually include deeply entrenched inequalities, a return to "normal" almost inevitably means continued, if slightly modified, conditions of inequality and marginalization.[88] As such, while crises may draw attention to these conditions crisis-born policy windows may be ill-suited to addressing crises' implications for or their manifestations among members of marginalized groups. Such policy windows may also obscure the relationship between the conditions that are constructed as the crisis and the ongoing bad things that create conditions of marginality. Crisis-born policies can therefore reinforce inequalities and reconstitute racial, gender, and economic identities, orders, and inequalities along other lines.

These processes are evident in the policy responses to the foreclosure crisis as well. In particular, the framing of the crisis as one primarily for lenders alongside the continued treatment of the problems facing women and people of color that both preceded and were exacerbated by it as non-crises were reflected and codified in the federal response to the meltdown.

First and most generally, although initial calls for intervention had focused on appropriating federal funds to help homeowners refinance their mortgages, in the end, federal programs emphasized funds for banks and lenders. Moreover, interventions aimed at helping borrowers involved little in the way of financial aid and instead once again emphasized individualized solutions like borrower education, more stringent standards for documentation, and the criminal prosecution of individual "bad apple" predatory lenders.[89] For example, among the early federal attempts to stem the flow of foreclosures on homes financed through subprime loans was emergency "cramdown" legislation proposed by Senator Richard Durbin (D-IL), which would have allowed judges to modify mortgages even if creditors objected to the proposed debt reorganization. This legislation was quickly blocked by lobbyists for the financial and lending industry, however.[90] As an alternative (and echoing the enduring racist and misogynist ideas that motivated and permeated the analogous earlier programs documented by Thurston and Taylor), in October 2007, the Bush administration announced the Hope Now Alliance, which offered foreclosure prevention counseling to homeowners via a 1-800 number. The Bush administration also promoted an industry-designed effort to "promote 'streamlined' voluntary loan modifications for a subset of subprime mortgages," but advocates estimated that only 3 to 12 percent of subprime borrowers were eligible for these modifications.[91]

The Borrower's Protection Act of 2007, introduced by Senators Charles Schumer (D-NY), Robert Casey (D-PA), and Sherrod Brown (D-OH), gained more traction than Durbin's proposal, but it was significantly weakened as it made its way through Congress. As introduced, the bill had two main components: (1) federal funding for default and foreclosure prevention counseling and outreach to homeowners for early intervention, to improve the communications between homeowners and servicers/lenders, and to negotiate modified loan agreements or refinances; and (2) "sealing the cracks in the regulatory system."[92] When Federal Reserve Chair Ben Bernanke and Secretary of Housing and Urban Development Alphonso Jackson endorsed the bill, however, they emphasized its borrower education components. As Jackson said in his prepared remarks supporting the bill,

> We also learned that while most people facing foreclosure are afraid of their banks, they are much more open to talking to a local non-profit counseling agency about their problems. That's why housing counseling and financial education are so important. This Administration has increased the budget for coun-

seling over 200 percent, with the President requesting another increase, to $50 million, in the coming fiscal year.[93]

While the budget for counselling was in the millions, in 2008, Congress began to authorize *trillions* of dollars to help financial and insurance companies.[94] There were indications that the proportion of funds for direct aid to homeowners might increase after President Obama took office. Together with Congress, in 2009 the Obama administration authorized $75 billion in incentives to lenders to encourage them to lower home loan payments for troubled borrowers, with the stated goal of preventing up to four million foreclosures.[95] Very little of this money was ever disbursed, however. The FHA's Short Refinance program, for example, was designed to help up to 1.5 million borrowers, but five months into its existence, it had helped only thirty-eight homeowners to refinance their mortgages.[96] Economist Nomi Prins estimated that by October 2010, however, Wall Street institutions had received $3.5 trillion and that government-sponsored enterprises had received $2.8 trillion, but that this had done little to help people stay in their homes.[97]

Similarly, the 2009 Home Affordable Modification Program (HAMP), part of the US Treasury Department's Troubled Asset Relief Program (TARP) also fell far short of its goals. Although HAMP was designed to help three to four million borrowers, by April 2011, it had helped only 630,000 borrowers get permanent loan modifications, a number that had increased to only one million by 2013.[98] Moreover, while HAMP was portrayed by policymakers and the media as aid for distressed borrowers, Daniel Immergluck explains that it is more accurately understood as "lender loss mitigation."[99] That is, HAMP did not mandate assistance for homeowners but essentially reimbursed mortgage servicers for the money they would arguably lose by allowing borrowers to refinance.[100] Most of the homeowners who were able to modify their loans under HAMP obtained reductions of less than 10 percent in their monthly mortgage payments. And although more than one-third of those helped by HAMP ultimately redefaulted, lenders and mortgage servicers collected $815 million in incentives for modifying these loans, often in cases in which borrowers were not able to stay in their homes.[101]

Too Little, Too Late

Most centrally, even these inadequate responses — as well as more robust ones such as the creation of the Consumer Financial Protection Bureau

(CFPB) in 2011—arrived too late to help the women and people of color who had been losing their homes for at least a decade before the crisis was declared and federal intervention was deemed warranted.[102] This is not to say that dominant political actors paid no attention to the disproportionate toll of the crisis on these and other marginalized groups. The 2008 Democratic platform, for example, stated that "minorities have been hit particularly hard" by "the housing crisis," noting that "in 2006, more than 40 percent of the home loans made to Hispanic borrowers were subprime, while more than half of those made to African Americans were subprime." But while the platform promised that the party would "ensure that the foreclosure prevention program enacted by Congress is implemented quickly and effectively so that at-risk homeowners can get help and hopefully stay in their homes," once in office, members of President Obama's administration also feared the potential backlash should the public perception be that policies were benefiting "underserving" borrowers, particularly undeserving borrowers of color. Rather than paying particular attention to those people their platform had acknowledged were "hit particularly hard," they instead eschewed the kinds of targeted policies that might have allowed those most affected by the meltdown to remain in their homes.[103]

Federal interventions became somewhat more effective at allowing people to stay in their homes after 2010, but, as Immergluck argues, these actions were taken too late to help members of the "vulnerable communities" who had been affected in the earlier stages of the crisis (and did nothing to help those who had been affected during the noncrisis era). As a consequence, "the more effective responses benefited households and communities impacted more heavily in the latter stages of the overall crisis" and the women and people of color who had been affected before 2007 "received effectively less assistance from the government than did middle-income homeowners." Insults were added to injuries and disparities were compounded by the fact that many properties lost during the earlier period "were sold off by lenders to private investors," often at healthy profits.[104]

Plus Ça Change, Plus C'est la Même Chose

Because aid arrived too late to help the people of color and sole-borrower women who experienced foreclosure before 2007, both the wealth and rates of homeownership among members of these groups were slower to recover than those of their white and male counterparts.[105] A study by researchers at the Pew Research Center found, for example, that by 2016, the rate of homeownership among African Americans had fallen to 41.3 percent, down from a peak of 49.1 percent in 2004 and also lower than it had been in 1994, when the rate was 42.3 percent. Although white households had experienced a decline from a peak of 76 percent in 2004, at 71.9 percent, that rate was nonetheless higher in 2016 than it had been in 1994, when 70 percent of white households owned their own homes.[106] Rates of homeownership among single parents (almost all of whom are women) declined from 51.3 percent in 2004 to 46.8 percent in 2016.

There is also evidence that many of the racial and gender disparities in rates of foreclosure evident in the 1990s persisted well past the end of the "crisis," due at least in part to ongoing and, by some measures, worsening discrimination in mortgage lending.[107] Using 2014 Home Mortgage Disclosure Act (HMDA) data, for example, Jacob Faber shows that, even after controlling for a range of individual- and community-level characteristics, Asian Americans, Latinos, and African Americans continue to be approved for mortgages at lower rates than their white counterparts. He shows further that Black and Latino borrowers continue to be significantly more likely to receive high-cost loans than white borrowers, and also that this disparity has actually *accelerated* in the years since the foreclosure crisis.[108] Using data from the Survey of Consumer Finance, Melanie Long finds similarly that sole-borrower low-income women have continued to carry higher mortgage debt than their male counterparts well after the crisis was said to have ended.[109]

There is also some evidence that lenders have returned to practices reminiscent of those used to deny credit to women before the passage of the Fair Housing and Equal Credit Opportunity Acts, and that these practices are once again being justified through controlling narratives about women's allegedly weak labor force attachment. These practices include denying mortgages to women who are pregnant or on parental leave (even paid parental leave) or requiring that they return from parental leave early. Some lenders are once again requiring that women submit the kinds of "baby letters" that had been typical before the passage of the ECOA, stipulating that they either pledge not to have children or promise that they will continue to engage in paid employment if they do.[110] Other practices include lender requirements that pregnant women sign "maternity contracts," which commit to a date by which they will return to work and which must be approved by both a doctor and the employer.[111]

In addition—and as if to confirm NCLC counsel Margot Saunders's assertion (quoted in chapter 4) that lenders are "ingenious in coming up with ways of avoiding the law" and "extremely imaginative in coming up with innovative ways to steal from borrowers"—there has also been a resurgence in extractive practices such as contract-for-deed home sales (also known as land installment contracts).[112] Under such sales, borrowers make down payments and monthly payments and are responsible for property taxes, insurance, and the maintenance and repair of properties (which are often uninhabitable at time of purchase) but they do not build equity or gain title to the home at purchase. Such sales are also not typically protected by the laws covering homeowners who buy homes with traditional mortgages.[113]

In other words, whatever policy windows were opened by the subprime and foreclosure "crisis" ultimately provided few opportunities to address the ongoing and structural inequalities that had fueled and been fueled by it. Instead, high rates of subprime lending and foreclosures among members of marginalized groups were naturalized as outside of the crisis and beyond the power of the state to remedy. Ending the crisis and returning to "normal" conditions therefore meant a return to continued—and in some ways exacerbated—non-crisis conditions of deeply entrenched inequalities and high levels of subprime mortgages and rates of foreclosure among members of these groups.[114]

Conclusion

I do not mean to equate the situation in the 1990s with conditions in 2007 and 2008. Among the important differences between the two periods was that, as Immergluck explains, "the overall scale of the subprime market was smaller on a national scale" and "much less extensive in high-cost metropolitan areas such as those in California and Florida" during the earlier period, and that the foreclosures of that period were consequently "both less severe and affected fewer neighborhoods and cities than did those in the late 2000s."[115] Also important, of course, is that the "first subprime boom did not cause major losses to the investment community," while the crisis period coincided with and helped to produce the Great Recession.[116] And in showing that rates of foreclosure during a period that came to be widely understood as a "foreclosure crisis" were, by some measures and among some groups, no worse than rates during what remains framed as a time of booming rates of homeownership, my point is not to argue that the "crisis" period was not, in fact, a "bad" time. I certainly do not mean to suggest that those borrowers who were helped by the government programs intended to stem the tide of foreclosures were unworthy of such assistance nor that the legislative and regulatory measures taken in the wake of the 2007 crisis were adequate. Indeed, as I explain above and as many scholars have shown, that policy response emphasized aid to banks and lenders and did far less than it could or should have to help borrowers.[117]

In addition, like all policy outcomes, the legislative and regulatory responses to the subprime crisis were overdetermined and complicated, and I am neither trying to provide a comprehensive account of those responses nor claiming that the crisis/non-crisis framework fully explains them.[118] Rather, I use these cases to illustrate the ways in which dominant assumptions about whose suffering is tolerable and whose is intolerable shape and determine which circumstances will be identified as crises demanding explanations and state intervention, and which are instead treated as inevitable and outside the reach of the state to ameliorate.

I also understand that political and economic resources are not infinite and that under some circumstances, it might seem pragmatic to prioritize issues that seem to have a "broader" impact. And certainly if we take the breadth of a problem as our metric of the concern, effort, and consideration that it warrants, the scant attention devoted to subprime mortgage lending and foreclosures before 2007 might not seem unreasonably low, the generally sanguine tone in policy deliberations and reporting about home buying and mortgage lending during that era might seem appropriate, and the failure to apply the language of crisis at that time might seem unremarkable. Likewise, the increased attention to, alarm about, and calls for state intervention into these issues beginning in 2007 might seem proportional to the rates of foreclosure in each era.

It may be impossible to determine a benchmark for the "correct" amount of media or political attention to a particular policy issue at a given moment. However, among the key lessons of scholarship about the dynamics of intersectional marginalization is that understanding and addressing the instantiation, functioning, and perpetuation of inequality demands that we take seriously the experiences of members of marginalized and intersectionally marginalized groups. It also requires that we transcend the very idea that things are worse, more alarming, or more worthy of attention and resources when they affect more people.[119] Indeed, as

Lani Guinier and Gerald Torres argue, at the very least, everyone should understand that it is in their interest to address issues that affect members of marginalized groups because these groups are often, in their words, the "canary in a coal mine" whose distress often portends trouble ahead for all.[120] Moreover, and as I have demonstrated in previous work, perceptions about the breadth and depth of an issue's impact are themselves subjective and influenced by the power and normativity of the groups affected by them. I have shown, for example, that even advocates for disadvantaged groups systematically overestimate the impact of issues affecting advantaged groups and systematically underestimate the effects of those issues affecting disadvantaged ones.[121] I have shown as well that this substitution of power for numbers in advocates' assessments of the breath of an issue's impact, in turn, is part of how they justify the vast disparities in the amount and kind of effort they devote to particular issues.[122]

The presence and absence of the terms *subprime crisis, mortgage crisis*, or *foreclosure crisis* may not, on their own, suffice to construct a crisis or a non-crisis. Likewise, the varying levels of attention devoted to subprime mortgage lending and foreclosure may not, on their own, be indicators that they were being constructed as non-crisis before 2007 and as crises after that date. I recognize as well that these variations are related to long-standing patterns in mainstream reporting on the economy that extend to issues beyond subprime lending and foreclosures.[123]

Nonetheless, these variations are indicators of the processes through which these issues were being constituted as non-crises during the first era and as crises during the second. That is, these differential levels of attention to subprime mortgages and to increasing foreclosures among dominant political actors and in the economic reporting of two of the most important and agenda-setting newspapers in the United States are indicators that the extractive lending practices and high foreclosure rates documented as affecting primarily sole-borrower women and people of color as early as 1996 did not suffice to constitute a crisis that merited and could be resolved through state intervention and resources.

Elvin Wyly and C. S. Ponder have characterized the resistance to taking seriously the experiences of Black women in the mortgage market as an example of the perils of the tendency to dismiss evidence offered by members of marginalized groups as unrepresentative "anecdotes" rather than as generalizable "data." "For almost 20 years," they write, "evidence from journalists' reports, Congressional testimony, and consumer protection litigation suggested that predatory practices in the subprime market were especially harmful for elderly African American women, many of them widows." But, they continue, "even amidst the collapse of the subprime industry in late 2006 and through the summer of 2007," much of this "voluminous evidence . . . was repeatedly dismissed as 'anecdotal.'"[124] In other words, even though activists, advocates, and state and local policymakers had made clear by the early 1990s that subprime mortgage lending was hurting marginalized communities, and even as many of these same actors tried very explicitly to frame these harms as crises, the harms suffered by women and people of color were dismissed as particular, unfixable, and problems of their own making. It was not until foreclosure rates among middle-class white male-breadwinner households reached levels typical of those among sole-borrower women and in communities of color and when foreclosures began to threaten the profitability of the lenders themselves that a "foreclosure crisis" was said to have begun. Only then did dominant economic reporters and political actors begin to treat subprime lending and foreclosures as policy problems that could and should be resolved by federal intervention. It was also then that they began to argue that such intervention was warranted, necessary, and likely to resolve these problems, even as they continued to treat high rates of subprime mortgages and foreclosures among women and people of color as natural, inevitable, and beyond the remedial power of the state.

Will These Crises Go to Waste?

Abby: You know, I love that we're supposed to call it "crisis." When it was crack in the inner cities it was a . . .
Kimara: Epidemic.
Abby: Epidemic. Right. Like it was the Black Plague. Now that it's heroin in the suburbs it's a crisis, just a bad thing that happens to good people. — *American Crime*, season 3, episode 2

The politics of crisis and non-crisis are defining elements of the early twenty-first-century American political landscape and among the key vehicles through which state intervention and resource allocation are (and are not) justified. But it has not always been thus: By revealing some of the ways in which the term *crisis* has come to do the political work that it does, the keyword analysis and the examinations of the foreclosure crisis and non-crisis expose processes that fuel both crisis politics and their role in reinforcing and perpetuating inequality and marginalization. By denaturalizing crisis politics, the analyses also demonstrate that the word itself began its political life in the US as a designator for bad things that happened rarely, suddenly, often elsewhere, and usually to others. Racial justice advocates used the language of crisis to try to persuade dominant political actors and the public that these groups' ongoing struggles were not inevitable facts of nature but instead problems worthy of and remediable through state action. Dominant political actors appropriated this meaning to justify state intervention to remedy bad things that happened to relatively privileged groups and to naturalize ongoing racialized, gendered, and other inequalities and treat them as non-crises.

Together, these processes underscore the malleability and constructedness of crisis and remind us that, contrary to dominant assumptions, it is not always self-evident when a crisis has begun or when it has ended. Instead, the political history of crisis makes clear that dominant understandings and assertions about when we have entered or exited a crisis are shaped as much by conventions about what is normal and about whose pain is tolerable as they are by the severity of the problems at hand. This history also makes clear that these conventions are not merely rhetorical and do not simply reflect efforts to draw attention to or raise the urgency of an issue. Instead, these conventions serve as arguments about and structure contestations over when and what kind of state intervention is acceptable to address which kinds of problems that affect which groups. These arguments rely on and create assumptions and practices that reflect, reproduce, and reconstitute prevailing attitudes and normative expectations about racialized, gendered, and other inequalities, at the same time as they justify policies that preserve and often reinforce their real material effects.

The paired analyses of the subprime mortgage crisis and its non-crisis analogue demonstrate further that neither the recognition nor the generativity of a crisis is foreordained. These matched cases also illuminate some of the processes through which problems come to be regarded as crises worthy of and remediable through state intervention and resources when they affect dominant groups even as analogous ones are treated as inevitable, immune to, and not warranting state intervention when they affect marginalized populations. They also provide a window onto the ways in which crisis politics work to naturalize structural inequalities and oppression by shaping how problems are understood as well as the policy solutions that are deemed reasonable to address them. In so doing, the cases also illuminate the ways in which the construction of crises and non-crises create path-dependent outcomes that can serve to further entrench conditions of marginalization for some groups even as they might alleviate hardships for others.

Recognizing this power of crisis not only to draw attention to an issue but also, more consequentially, to justify state intervention and resources to address it, advocates and activists associated with a range of issues, groups, and movements have continued to reframe an ever-expanding array of naturalized conditions as intervention-worthy crises. And as they have done so, crisis politics have become ever-more woven into the fabric of American politics and policymaking, ever-more integral to domestic policy agenda setting and problem definition, and ever-more central to battles over and justifications for or against state intervention. In the 1970s, for example, feminists introduced the term *rape crisis center*, in part to shift understandings of sexual violence from an individualized and private issue to an emergency that deserved and demanded resources and a response. In the 1980s, AIDS activists formed the Gay Men's Health Crisis to draw attention to the Reagan administration's failed response to the HIV epidemic.[1] The 1980s and 1990s saw increasing calls for community and government interventions and resources to address what many advocates characterized as a "crisis of the Black male."[2] On the right, "crisis pregnancy centers" became a staple of the anti-abortion movement's tactics.

And depending on where you are and on when you have found your way to this book, any number of other crises (and non-crises) might come to mind as well. In the years after the Great Recession and the foreclosure crisis that are the subject of the previous two chapters, for example, the zeitgeist within which Rahm Emanuel championed the productive uses to which crises could be put continued apace, as the list of calamitous events and phenomena labeled crises continued to grow. In late 2013, doctors, public health officials, and policymakers began to describe an "opioid crisis" that was ravaging many communities, while 2014 witnessed a "water crisis" in Flint, Michigan as well as increasing attention to what many observers described as a "border crisis" in the Southwest. A year later, concerns intensified about a global "refugee crisis." References to a "climate crisis" spiked in 2019, as climate scientists warned that the earth had seen its warmest and wettest year on record. In a somewhat different register, the advent of antiretroviral drug cocktails in the 1990s and pre-exposure prophylaxis (PrEP) in the 2010s led many to declare that the "AIDS crisis was over," even as persistent racial, economic, and regional inequalities in access to these treatments meant that, as Jonathon Catlin observed, there "was a higher per capita rate of AIDS for Black people some two decades after medicine was available than there ever was for white people when there were no effective drugs."[3]

The foregoing examples crystallize some of the lessons and arguments in this book and about the politics of crisis and non-crisis more generally. The border crisis exemplifies the ways in which different understandings of crises are part of political contestations that bring with them their own implications for problem definition and for whether and how the state should respond.[4] For some, the crisis had to do with alleged increases in the numbers of people trying to enter the United States from Mexico, Central, and South America. For those who held this belief, the appropriate solution demanded and justified the marshalling of state resources and power to increase border patrolling and to build a wall. For those who saw the crisis as one produced by political and economic conditions in migrants' countries of origin (themselves produced by histories of colonization and by contemporary American hegemony in the region) and by the discriminatory and often inhumane and even lethal treatment they faced when they tried to enter the United States, the situation demanded state action and resources to treat them fairly, humanely, and with compassion.

The climate crisis illustrates the invocation of crisis as an attempt to denaturalize a problem and to shift the timeframe within which it is understood, reframing it from an inevitability that will simply continue to unfold to an intervention-worthy problem that is the product of human action and can thus be remedied through human agency as well. Like the mortgage foreclosure crisis and non-crisis, the declarations about the end of the AIDS crisis reveal the ways in which racialized norms and expectations effectively disappeared what might be understood as an ongoing crisis-level prevalence of infections and illness in some Black communities. "For such acutely affected groups in the United States and around the world," Catlin writes, "the AIDS epidemic is still experienced as a 'crisis'" even as "most Americans—even within queer communities—may not conceive of AIDS as a crisis."[5]

Juxtaposing the "opioid crisis" against the non-crisis of the "crack epidemic" is another example in which analogous problems are treated differently when they are perceived to affect different groups. In this case, while the effects of the so-called crack epidemic had been understood as being felt primarily among low-income Black people living in cities, the rise in opioid addiction was understood to affect mainly white people in suburban and rural areas. While the state response to the crack epidemic focused on punitive and carceral interventions and resources, those responding to the opioid epidemic questioned these solutions and in many cases rejected them in favor of treatment (at least, as Rebecca Tiger argues, for middle-class white people) and, eventually, regulation and punishment of pharmaceutical companies.[6] And as public health authorities began to pay more attention to opioid use in rural and suburban areas, advocates argued that "the emphasis on the opioid crisis as a plague of the white rural and Rust Belt underclass has obscured the toll the problem has taken in major cities and among the urban poor."[7] That is, while opioid use among rural and suburban whites has been treated as a crisis that can and should be resolved, its manifestations among poor people and people of color in cities have been naturalized as non-crises within the crisis.

Most generally, the designation of such widely ranging "bad things" as crises underscores the ongoing centrality and escalation of crisis politics as an arena for problem definition, agenda setting, and for competing ideas about the role of the state. It suggests that American politics are now, to some degree, always crisis politics: Not only has the term so permeated American politics and culture that they are almost unimaginable without it, but the actual and the perceived generativity of crises have become staples of both policymaking and movement politics in the United States. The persistent and recurring battles over which bad things are crises, which are non-crises, and what the state can and should do about them have become defining features and pivot points in American politics and policymaking.

COVID-19 Crisis and Non-Crisis

In each of the foregoing cases and in many others, political actors and activists have tried to use the idea that a problem is a crisis as a way to justify state intervention and resources. Many of these contests and conflicts were heightened by the 2016 election of Donald Trump, which was itself deemed by many to be a crisis. His presidency also brought with it or heightened the salience of a basket of issues and problems to which the label *crisis* was appended, several of which came to a head in 2019 and 2020 during what was routinely referred to as the "constitutional crisis" of his (first) impeachment.

As the impeachment hearings unfolded in late 2019, reports began to emerge about what was described at first as a pneumonia-like illness in the Wuhan Province of China. By January 2020, news accounts were describing a "coronavirus crisis" in that country and, soon after, in the Lombardy region of Italy. In late February, infections in Seattle earned this designation, and not long after that, so, too, did levels in several Californian cities. By early March of that year, reporters, political observers, and policymakers began to use the term *crisis* more broadly to describe COVID-19 and its implications for the United States. This practice intensified as the numbers of infections and deaths increased, as the health and economic effects of the virus and its spread became clearer and widened, and as anti-lockdown demonstrators—many of whom were following the president's lead—refused to wear masks and defied the stay-at-home orders that health officials argued were necessary to slow the spread of the virus.

And then, in the midst of these stay-at-home orders, the murders of Ahmaud Arbery, George Floyd, and Breonna Taylor by police and others prompted widespread and massive mobilization for racial justice in cities across the United States and the world. By early June 2020, journalists and political observers were referring to the "double" and even "triple crises" of the pandemic, its economic effects, and the uprisings.

Two Clear-Cut Crises?

In its early days and at first glance, the scope, scale, and trajectory of the COVID-19 pandemic bore all the markers of a classic, easily recognizable, and self-evident clear-cut crisis: an apparently unambiguously urgent problem that was triggered by a seemingly exogenous cause, one that arrived suddenly and unexpectedly and that brought with it a set of quick, discrete, and episodic shocks that were ostensibly universal in their effects. This latter characteristic was evident in the proliferation of references in advertising and social media to ideas such as "we are all in this together" (Gucci and PCI Security Standards Council), "the virus does not discriminate" (Seattle and King County, WA), we are "apart, but united" (Mastercard), and "staying apart is the best way to stay united" (Coke).[8] The pandemic was also treated (borrowing Murray Edelman's previously referenced characterization) as "unique and threatening," as a turning point at which action or inaction would determine life or death—in this case, the life or death of individuals, of institutions, and of the economy. State, local, and federal political actors and observers also began to recognize and act on the need for intervention to address the pandemic. Similarly, the disruptiveness of the racial justice protests seemed to many observers to arrive as if out of nowhere, and they were met in many cities with exceptional and extreme police and even military force that, President Trump insisted, was necessary to contain the unrest and restore what he referred to increasingly as "law and order" in American cities.[9]

Together, the pandemic's clear, life-threatening, and ostensibly universal and unprecedented health and economic effects alongside the upheaval of the protests might seem to cast doubt on some of the claims that I have made in this book: for example, that crisis is a construct or that what constitutes a crisis is politically determined. Conversely, the pandemic might also seem to confirm the assumption that some bad things are, in fact, much worse than others and therefore truly are crises. But the seeming self-evidence that the events of the spring and summer of 2020 were clear-cut crises becomes murkier if we consider them in the context of longer-term problems and processes. Doing so, as Antonio Vázquez-Arroyo argues, entails not only coming to terms with "what is currently unfolding" but also requires that we try to "grasp the ways in which the current pandemic is advancing through an already catastrophic situation," one structured by, inter alia, white supremacy, heteropatriarchy, ableism, and economic precarity.[10] It also underscores several key points about the subject of this book: the relationships among crisis politics, episodic hard times, and the kinds of ongoing and quotidian hard times that routinely affect and structure the lived experiences of marginalized groups.

It is too soon, and these events are too numerous and too varied, for thorough and nuanced analyses of the relationships among the pandemic, police violence, racial justice protests, and the politics of marginalization in the United States, and it is not possible to do justice to these issues in one chapter or even one book. Even in the course of writing this epilogue, the contours and implications of the pandemic, the protests, and their intersections have continued to evolve and to come into view. Rather than a comprehensive assessment of the many important questions about crisis politics and marginalized groups raised by these events—questions that will undoubtedly be asked, analyzed, and assessed for many years—I suggest three interrelated clusters of issues that are brought into focus through the lenses offered in this book: that both the material effects and the definition of crises are often endogenous to politics; that the events and phenomena deemed crises by dominant political actors are often ones that affect or are exacerbated by bad things that affect marginalized groups even in ostensibly good times; and that although faith in the generativity of crisis remains complicated when it comes to addressing marginalization, oppression, and subordination, that activists and advocates have used the confluence of the pandemic, police violence, and racial justice protests to reframe understandings of systemic racism and other forms of marginalization in ways that bring us back to its origins, particularly to the NAACP's decision to name its magazine *The Crisis*.

Crisis as Endogenous

It is almost certainly the case that COVID-19 would have had calamitous effects regardless of political leaders' responses to it. It is also true that police violence against Black people is not new and also that it has long prompted mass mobilization and sustained action.[11] But just as there is "no such thing as a 'natural disaster,'" so, too, is it the case that neither the causes nor the consequences of the pandemic or white supremacist police violence were inevitable or "defined by an autonomous natural order."[12] Instead, like disasters, crises "have histories, they are products of time and place," and what gets called a crisis "is itself a political act."[13] Likewise, that the coronavirus pandemic and racist policing became crises in the United States illustrates some of the ways in which crises are dependent variables, the products of state action and inaction, and the outcomes of political decisions and policy processes.

For example, in both the United States and elsewhere, at least some portion of what was understood to be the "crisis" of the coronavirus crisis resulted from political and policy decisions in both the short and long terms. Among the clear and painfully direct short-term decisions that led to some of the defining features of its crisis-ness in the United States were President Trump's now well-documented minimization of and denial about the threat posed by the virus. This minimization was evident, for example, in his failure to take seriously the early 2020 security briefings that warned infections likely would spread in the absence of interventions.[14] That the pandemic resulted from not only policy decisions but also partisan politics became clear when the committee headed by President Trump's son-in-law Jared Kushner crafted but then abandoned a national plan because its members concluded that the pandemic's effects were likely to be concentrated in states with Democratic governors, on whom they hoped they could—and on whom they in fact tried to—pin the blame.[15] The effects of this inaction were likely exacerbated by those actions that the Trump administration did take, including its focus on "closing the border to China," its continued assaults on the Affordable Care Act, and its neglect of the deadly conditions in detention centers and other carceral institutions. The administration's failure to take seriously early reports about the virus also likely contributed to and exacerbated the effects of state and local officials' decisions and actions as well, such as New York City mayor Bill DeBlasio's mid-March assurances that residents of that city should continue to live their lives, to send their children to school, and to take public transportation.[16]

Among the longer-term actions, inactions, and decisions that likely played important roles in constituting the contours of the crisis in the United States were the Trump administration's failure to replenish the so-called national stockpile of emergency medical supplies and its jettisoning the Obama administration's plans for doing so.[17] Also likely important was President Trump's decision in 2017 to reduce the size of the White House National Security Council (NSC) Directorate for Global Health Security and Biodefense by absorbing it into another NSC directorate, and jettisoning the previous administration's plans.[18]

But as the scale of the pandemic escalated, and as it became ever clearer that the United States was becoming an outlier in both rates of infection and mortality and also in the economic toll it was taking, observers increasingly noted the contributions of broader and longer-term factors as well. Among those frequently referenced among liberals and progressives were neoliberal developments such as the deregulation and privatization of for-profit health care and insurance alongside large numbers of uninsured people. For example, because many Americans lack access to paid medical leave and child care and in the face of a patchwork of inadequate state-administered unemployment insurance systems, many people avoided or lacked access to testing and treatment and could not afford to stay home from work even if they suspected that had been exposed to the virus or were experiencing symptoms.[19]

Similarly, the crises associated with the murders of Arbery, Taylor, and Floyd, the protests against them, and the police response to those protests were themselves also, in important ways, the products of short-term and long-term political action and policy decisions. Among the important long-term foundations were policies related to the wars on crime and drugs that relicensed racist and aggressive policing tactics, the militarization of police forces, and long histories of both white supremacist violence and mobilization against it.[20]

Same Storm, Different Boats: Disparities and Discrimination

These relatively straightforward ways in which politics and policy produced the crises of the pandemic, police violence, and racial justice protests point, in turn, to more subtly endogenous aspects of their crisis-ness. They point in particular to features related to the fact that the kinds of things that are deemed crises are often ones exacerbated by bad things that structure the lives of members of marginalized groups even in ostensibly good times. In the case of the COVID-19 pandemic, it seemed at first that many of the earliest diagnosed infections in the United States were clustered in relatively affluent communities. Once infection and mortality data were available by race and other demographic indicators, however, it became clear that both the illness and its economic implications were taking a disproportionate toll on members of marginalized groups. That is, many of the worst effects of the pandemic were products of white supremacy, economic precarity, heteropatriarchy, and other forms of inequality, marginalization, and oppression.

In something of a departure from the case of foreclosures and from other recent crises (and perhaps reflecting increased attention to inequalities and even to intersecting forms of marginalization in the wake of the 2016 election), dominant political actors and news outlets began to pay some attention to many of these disparities at a relatively early stage of the pandemic. Among the COVID-19-related headlines of stories published in mainstream news outlets in the spring of 2020 included:

- "As Coronavirus Deepens Inequality, Inequality Worsens Its Spread" (*New York Times*, 15 March 2020)
- "They Clean the Buildings: Workers Are Fleeing, but Who's Protecting Them?" (*New York Times*, 18 March 2020)
- "The Coronavirus Is a Disaster for Feminism: Pandemics Affect Men and Women Differently" (*Atlantic*, 19 March 2020)
- "Coronavirus May Disproportionately Hurt the Poor—And That's Bad for Everyone" (*Time* magazine, 11 May 2020)

Several news stories reported on the findings of a May 2020 study conducted by amfAR, for example, which found that US counties in which at least 13 percent of the population was Black accounted for 52 percent of COVID-19 cases nationwide.[21] In Michigan, where African Americans comprise approximately 14 percent of the population, by May 2020 they constituted 41 percent of cases in that state. Disparities in mortality rates were even more alarming. A *Washington Post* study conducted in April of that year found that "majority-Black counties faced three times the COVID-19 infection rate, and nearly six times the mortality rate from the virus, that majority-white counties did."[22] Reports also began to document high rates of infection and mortality among people incarcerated in prisons, jails, and detention centers, as well as patterns of discrimination such as refusals to treat LGBTQ people and the rationing of care and supplies that seemed to be leading to denials of treatment to people with disabilities.[23]

These disparities in rates of and vulnerability to infection, access to health care, and mortality mapped onto and were exacerbated by racial, gender, and other disparities in the pandemic's economic impact as well. Among these exacerbating factors were that women, people of color, and women of color in particular have long been more likely to be employed in occupations or in positions that did not allow them to work from or to stay home.[24] The resulting increased risk of exposure was further exacerbated by the fact that members of these same groups were also more likely to be employed in sectors that were deemed "essential," making those employed in such jobs ineligible for unemployment benefits.[25] At the same time, and despite the fact that so much of their work was more likely to be deemed "essential," women, low-income people, and people of color nonetheless also lost their jobs at higher rates than their white and male counterparts. Other gendered patterns began to become clear as well, such as ones in which women were shouldering disproportionate shares of care work and domestic labor, particularly when it came to elder care, child care, and at-home schooling.[26]

In addition to the foregoing health and economic disparities, each day seemed to bring evidence of other pandemic-related disparities and discrimination, such as verbal and physical attacks against Asian Americans, as Trump and other conservative elites scapegoated and demonized China through their persistent references to COVID-19 as the "China virus" and the "Kung Flu." There was also evidence of discriminatory enforcement of social-distancing and mask-wearing rules, prompting some observers to characterize it as the new "stop-and-frisk." Journalist Adam Serwer reported, for example, that "in East New York, police assault black residents for violating social-distancing rules; in Lower Manhattan, they dole out masks and smiles to white pedestrians."[27]

Like the intersecting raced and gendered disparities that were both thrown into relief and exacerbated by the foreclosure crisis and noncrisis, the disparities and discrimination laid bare by the coronavirus pandemic are troubling examples of the ways in which hard times so often inflict disproportionate harm and suffering on members of marginalized groups. And there is no doubt that the disproportionately high rates of infection, mortality, and economic precarity and exploitation experienced by women, people of color, low-income people, incarcerated people, and immigrants in the midst of the broader pandemic is another chapter in the ongoing saga of racial, gender, and economic inequality in the United States, in which the effects of crises are more pronounced among members of marginalized and intersectionally marginalized groups, who "get pneumonia when the rest of the country has a particularly bad cold." As

Keeanga-Yamahtta Taylor put it even more pointedly in an April 2020 column in the *New Yorker*, "The old African-American aphorism 'When white America catches a cold, black America gets pneumonia' has a new, morbid twist: when white America catches the novel coronavirus, black Americans die."[28] But as was also true in the cases of subprime lending and foreclosures, although this narrative captures crucial aspects of the many ways in which what Susan Sterett and Laura Mateczun call the "disaster cascade" of the pandemic were exponentially harder for members of marginalized and subjugated groups, it is only the tip of the iceberg when it comes to understanding the relationships among COVID-19, crisis construction, and the politics of marginalization.[29]

In this particular case, considering these early framings about the impact of the pandemic on marginalized groups suggests that there is an important difference between the idea that such inequalities are *laid bare by* a crisis and treating those inequalities *as themselves* a crisis. It suggests as well that there are important differences between questioning, as Judith Butler asks, whose lives are grievable and asking what it would take to prevent the harm that creates the grief.[30] Once again, these distinctions are more than rhetorical and also deeper than simply saying that something is bad or arguing that it is urgent. The issue also cannot be reduced to the idea that dominant political actors did not care about an issue that affects marginalized groups, although that was certainly a contributing factor, with observers such as Serwer going as far as to suggest that President Trump simply stopped caring about the pandemic once he "found out who was dying."[31] Rather, it suggests that understanding the relationship between crises and marginalization entails reckoning with what it means that some inequalities are buried in the first place. It also entails exploring whether, once an inequality has been laid bare by a crisis, it is then treated as itself resolvable through and therefore worthy of state intervention and resources or whether it is normalized and treated as a non-crisis within the crisis. Even if people and political actors become concerned about or troubled by the "wake up call," as Chester Hartman and Gregory Squires put it, that is delivered by a bad thing, it matters whether they think the problem can be fixed, and if so, by who and through what means.[32] In these ways, the distinction is between different understandings of a problem and, most crucially, different approaches to whether and how a problem can, should, and will be addressed.

In the tethered cases of COVID-19, racist police violence, and the mobilization against that violence, the framework of crisis and non-crisis reminds us that at issue is not only that members of marginalized groups were already more likely to be affected by problems including unemployment, a lack of or inadequate health insurance, eviction, foreclosure, and police violence before the crises had begun. Also important are questions about the ways in which such disparities and exacerbations were understood, framed, and addressed: Which problems were universalized and treated as parts of the crises that could be solved by state intervention and resources, and which were particularized and naturalized as endemics that were outside the crisis and beyond the power of the state to remedy? Although dominant media and political actors seemed to be more troubled by these patterns than they had been in the cases of subprime mortgages and foreclosures, many nonetheless normalized the deep and structural inequalities that produced these uneven effects of the pandemic, continuing to treat them as non-crises—the unfortunate but nonetheless natural and inevitable results of unremarkable conditions that are immune to, and therefore do not warrant, state intervention.

One example of such differential treatment was evident in the early months of the pandemic. Asked at a 7 April 2020 press conference about the racialized health and economic disparities that were translating into disproportionate rates of infection and death among African Americans, for example, Anthony Fauci, Director of the National Institute of Allergy and Infectious Diseases and a member of President Trump's Coronavirus Task Force, replied:

> We have a particularly difficult problem of an exacerbation of a health disparity. We've known, *literally forever*, that diseases like diabetes, hypertension, obesity, and asthma are disproportionately afflicting the minority populations, particularly the African Americans. . . . Unfortunately, when you look at the predisposing conditions that lead to a bad outcome with coronavirus—the things that get people into ICUs that require intubation and often lead to death—they are just those very comorbidities that are, unfortunately, disproportionately prevalent in the African American population. . . . So we're very concerned about that. *It's very sad. There's nothing we can do about it right now*, except to try and give them the best possible care to avoid those complications (italics added).[33]

Dr. Fauci made clear in his statement that he recognized and was troubled by the racialized health and economic disparities he described. However, his characterization of the health disparities as something "we've known, literally forever" alongside his assertion that while the situation might be "very sad," that "there's nothing we can do about it right now" framed them as outside of the crisis and beyond the power of the federal government to remedy. Though sympathetic, his language nonetheless echoed the sentiments of Mortgage Bankers Association researcher Michael Fratantoni, the witness quoted in chapter 5, who argued that the rising rates of foreclosure that were the subject of the hearings were not at "crisis levels" because they were "still caused by the same things that have historically caused mortgage delinquencies." Unlike Fratantoni, Fauci did not dismiss concerns about the disparities in rates of infection and mortality. He did, however, treat these "endemics" very explicitly as a non-crisis: as long-standing problems that were natural and inevitable, that affected a particular group we might have predicted would bear a disparate impact, and that, although unfortunate and tragic, were caused by *un*alarming conditions *un*remediable through and therefore *un*warranting of federal action.[34]

Conditions-as-Crises

While many dominant political actors and reporters initially treated these inequities as outside of both the crisis and beyond the power of the government to remedy, others did just the opposite. Representative Alexandria Ocasio-Cortez (D-NY), for example, framed the conditions that fueled and were fueled by COVID-19 as part of and integral to how the crisis of the pandemic should be understood and addressed, and as just as much a product of state action and inaction as the disease itself. Speaking to *New York Times* reporter Mark Leibovich in late April 2020 about the pandemic's particularly devastating effects on her constituents in New York's 14th Congressional District, Ocasio-Cortez said, "this crisis is not really creating new problems. It's pouring gasoline on our existing ones."[35]

Ocasio-Cortez's framing of the pandemic's effects as constituted by ongoing issues of access to health care, income inequity, and racial injustice were echoed and amplified by activists and advocates. As critical race feminist legal scholar Kimberlé Crenshaw put it in a column published in the *New Republic*,

On paper, Covid-19 may fit the profile of an equal opportunity assassin, but the trajectory of its rampage throughout the United States strongly indicates otherwise.... Confronting these disparities squarely reveals a further truth: that the conditions of disparate vulnerability are not just there, but rather reflect the long-term consequences of the nation's racially and economically disparate response to earlier crises. Rescues past and present illuminate in striking clarity whose vulnerability warrants robust interventions and whose does not.[36]

Many political actors, activists, and observers echoed Ocasio-Cortez's and Crenshaw's analyses situating the pandemic within broader contexts of inequality, marginalization, and oppression. They also engaged in even more explicit examples of the broad and long-standing practice of treating crises as generative of policy windows that can provide opportunities to address long-standing goals. Many echoed and even quoted Rahm Emanuel's 2008 admonition that we should not let a "serious crisis to go to waste." In some cases, they did so as calls to action, in other cases, as cautionary tales. Examples of the latter include an article published in *Jacobin* titled, "Why the Neoliberals Won't Let This Crisis Go to Waste," which opened with the following statement:

> Many observers expected that the 2008 financial crisis would mark the end of neoliberalism. Instead, we saw a wave of privatization and sharp cuts in public services. Today, the forces best placed to exploit the coronavirus pandemic are still those who already have power: the neoliberals who've been shaping the economic policy agenda for decades.[37]

Examples of the former include a self-referential 25 March 2020 *Washington Post* op-ed authored by Emanuel himself titled "Let's Make Sure This Crisis Doesn't Go to Waste":

> Today, faced with another crisis, we need to think strategically not only about how to address the virus but also about how the United States can come out stronger on the other side. We all know this won't be the last time we confront a pandemic. But it should be the last time a public health emergency provokes an economic depression. We need to prepare for tomorrow, starting today.[38]

Racism Is a Crisis

Three COVID-era developments help to illustrate these attempts to denaturalize the ongoing and normalized conditions of marginalization made evident in the pandemic and the protests and to reframe them as crises

that are remediable through state intervention. First among these was a proliferation of dozens of statements and resolutions issued by a wide range
of cities, counties, and professional organizations declaring that racism was
itself "a crisis" or a "public health crisis."[39] Although the first such declarations were issued in 2019, they increased steeply in tandem with the pandemic, and their proliferation accelerated in the wake of the racial justice
protests that summer. The content of these statements varied widely, with
some doing little more than acknowledging the disparities or, like Fauci's
statement above, averring that racism and racialized police violence are
troubling and unfortunate. For example, the city council of Goleta, CA's
resolution "Condemning Police Brutality and Declaring Racism a Public
Health Emergency" merely stated that it is "committed to making Goleta
a welcoming, inclusive, and safe community for everyone," that it both pro-
motes "free thought and speech" and also condemns "racism and police
brutality, hate speech, bigotry, violence and prejudice," and that is stands
"in solidarity with the people of Goleta and the Black Lives Matter movement" in its dedication "to creating a community where all people can
safely, freely and fully engage in our democracy without the fear of those
that have sworn to protect them."[40]

While statements such as the Goleta city council's were quite short and
general, others drew explicit links between long-standing racial disparities and injustices and the disparities in COVID-19 rates of infection and
death and police violence and even laid out some explicit measures that
would be taken to address them. The preamble to the Hamden, CT city
council's "Resolution Declaring Racism as a Public Health Crisis," stated,
for example,

> How is racism a public health emergency? The trauma inflicted by racism and
> the purposeful disinvestment in social and economic well-being, people of color
> live with disproportionately higher cortisol levels, higher rates of chronic stress,
> higher rates chronic disease, lower infant birth rates, higher rates of COVID-19
> infection and death and pay the ultimate price with their lives. This time of a
> global pandemic, we can put these efforts toward immediate and life savings
> action.

The resolution also enumerated seven measures it argued would "catalyze
and authorize data analysis, policy analysis to prevent unintentional injustices, and implementation of policies and actions to dismantle or course-
correct problematic systems."[41] Taken together, these statements harken

back to the ideas motivating the NAACP's decision (described in chapter 2) to name its magazine *The Crisis*. That is, they harness the language of crisis as part of efforts to change the way in which racism is understood and addressed: not as natural or inevitable, but as worthy of and ameliorable through state intervention and resources.

The First "Shecession"?

A second example of the ways in which the events of 2020 might serve to denaturalize ongoing and normalized conditions of marginalization is evident in the unprecedented attention paid to labor force issues faced by women in the midst of the coronavirus pandemic. Much of this attention was prompted by the fact that the pandemic had led to "an economic downturn where job and income losses are affecting women more than men," or what some referred as the "first female recession."[42] As Amanda Holpuch explained in an August 2020 article in the *Guardian*, "from February to May, 11.5 million women lost their jobs compared with 9 million men. . . . By the end of April, women's job losses had erased a decade of employment gains."[43]

It might seem unremarkable that journalists would pay attention to these developments, but such reports stand in stark contrast to the ways in which gendered norms and expectations regarding income inequality and labor force participation have typically been framed in mainstream economic reporting. As I discuss briefly at the outset of chapter 4, for example, such norms and expectations marked ideas about both the depth and gravity of the Great Recession as well as the indicators that it was over. In particular, policymakers and economic reporters had treated high rates of white male unemployment as the defining indicator of that economic crisis. This approach naturalized ongoing high rates of unemployment among men of color and women of all races as a non-crisis and as already accounted for in long-standing ideological tropes and infrastructures, thereby making these statistics irrelevant to the metrics used to determine economic recovery.[44]

Much was made, for example, of the fact that unemployment rates for men reached 10.5 percent in May 2009 (up from 5 percent in 2007) and that the analogous rate for women had increased to only 8 percent (from 4.8 percent in 2007).[45] But it was also true that rates of women's unemployment were not actually declining but were instead remarkably high.

Women also continued to endure inequalities that had affected them long before the recession had begun: They remained concentrated in lower-paying service positions, average wages for white men remained higher than those for white women, and white men with high school diplomas continued to earn about as much as white women with college degrees.[46] But while some observers and analysts at that time noted these dispari-ties, there was scant acknowledgment of the fact that women's lower rates of unemployment were at least in part an artifact of long-standing norms about women's paid labor, whereby the proportion of women in the labor force was far lower than the proportion of men. Lawrence Mishel and his colleagues estimated for example, that in 2007, before the recession began, 90.9 percent of men between the ages of twenty-five and fifty-four, but only 75.4 percent of women in this same group, were in the labor force.[47] In other words, it was true that among all those in the paid labor force, a greater proportion of men were unemployed compared to the propor-tion of women. But even when the gap between the rates of men's and women's unemployment was at its peak, a greater proportion of Ameri-can men than American women was nonetheless employed.[48] The abso-lute value of the number of men working also remained higher than the number of women, those men continued to earn more than their female counterparts, and they also continued to hold higher-paid jobs than more highly educated women. Yet these long-term structural inequities were not factored into the constitution of the Great Recession as a crisis; rather, it was the suggestion that gendered norms were being challenged and gen-dered disparities possibly narrowing or reversing that was deemed the sign of trouble and the problem worthy of attention.

It was in that context that an upturn in which 90 percent of the jobs created went to (mostly white) men was construed as a "recovery"—the central and symbolically powerful verdict rendered—and these racial-ized and gendered realities were at once subsumed, made invisible, and neutralized by the official end to crisis. Indeed, that the disproportion-ate benefits of that recovery went to white male workers was—and has long been—one of the conditions that "make our sense of normalcy pos-sible."[49] But whereas in 2009 the notion that the economy had entered a recovery was not questioned, even as—or perhaps because—women and people of color fared worse, in 2020, the fact that these groups were suf-fering more was treated as an important and at times even integral factor in many analyses of the economic implications of the pandemic. Articles such as those referenced at the outset of this section, for example, even used these disparities as points of entry into discussions about broader and longer-standing structural economic issues facing women and particularly women of color. The *Guardian* article, for example, contextualized women's unemployment rates by arguing that they

> have underlined the changing nature of the workforce and brought into focus the overlooked issues attached to that shift. Women, especially women of color, are more vulnerable to sudden losses of income because of the gender pay gap and are more dependent on childcare and school to be able to work.[50]

The article concludes by quoting Institute for Women's Policy Research president Nicole Mason, who stated that "what we're realizing now is that what is happening now is the result of broken systems that were not working for the majority of Americans and people." In so doing, Mason tried to use the pandemic and the raced and gendered economic conditions that it has thrown into relief to denaturalize ongoing conditions of marginalization and reframe them as part of the crisis: that is, as problems that can and must be remedied by the state if the crisis is ever to truly end.

Conclusion: "Normal Wasn't Working"

The foregoing point relates to the final illustration of the ways in which advocates and activists tried to denaturalize the ongoing and normalized conditions of marginalization made evident in the pandemic and the protests. In particular (and echoing "Normalcy, Never Again," the working title of what would come to be known as Martin Luther King Jr.'s 1963 "I Have a Dream" speech), among the earliest, most common, and most enduring refrains about the pandemic and the protests were admonitions that ending the crises should not mean a return to "normal" because "normal wasn't working" and that going back to "normal" would mean a return to conditions of deep structural inequalities.[51] "Unprecedented crises demand unprecedented action," political scientist Daniel Carpenter and economist Darrick Hamilton wrote in an April 2020 white paper for the Scholars Strategy Network. "Far from a temporary state of affairs," they continued, "the COVID-19 pandemic crisis instead exposes the rot in our republic, the severe weakness of our society, and the frailty of a purportedly robust economy."[52] Speaking a few months later at a World Economic Forum event that was part of its "Great Reset" series, former secretary of state John Kerry opened his remarks by saying "the normal was a crisis; the normal was itself not working."[53] And in a January 2021 column published in honor of the inauguration of President Joe Biden and Vice President Kamala Harris, Alicia Garza, co-creator of the Black Lives Matter Global Network, reminded readers that

> The truth is, things weren't great before the pandemic hit and they certainly were tenuous before Trump's election. White supremacy has always been normalized in this country. . . . The reckoning that this country is facing is not just a racial justice one. America is deciding who it will be, not just for ourselves, but for the rest of the world. This is the time when we get to decide whether we will go forwards and act on the painful lessons we've learned, or if we will downshift into complacency and normalcy that was anything but normal.[54]

Through formulations such as these, activists and advocates have recognized the limits of treating crisis itself as generative. Rather than Emanuelian strategies that try to use the crisis to "do things you could not do before," they have tried instead to disrupt and blur the lines between crisis and non-crisis by using the moment to question the containability of both and to problematize the very meaning, conditions, and desirability of "before." That is, they have tried to use the confluence of the health pandemic, the economic crisis, and the increased attention to racist police violence and other inequalities to address the ongoing and deeply entrenched forms of oppression that these events have both revealed and fueled. In so doing, they have attempted to shape and provide some context for the ways in which racial injustice, misogyny, and possible remedies for them are understood and to make it more difficult to continue to naturalize them as the "normal" conditions that would signal an end to the crises.

There are still many reasons to worry that harnessing redistributive and liberatory agendas to the twinned crises of the pandemic and police violence will do more to reorganize or reinforce unjust racial, gender, economic, and other orders than it will do to alleviate or end them. Indeed, as I put the finishing touches on this book, policymakers are dismantling many COVID-19-related provisions and police violence continues unabated. But there are also signs that these challenges have made clearer to increasing numbers of people and policymakers that there are costs associated with treating structural inequalities as non-crises. There may therefore also be reasons to hope, then, that if and when these crises "end," it might not mean, as it has so often, a return to "normal" pre-crisis conditions of continued—or exacerbated—deeply entrenched inequality and normalized injustice that are treated as outside the power of the state to remedy.[55]

Overview of Sources and Methods

The arguments and analyses in this book draw on evidence and data that I collected from a wide range of sources, including print media and political and government documents. I describe many important features of these sources and detail the methods that I used to collect and code the data in the notes that accompany the tables and figures and in the body and endnotes of the relevant chapters. Here, I assemble and elaborate on these considerations and decisions in order to present a more holistic account of my approach and reasoned justifications for my decisions for readers who want more details about them.

I begin in appendix A with a discussion about some of the caveats and considerations associated with my approach to working with textual evidence. In appendix B, I describe key aspects of the methods I used to collect and code the data from the various sources and report the results of supplementary searches and analyses that I conducted. Appendix C provides a list of the main sources of evidence used in the book, and appendix D contains several supplementary figures and tables.

Working with Textual Data: Caveats and Considerations

"For much of its history," Justin Grimmer, Margaret Roberts, and Brandon Stewart write in a 2021 review essay about machine learning in the social sciences, "empirical work in the social sciences has been defined by scarcity." Whereas data were previously "hard to find, surveys were costly to field, and record storage was close to impossible," they continue, "abundance now defines the social sciences."[1] This description is particularly true of textual data: The digitization of newspapers, government publications, political documents, and other sources enables, at least in theory, easier, more comprehensive, and more systematic searching of a broader range of sources than is possible using hard copies.[2] Researchers now take for granted, for example, that they can type a word like *crisis* into a search engine to see how it has been used in hundreds of newspapers published for over a century, something that previously would have been like searching for a needle in a haystack.

But for all that digitization has made possible, a growing body of scholarship also alerts researchers to several caveats and tradeoffs associated with searchable and machine-readable sources, some of which can introduce problems and sources of error into our work.[3] Below, I discuss seven such issues that were particularly salient in doing the research for this book, explaining some of the ways in which I grappled with and ultimately addressed each one.

Textual Data vs. Text-as-Data

First, and most generally, while most of the analyses in this book rely on "textual data," and although I draw on and am indebted to ideas and methods

associated with "text-as-data" approaches, I do not treat text as data in the
sense that data scientists and social science methodologists use this term.
As Kenneth Benoit explains, "textual data" is "text that has undergone selection and refinement for the purpose of more analysis." Treating text as
data, however "means converting [that text] into features of data and analysing or mining these features for patterns, rather than making sense of a
text directly."[4] Moreover, as Laura Nelson, Derek Burk, Marcel Knudsen,
and Leslie McCall explain, "in contrast to computer scientists and compu-
tational linguists," even social scientists who do take a "text-as-data" approach are typically less interested in "classifying a massive amount of text
into their dominant categories" than they are "in identifying complex, socially constructed, and unsettled theoretical concepts, often with ill-defined
boundaries, such as populism, rationality, ambiguity, and inequality" or, as is
the case in this book, crisis.[5] Nelson and her coauthors go on to explain that
the kind of "dictionary methods" (which they define as searching "through
a corpus of documents for a list of words or phrases predetermined by the
researcher") on which many of the analyses in this book rely are particularly appropriate "when specific phrases are of interest."[6] In their piece, for
example, they argue that "tracking the use of the term 'inequality'" can reveal "shifts in the way that the underlying concept of inequality is being represented," in ways that allowed them to explore whether "the deployment
of the inequality term itself has substantively meaningful consequences,"
such as "for understanding how public discourse reflects or shapes public
perceptions and views about inequality."[7] More generally, the combination
of dictionary method keyword searching and hand-coding allows for what
they describe as "a more flexible approach to identifying and classifying
subject matter that varies in form (i.e., the particular words or phrases used)
but not necessarily in content (i.e., the concept of interest)."[8]

Limits and Selectivity of Digitization

A second broad issue is that only a fraction of potentially relevant and
illuminating sources have been digitized or collected in systematic, comprehensive, and easily accessible formats and repositories. Particularly relevant to research addressing issues of power and marginalization is that
many of the biases in what is and is not available replicate long-standing
biases toward dominant sources and groups. For example, while the full
digitized corpus of the *New York Times* is accessible to researchers (it

is available from 1851–2015 through ProQuest Historical Newspapers, and ProQuest US Newsstream makes its full text available from 1980 through the present), full digitized runs of even the most prominent African American papers and magazines such as the *Chicago Defender* and the NAACP's *Crisis* magazine are far more difficult to access. Even when digitized copies of every issue in a publication's run can be located, scholars must often piece them together from different sources. As I note in chapter 2, for example, *The Crisis* magazine is available from 1910–1922 in PDF form via the Modernist Journal Project, and through 1923 from the Internet Archive. Later issues are available through Google Books, but that platform does not allow users to download or even to print the issues, so searches must be done online using the (not very flexible) Google Books interface. Similarly, the archive of national political party platforms available through the University of California, Santa Barbara's American Presidency Project (UCSB APP) is invaluable but includes platforms only of parties receiving electoral votes. As such, while it includes the platforms of some minor parties in some years (such as the Constitutional Union Party and the Southern Democratic Party in 1860, the Populist Party in 1892, the Progressive Party in 1912, and the States' Rights Party in 1948), it excludes the platforms of many minor parties.

The unevenness in digitation means more generally that the time periods covered by the data sources on which I draw vary considerably, and also that many are periodized in their own, somewhat different, ways. For example, the Google Books data summarized in figures 2.1 and 2.7 begin in 1810 and are classified by decade—"1810s," "1820s," and so forth. The *New York Times* data in figure 2.2 begin in 1851 and are classified as "1851–59," "1860–69," etc.).

Abundance of Digitization

Another digitization-related issue with implications for the research in this book is the flip-side of the foregoing one, which is that even with the acknowledged foregoing limitations, there is nonetheless an overabundance of searchable text. Scholars must therefore make decisions about which of the many available and relevant sources they will include, as every additional corpus requires extra time and resources for processing, cleaning, and analyzing text. Though I chose to focus my analysis in chapter 5 on economic reporting in the *New York Times* and the *Wall Street Journal*, for example, I could have conceivably included up to hundreds more individual sources or I could have used a collection of many sources such as the *Readers' Guide to Periodical Literature* (which, as I explain in chapter 5 and at greater length below, I did use to replicate several key searches and analyses). I also could have included analyses of news sources and policy deliberations in select states and localities. My decision to focus on two particularly important and revealing mainstream national newspapers was guided by several considerations. First, it reflects the emphasis that a keyword approach places on understanding the context in which words are used. While additional sources would certainly have added additional information, expanding the corpus in this way would have also made it more difficult to engage deeply with their substance in a manner that is in the spirit of a keyword approach.

My decision to focus on the *New York Times* and the *Wall Street Journal* also reflects my related attempt to conduct a keyword analysis in a way that also heeds the lessons of mixed-methods approaches, which encourage scholars to harness both the breadth that is possible through large-N research and the nuance available through more in-depth case studies. Treating the entire universe of relevant articles in these two newspapers as the population of interest for the analyses allowed me to combine text searching and computer-assisted coding with hand coding and close reading, bringing the lens up to identify trends as a "large-N" analysis allows and lowering it for the kind of detailed and context-sensitive discussions of illustrative and representative examples that are in the spirit of a qualitative keyword approach. And although some researchers argue that automated coding is less prone to the subjective assessments of human coders, Nelson and her coauthors remind us that automated and computer-assisted dictionary methods cannot be "mechanistically applied" either. Instead, "their output is typically tested by hand post facto," as hand coders typically "go back through a sample of the corpus to test the validity of the computer-assisted codes." As such, "dictionary and fully automated methods rely to a nontrivial degree on the judgment of the analyst to interpret and verify the results." In other words (and not unlike the credit scoring I discuss in chapters 4 and 5), automated methods do not "replace the human researcher in the content analysis workflow," and "regardless of technique, the researcher is making decisions every step of the way based on their deep substantive knowledge of the domain."[9]

Finally, my decision to draw specifically on the *New York Times* and the *Wall Street Journal* is based on their status as national news sources and "papers of record," which make them particularly important and appropriate parts of the transcript of dominant politics. As communications scholar Nikki Usher writes,

> *The Times* is a pivotal institution in American democracy. Since 1851, it has shaped the contours of elite political discussion and provided substantive reporting from across the world and the nation. . . . So why should we care about *The New York Times*? Fundamentally, *The New York Times* is a special place; its stature, its size, its place in the public imagination, and maybe even its sense of its own importance make its transition to the digital age notable. It has won more Pulitzer Prizes than any other newspaper (over one hundred and ten and counting). . . . Even for critics, *The New York Times* remains the most important newspaper in the United States.[10]

At the same time that the *New York Times* is distinct in these important ways, Frank Baumgartner, Suzanna De Boef, and Amber Boydstun also find that it tracks "closely with alternate papers," and argue that it can be treated as a representative source.[11] The *Wall Street Journal* is similarly considered the "financial newspaper of record."[12] In addition, while the *Wall Street Journal* does not capture the overtly racist vilification of subprime borrowers that characterized more extreme-right news outlets such as Fox News or the *New York Post*, the *Wall Street Journal* is nonetheless typically more conservative in both its news coverage and its editorial positions than the more centrist *New York Times*.[13] That the *Wall Street Journal* is typically less explicitly racist than other conservative outlets also makes it a harder test of my arguments about the ways in which race and gender were and were not at play in coverage of subprime mortgages and foreclosures than sources like Fox or the *New York Post*.

Challenges of Text Recognition

Fourth, like most technologies, optical text recognition (OCR) is far from perfect, and research suggests that some text-recognition errors occur in systematically problematic ways.[14] These errors are less pervasive in text that originates in digital form (although these sources can still contain misspellings and the like) than they are in sources that began as hard copies that were then scanned into PDFs (as is true of much of the *Congressional Record*) or sources that are transcripts of audio and video

FIGURE A.1. The "medial S."

recordings (also true of the oral portions of congressional hearings in the *Congressional Record*).

One particular issue that scholars have identified and that had implications for the research for this book has to do with OCR's tendency to misrecognize the "medial s" by confusing it for an "f" (see figure A.1). As Google explains in "What Does the Ngram Viewer do," "When we generated the original Ngram Viewer corpora in 2009, our OCR wasn't as good as it is today. This was especially obvious in pre-nineteenth century English, where the elongated medial-s (ſ) was often interpreted as an *f*."[15] For example, *best* was often read by OCR scanners as *beft*. Although the technology has improved significantly over the last decade, I avoided systematic errors by searching for *crifif* and *crifef*. Doing so produced only two hits in the many sources I use in this project (two congressional hearings, the first one from 1969 and the other from 1971), neither of which ended up being germane and neither of which has ended up in the data I compiled and analyzed.

Challenges of Working with PDFs

In addition, and as I note in chapter 2, PDFs are cumbersome, particularly when they are very long (many records of congressional hearings exceed 1,000 pages), and they are consequently difficult to work with. This is true even when it comes to more recent parts of the *Congressional Record*, in which the PDFs originated as digital text. Although the Government Printing Office (GPO) publishes online text versions of some hearings, these are available beginning only for those held in 1997. Moreover, even within this limited timeframe, the GPO does not publish all hearings. ProQuest is consequently the most compressive source of digitized congressional documents, but in the period during which I was doing the research and analyses for this project, it imposed an additional impediment by locking its PDFs so that they cannot be easily uploaded into data or text analysis and management programs. Although scholars could purchase text files and metadata derived from these PDFs, at the time that I conducted the research for this book, those data were prohibitively expensive and also required extensive processing before they could be usable. As a consequence, while it was possible to analyze the full text of some documents—such as the party platforms and State of the Union addresses that I use in chapter 2—doing so in some analyses of congressional hearings and bills proved prohibitive. Consultations with several colleagues who employ text analysis (including several data scientists) convinced me that the costs of the additional time and resources necessary to conduct full-text analyses of the use of *crisis* in the full text of congressional hearings would outweigh the additional benefits possible by analyzing its use in the titles of hearings and bills (although I do conduct full-text searches in the case of some of the more constrained searches in chapter 5). A full-text analysis would no doubt be revealing, and since ProQuest has recently begun to make the full text of these and other government sources more usable through TDM Studio, I hope to replicate the analyses of hearing and bill titles and summaries for the full text of these sources in the future.

Keyword Analysis vs. Keyword Searches and Keyword vs. Subject Searches

A sixth set of issues has to do with the term *keyword* itself. The first issue in this cluster of considerations is that this book contains frequent references to three uses of that term—*keyword analysis, keyword approach,* and *keyword search*—and relies heavily on keyword *searches* as the basis for its keyword *analyses.* The term *keyword analysis* describes an analytic approach that, as Bruce Burgett and Glenn Hendler write, tells a story about "how the meanings of words change through time and across space, how they have shaped our thinking," and how they are deployed in "relation to debates."[16] A *keyword search,* in contrast, is a tool "for information retrieval within various archiving systems," and the term describes the mechanics of using "natural language" to search sources such as databases or the internet to look for instances of particular words or phrases, either in the full text of documents or in particular search or metadata fields such as titles, abstracts, and even, in some cases, keywords.[17] Keywords can also be used in conjunction with Boolean searching, using operators such as AND, OR, and NOT to refine search terms and return more specific or germane results.

A second and related issue has to do with the tradeoffs between keyword searches and subject searches. As Pablo Barbera, Amber Boydstun, Suzanna Linn, Ryan McMahon, and Jonathan Nagler explain in a 2021 article, the ability to conduct keyword searches gives researchers more control, is more transparent, and returns more comprehensive results than is possible through subject classifications.[18] For example, a subject search for "subprime mortgage" in the *New York Times* from 1980 through 2006 returned only 17 results, compared with 72 using the keyword search. But keyword searches also typically sweep up a lot of irrelevant or redundant observations. To make sure to the extent possible that all observations included in all analyses were substantively germane, I went through the results of each search to identify and delete false positives as well as duplicate entries for the same observation, adjusting search parameters to minimize irrelevant observations and then going through the results again to eliminate any remaining problems before conducting analyses. In the case of the aforementioned search for articles about "subprime mortgages", for example, I determined that four of the original 72 observations returned for the *New York Times* from the period 1980 through 2006 and 21 of the original 210 for the *Wall Street Journal* were out of scope and were therefore excluded (see table 5.1).

I also relied on keyword searches of the full text of party platforms and State of the Union addresses (see tables 2.1, 2.2, and 2.3), and used ProQuest Congressional to conduct keyword searches of congressional hearings and bills for some of the more narrowly tailored searches I conducted, such as tracking use of the terms *subprime crisis, mortgage crisis,* and *foreclosure crisis.* Keyword searching the full text of these sources was too unwieldy for broader searches, however, such as for the unmodified terms *crisis, mortgage,* and *foreclosure.* In addition, ProQuest's subject terms do not include ones that would be necessary to use that feature to search the full text of these documents in an effective way. The subject coding done by the US Policy Agendas Project (USPAP), however, provided reliable and valid coding and measures to assess how much and what kind of attention dominant political actors devoted to these issues and how this has varied over time, which I present in tables 5.4 and 5.5. In the case of the use of the term *crisis,* I used ProQuest to search the titles of hearings and titles and summaries of bills (see figs. 2.8 and 2.10 and tables 3.1 and 3.2) and used Legacy CIS numbers (the only record indenti-fier variable common to both ProQuest and USPAP) to match each result with its coded US Policy Agendas Project entry. I provide a more detailed descriptions of my use of USPAP in appendix B.

Google Ngram Data

Several of the foregoing issues converge in debates about the reliability and validity of Google Ngram data. As Nadja Younes and Ulf-Dietrich Reips explain, the Google Books Ngram Viewer, known as Google Ngram, "is a search engine that charts word frequencies from a large corpus of books that were printed between 1500 and 2008," generating charts "by dividing the number of a word's yearly appearances by the total number of words in the corpus in that year."[19] Since its introduction in 2009, Ngram has be-come "a valuable tool for exploring . . . important socioeconomic trends and assessing public reactions to major natural or social events."[20]

But while Ngram has become "a widely used tool in the current 'com-putational turn' in many social sciences and humanities disciplines," schol-ars have also raised a range of concerns about it and possible biases in its data.[21] Alexander Koplenig has raised concerns, for example, about the fact that scientific texts—and, therefore, academic language—are over-represented in the corpus; about the lack of metadata about the books included the corpus (including information about the authors and titles that are included in it); that the data lag actual usage because books take longer to publish than other kinds of texts; and about the unevenness of the sampling of works spanning two centuries and the consequent over-representation of more recent texts.[22] In other words, as Eitan Pechenick, Christopher Danforth, and Peter Dodds argue, we cannot assume an un-biased sampling of books; they advise that "much caution must be used when employing these data sets to draw cultural conclusions from the fre-quencies of words or phrases in the corpus."[23]

Junyan Jiang, Tianyang Xi, and Haojun Xie acknowledge these con-cerns, but based on their own analyses and their review of several oth-ers, they contend that Google Ngram counts track closely with and are reliable indicia of real-world events.[24] Sean Richey and J. Benjamin Tay-lor, too, conducted a range of validity tests and argue that Ngram data have "content validity and can be used as a proxy measure for previ-ously difficult-to-research phenomena and questions" and can be effective proxies for novel, difficult-to-measure variables." Richey and Taylor argue that Ngrams should be thought of as "an extension of coding the running record, such as *The New York Times* and other notable newspapers," in this case, the "running record in books."[25] For my purposes, and as I explain in chapter 2, I treat the results of the Ngram and Google Books searches as initial and rough measures of language usage and as preliminary and general indicators of the introduction and trajectory of the term *crisis* as a staple of mainstream American political vocabulary. Similarly, I regard the differences among the incidence of *crisis, poverty*, and *accident* in figure 2.1 as evidence that the changes in the over-time use of the term *crisis* are not a function of general increases in the use of all words. I also try to follow Koplenig's suggestion that rather than characterizing claims based on Google Books data as evidence of "general linguistic or cultural change," scholars should "explicitly restrict any results to linguistic or cultural change 'as it is represented in the Google Books Ngram data.' "[26]

*   *   *

I acknowledge the implications of the foregoing issues, and I have tried to both present reasoned justifications for my choices about the sources and searches I use in each chapter and to acknowledge the limitations of any findings and my claims about them.

Sources, Methods, and Coding Protocols

Much of the research for this book relies on systematic searches and content analyses of text-based sources, and many of these analyses combine inductive and deductive approaches and a combination of keyword searches, "dictionary method" searching and coding, hand coding, and close reading. I discuss and describe most of the key methodological, search, and coding decisions in the body and footnotes of the relevant chapters. In what follows, I collect these discussions and descriptions and provide additional details about several coding protocols that were not appropriate for inclusion in the main text.

The Crisis Magazine: Coding Process and Protocol

As I note in chapter 2 and discuss briefly in appendix A, searchable PDF copies of *The Crisis* are available only from 1910–23 (from 1910–22 via the Modernist Journal Project and through 1923 from the Internet Archive). Although later issues are available through Google Books, it is not possible to download or scrape those issues, and so searches must therefore be done online using the Google Books interface and search engine. To code the use of the terms *crisis* and *crises* on the part of *Crisis* magazine writers, I therefore searched for each instance of those terms in all available PDFs from 1910–23 and in Google Books from 1924–59. After deleting eponymous references to the magazine itself, a research assistant used the following protocol to code each valid observation of terms *crisis* and *crises* in all issues of the magazine from that period, focusing on criteria including the type of article in which the term was used, type of issue to which it referred (domestic or international), whether the issue pertained to race/racial inequality, whether it was being used to describe a clear-cut crisis and/or in a way that suggests that the issue in question faced some kind of turning point, and if so, whether there is a call for government action or resources to address it.

1. #Crisis/es (not as reference to magazine itself): How many real instances or "hits?"
2. Crisis1Page#: On what page does the first instance appear?
3. Crisis1Text: Copy enough of the text of the place it's used to give a sense about its context.
4. Crisis1ArticleType: What kind of piece is it? Article? Editorial? Letter? Look at the extant entries for other possibilities.
5. Crisis1.FictionOrAd? (1=yes): Indicate whether the Article Type is an advertisement or piece of fiction or poetry.
6. Crisis1.Context&Description: Briefly describe the use.
7. Crisis1.TurningPointCriticalJuncture? (0=No, 1=Yes): Is the term being used in a way that suggests that the issue in question faced some kind of turning point?
8. Crisis1.Long-termIntoCriticalJuncture (0=No, 1=Yes): If so, is it some kind of long-term problem?
9. Crisis1.StateActionNecessaryOrJustified (0=No, 1=Yes): Is there some call for government action or resources to address the crisis?
10. Crisis1.Domestic (1) or International (2): Is whatever being described as a crisis a domestic issue or an international one?
11. Crisis1.AboutRace? (0=No, 1=Yes): Does whatever being described as a crisis have to do with race?

Corpora Project's Google Books Ngram Data

Figure 2.1 depicts data from Google Books (American). Rather than using Google's "Ngram" interface, I accessed the data through Brigham Young University's Corpora Project (corpus.byu.edu). BYU Corpora allow users to download and manipulate a wide range of textual data, including Google Books data. I compiled the data by searching the database for the following terms: "crisis OR crises", "accident", and "poverty". I chose to compare the incidence of the word *crisis* to other words to provide some visual context for its variation over time. Like *crisis, poverty* and *accident* are both nouns that have long been part of the English language: The *Oxford English Dictionary* records *poverty* as having entered English in 1225 and *accident* as having entered in 1395 (*crisis* entered a bit later, in 1545). The key point here, however, is that the differences among the levels of use of these three words provide strong evidence that the changes observed when it comes to *crisis* are likely not a function of general increases in the use of all words.

The *New York Times* and the *Wall Street Journal*

Chapters 2 and 5 make extensive use of evidence from the *New York Times* and the *Wall Street Journal*. Chapter 2 traces the evolution of crisis language and politics beginning in the nineteenth century, and the data in figure 2.2 were compiled by searching ProQuest Historical Newspapers database for the following terms in the titles of editorials or in articles appearing on the front page: "crisis OR crises", "accident", and "poverty". Note that because it proved prohibitive to tabulate the total number of editorials and front-page stories in the *New York Times*, unlike the data depicted in other figures, figure 2.2 depicts only the number of observations of the terms *crisis* and *crises* in these pieces and not the proportion of the total that they comprise.

I relied on ProQuest US Newsstream for all *New York Times* and *Wall Street Journal* data presented in chapter 5. As I explain in appendix A, I used keyword searches rather than ProQuest's or the newspapers' subject classifications for these searches. Unless otherwise specified, all *New York Times* and *Wall Street Journal* data presented in that chapter were drawn from searches of full text and titles of documents for all available years (beginning in 1980 for the *Times* and in 1982 for the *Wall Street Journal*). In the case of the *Wall Street Journal*, I further specified that the searches ignore items in several regular features—"New Securities Issues," "New Stock Listings," and "Bids and Offers"—as these are not substantive articles but rather, as their names suggest, simply listings of securities and stocks for sale and offers made to purchase companies.

I downloaded all of the resulting data and metadata into a spreadsheet and downloaded and cleaned the full text of all articles as well, using Nvivo and Linguistic Inquiry and Word Count (LIWC) to conduct keyword searches (a version of what Nelson and her coauthors call a "dictionary method") that generated analyzable data. As I explain in appendix A, searching by keyword gives researchers more control and returns more comprehensive results than subject searching, but also typically sweeps up a lot of irrelevant or redundant observations. Although the items returned through this approach are generally germane, they are also likely to include more "false positives" than would be returned by a subject search. To make sure to the extent possible that all observations included in all analyses were substantively germane, I went through the results of each search to identify and delete duplicate entries for the same observation and patterns of false positives, adjusting search parameters to minimize irrelevant observations and then going through the results again to eliminate any remaining problems before conducting analyses.

The particular keywords and specific search strings that I used are detailed in the endnotes and in the captions and notes for each table and figure, but details about the coding and data used in three tables bear elaboration here.

Coding Characterizations of Subprime Mortgage Lending and Rising Rates of Foreclosure

Tables 5.1 and A.3 depict the terms used to characterize the credit of borrowers who took out subprime mortgages and who lost their homes to foreclosure, comparing those characterizations used during the non-crisis era with those used during the crisis era. I used a two-step process to identify and code these data. First, I used ProQuest US Newsstream to search the *New York Times* and *Wall Street Journal* for "subprime NEAR mortgage" and "rising NEAR foreclosure" or "increasing NEAR foreclosure", which returns documents that contain the two search terms, in any order, within four words apart. After removing duplicate or irrelevant observations, I then used Nvivo to identify and compile a list of all descriptors accompanying "credit" in these articles and calculated the proportion of articles that contained any of these (mostly) bi-grams.

Determining and Coding Whether a Story Addresses Race and/or Gender

Tables 5.2 and A.3 include data indicating whether articles about subprime mortgages and about rising rates of foreclosures focused on the

TABLE A.I. *New York Times (NYT), Wall Street Journal (WSJ), Readers' Guide to Periodical Literature (RG), Ethnic NewsWatch (ENW), Alt-Press Watch (APW), and GenderWatch (GW) articles addressing subprime mortgages, increasing foreclosures, and mortgage, subprime, or foreclosure crisis, 1995–2008*

Year	Subprime mortgage[a]						Increasing foreclosures[b]						Mortgage, subprime, or foreclosure crisis[c]					
	NYT	WSJ	RG	ENW	APW	GW	NYT	WSJ	RG	ENW	APW	GW	NYT	WSJ	RG	ENW	APW	GW
1995	0	0	0	0	0	0	0	1	0	0	0	0	0	0	0	0	0	0
1996	0	2	2	0	0	0	0	0	0	0	0	0	2	1	0	0	0	0
1997	4	11	0	0	1	0	1	0	0	0	0	0	0	0	1	1	0	0
1998	7	8	4	3	1	0	0	0	0	0	0	0	0	0	0	1	1	0
1999	10	4	2	1	0	0	1	1	1	1	0	0	0	0	1	0	0	0
2000	22	6	2	12	5	0	0	0	0	2	0	0	0	0	0	1	0	0
2001	14	4	2	11	3	0	2	2	0	0	1	0	0	0	1	1	0	0
2002	13	3	3	14	15	0	2	3	1	2	2	0	0	0	0	0	1	1
2003	12	10	0	2	6	0	0	4	0	0	2	0	0	0	0	0	1	0
2004	10	9	1	3	4	0	1	0	0	2	1	0	0	0	0	0	3	0
2005	14	12	1	9	4	0	1	1	0	4	0	0	0	0	0	1	0	0
2006	27	30	6	14	7	0	2	10	3	6	6	0	1	0	0	0	3	0
2007	731	1805	236	148	100	2	186	247	12	28	20	0	239	319	75	57	41	1
2008	663	1156	368	229	302	16	345	367	24	56	23	3	565	546	228	243	281	12

[a] For the *New York Times, Wall Street Journal*, Ethnic NewsWatch, Alt-Press Watch, and GenderWatch, search was for "subprime N4 mortgage", which returns documents that contain the two search terms, in any order, within four words apart. *Readers' Guide* search was for "subprime N4 mortgage". After removing irrelevant observations, I then used Nvivo to identify and compile a list of all descriptors accompanying "credit" in these articles and calculated the proportion of articles that contained any of these (mostly) bi-grams.

[b] For the *New York Times, Wall Street Journal*, Ethnic NewsWatch, Alt-Press Watch, and GenderWatch, search was for "rising N4 foreclosure" or "increasing N4 foreclosure", which returns documents that contain the two search terms, in any order, within four words apart. *Readers' Guide* search was for "rising N4 foreclosure" or "increasing N4 foreclosure". After removing irrelevant observations, I then used Nvivo to identify and compile a list of all descriptors accompanying "credit" in these articles and calculated the proportion of articles that contained any of these (mostly) bi-grams.

[c] For all sources, search was for "'mortgage crisis' OR 'foreclosure crisis' OR 'subprime crisis' ".

Sources: ProQuest US Newsstream, ProQuest Ethnic NewsWatch, ProQuest Alt-Press Watch, ProQuest GenderWatch; *Readers' Guide to Periodical Literature Full Text Mega* (H. W. Wilson).

TABLE A.2. Correlations among *New York Times, Wall Street Journal, Readers' Guide to Periodical Literature*, Ethnic NewsWatch, Alt-Press Watch, and GenderWatch articles addressing subprime mortgages, increasing foreclosures, and mortgage, subprime, or foreclosure crisis, 1995–2008

	New York Times	Wall Street Journal	Readers' Guide
Subprime mortgages[a]			
New York Times	1.00	.984**	.959**
Wall Street Journal	.984**	1.00	.893**
Readers' Guide	.959**	.893**	1.00
Ethnic NewsWatch	.957**	.890**	.998**
Alt-Press Watch	.847**	.738**	.962**
GenderWatch	.730**	.596*	.894**
Increasing foreclosures[b]			
New York Times	1.00	.994**	.992**
Wall Street Journal	.994**	1.00	.985**
Readers' Guide	.992**	.985**	1.00
Ethnic NewsWatch	.913**	.984**	.996**
Alt-Press Watch	.973**	.974**	.956**
GenderWatch	.639*	.817**	.885**
Mortgage, subprime, or foreclosure crisis[c]			
New York Times	1.00	.991**	.996**
Wall Street Journal	.991**	1.00	.975**
Readers' Guide	.996**	.975**	1.00
Ethnic NewsWatch	.984**	.951**	.996**
Alt-Press Watch	.965**	.920**	.984**
GenderWatch	.947**	.894**	.971**

[a] For the *New York Times, Wall Street Journal*, Ethnic NewsWatch, Alt-Press Watch, and GenderWatch, search was for "subprime NEAR mortgage", which returns documents that contain the two search terms, in any order, within four words apart. *Readers' Guide* search was for "subprime N4 mortgage". After removing irrelevant observations, I then used Nvivo to identify and compile a list of all descriptors accompanying "credit" in these articles and calculated the proportion of articles that contained any of these (mostly) bi-grams.

[b] Search was for "rising NEAR foreclosure" or "increasing NEAR foreclosure", which returns documents that contain the two search terms, in any order, within four words apart. *Readers' Guide* search was for "rising N4 foreclosure" or "increasing N4 foreclosure". After removing irrelevant observations, I then used Nvivo to identify and compile a list of all descriptors accompanying "credit" in these articles and calculated the proportion of articles that contained any of these (mostly) bi-grams.

[c] For all sources, the search was for "'mortgage crisis' OR 'foreclosure crisis' OR 'subprime crisis'".

Sources: ProQuest US Newsstream ProQuest Ethnic NewsWatch, ProQuest Alt-Press Watch, ProQuest Gender-Watch, and *Readers' Guide to Periodical Literature Full Text Mega* (H.W. Wilson).

** Correlation is significant at the 0.01 level (2-tailed).

* Correlation is significant at the 0.05 level (2-tailed).

implications of such loans for people of color and for women. To determine whether an article addressed people of color or race and whether these issues could be said to be the story's focus, I used a two-step process to identify and code these data as well. First, I searched each relevant article and coded it "1" if it included (and "0" if it did not include) any of the following terms: *African American, American Indian, Asian American, Black, Hispanic, "inner city," Latino, minority/minorities, Native American.*

Similarly, to determine whether articles addressed women or gender and whether such issues were the focus of the story, I searched each relevant article and coded it "1" if it included (and "o" if it did not include): *female, gender, lady/ladies,* and *woman/women.* I also searched for the terms *discriminate* and *discrimination.*

After conducting these "dictionary" searches, I then read each story in which these terms were observed to determine whether it did, in fact, address these issues. An example of a story that was coded as focusing on race was one published on 14 November 1999 in the *New York Times* titled "Study Discerns Disadvantage for Blacks in Home Mortgages." An example of a story that was coded as addressing race in a *secondary* way was one published on 29 June 2000 in the *New York Times* titled "New State Rules Aim to Curb Loan Abuses." Though the story does not *focus on* people of color, it notes that "predatory lenders typically use high-pressure tactics to talk home-owners into exorbitant loans that often force them into bankruptcy or foreclosure. The most frequent victims are the elderly, women, and residents of minority neighborhoods."

To ensure to the extent possible that the patterns of attention to the issues in these two newspapers were representative of more general trends, I replicated several key searches using the *Readers' Guide to Periodical Literature.* I report the search results by year in table A.1 and the (strongly significant) correlations among the results for all three sources in table A.2.

Patterns of Attention in Publications Focused on Issues of Race, Gender, and Inequality

Among the key findings in part 1 of this book is that the word *crisis* entered the lexicon of domestic politics through movements of marginalized groups but that *crisis politics* is the creation and purview of dominant political actors. Nonetheless, as I have explained, advocates for and movements of marginalized groups have often tried to advance their goals by framing issues facing their constituents as crises or by attaching these issues to crises constructed by dominant political actors. While it is beyond the scope of the analyses and arguments in this book to examine these dynamics in depth, to explore whether the patterns of attention in publications focused on issues of race, gender, and inequality offered alternatives to those in mainstream reporting, I replicated several key searches using three additional ProQuest databases: (1) GenderWatch, a full-text database of over 300 scholarly and popular publications that focus on gender issues; (2) Alt-Press Watch, a full-text database of over 230 alternative and independent scholarly and popular publications; and (3) Ethnic NewsWatch, a full-text database of over 340 scholarly and popular publications covering "ethnic communities."[1]

As I discuss at greater length above in appendix A, databases such as these do not include all relevant and important periodicals and often do not include full runs of those that are included. In the case of Ethnic NewsWatch, I therefore specified that the searches include only newspapers and magazines, and only ones for which the database covered the full run of issues during the period of interest (1995 through 2008), and only those described as focusing on African American, Asian American, Latino, and Indigenous communities and on issues in the United States. In the case of Alt-Press Watch, I likewise restricted the search to news sources for which the database covered the full period (I also excluded the conservative publications that this database includes under its "alternative" label). The GenderWatch database's American newspaper and magazine holdings are far more limited than those in Ethnic NewsWatch or Alt-Press Watch, and so in that case, I did not limit the searches except to specify that they should include only magazines and newspapers.

The results of these searches and analyses are reported in tables A.1–A.3. The data in tables A.1 and A.2 make clear that the general levels of attention to these issues on the part of the news outlets included in these three databases are highly correlated with those for dominant economic reporting in the *New York Times*, *Wall Street Journal*, and *Readers' Guide to Periodical Literature*. For example, there is very little attention (and in the case of GenderWatch, no attention) to subprime mortgage lending and rising rates of foreclosure and very few instances (and in the case of GenderWatch, zero instances) of the terms *mortgage crisis*, *foreclosure crisis*, or *subprime crisis* from 1995–2006 followed by exponential increases in 2007 and 2008. Table A.3, however, illuminates both telling similarities and revealing differences in patterns of attention devoted to and characterization of subprime mortgages and foreclosures in news sources that center issues of race, gender, and inequality. For example, of the sixty-nine articles addressing subprime mortgages in the Ethnic NewsWatch database from 1995–2006, almost 65 percent used damning descriptors (such as *weak*, *poor*, *tarnished*, *damaged*, or *questionable*) to characterize the credit of people who took out such loans published, a proportion that is extremely similar to those in the *New York Times* and *Wall Street Journal* (this

	Ethnic NewsWatch			Alt-Press Watch			GenderWatch		
	1995–2006	2007	2008	1995–2006	2007	2008	1995–2006	2007	2008
Total number of stories about subprime mortgages during period (N)[a]	69	147	229	43	50	120	0	0	6
Percent of stories about subprime mortgages suggesting that they are sold to borrowers with bad (or "weak," "poor," "dicey," "tarnished," "rocky," "damaged," "questionable," "scuffed," or "no") credit	63.7%	36.7%	8.3%	46.5%	28%	17.6%	NA	NA	0
Percent of stories about subprime mortgages during period addressing people of color/race	60%	27%	26%	11.6%	4%	5.8%	NA	NA	50%
Secondary way	10%	23%	12.2%	20.1%	28%	11.7%	NA	NA	33%
Percent of stories about subprime mortgages during period addressing women/gender	2.8%	0%	0.8%	0%	0%	0%	NA	NA	83%
Secondary way	1.4%	2%	0.4%	0.2%	0%	1.6%	NA	NA	16%
Total number of stories about rising rates of foreclosures during period (N)[b]	16	28	56	10	12	10	0	0	0
Percent of stories about rising rates of foreclosures during period addressing people of color/race	37.5%	21.4%	17%	0%	16.7%	0%	NA	NA	NA
Percent of stories about rising rates of foreclosures during period addressing women/gender	0%	0%	0%	0%	8.3%	0%	NA	NA	NA
Total number of stories using terms *mortgage crisis, foreclosure crisis,* or *subprime crisis* during period (N)[c]	3	54	241	3	30	167	0	0	6
Percent of stories using terms *mortgage crisis, foreclosure crisis,* or *subprime crisis* during period addressing people of color/race	33%	27.8%	32.7%	33.3%	3.3%	4%	NA	NA	33%
Percent of stories using terms *mortgage crisis, foreclosure crisis,* or *subprime crisis* during period addressing women/gender	0%	1.8%	1.7%	0%	0%	0%	NA	NA	83%

Note: Data are organized to depict the periodization of two eras: (1) the non-crisis period that begins the year after the passage of HOEPA in 1995 and ends in 2006; and (2) the crisis period of 2007–8.

[a] Search was for "subprime NEAR mortgage", which returns documents that contain the two search terms, in any order, within four words apart. After removing irrelevant observations, I then used Nvivo to identify and compile a list of all descriptors accompanying "credit" in these articles and calculated the proportion of articles that contained any of these (mostly) bi-grams.

[b] Search was for "rising NEAR foreclosure" or "increasing NEAR foreclosure", which returns documents that contain the two search terms, in any order, within four words apart. After removing irrelevant observations, I then used Nvivo to identify and compile a list of all descriptors accompanying "credit" in these articles and calculated the proportion of articles that contained any of these (mostly) bi-grams.

[c] Search was for "mortgage crisis" OR "foreclosure crisis" OR "subprime crisis".

I used Nvivo to search articles retrieved through the foregoing searches, coding them as "1" if they included (and "0" if they did not include) the following terms: *African American, American Indian, Asian American, Black, Hispanic, "inner city," Latina, minority/minorities, Native American, female, gender, lady/ladies, woman/women, discrimination,* and *discrimination.* I read each story in which these terms were observed to determine whether it did, in fact, address people of color or race and women or gender. For additional information, see appendices A, B, and C, and note 21 in chapter 5.

Source: ProQuest US Newsstream, ProQuest Ethnic NewsWatch, ProQuest Alt-Press Watch, and ProQuest GenderWatch.

proportion also maps closely onto the results for the *Readers' Guide* replication).

While non-crisis-era levels of attention to subprime lending and fore-closures were as low as (and in the case of GenderWatch, seemingly lower than) they were in mainstream outlets, the substance of the coverage in Ethnic NewsWatch reveals that the publications included in that database were also far more likely to examine the implications of such loans for people of color during both periods, and that some of these difference are particularly pronounced during the non-crisis period (see table A.3; for details about how I determined and code whether a story addressed race or gender, see the previous section, "Determining and Coding Whether a Story Addresses Race and/or Gender"). For example, whereas only 15 percent of *New York Times* articles and 10 percent of *Wall Street Journal* articles about subprime mortgages published during the non-crisis period focused on their implications for people of color, this was true of 60 percent of stories about such loans published in the Ethnic NewsWatch articles during this era. And while only 1.8 percent of *New York Times* articles that used the term *mortgage crisis, subprime crisis,* or *foreclosure crisis* in 2007 focused on the racialized patterns in foreclosures, this was the case for 27.8 percent of analogous stories retrieved by the Ethnic News-Watch search. Similar patterns and disparities are evident across the other searches and years as well.

Articles in the Ethnic NewsWatch publications were also more likely during both the non-crisis and crisis periods to contextualize such credit problems as manifestations of discrimination, to note the possibility of more direct forms of state intervention, and to acknowledge that, zombie facts notwithstanding, many subprime borrowers did, in fact, qualify for "prime" mortgages. A 2006 article in *Mother Jones*, for example, noted:

> What began as a way for borrowers with poor credit to get loans, albeit at higher interest rates and with extra fees, has become a booming business that often targets customers who could qualify for less expensive "prime" mortgages but don't know it.[2]

It is perhaps not surprising that publications devoted to addressing issues that affect communities of color paid more attention to the racial implications of these issues than mainstream reporters. Indeed, Catherine Squires and others have shown that this has long been the case for African Americans newspapers. The differences in the extent to which and the ways in which these issues were addressed in these publications are nonetheless significant, however, as combined with the reports cited in chapter 4, these data provide additional evidence that the ways in which mainstream economic reporters framed these issues were not inevitable.

Although the data from the publications in Ethnic NewsWatch (and, to a lesser degree, in Alt-Press Watch) make clear that alternative understandings of the role of racism in subprime mortgage lending were available during both the non-crisis and crisis periods, these and other nondominant media provide almost no evidence of any such attention or alternatives when it comes to gender. As I note above, searching GenderWatch revealed no attention to subprime mortgage lending and rising rates of foreclosure and no instances of the terms *mortgage crisis, foreclosure crisis*, or *subprime crisis* during the non-crisis era. One exception to this near-ubiquitous rule was a very short piece that was published in the Black women's magazine *Essence* in 2001. Titled "Lending Traps!" the brief article explained:

> Got spotty credit? Need to borrow some quick cash? Beware! There's a growing industry of "fringe" finance companies eager to give you a no-credit-check loan with stick-'em-up interest rates—up to a 390 annual percentage rate (APR). Unsuspecting cash-strapped sisters are losing homes, cars and property to aggressive lending companies that prey on those whose credit histories are classified as subprime. Usury and disclosure laws in many states don't apply, because lawmakers have defined the interest charged as costs, according to the Public Interest Research Group. . . . If you have equity in your home, lenders will gladly make a high-interest loan based not on your ability to repay but on the equity. Monthly payments can often amount to nearly all your income, making foreclosure almost certain.[3]

This very short (and uncredited) piece is exceptional not only for making clear that Black women were being targeted by subprime lenders but also because it provides a fair bit of context and detail, explaining, for example, that subprime loans are unregulated and extractive. I could find almost no other evidence of such efforts, however.

In addition, of the sixty-nine articles returned in the Ethnic NewsWatch search for subprime mortgages from 1995–2006, only 2.8 percent noted anything about the ways in which gender might matter for this issue. And as in the case of their mainstream counterparts, I could identify no articles in these alternative sources that acknowledged that women who took out subprime mortgages had better rather than worse credit, on average, than their white male counterparts who took out prime loans. Also like their mainstream counterparts, even those non-crisis period articles that focused on the experiences of women borrowers failed to thematize gender as an axis along which these issues played out or to draw any connections to gender discrimination or inequality. Combined with the lack of evidence of any real attention to subprime mortgage lending and rising rates of foreclosure in the news sources included in GenderWatch, these elisions confirm and reinforce the more general failure to recognize the misogynist origins of and gendered patterns in rates of subprime lending and foreclosures as well as the implications of these problems for women during either the non-crisis or crisis period.

Coding Protocol for *New York Times* and *Wall Street Journal* Editorials and Op-Eds

Table 5.6 summarizes content-coded data from editorials and op-ed pieces addressing rising or increasing rates of foreclosure, noting whether and how they address the possibility of federal intervention. I retrieved all *New York Times* and *Wall Street Journal* editorials and op-ed pieces addressing rising or increasing rates of foreclosure, and, after deleting duplicates and false positives, a research assistant used the following protocol to code each valid observation to indicate whether it mentioned federal, state, or local intervention or the possibility for it and, for each positive observation, for whether these mentions are supportive, unsupportive, or neutral with regard to said intervention:

1. FedInt? (0=No, 1=Yes): Does piece mentions federal intervention or possibility for it?
2. ProFedInt (0=No, 1=Yes): Is the mention supportive of federal intervention?
3. AntiFedInt (0=No, 1=Yes): Is the mention unsupportive of federal intervention?
4. NoPosFedInt (0=No, 1=Yes): Does piece simply describe intervention without taking a position?
5. StateInt? (0=No, 1=Yes): Does piece mention state intervention or possibility for it?
6. ProStateInt (0=No, 1=Yes): Is the mention supportive of state intervention?
7. AntiStateInt (0=No, 1=Yes): Is the mention unsupportive of state intervention?

8. NoPosStateInt (o=No, 1=Yes): Does piece simply describe intervention without taking a position?

9. LocalInt? (o=No, 1=Yes): Does piece mention local intervention or possibility for it?

10. ProLocInt (o=No, 1=Yes): Is the mention supportive of local intervention?

11. AntiLocInt (o=No, 1=Yes): Is the mention unsupportive of local intervention?

12. NoPosLocInt (o=No, 1=Yes): Does piece simply describe intervention without taking a position?

13. Pro-IntText: Some lines of text illustrating pro-intervention position.

14. Anti-IntText: Some lines of text illustrating anti-intervention position.

Party Platforms, Congressional Hearings, Congressional Bills, and State of the Union Addresses

Chapters 2, 3, 4, and 5 use evidence from party platforms, congressional hearings, congressional bills, and State of the Union addresses. These data are drawn from full-text sources as well as from data available through the US Policy Agendas Project (USPAP).

In chapters 2 and 3, I use USPAP data to trace the evolution of crisis language and crisis politics beginning in the nineteenth century. To compile the data in tables 2.1 and 2.2 and figures 2.4a and 2.4b, for example, I downloaded the full text of all major party platforms from the University of California, Santa Barbara's American Presidency Project (UCSB APP), compiled by Gerhard Peters and John T. Woolley. After cleaning the text, I used Linguistic Inquiry and Word Count (LIWC) to search each platform for all instances of the terms *crisis* or *crises*, creating a spreadsheet with the contextualizing text for each observation (presented in table 2.1; figures 2.4a and 2.4b summarize the number of observations by year) and using Nvivo to code them substantively (see table 2.2).

I also used the full text of the platforms from the UCSB APP to compile the "first observations" data in table 2.3. The data in this table also use the full text files of all State of the Union addresses, which I downloaded from Brad Borevitz's State of the Union website (stateoftheunion.one twothree.net). With the help of research assistant Andrew Proctor, I coded the "first mentions" in these two sources using the "kwic" command (key words in context) in the R quanteda package. Doing so produces an output file that identifies the year, row in data, context before the word, and context after the word, from which bi-gram and tri-grams were identified.

This list was then sorted alphabetically and by source and year to identify the earliest observation for each bi-gram and tri-gram. I used the State of the Union text files to compile the data in figure 2.6 as well, searching these for and coding all instances of the terms *crisis* or *crises*.

As I explain above, it was not feasible at the time that I conducted this research to conduct analyses of the full text of congressional hearings and bills, so I instead used keyword searches of ProQuest Congressional to compile the data that track the use of *crisis/es* in the titles of congressional hearings (figure 2.4 and table 3.1) and bill titles and summaries (figure 2.5).

Chapter 5 likewise used both inductive and deductive approaches and a combination of systematic keyword searches, computer-assisted and hand coding, and close reading of both full-text sources and data from the US Policy Agendas Project, in this case to compare the amount and type of attention dominant political actors paid to subprime mortgage lending and housing foreclosures in the non-crisis and crisis eras. For example, as in the case of the *New York Times* and *Wall Street Journal* data, I searched the full text of all party platforms, State of the Union addresses, hearings, and bills for the terms *subprime mortgage*, *nonconforming mortgage*, and *predatory mortgage*, as well as the full text of all party platforms and State of the Union addresses for any instances of the words *mortgage* and *foreclosure*. Because of their limited numbers and manageable length, I was also able to read each platform and address to search for *any* discussion related to homeownership, coding those that address subprime mortgages and foreclosure.

Chapters 2 through 5 also used evidence that combines the data derived from the foregoing searches with data from the USPAP. I describe the steps that I used to code and assemble these data below.

US Policy Agendas Project

In several analyses, I combined the full-text searches described above with data from the US Policy Agendas Project. The University of Texas–based USPAP uses data from archived sources to classify the policy activities and outputs of a range of policy actors into 20 major topics and over 200 subtopics, allowing scholars to track and compare them over time. USPAP hearings, bills, party platforms, executive orders, and State of the Union data were invaluable to this project. In the case of bills and hearings, USPAP codes each document in its entirety. In the case of party platforms and State of the Union addresses, USPAP codes each "quasi-sentence" in each document.[4] (The USPAP is hosted by the University of Texas at Austin, where Bryan Jones is the principal investigator, and most of the data are collected there as well. The party platform data were collected by Christina Wolbrecht, and the congressional bill data were collected by E. Scott Adler and John Wilkerson.)

In chapter 2, I used these data to determine the topics to which dominant political actors attached crisis language and to track over-time shifts in this usage as one indicator of the evolution of *crisis politics*. More specifically, USPAP data allowed me to identify the topics addressed by each hearing and bill with *crisis* or *crises* in its title and the topic associated with each observation of these words in the full text of party platforms and State of the Union addresses. These data allowed me to track the absolute number of topics with which *crisis* is associated and to trace how these have changed over time, as well as to gauge their relative incidence compared to the proportions of the bills, hearings, and "quasi-sentences" in each State of the Union address and party platform as well. To do so, I first used ProQuest Congressional to search for the terms *crisis* and *crises* in bill and hearing titles. I then used the Legacy CIS numbers (the only record identifier variable common to both ProQuest and USPAP) to match these data with their coded USPAP entries, using a Python script to aggregate those to the year level. In the case of party platforms and State of the Union addresses, with the help of then-Policy Agendas Project Graduate Research Fellow Maraam Dwidar (later updated by Andrew Proctor), I created an indicator variable to identify instances of variations of the word *crisis/es* (*CRISIS, CRISES, Crises, Crisis, crises, crisis,* and so on) in USPAP party platforms and State of the Union data, and then aggregated those to the year level as well. I used these year-level data to calculate the percent of the bill titles and summaries (excluding private bills), hearing titles, platform statements, and State of the Union statements containing *crisis/es* by topic for all available years (which varied by data source), repeating this calculation for the period up to and then post 1967 (see figures 2.8–2.11 and table 3.2). Although USPAP hearings, Democratic Party platform, and State of the Union data are available through 2020, at the time of publication, the data for congressional bills were reliable only through only 2014 and were available for Republican Party platforms only through 2016. To keep the analyses relatively comparable, figures 2.8, 2.9, and 2.11 depict data through 2016 while figure 2.10 depicts data through 2015.

In chapter 3, I followed a similar procedure to collect and code the data in table 3.1, using the Legacy CIS numbers to match each result from the ProQuest hearing title search with its coded USPAP entry, and then using

USPAP topic codes to determine whether the issue being addressed in each hearing was primarily domestic.

The comprehensiveness of USPAP's coding of party platforms and State of the Union addresses made it possible to conduct an analysis of the subject of every observation of the word *crisis* or *crises* in the full text of each plank (in the case of platforms) or sentence (in the case of State of the Unions addresses) beginning in 1952 in the case of the former and 1946 in the case of the latter, and to track how these have changed over time, and to gauge their relative incidence as a proportion of the planks and quasi-sentences that address these topics as well. As I explained in appendix A, although I conducted full-text searches in the case of some of the more narrowly tailored searches in chapter 5, conducting analogous analyses of the use of the words *crisis* and *crises* in the full text of congressional hearings and bills proved prohibitive. The documents in these two sources are not only far more numerous and much longer, but at the time that I conducted this research, the full text of congressional bills and hearings was also available mainly through scanned PDFs that, as I explained previously, require extensive processing before they are usable.

In chapter 5, I used USPAP data to examine the ways in which dominant political actors addressed subprime mortgages, foreclosures, and issues related to mortgage lending and homeownership more generally. With help from Maraam Dwidar, we first searched USPAP data for bills, hearings, public laws, executive orders, and State of the Union address and party platform quasi-sentences for those falling under the following categories:

1400: General Community Development and Housing Issues

1401: Housing and Community Development

1403: Urban Economic Development and General Urban Issues

1404: Rural Housing and FmHA Housing Assistance Programs

1405: Rural Economic Development

1406: Low and Middle Income Housing Programs and Needs

1407: Veterans Housing Assistance and Military Housing Programs

1408: Elderly and Handicapped Housing

1409: Housing Assistance for Homeless and Homeless Issues

1410: Secondary Mortgage Market

1501: US Banking System and Financial Institution Regulation

1504: Consumer Finance, Mortgages, and Credit Cards

1525: Consumer Safety and Consumer Fraud

We dropped observations outside of the timeframe of interest (1980–2014) and created binary variables intended to identify whether each observation in each file discussed mortgage lending, subprime lending, predatory mortgages, homeownership and/or home buying, and/or foreclosure. We next coded each observation as either 0 or 1 for each of these five variables. These determinations were made by keyword searching each file for the following search terms and then spot-checking every tenth observation for accuracy:

- "mortgage"
- "subprime" "sub-prime" "sub prime"
- "'foreclos*' NEAR rising or increasing"
- For predatory lending: "predator*", "reverse redlining", "abusive NEAR mortgage", "unscrupulous lenders", or "usurious NEAR mortgage" (These five measures were aggregated into one variable that identified whether an observation mentioned either predatory mortgage-lending practices.)
- "homeown" and "home buy" (These two measures were aggregated into one variable that identified whether an observation mentioned either homeownership or home buying.)

We next ran cross-tabulations in Stata that returned a raw count of the total number of observations in each file pertaining to each topic by year (mortgage lending, subprime lending, predatory mortgages, and/or foreclosure, and homeownership/buying). We then used these counts to calculate two percentages: (1) the percentage of observations addressing mortgage lending, subprime lending, predatory mortgage lending, home buying/homeownership, and foreclosure in a given year as a percentage of *all* hearings, bills, laws, executive orders, and platform and State of the Union quasi-sentences in a given year (so, e.g., the total number of congressional hearings addressing subprime mortgages in 1998/total number of hearings conducted in 1998, and so on, for each year, each topic, and each source); and (2) the percentage of observations addressing mortgage lending, subprime lending, predatory mortgage lending, foreclosure, and home buying/homeownership in a given year as a percentage of hearings in each subtopic category (so, e.g., the total number of congressional hearings addressing subprime mortgages in 1998/total number of all hearings on the USPAP topics listed above; the executive orders turned up no attention to subprime lending and foreclosure, so they do not appear in the tables or figures).

Robustness Check

To be sure that our search parameters yielded accurate and unbiased observations and counts (i.e., that they included neither false positives nor false negatives), we also conducted a robustness check by repeating the foregoing steps for each of the foregoing searches, this time for all USPAP topics in the bills, hearings, public laws, party platforms, executive orders, and State of the Union address datasets. If our original search parameters— i.e., the search terms and USPAP topics we searched—were accurate, the robustness checks should have produced few additional observations, and any additional hits should not have been topically germane.

Happily, this is by and large what we found across all searches and data sources, evident in the correlations in table A.4, which reveals mainly negligible differences between the number of observations in the topic-specific searches used to collect the data for the substantive analyses and the counts in the searches across all USPAP topics. Figures A.2 to A.5

TABLE A.4. **Correlations among topic searches and robustness checks**

	Mortgage lending[a]	Subprime lending[b]	Foreclosure[c]	Predatory mortgages[d]
Hearings	0.99**	1.00**	1.00**	0.60**
Democratic platforms	0.98**	1.00**	0.94**	0.36
Republican platforms	0.89**	‡	0.91**	0.33
State of the Union addresses	0.92**	‡	1.00**	0.45**

‡ No observations in either the topic search or robustness check.
[a] Search was for "mortgage", i.e., the same terms used in figure A.2.
[b] Search was for "subprime", "sub-prime", and "sub prime", i.e., the same terms used in figure A.3.
[c] Search was for " 'foreclos*' NEAR rising or increasing", i.e., the same terms used in figure A.4.
[d] Search was for "predator*", "reverse redlining", "abusive NEAR mortgage", "unscrupulous lenders", or "usurious NEAR mortgage", i.e., the same terms used in figure A.5. Like figure A.5, the results of these searches were aggregated into one variable that identified observations mentioning predatory mortgage-lending practices.
** Correlation is significant at the 0.01 level (2-tailed).
Source: US Policy Agendas Project.

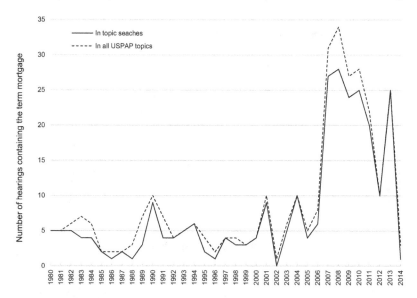

FIGURE A.2. Robustness check for USPAP search of congressional hearings addressing mortgage lending, 1980–2014. *Note:* The black line tracks mentions of the term *mortgage* in USPAP hearings data categorized by the US Policy Agendas Project's coding scheme as falling under 1400 (General Community Development and Housing Issues), 1401 (Housing and Community Development), 1403 (Urban Economic Development and General Urban Issues), 1404 (Rural Housing and FmHA Housing Assistance Programs), 1405 (Rural Economic Development), 1406 (Low and Middle Income Housing Programs and Needs), 1407 (Veterans Housing Assistance and Military Housing Programs), 1408 (Elderly and Handicapped Housing), 1409 (Housing Assistance for Homeless and Homeless Issues), 1410 (Secondary Mortgage Market), 1501 (US Banking System and Financial Institution Regulation), 1504 (Consumer Finance, Mortgages, and Credit Cards), and 1525 (Consumer Safety and Consumer Fraud). The dotted line tracks this term across all USPAP hearing topics. *Source:* US Policy Agendas Project.

likewise graph the results of the original substantive searches of the hearings data alongside the results of the robustness check searches, with almost indistinguishable trendlines in most cases. On the topic of subprime lending, for example, there is no difference between the original and robust data in the hearings or in either the Democratic or Republican Party platforms. In cases where the robustness check revealed major discrepancies, we did our best to determine whether the additional observations were germane and adjusted accordingly.

The one exception is the search results for predatory mortgage lending (see figure A.5), for which the correlations between the topic searches and the robustness checks are very low, and for which the trendlines do not overlap at all. These low correlations are due to the fact that, unlike most

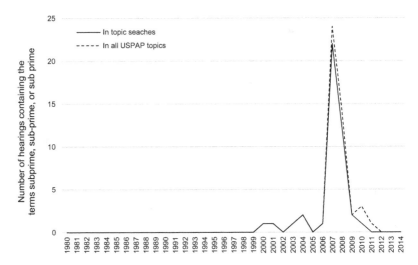

FIGURE A.3. Robustness check for USPAP search of congressional hearings addressing sub-prime mortgage lending, 1980–2014. *Note:* The black line tracks mentions of the terms *sub-prime, sub-prime, sub prime* in USPAP hearings data categorized by the US Policy Agendas Project's coding scheme as falling under 1400 (General Community Development and Housing Issues), 1401 (Housing and Community Development), 1403 (Urban Economic Development and General Urban Issues), 1404 (Rural Housing and FmHA Housing Assistance Programs), 1405 (Rural Economic Development), 1406 (Low and Middle Income Housing Programs and Needs), 1407 (Veterans Housing Assistance and Military Housing Programs), 1408 (Elderly and Handicapped Housing), 1409 (Housing Assistance for Homeless and Homeless Issues), 1410 (Secondary Mortgage Market), 1501 (US Banking System and Financial Institution Regulation), 1504 (Consumer Finance, Mortgages, and Credit Cards), and 1525 (Consumer Safety and Consumer Fraud). The dotted line tracks these terms across all USPAP hearing topics. *Source:* US Policy Agendas Project.

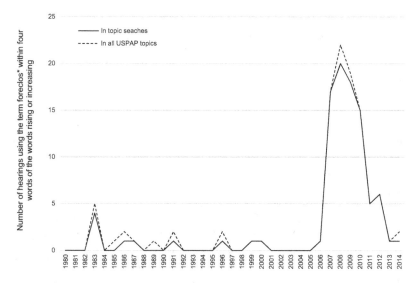

FIGURE A.4. Robustness check for USPAP search of congressional hearings addressing rising rates of foreclosure, 1980–2014. *Note:* The black line tracks mentions of the term "'foreclos*' NEAR rising or increasing" in hearings categorized by the US Policy Agendas Project's coding scheme as falling under 1400 (General Community Development and Housing Issues), 1401 (Housing and Community Development), 1403 (Urban Economic Development and General Urban Issues), 1404 (Rural Housing and FmHA Housing Assistance Programs), 1405 (Rural Economic Development), 1406 (Low and Middle Income Housing Programs and Needs), 1407 (Veterans Housing Assistance and Military Housing Programs), 1408 (Elderly and Handicapped Housing), 1409 (Housing Assistance for Homeless and Homeless Issues), 1410 (Secondary Mortgage Market), 1501 (US Banking System and Financial Institution Regulation), 1504 (Consumer Finance, Mortgages, and Credit Cards), and 1525 (Consumer Safety and Consumer Fraud). The dotted line tracks these terms across all USPAP hearing topics. *Source:* US Policy Agendas Project.

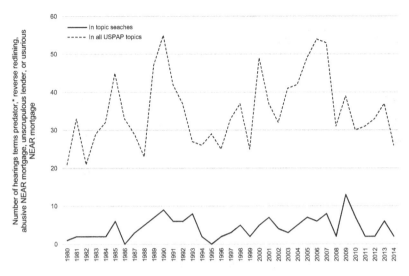

FIGURE A.5. Robustness check for USPAP search of congressional hearings addressing predatory mortgage lending, 1980–2014. *Note:* The black line tracks mentions of the terms "predator*", "reverse redlining", "abusive NEAR mortgage", "unscrupulous lender", and "usurious NEAR mortgage" in hearings categorized by the US Policy Agendas Project's coding scheme as falling under 1400 (General Community Development and Housing Issues), 1401 (Housing and Community Development), 1403 (Urban Economic Development and General Urban Issues), 1404 (Rural Housing and FmHA Housing Assistance Programs), 1405 (Rural Economic Development), 1406 (Low and Middle Income Housing Programs and Needs), 1407 (Veterans Housing Assistance and Military Housing Programs), 1408 (Elderly and Handicapped Housing), 1409 (Housing Assistance for Homeless and Homeless Issues), 1410 (Secondary Mortgage Market), 1501 (US Banking System and Financial Institution Regulation), 1504 (Consumer Finance, Mortgages, and Credit Cards), and 1525 (Consumer Safety and Consumer Fraud). The dotted line tracks these terms across all USPAP hearing topics. *Source:* US Policy Agendas Project.

of the other search terms, which are relatively specific to issues of housing and lending, the terms *predatory, abuse,* and *fraud* are frequently used with regard to several other policy issues. More specifically, the robust data included nongermane hearings about seven issues: (1) policies intended to address sexual predators; (2) predator threats to livestock (under agricultural policy); (3) predatory funds targeting developing countries; (4) drug/alcohol abuse; (5) domestic abuse; (6) identity/credit card/Medicare and Medicaid fraud; and (7) fraudulent trade practices. As such, while we might be troubled by this divergence in the case of our searches for *mortgage* or *subprime,* in this case we interpret this divergence as evidence that our search terms do a good job of retrieving only relevant observations.

Main Sources of Data and Evidence

B elow is a list of the main sources of newspaper, government, and political documents from which I compiled the data for this project:

1. The American Presidency Project, compiled by Gerhard Peters and John T.
   Woolley and hosted by the University of California, Santa Barbara: I downloaded the full text of all major party platforms, which are available beginning
   with the 1840 presidential election.
2. Corpora Project, compiled by Mark Davies and hosted by Brigham Young University (corpus.byu.edu): BYU Corpora allow users to download and manipulate a wide range of textual data, including Google Books data.
3. State of the Union (stateoftheunion.onetwothree.net), created by Brad Borevitz: State of the Union allows users to download the full text of all State of the
   Union addresses.
4. The US Policy Agendas Project (USPAP), Bryan Jones PI, hosted by the
   University of Texas at Austin: USPAP collects data from archived sources to
   trace changes in the national policy agenda and public policy outcomes, classifying policy activities into 20 major topics and over 200 subtopics allowing
   scholars to track and compare them over time. I also used the party platform
   data compiled by Christina Wolbrecht and the congressional bills data compiled by E. Scott Adler and John Wilkerson, both of which are hosted by
   USPAP.
5. *The Crisis* magazine: 1910–1922 from the Modernist Journal Project from the
   Internet Archive through 1923, and from Google Books for later dates.
6. ProQuest: I made extensive use of several ProQuest sources, including Pro-
   Quest US Newstream, ProQuest Ethnic NewsWatch, ProQuest Alt-Press
   Watch, ProQuest GenderWatch, ProQuest Historical Newspapers, and Pro-
   Quest Congressional.

7. *Readers' Guide to Periodical Literature*: Used to replicate several key searches and analyses in chapter 5.

8. Project Gutenberg: The full text of the *Federalist Papers* and of Thomas Paine's *The American Crisis*.

Supplementary Figures and Tables

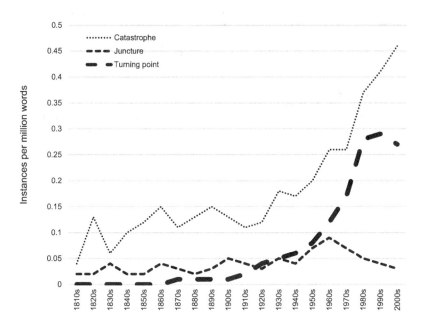

FIGURE A.6. Focus on the instances of the terms *catastrophe, juncture,* and *turning point* in English-language American books (per million words), 1810s–2000s, which were difficult to see in figure 2.7. *Note:* Search was for "catastrophe", "juncture", "turning point". *Source:* Mark Davies, 2011–. *Google Books Corpus* (based on Google Books Ngrams).

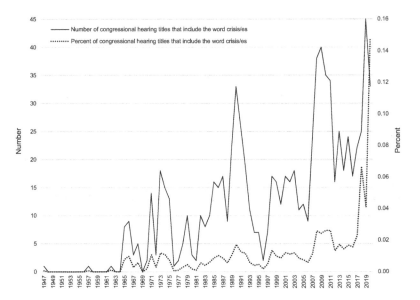

FIGURE A.7. Instances of the terms *crisis* and *crises* in the titles of congressional hearings (by year), 1947–2020 (number and as a percent of all hearings). *Notes:* Search was for "crisis" or "crises". ProQuest Congressional makes hearings searchable beginning in 1824, but figure begins in 1947 because there are no observations prior to 1947. *Source:* ProQuest Congressional.

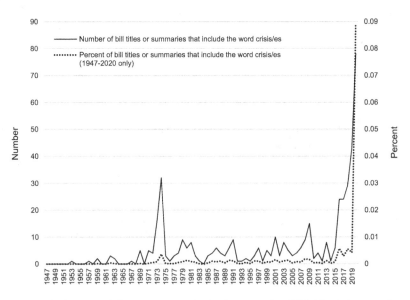

FIGURE A.8. Instances of the terms *crisis* and *crises* in congressional bill titles and summaries (by year), 1947–2020 (number and as a percent of all bills). *Notes:* Search was for "crisis" or "crises". *Source:* ProQuest Congressional.

Topics of bill titles and summaries, party platform quasi-sentences, and State of the Union quasi-sentences containing *crisis* **or** *crises*, **1965–79**

US Policy Agendas Project category	Bills		Party platforms		State of the Union addresses	
	N	% of titles containing *crisis/crises*	N	% of quasi-sentences containing *crisis/crises*	N	% of quasi-sentences containing *crisis/crises*
Agriculture	0	0	1	2.6	0	0
Banking, Finance, and Domestic Commerce	6	8.6	1	2.6	0	0
Civil Rights, Minority Issues, and Civil Liberties	0	0	0	0	0	0
Community Development and Housing Issues	0	0	8	20.5	1	4.5
Defense	13	18.6	6	15.4	5	22.7
Education	5	7.1	2	5.1	0	0
Energy	20	28.6	3	7.7	5	22.7
Environment	0	0	3	7.7	0	0
Foreign Trade	1	1.4	3	7.7	0	0
Government Operations	2	2.9	0	0	4	18.2
Health	2	2.9	0	0	0	0
Immigration	0	0	0	0	0	0
International Affairs and Foreign Aid	1	1.4	9	23.1	6	27.3
Labor, Employment, and Immigration	11	15.7	0	0	0	0
Law, Crime, and Family Issues	0	0	0	0	0	0
Macroeconomics	0	0	1	2.6	1	4.5
Public Lands and Water Management	0	0	0	0	0	0
Social Welfare	0	0	0	0	0	0
Space, Science, Technology, and Communication	0	0	0	0	0	0
Transportation	9	12.9	2	5.1	0	0
Total	70	100	39	100	22	100

Note: Search was for "crisis" or "crises". These data are a subset of those depicted in figures 2.9–2.11. The bills data were compiled by using the Legacy CIS numbers to match each result of each search with its coded US Policy Agendas Project entry. For additional information, see appendix B, appendix C, and notes 4, 18, and 19 in chapter 2.
Sources: ProQuest Congressional; US Policy Agendas Project.

Notes

Introduction

1. "Rahm Emanuel on the Opportunities of Crisis," video available at https://www.youtube.com/watch?v=_mzcbXi1Tkk.

2. Neil deMause, "The Recession and the Deserving Poor: Poverty Finally on Media Radar—But Only When It Hits the Middle Class," *Fairness and Accuracy in Reporting*, 1 February 2009, https://fair.org/extra/the-recession-and-the-deserving-poor/; Lani Guinier and Gerald Torres, *The Miner's Canary: Enlisting Race, Resisting Power, Transforming Democracy* (Cambridge, MA: Harvard University Press, 2002); John Kingdon, *Agendas, Alternatives, and Public Policies* (New York: Harper Collins, [1984] 1995). See also Sally J. Kenney, "Where Is Gender in Agenda Setting?" *Women & Politics* 25 (2003): 179–207; Barbara J. Nelson, *Making an Issue of Child Abuse: Political Agenda Setting for Social Problems* (Chicago: University of Chicago Press, 1984).

3. Following Bronwen Lichtenstein and Joe Weber, I use the terms "women as sole borrowers," "sole women," or "women alone" rather than "single women" or "unmarried women." Bronwen Lichtenstein and Joe Weber, "Women Foreclosed: A Gender Analysis of Housing Loss in the US Deep South," *Social & Cultural Geography* 16 (2015): 6.

4. Robert Cotterman, *New Evidence on the Relationship between Race and Mortgage Default: The Importance of Credit History Data*, Unicon Research Corp., 23 May 2002, https://www.huduser.gov/portal/Publications/PDF/crhistory.pdf; de Mause, "Deserving Poor"; "The State and the Nation's Housing 2009," Joint Center for Housing Studies of Harvard University (2009), http://www.jchs.harvard.edu/sites/jchs.harvard.edu/files/son2009.pdf.

5. Algernon Austin, *Uneven Pain* (Washington, DC: Economic Policy Institute, 2010); Lawrence Mishel et al., *The State of Working America* (Ithaca, NY: Cornell University Press, 2012).

6. Leah Bassel and Akwugo Emejulu depict a similar situation for women of color in France and Britain: "The 2008 economic crisis . . . is not necessarily a new

experience for these women. In pre-crisis France and Britain, minority women were already in precarious social and economic circumstances. Regardless of their educational outcomes, minority women were . . . more likely to be unemployed, underemployed or over-concentrated in low-skilled, low-paid, insecure employment. A striking feature of the crisis is that more privileged groups are now starting to experience the routine crises and precarity that minority women have long had to negotiate. On the other hand, however, crisis and austerity do represent an important change in the material circumstances of minority women. Due to the asymmetrical impacts of austerity, minority women are disproportionately disadvantaged by cuts to public spending thus sharpening and deepening their existing inequalities." Leah Bassel and Akwugo Emejulu, *Minority Women and Austerity: Survival and Resistance in France and Britain* (Bristol, UK: Bristol University Press, 2017), 1.

7. As Arjen Boin, Paul 't Hart, and Sanneke Kuipers write, "a crisis rarely, if ever, 'speaks for itself.'" Instead, "the definition of a situation is . . . the outcome of a subjective process" in which "crisis definitions are continuously subjected to the forces of politicization." Arjen Boin, Paul 't Hart, and Sanneke Kuipers, "The Crisis Approach," in *Handbook of Disaster Research*, ed. Havidán Rodríguez, William Donner, and Joseph E. Trainor (New York: Springer International, 2017), 29.

8. Bassel and Emejulu, *Minority Women and Austerity*, 40. Jeffrey Alexander makes a related but somewhat different point about what he calls the "societalization of social problems." How, he asks, do "endemic, ongoing institutional strains suddenly burst their sphere-specific boundaries and become explosive scandals in society at large?"

> Problems become crises, I suggest, only when they move outside their own spheres and appear to endanger society at large. I call this sense of broader endangerment, and the responses it engenders, "societalization." Societalization occurs when the discourses and material resources of the civil sphere are brought into play. It is only when sphere-specific problems become societalized that routine strains are carefully scrutinized, once lauded institutions ferociously criticized, elites threatened and punished, and far-reaching institutional reforms launched, and sometimes made."

"Societalization is blocked or stalled," however, "to the degree that those subject to institutional strain and dysfunction are subaltern groups" because "the strains they are subjected to, and the social techniques they have devised for addressing them, are invisible to, or ignored by, those whose perceptions are mediated by the communicative institutions of the dominant civil sphere and whose actions are regulated thereby." Jeffrey C. Alexander, *What Makes a Social Crisis? The Societalization of Social Problems* (Medford, MA: Polity Press, 2019), 3, 20.

9. E. E. Schattschneider, *The Semisovereign People* (New York: Holt, Rinehart and Winston, 1960); Frank Baumgartner and Bryan Jones, *Agendas and Instability*

in American Politics (Chicago: University of Chicago Press, 1993); Kingdon, *Agendas.* As Boin, Hart, and Kuipers write,

> before anything can be done to prevent a crisis from materializing, an emerging threat must be explicitly recognized. [But] threats to shared values or life-sustaining functions cannot always be recognized before their disastrous consequences materialize. As the crisis process begins to unfold, policy makers often do not see anything out of the ordinary. Everything is still in place, even though hidden interactions eat away at the pillars of the system. It is only when the crisis is in full swing and becomes manifest that policy makers can recognize it for what it is. . . . Even if consensus would exist that a serious threat is emerging, the status of this new problem is far from assured. Governments deal with urgent problems everyday; attention for one problem takes away attention from another. For a threat to be recognized as a crisis, it must gain sufficient societal and political attention to earn a place on overcrowded policy agendas.

Boin, Hart, and Kuipers, "Crisis Approach," 29.

10. Bassel and Emejulu define "routinised crises" as "persistent, institutionalised and ordinary hardships in everyday life." For example, they explain, "their persistently high unemployment and poverty rates are not 'exceptional' and not necessarily problems to be addressed, since they are indicators of capitalism, patriarchy and white supremacy operating as intended." Bassel and Emejulu, *Minority Women and Austerity*, 40.

11. Marc Raboy and Bernard Degenais, *Media, Crisis, and Democracy* (Thousand Oaks, CA: Sage, 1992); Antonio Vázquez-Arroyo, "The Antinomies of Violence and Catastrophe: Structures, Orders, and Agents," *New Political Science* 34, no. 2 (2012): 211–21; Antonio Vázquez-Arroyo, "How Not to Learn from Catastrophe: Critical Theory and the Catastrophization of Political Life," *Political Theory* 4, no. 1 (2013): 738–65.

12. Khalilah L. Brown-Dean, "From Exclusion to Inclusion: Negotiating Civic Engagement When Times are Always Hard" (paper presented at the 2010 Annual Meeting of the American Political Science Association, Washington, DC, 2–5 September 2010).

13. Ruth Wilson Gilmore, *Golden Gulag: Prisons, Surplus, Crisis and Opposition in Globalizing California* (Berkeley: University of California Press, 2007), 28. Michel Foucault contrasts endemics with epidemics. He defines the latter as "temporary disasters that caused multiple deaths" at "times when everyone seemed to be in danger of imminent death" and argues that their threat had "haunted political powers ever since the early Middle Ages." Endemics, in contrast, are "permanent factors . . . [that] sapped the population's strength, shortened the working week," and "cost money." This late eighteenth-century shift meant that death "was

no longer something that suddenly swooped down on life-as in an epidemic," but instead something permanent "that slips into life, perpetually gnaws at it, diminishes it and weakens it." Michel Foucault, *Society Must Be Defended* (New York: Picador, 2003), 243, 244.

Drawing on Foucault, Lauren Berlant describes slow death as the "physical wearing out of a population in a way that points to its deterioration as a defining condition of its experience and historical existence." Lauren Berlant, *Cruel Optimism* (Durham, NC: Duke University Press, 2011), 95. "The focus is on the articulation of the structural and the experiential. Not defining a group of individuals merely afflicted with the same ailment, slow death describes populations marked for wearing out" (278). Rob Nixon describes "slow violence" as "a violence that occurs gradually and out of sight, a violence of delayed destruction that is dispersed across time and space, an attritional violence that is typically not viewed as violence at all. It is incremental and accretive, playing out across temporal scales. The effects of slow violence are delayed such that the causes and the memory of catastrophe readily fade, making it difficult to secure effective legal measures for prevention, restitution, and redress." Robert Nixon, *Slow Violence and the Environmentalism of the Poor* (Cambridge, MA: Harvard University Press, 2011), 6–9. Scott Knowles uses the term "slow disaster" as "a way to think about disasters not as discrete events but as long-term processes" that stretch "both back in time and forward across generations to indeterminate points, punctuated by moments we have traditionally conceptualized as 'disaster,' but in fact claim much more life, health, and wealth across time than is generally calculated." 2020. Scott Knowles, "Slow Disaster in the Anthropocene: A Historian Witnesses Climate Change on the Korean Peninsula." *Daedalus* 149 (2020): 197.

14. Janet Roitman, *Anti-Crisis* (Durham, NC: Duke University Press, 2013), 39.

15. Sascha Engel, "A Crisis of Crisis Narratives?" *New Political Science* 36, no. 2 (2014): 266; Michel Serres, *Times of Crisis: What the Financial Crisis Revealed and How to Reinvent our Lives and Futures* (New York: Bloomsbury, 2014).

16. Reinhart Koselleck, "Crisis," *Journal of the History of Ideas* 67, no. 2 (2006): 399.

17. Koselleck, "Crisis," 399.

18. Peter Schuck, "Crisis and Catastrophe in Science, Law, and Politics: Mapping the Terrain," in *Catastrophe: Law, Politics, and the Humanitarian Impulse*, ed. Austin Sarat and Javier Lezaun (Amherst: University of Massachusetts Press, 2009), 19.

19. Roitman, *Anti-Crisis*, 3.

20. Roitman, *Anti-Crisis*, 3.

21. I am not arguing that the crisis frame is new. In the 1970s, for example, dominant political actors spoke about an "urban crisis"; in the 1980s and 1990s, they applied the term *crisis* to, inter alia, the Iranian revolution; HIV/AIDS; US military interventions in Panama, Haiti, Nicaragua; the first Gulf War; welfare;

and the United Nations. As I show in chapter 3, however, insofar as dominant political actors applied the term *crisis* to affected marginalized groups, it was more typically through discourses about, for example, "crime crises" or "urban crises" — presumptively race-neutral shorthands and coded language that have long worked to pathologize low-income marginalized populations of color. And to the extent that they have invoked crisis as a way to justify state action to address these issues, it has typically been in ways that have blamed and punished members of marginalized communities for creating problems that affect dominant groups. See Stuart Hall et al., *Policing the Crisis: Mugging, the State, and Law and Order* (London: Macmillan 1978); Willie Legette, "The Crisis of the Black Male: A New Ideology of Black Politics," in *Without Justice for All: New Liberalism and Our Retreat from Racial Equality*, ed. Adolph Reed (Boulder, CO: Westview Press, 1999); Thomas Sugrue, *The Origins of the Urban Crisis: Race and Inequality in Postwar Detroit* (Princeton, NJ: Princeton University Press, 1996); Keeanga-Yamahtta Taylor, *Race for Profit: How Banks and the Real Estate Industry Undermined Black Homeownership* (Chapel Hill: University of North Carolina Press, 2019).

22. Randolph Starn, "Historians and 'Crisis,'" *Past and Present* 52 (1971): 3–22. As Jonathon Catlin notes, Walter Benjamin and Theodor Adorno developed a theory of history as a "permanent catastrophe." Jonathon Catlin, "Catastrophe Now," *History and Theory* 60 (2021): 581.

23. Edgar Morin, "Pour une crisologie," *Communications* 25 (1976): 149. "Pour une crisologie" translates somewhat awkwardly in English to something along the lines of "an argument for the study of crisis." See also Alvin Gouldner, *The Coming Crisis of Western Sociology* (New York: Basic Books 1970).

24. Colin Hay, "Crisis and the Structural Transformation of the State: Interrogating the Process of Change," *British Journal of Politics and International Relations* 1, no. 3 (1999): 317–18.

25. Morin, "Crisologie," 149.

26. Austin Sarat and Javier Lezaun, eds., *Catastrophe: Law, Politics, and the Humanitarian Impulse* (Amherst: University of Massachusetts Press, 2009), 1.

27. Bruce Norton, "Economic Crises," *Rethinking Marxism* 25, no. 1 (2013): 10–22. See also Antonio Gramsci, *The Prison Notebooks* (New York: International, 1971), 276: "The crisis consists precisely in the fact that the old is dying and the new cannot be born; in this interregnum a great variety of morbid symptoms appear."

28. Norton, "Economic Crises," 10. Norton explains that while Marx and others such as Eduard Bernstein came to question the transformative potential of crises to shake the present in ways that would "unlock the future," "from the 1870s into the twenty-first century," other socialist thinkers (including, notably, Rosa Luxemburg), "took as their central task the demonstration that capitalist development inevitably produces ever-deepening crisis tendencies," ideas that continued to hold sway into the 1970s. Norton, "Economic Crises," 10–13. See also Herbert Marcuse on the anti-capitalist revolutionary potential of the "catastrophe of liberation."

Herbert Marcuse, *One-Dimensional Man: Studies in the Ideology of Advanced Industrial Society* (London: Routledge, 2006), 232.

29. Kevin Rozario, *The Culture of Calamity: Disaster and the Making of Modern America* (Chicago: University of Chicago Press, 2007), 3.

30. Milton Friedman, *Capitalism and Freedom* (Chicago: University of Chicago Press, [1962] 1982), xiv.

31. The frequency of pronouncements that we are in crisis may be matched only by declarations that "everything changed" or that we are observing the "biggest step forward."

32. Naomi Klein, *The Shock Doctrine: The Rise of Disaster Capitalism* (New York: Metropolitan Books 2007).

33. Rozario, *Culture of Calamity*, 3. In his description of the book, Rozario further attributes disaster's role to the ways in which "destruction leads naturally to rebuilding," making disasters "a boon to capitalism" and consequently "indispensable to the construction of dominant American ideas of progress".

34. Ian Bremmer, *The Power of Crisis: How Three Threats—and Our Response— Will Change the World* (New York: Simon and Schuster, 2022).

35. Baumgartner and Jones, *Agendas and Instability*; Thomas Birkland, *After Disaster* (Washington: Georgetown University Press, 1997); Thomas Birkland, *Lessons of Disaster* (Washington: Georgetown University Press, 2006); Michele Dauber, *The Sympathetic State: Disaster Relief and the Origins of the American Welfare State* (Chicago: University of Chicago Press, 2013).

36. Daniel Aldrich, "Fixing Recovery: Social Capital in Post-Crisis Resilience," *Journal of Homeland Security* 6 (2010): 1–10; Daniel Aldrich, "The Externalities of Social Capital: Post-Tsunami Recovery in Southeast India," *Journal of Civil Society* 8, no. 1 (2011a): 81–99; Daniel Aldrich, "The Power of the People: Social Capital's Role in Recovery from the 1995 Kobe Earthquake," *Natural Hazards* 56, no. 3 (2011b): 595–611; Daniel Aldrich, "Social, Not Physical, Infrastructure: The Critical Role of Civil Society in Disaster Recovery," *Disasters: The Journal of Disaster Studies, Policy and Management* 36 (2012a): 398–419; Daniel P. Aldrich, *Building Resilience: Social Capital in Post-Disaster Recovery* (Chicago: University of Chicago Press, 2012); Daniel Aldrich and Kevin Crook, "Strong Civil Society as a Double-Edged Sword: Siting Trailers in Post-Katrina New Orleans," *Political Research Quarterly* 61, no. 3 (2008): 279–389; Allen M. Omoto, Mark Snyder, and Justin D. Hackett, "Everyday Helping and Responses to Crises: A Model for Understanding Volunteerism" (Working paper, California University of Pennsylvania, 2011); Adam Berinsky, *In a Time of War* (Chicago: University of Chicago Press, 2009); Leonie Huddy and Stanley Feldman, "Americans Respond Politically to 9/11: Understanding the Impact of the Terrorist Attacks and their Aftermath," *American Psychologist* 66, no. 6 (2011): 455–67; Leonie Huddy, Stanley Feldman, and Christopher Weber, "The Political Consequences of Perceived Threat and Felt Insecurity," *Annals of the American Academy of Political and Social Science* 614

(2007): 131–53; Kingdon, *Agendas*; Theda Skocpol, "Will 9/11 and the War on Terror Revitalize American Civic Democracy?," *PS: Political Science and Politics* 35, no. 3 (2002): 537–40; Patricia Strach and Virginia Sapiro, "Campaigning for Congress in the '9/11' Era," *American Politics Research* 39, no. 2 (2011): 264–90; Elizabeth Zechmeister and Jennifer Merolla, *Democracy at Risk: How Terrorist Threats Affect the Public* (Chicago: University of Chicago Press, 2009).

37. Sanneke Kuipers, *The Crisis Imperative: Crisis Rhetoric and Welfare State Reform in Belgium and the Netherlands in the Early 1990s* (Amsterdam: Amsterdam University Press, 2006).

38. Klein, *Shock Doctrine*; Berinsky, *Time of War*; Zeichmeister and Merolla, *Democracy at Risk*; Leonie Huddy, Stanley Feldman, Charles Taber, and Gallya Lahav, "Threat, Anxiety, and Support of Antiterrorism Policies," *American Journal of Political Science* 49 (2005): 593–608; Steven Levitsky and Daniel Ziblatt, *How Democracies Die* (New York: Broadway Books, 2018); Darren W. Davis and Brian D. Silver, "Civil Liberties vs. Security: Public Opinion in the Context of the Terrorist Attacks on America," *American Journal of Political Science* 48 (2004): 28–46; Kenneth Lowande and Jon C. Rogowski, "Executive Power in Crisis," *American Political Science Review* 115 (2021): 1406–23; William G. Howell, Saul P. Jackman, and Jon C. Rogowski, *The Wartime President: Executive Influence and the Nationalizing Politics of Threat* (Chicago: University of Chicago Press, 2013); William G. Howell and Faisal Z. Ahmed, "Voting for the President: The Supreme Court during War," *Journal of Law, Economics, & Organization* 30 (2014): 39–71; Clinton Rossiter, *Constitutional Dictatorship: Crisis Government in the Modern Democracies* (New York: Transaction, [1948] 2005); Robert P. Saldin, "Executive Power and the Constitution in Times of Crisis," *White House Studies* 4 (2004): 489–504; Stephen M. Sales, "Threat as a Factor in Authoritarianism: An Analysis of Archival Data," *Journal of Personality and Social Psychology* 28 (1973): 44–57; Phillip E. Stebbins, "Truman and the Seizure of Steel: A Failure in Communication," *Historian* 34 (1971): 1–21; Albert L. Sturm, "Emergencies and the Presidency," *Journal of Politics* 11 (1949): 121–44.

39. Arjen Boin, Allan McConnell, and Paul 't Hart, *Governing after Crisis: The Politics of Investigation, Accountability, and Learning* (London: Cambridge University Press, 2008); Nolan McCarthy, Keith Poole, and Howard Rosenthal, *Polarized America: The Dance of Ideology and Unequal Riches* (Cambridge, MA: MIT Press, 2013); David Runciman, *The Confidence Trap: A History of Democracy in Crisis from World War I to the Present* (Princeton, NJ: Princeton University Press, 2013). In addition to this and other work in political science, history, sociology, and related disciplines, there are large bodies of both scholarly and applied research about what is often called "emergency management," "disaster management," or "crisis management." For example, the many periodicals on these and related topics include the *Journal of Contingencies and Crisis Management*, *Journal of Homeland Security and Emergency Management*, *Journal of Emergency Management*,

266 NOTES TO INTRODUCTION

Australian Journal of Emergency Management, International Journal of Mass Emergencies and Disasters, International Journal of Disaster Risk Reduction, Journal of Homeland Security, Disaster Prevention and Management, International Journal of Emergency Management, and *Journal of Disaster Research*. In addition, the Federal Emergency Management Agency (FEMA) maintains a Higher Education College List, which includes 350 Emergency and Disaster Management programs (324 in the United States alone). See https://training.fema.gov/hiedu/collegelist/. For essays that provide helpful overviews of much of this work, see, for example, Rodríguez, Donner, and Trainor, *Handbook of Disaster Research*. Ronald W. Perry's essay in that volume provides a very helpful history of disaster studies, and also traces its evolving definitions, from "accidental or uncontrollable events, actual or threatened" that "seriously disrupt normal activities" and lead to physical destruction to ones that emphasize their social aspects and the ways in which vulnerability to disaster can be modified through social change. Ronald W. Perry, "Defining Disaster: An Evolving Concept," in Rodríguez, Donner, and Trainor, *Handbook of Disaster Research*, 7–10. See also Kathleen Tierney, *Disasters: A Sociological Approach* (Medford, MA: John Wiley and Sons, 2019). See also, inter alia, Ben Wisner, Piers Blaikie, Piers M. Blaikie, Terry Cannon, and Ian Davis, *At Risk: Natural Hazards, People's Vulnerability and Disasters* (New York: Routledge, 2004).

40. Gwen Prowse, "Three Essays on Racialized Disaster and Grassroots Resistance in U.S. Politics" (PhD diss., Yale University, 2022), 3.

41. Bob Bolin and Liza Kurtz, "Race, Class, Ethnicity, and Disaster Vulnerability," in Havidán, Donner, and Trainor, *Handbook of Disaster Research*, 181–204.

42. Austin, *Uneven Pain*; Akwugo Emejulu and Leah Bassel, "Whose Crisis Counts? Minority Women, Austerity and Activism in France and Britain," in *Gender and the Economic Crisis in Europe*, ed. Johanna Kantola and Emanuela Lombardo (London: Palgrave Macmillan), 185–208.

43. William Sundstrom, "Last Hired, First Fired? Unemployment and Urban Black Workers during the Great Depression," *Journal of Economic History* 52, no. 2 (1992): 415–29.

44. Austin, *Uneven Pain*. Subtracting the rate of white unemployment (5.1) from the rate of Black unemployment (15.7) suggests that gap is 10.6 percent, but because of rounding, the number reported in *Uneven Pain* is 10.5 percent.

45. Reflecting their popular use and relatively equal prevalence, I use the terms *COVID-19 crisis* and *coronavirus crisis* relatively interchangeably. COVID-19 is the acronym given to "coronavirus disease 2019," which is the name of the disease caused by the novel coronavirus called "severe acute respiratory syndrome coronavirus 2," or SARS-CoV-2. https://www.who.int/emergencies/diseases/novel-coronavirus-2019/technical-guidance/naming-the-coronavirus-disease-(covid-2019)-and-the-virus-that-causes-it

46. Jamila Michener and Margaret Teresa Brower, "What's Policy Got to Do with It? Race, Gender & Economic Inequality in the United States," *Daedalus* 149 (2020): 100–118.

47. UN Women and David Snyder, "COVID-19 and the Care Economy: Immediate Action and Structural Transformation for a Gender-Responsive Recovery" (2020), https://www.unwomen.org/en/digital-library/publications/2020/06/policy-brief -covid-19-and-the-care-economy#view. In addition to these effects, Elaine Enarson, Alice Fothergill, and Lori Peek note that disasters often exacerbate gendered inequalities in mortality, health and well-being, and gender-based violence, as well as the heightened risks and vulnerabilities faced by LGBTQ people. See Elaine Enarson, Alice Fothergill, and Lori Peek, "Gender and Disaster: Foundations and New Directions for Research and Practice," in Havidán, Donner, and Trainor, *Handbook of Disaster Research*, 205–24.

48. Jeffrey Berry, *The New Liberalism* (Washington, DC: Brookings Institute Press, 1999); Bonnie Honig, *Emergency Politics: Paradox, Law, Democracy* (Princeton, NJ: Princeton University Press, 2009); Ronald Ingelhart, "The Silent Revolution in Europe: Intergenerational Change in Post-Industrial Societies," *American Political Science Review* 65, no. 4 (1971): 991–1017; Ronald Ingelhart, *The Silent Revolution: Changing Values and Political Styles in Advanced Industrial Society* (Princeton, NJ: Princeton University Press, 1977); Ronald Ingelhart, "Changing Values among Western Publics from 1970 to 2006," *West European Politics* 31, nos. 1–2 (2008): 130–46.

49. Lee Ann Banaszak, *Why Movements Succeed or Fail: Opportunity, Culture and the Struggle for Woman Suffrage* (Princeton, NJ: Princeton University Press, 1996); Tony Kennedy and David Phelps, "NWA Will Lay Off 10,000; $15 Billion Airline Aid OK'd," *Star Tribune*, 22 September 2001, 1.

50. Giorgio Agamben, *State of Exception* (Chicago: University of Chicago Press, 2005); Jill M. Bystydzienski, Jennifer Suchland, and Rebecca Wanzo, "Introduction to Feminists Interrogate States of Emergency," *Feminist Formations* 25 (2013): vii–xiii; Klein, *Shock Doctrine*; Berinsky, *Time of War*; Zeichmeister and Merolla, *Democracy at Risk*; Honig, *Emergency Politics*; Huddy, Feldman, Taber, and Lahav, "Threat, Anxiety, and Support"; Dara Strolovitch, "Advocacy in Hard Times," in *Nonprofit Advocacy*, ed. Steven Smith, Yutaka Tsujinaka, and Robert Pekkanen (Baltimore: Johns Hopkins University Press, 2014), 137–69; Levitsky and Ziblatt, *How Democracies Die*; Davis and Silver, "Civil Liberties vs. Security." See also Lowande and Rogowski, "Executive Power in Crisis"; Howell, Jackman, and Rogowski, *Wartime President*; Howell and Ahmed, "Voting for the President"; Rossiter, *Constitutional Dictatorship*; Saldin, "Executive Power"; Sales, "Threat"; Stebbins, "Truman"; Sturm, "Emergencies and the Presidency."

51. Kyle Whyte, "Against Crisis Epistemology" in *The Routledge Handbook of Critical Indigenous Studies*, ed. Brendan Hokowhitu, Aileen Moreton-Robinson, Linda Tuhiwai-Smith, Chris Andersen, and Steve Larkin (New York: Routledge, 2020), 52.

52. David Sanger, *The Inheritance: The World Obama Confronts and the Challenges to American Power* (New York: Broadway Books 2009), 448.

53. Whyte, "Against Crisis Epistemology," 52.

54. Stuart Hall et al., *Policing the Crisis: Mugging, the State, and Law and Order* (London: Macmillan, 1978).

55. David Pellow, "We Didn't Get the First 500 Years Right, So Let's Work on the Next 500 Years: A Call for Transformative Analysis and Action," *Environmental Justice* 2, no. 1 (2009), 4.

56. Birkland, *After Disaster*; Birkland, *Lessons of Disaster*; Thomas Homer-Dixon, *The Upside of Down: Catastrophe, Creativity, and the Renewal of Civilization* (Washington, DC: Island Press, 2010).

57. Kingdon, *Agendas*; Schattschneider, *Semisovereign People*.

58. Mary Dudziak, *Cold War Civil Rights* (Princeton, NJ: Princeton University Press, 2000); Eleanor Flexner and Ellen Fitzpatrick, *Century of Struggle: The Women's Rights Movement in the United States* (Cambridge, MA: Harvard University Press, 1996); Robert Grader, *A Scientific Model of Social and Cultural Evolution* (Kirksville, MO: Thomas Jefferson University Press, 1995); Philip Klinkner and Rogers Smith, *The Unsteady March* (Chicago: University of Chicago Press, 1999); Daniel Kryder, *Divided Arsenal* (New York: Cambridge University Press, 2001); David Mayhew, *Divided We Govern: Party Control, Lawmaking, and Investigations, 1946–2002* (New Haven, CT: Yale University Press, 2005); Gretchen Ritter, "Gender and Politics over Time," *Politics & Gender* 3, no. 3 (2007): 386–97.

59. Dauber, *Sympathetic State*; Dudziak, *Cold War*; Michael Goldfield, "Worker Insurgency, Radical Organizations, and New Deal Labor Legislation," *American Political Science Review* 83, no. 4 (1989): 1257–82; Ira Katznelson, *Fear Itself: The New Deal and the Origins of Our Time* (New York: Liverlight, 2013); Klinkner and Smith, *Unsteady March*; Julie Novkov, "Sacrifice and Civic Membership: Race, Gender, Sexuality and the Acquisition of Rights in Times of Crisis" (paper presented at the annual meeting of the Midwest Political Science Association, Chicago, IL, 22–25 April 2010); Christopher Parker, *Fighting for Democracy* (Princeton, NJ: Princeton University Press, 2009); Frances Fox Piven and Richard Cloward, *Poor People's Movement* (New York: Vintage Books, 1977); Theda Skocpol, *Protecting Soldiers and Mothers* (Cambridge, MA: Harvard University Press, 1992).

60. Flexner and Fitzpatrick, *Century of Struggle*; Mayhew, *Divided*; Skocpol, *Soldiers*; Eleanor Flexner, *Century of Struggle: The Woman's Rights Movement in the United States* (Cambridge, MA: Harvard University Press, 1959).

61. Rebecca Solnit, *A Paradise Built in Hell* (New York: Viking 2009); Martin Gilens, *Why Americans Hate Welfare* (Chicago: University of Chicago Press, 1999); Goldfield, "Worker Insurgency"; Leslie McCall, "Increasing Class Disparities among Women and the Politics of Gender Equity," in *The Sex of Class: Women Transforming American Labor*, ed. Sue Cobble (Ithaca, NY: Cornell University Press, 2007), 15–34; Suzanne Mettler, *Soldiers to Citizens* (New York: Oxford University Press, 2007); Parker, *Fighting for Democracy*; Piven and Cloward, *Poor Peoples Movement*; Skocpol, *Soldiers*; Skocpol, "War on Terror."

62. Matthew Roberts, "Emergence of Gay Identity and Gay Social Movements

in Developing Countries: The AIDS Crisis as a Catalyst," *Alternatives: Global, Local, Political* 20, no. 2 (1995): 243–64; Cathy Cohen, *The Boundaries of Blackness* (Chicago: University of Chicago Press, 1999).

63. Dauber, *Sympathetic State*, 257. See also Susan Sterett, "New Orleans Everywhere: Bureaucratic Accountability and Housing Policy after Katrina," in *Catastrophe: Law, Politics, and the Humanitarian Impulse*, ed. Austin Sarat and Javier Lezaun (Amherst: University of Massachusetts Press, 2009), 83–115. As Dauber's work helps to makes clear, disaster can function somewhat differently than crisis, as classification as a "disaster" has often had official force. For an account of the political construction of the related concept of "national calamity" in the United States and the role of the American Red Cross in its exportation, see Marian Moser Jones, *The American Red Cross from Clara Barton to the New Deal* (Baltimore: Johns Hopkins University Press, 2013).

64. Rozario, *Culture of Calamity*, 3.

65. Morin, "Crisologie," 149.

66. Leslie McCall, *The Undeserving Rich: American Beliefs about Inequality, Opportunity, and Redistribution* (New York: Cambridge University Press, 2013), 14. Jeffrey Alexander notes similarly that "a vast social science literature" conceptualizes "social reactions to social problems . . . as responses to objective, actually existing strain." Social science, he argues, "must attenuate the putative relationship between strain and response. It is not strains that generate social crises, but societalization, a process triggered by cultural logic and media representation." Alexander, *What Makes a Social Crisis?*, 111–12.

This way of thinking about crisis as an outcome is different from the way in which scholars such as McCarty, Poole, and Rosenthal treat crisis as endogenous by showing how politics and policies create the conditions that generate or exacerbate the conditions that we come to identify as economic crises. See Nolan McCarty, Keith Poole, and Howard Rosenthal, *Polarized America: The Dance of Ideology and Unequal Riches* (Cambridge, MA: MIT Press). It is also different from the way in which Desmond King conceptualizes "designated" crisis, which he describes as "an endogenous event or continuing problem deemed a crisis for political and electoral reasons." See Desmond King, "Against the State"(unpublished manuscript, n.d.): 11; Desmond King, "The American State and the Obama Presidency: A Preliminary Discussion," *DMS: Der Modern Staat* 5 (2011): 269–81. As Rachel Luft writes, "The social construction of disaster is a foundational concept in the sociology of disaster" in which scholars have argued that "disasters are fundamentally human constructs that reflect the global distribution of power and human uses of our natural and built environments," treating race and, more recently, gender as categories of "social vulnerability" within these distributions. Rachel E. Luft, "Racialized Disaster Patriarchy: An Intersectional Model for Understanding Disaster Ten Years After Hurricane Katrina," *Feminist Formations* 28 (2016): 7. For a review of scholarship addressing gender, sexuality, and disaster, see Enarson,

Fothergill, and Peek, "Gender and Disaster." For a review of scholarship addressing race, ethnicity, class, and disaster, see Bolin and Kurtz, "Race, Class, Ethnicity,"
181–204. Similarly, Andy Horowitz and Jacob A. C. Remes note in the introductory
essay to their 2021 edited volume *Critical Disaster Studies*, "scholars have come to
accept the once controversial maxim that there is no such thing as a natural disaster." Remes and Horowitz distinguish critical disaster studies from this work and
from "work in the field of disaster risk reduction and much of traditional disaster
studies in general" by insisting "that 'disaster' itself is an analytical conceit." That
is, "there are floods and earthquakes, wars and famines, engineering failures and
economic collapses, but to describe any of these things as a disaster represents an
act of interpretation." Jacob A. C. Remes and Andy Horowitz, "Introducing Critical
Disaster Studies," in *Critical Disaster Studies: New Perspectives on Disaster, Risk,
Vulnerability, and Resilience*, ed. Jacob A. C. Remes and Andy Horowitz (Philadelphia: University of Pennsylvania Press, 2021), 1–2.

Approaching the question of the role of disaster from a somewhat different perspective, Michele Dauber demonstrates the corollary to some of these claims, showing that the history of the federal government's disaster relief itself makes clear that
it has been defined to include "both natural and man-made disasters, including relief
for victims of the Whiskey Rebellion in western Pennsylvania and for various Indian
attacks on white settlers." In establishing claims for disaster relief," she continues,
"nature is less a gatekeeper than a particularly useful ally in making the case that
a loss was beyond the victim's control to prevent." Dauber observes further that
the "fluidity" around what constitutes a disaster means that we would "do better
to observe these contests over the meaning and content of the concept of disaster
than to enroll ourselves as partisans on one side or the other of the question of what
constitutes a true 'disaster.' " Dauber, *Sympathetic State*, 14. For more work on the
sociology of disaster, see Kai Erikson, *A New Species of Trouble: The Human Experience of Modern Disasters* (New York: Norton, 1994); Lawrence J. Vale and Thomas J.
Campanella, eds., *The Resilient City: How Modern Cities Recover from Disaster*
(New York: Oxford University Press, 2005); Kai Erikson, *Everything in Its Path: Destruction of Community in the Buffalo Creek Flood* (New York: Simon and Schuster, 1978); Charles Perrow, *Normal Accidents: Living with High-Risk Technologies*
(Princeton, NJ: Princeton University Press, 1999); Eric Klinenberg, *Heat Wave: A Social Autopsy of Disaster in Chicago* (Chicago: University of Chicago Press, 2003). For
a history of disaster management, see Scott. Knowles, *The Disaster Experts: Mastering Risk in Modern America* (Philadelphia: University of Pennsylvania Press, 2011).

67. As Pellow puts it, "Modern market economies are supposed to produce social
inequalities and environmental inequalities. Is this a crisis? That depends on whom
you ask." Pellow, "Call for Transformative Analysis," 4. See also Dara Strolovitch,
"Of Mancessions and Hecoveries: Race, Gender, and the Political Construction of
Economic Crises and Recoveries," *Perspectives on Politics* 13 (2014): 167–76.

68. Louis Althusser, "Ideology and Ideological State Apparatuses," *La Pensee*
151 (1970); Hall et al., *Policing the Crisis*.

69. On "societalization," see Alexander, *What Makes a Social Crisis?* Dauber makes a related point about disaster, writing that "the boundary between natural and man-made events has proven in practice to be of only secondary importance to decisions about whether to provide disaster relief," and that political actors, particularly Democrats, have tried to make the case that widely ranging events "constitute a force larger than and outside the control of their victims," such as proponents of the New Deal who represented "the 'Depression' as a national calamity overwhelming the ability of Americans to provide for themselves." Dauber, *Sympathetic State*, 14. That said, while Dauber demonstrates that, like crisis, disaster can also be constructed, it is also important that some definitions of both "disaster" and "emergency" have official force in a way that is not true of "crisis."

70. Iain White and Gauri Nandedkar, "The Housing Crisis as an Ideological Artefact: Analysing How Political Discourse Defines, Diagnoses, and Responds," *Housing Studies* 36 (2019): 214.

71. Hall et al., *Policing the Crisis*.

72. Hannah Arendt, *On Revolution*, 1963, 94, as quoted in Murray Edelman, *Political Language: Words that Succeed and Policies that Fail* (New York: Academic Press, 1977), 15–16.

73. Edelman, *Political Language*, 15–16.

74. Daniel Rodgers, *Contested Truths: Keywords in Politics* (Cambridge, MA: Harvard University Press, 1987).

75. Raymond Williams, *Keywords* (New York: Oxford University Press, 1976). This book makes frequent reference to the terms *keyword analysis*, *keyword approach*, and *keyword search*, and relies heavily on keyword *searches* as the basis for its keyword *analyses*. The term *keyword analysis* describes an analytic approach that, as Bruce Burgett and Glenn Hendler write, tells a story about "how the meanings of words change through time and across space, how they have shaped our thinking," and how they are deployed in "relation to debates." A *keyword search*, in contrast, is a tool "for information retrieval within various archiving systems," and the term describes the mechanics of using "natural language" to search sources such as databases or the internet to look for instances of particular words or phrases, either in the full text of documents or in particular search or metadata fields such as titles, abstracts, and even, in some cases, keywords. Keywords can also be used in conjunction with Boolean searching, using operators such as AND, OR, and NOT to refine search terms and return more specific or germane results. Bruce Burgett and Glenn Hendler, "Keywords: An Introduction," in *Keywords for American Cultural Studies*, 3rd ed., ed. Bruce Burgett and Glenn Hendler (New York: New York University Press, 2020), vii.

76. Williams, *Keywords*, 15.

77. Nancy Fraser and Linda Gordon, "'Dependency' Demystified: Inscriptions of Power in a Keyword of the Welfare State," *Social Politics: International Studies in Gender, State & Society* 1, no. 1 (1994): 5.

78. Rodgers, *Contested Truths*.

79. Fraser and Gordon, "Dependency" Demystified"; Hall et al., *Policing the Crisis.*

80. Patricia Strach, *All in the Family* (Palo Alto, CA: Stanford University Press, 2007); Sarah Churchwell, *Behold America: The Entangled History of "America First" and "the American Dream"* (New York: Basic Books 2018).

81. There has been, in recent years, a proliferation of edited "keyword" volumes on a wide range of general and more specialized areas. Many of these have been published as part of New York University Press's *Keywords* series, which includes volumes on African American studies, American cultural studies, Asian American studies, children's literature, disability studies, environmental studies, Latina/o studies, media studies, and a forthcoming volume on gender and sexuality studies. Keyword volumes on anti-capitalism, India, Southern studies, and big data have been published by other presses as well. None of these, however, include entries for "crisis." See Rachel Adams, Benjamin Reiss, and David Serlin, *Keywords for Disability Studies* (New York: New York University Press, 2015); Joni Adamson, William Gleason, and David Pellow, *Keywords for Environmental Studies* (New York: New York University Press, 2016); Bruce Burgett and Glenn Hendler, *Keywords for American Cultural Studies* (New York: New York University Press, 2007); Erica Edwards, Roderick Ferguson, and Jeffrey Ogbar, *Keywords for African American Studies* (New York: New York University Press, 2018); Kelly Fritsch, Clare O'Connor, and AK Thompson, *Keywords for Radicals: The Contested Vocabulary of Late-Capitalist Struggle* (Chico: AK Press, 2016); Craig Jeffrey and John Harriss, *Keywords for Modern India* (New York: Oxford University Press, 2014); Colin MacCabe and Holly Yanacek, *Keywords for Today: A 21st Century Vocabulary* (New York: Oxford University Press, 2018); Rukmini Bhaya Nair and Peter Ronald deSouza, *Keywords for India: A Conceptual Lexicon for the 21st Century* (New York: Bloomsbury Academic, 2020); Philip Nel, Lissa Paul, and Nina Christensen, *Keywords for Children's Literature*, 2nd ed. (New York: New York University Press, 2021); Laurie Ouellette and Jonathan Gray, *Keywords for Media Studies* (New York: New York University Press, 2017); Scott Romine and Jennifer Rae Greeson, *Keywords for Southern Studies* (Athens: University of Georgia Press, 2016); Cathy Schlund-Vilas, Linda Trinh Võ, and K. Scott Wang, *Keywords for Asian American Studies* (New York: New York University Press, 2015); Nanna Bonde Thylstrup, Daniela Agostinho, and Annie Ring, *Uncertain Archives: Critical Keywords for Big Data* (Cambridge, MA: MIT Press, 2021).

82. Hall et al., *Policing the Crisis*; Edelman, *Political Language*; Deborah A. Stone, "Causal Stories and the Formation of Policy Agendas," *Political Science Quarterly* 104, no. 2 (1989): 281–300; Joseph Gusfield, *Contested Meanings: The Construction of Alcohol Problems* (Madison: University of Wisconsin Press, 1996); Ange-Marie Hancock, *The Politics of Disgust* (New York: New York University Press, 2004); George Lakoff, *Moral Politics* (Chicago: University of Chicago Press, 1996).

83. To paraphrase Judith Butler, why are the bad things that happen to some

groups grievable, while bad things that befall others lead to outcomes such as punishment and blame? See Judith Butler, *Frames of War: When Is Life Grievable?* (New York: Verso, 2009). See also Julie Novkov, "Rights, Race, and Manhood: The Spanish American War and Soldiers' Quests for First Class American Citizenship" (2009), http://works.bepress.com/ulie_novkov/6/. Mary Dudziak (2012) asks a related set of questions about "wartime," arguing that it is far less discrete or defined than official indicators and "declarations" would suggest. See Mary Dudziak, *War Time: An Idea, Its History, Its Consequences* (NY: Oxford University Press, 2012). Note, too, that Reinhart and Rogoff's conception of crisis diverges from but overlaps with the one that I sketch here. Writing specifically about financial crises, those authors argue that Americans typically conceive of them as things that happen "elsewhere." See Carmen Reinhardt and Kenneth Rogoff, *This Time Is Different: Eight Centuries of Financial Folly* (Princeton, NJ: Princeton University Press, 2010).

84. Elizabeth Cohen, *The Political Value of Time: Citizenship, Duration, and Democratic Justice* (New York: Cambridge University Press, 2018).

85. See previous note 13. On endemics, see Foucault, *Society Must Be Defended*; Berlant, *Cruel Optimism*. On slow death, see Berlant, *Cruel Optimism*. On premature death, see Gilmore, *Golden Gulag*. On uneventful catastrophe and the everyday state of emergency, see Saidiya Hartman, "The Death Toll." *Los Angeles Review of Books*, 14 April 2020. Eva Horn writes similarly of "a catastrophe without disaster" and "a catastrophe without event." Eva Horn, *The Future as Catastrophe: Imagining Disaster in the Modern Age.* (New York: Columbia University Press, 2018). On routinized crises, see Bassel and Emejulu, *Minority Women and Austerity*, 40. On slow disaster, see Knowles, "Slow disaster." On slow violence, see Nixon, *Slow Violence*. On withheld violence, see Ariella Azoulay and Adi Ophir, "The Order of Violence," in *The Power of Inclusive Exclusion*, ed. Adi Ophir, Michal Givoni, and Sari Hanfi (New York: Zone Books 2009), 99–140. *Non-crisis* might also be understood as the way in which problems are treated before they are, in Alexander's terminology, "societalized." As he writes, "social strains are real; they have material consequences, and sometimes, as in economic crisis or war, such consequences can be very harsh indeed. Nonetheless, it is not the substance of strain that causes societalization but, rather, how such strains are understood." Alexander, *What Makes a Social Crisis*, 8. Or, as Walter Benjamin summed it up, "that things 'just go on' *is* the catastrophe." Walter Benjamin, "Central Park," *New German Critique* 34 (Winter 1985), 50.

86. Luft, "Racialized Disaster Patriarchy," 3.

87. On non-issues and suppressed issues, see Frederick Frey, "Comment: On Issues and Nonissues in the Study of Power," *American Political Science Review* 65, no. 4 (1971): 1081–1101; John Gaventa, *Power and Powerlessness* (Champagne: University of Illinois Press, 1980). On un-politics, see Matthew Crenson, *The Unpolitics of Air Pollution* (Baltimore: Johns Hopkins University Press, 1971). On semantically masked crises, see Edelman, *Political Language*, 47. On the idea that

issues are "organized into" or "out of" politics, see Schattschneider, *Semisovereign People*.

88. See, for example, Annie Menzel, "Crisis and Epistemologies of Ignorance" (paper presented at the American Political Science Association conference, Washington, DC, 2–5 September 2010); Paul Pierson, *Politics in Time* (Princeton, NJ: Princeton University Press, 2004); Shannon Sullivan, "White Ignorance and Colonial Oppression: Or, Why I Know so Little about Puerto Rico," in *Race and Epistemologies of Ignorance*, ed. Shannon Sullivan and Nancy Tuana (Albany: SUNY Press, 2007), 153–71; Vázquez-Arroyo, "How Not to Learn" and "Orders of Violence."

89. Rebecca Jordan-Young and Katrina Karkazis use "zombie facts" to describe "a fact that seemingly can't be killed with new research of even new models that would make old research irrelevant or subject to new interpretations." Zombie facts are particularly hard to "kill," they argue, when they have a "strong resonance between a scientific finding and familiar cultural stories, timed precisely at a moment when this new finding seems to answer an important social question." See Rebecca M. Jordan-Young and Katrina Karkazis, *Testosterone: An Unauthorized Biography* (Cambridge, MA: Harvard University Press, 2019), 54, 104. See also Monica Prasad, *The Land of Too Much: American Abundance and the Paradox of Poverty* (Cambridge, MA: Harvard University Press, 2012); Greta Krippner, *Capitalizing on Crisis: The Political Origins of the Rise of Finance* (Cambridge, MA: Harvard University Press, 2011); Greta Krippner, "Democracy of Credit: Ownership and the Politics of Credit Access in Late Twentieth-Century America," *American Journal of Sociology* 123 (2017): 1–47; Abbye Atkinson, "Borrowing Equality," *Columbia Law Review* 120 (2020): 1403–70.

90. As Nicola Smith writes, "'Crisis' is often understood as a material fact—as some kind of exogenous reality that must be responded to—rather than as a discursive construction through which neoliberal capitalism is being reforged. But neoliberal discourse might instead be understood as internal to the crisis itself, a part of the way in which the crisis becomes articulated and understood, indeed a language through which 'crisis' becomes recognized as such." Nicola Smith, "Toward a Queer Political Economy of Crisis," in *Scandalous Economics: Gender and the Politics of Financial Crises*, ed. Aida Hozić and Jacqui True (New York: Oxford University Press, 2016), 246.

91. With gratitude and apologies to Rabbi Harold Kushner, the title of this book—and of this section—takes its wording from the title of his 1981 best-selling book, *When Bad Things Happen to Good People* (New York: Schocken Books, 1981). The book addresses the broad question "why do the righteous suffer?" As Kushner writes in the preface to the twentieth-anniversary edition of the book, he wrote it, in part, to articulate what he had come to understand about "G-d's role in an unfair and pain-filled world," and that in the decades since its publication its title has "entered the language as the way to refer to world's unfairness."

92. "The same logic," Dauber continues, "that put $2,000 government-issued

debit cards into the hands of poor black residents of New Orleans propelled the success of welfare reform," based on the idea although they may not have been "responsible for the hurricane, surely they were responsible for their own poverty if they failed to become self-supporting after five years on welfare." Dauber, *Sympathetic State*, 15. See also, inter alia, Chester Hartman and Gregory Squires, *There Is No Such Thing as a Natural Disaster: Race, Class, and Hurricane Katrina* (New York: Routledge, 2006); and Paul Frymer, Dara Z. Strolovitch, and Dorian Warren, "New Orleans Is Not the Exception," *Du Bois Review* 3 (2006): 37–57.

93. Luft, "Racialized Disaster Patriarchy," 7.

94. Whyte, "Against Crisis Epistemology," 56–57.

95. Margot Canaday, *The Straight State* (Princeton, NJ: Princeton University Press, 2009); Cohen, *Boundaries of Blackness*; Novkov, "Sacrifice and Civic Membership"; Jasbir Puar, *Terrorist Assemblages* (Durham, NC: Duke University Press, 2007); Stratch and Sapiro, "Campaigning." See also M. David Forrest, *Giving Voice without Power? Organizing for Social Justice in Minneapolis* (Minneapolis: University of Minnesota Press, 2022).

96. Paula Treichler, *How to Have Theory in an Epidemic* (Durham, NC: Duke University Press, 1999), 1.

Chapter One

1. Barack Obama, "Guns Are Our Shared Responsibility," *New York Times*, 8 January 2016, A23. The only op-ed in that day's issue that did not make explicit references to a crisis was a column about North Korea's "nuclear threat."

2. The Crime Prevention Research Center defines "mass shootings" as ones in which four or more people are killed "in a public place, and not in the course of committing another crime, and not involving struggles over sovereignty." Crime Prevention Research Center, "Comparing Death Rates from Mass Public Shootings and Mass Public Violence in the US and Europe," 23 June 2015, http://crimere search.org/2015/06/comparing-death-rates-from-mass-public-shootings-in-the-us -and-europe/.

3. This piece was President Obama's sixth *New York Times* op-ed, his fourth while serving as president, and the only one that was published during his second term. President Obama's previous contributions had addressed a range of high-profile and controversial issues, including the threat posed by avian flu (2005, written while he was serving in the US Senate and coauthored with Senator Richard Lugar [R-IN]), his plan for Iraq (2008, written during his first presidential campaign), the Affordable Care Act (2009), expanding trade with Asia-Pacific Economic Cooperation countries (2010), and Southern Sudanese independence (2011). Of these six pieces, three invoked crisis to characterize the issues at stake.

4. See, for example, "Frustrated Obama on Oregon Shooting: 'We've Become Numb to This,'" *Chicago Tribune*, 2 October 2015, http://www.chicagotribune

.com/news/ct-obama-oregon-community-college-shooting-20151001-story.html; Jon Sopel, "Obama's 'Frustration' at US Gun Laws," *BBC*, 2 October 2015, http://www.bbc.com/news/av/world-us-canada-34427292/oregon-college-shooting -obama-s-frustration-at-us-gun-laws; Scott Horseley, "President Obama's Tone on Mass Shootings Grows More Frustrated," National Public Radio, 13 June 2016, https://www.npr.org/2016/06/13/481914458/president-obamas-tone-on-mass -shootings-grows-more-frustrated.

5. Daniel Rodgers, *Contested Truths: Keywords in American Politics Since Independence* (Cambridge, MA: Harvard University Press, 1987).

6. Rodgers, *Contested Truths*, 3.

7. Nancy Fraser and Linda Gordon, "A Genealogy of Dependency: Tracing a Keyword of the U.S. Welfare State," *Signs: Journal of Women in Culture and Society* 19, no. 2 (1994): 310; Pierre Bourdieu, *Outline of a Theory of Practice* (New York: Cambridge University Press, 1977).

8. Michel Foucault, "Nietzsche, Genealogy, History," in *The Foucault Reader*, ed. Paul Rabinow (New York: Pantheon), 76–100.

9. Fraser and Gordon, "Genealogy of Dependency," 310. Fraser and Gordon explain that their approach "differs from Foucault's, however, in two crucial respects: we seek to contextualize discursive shifts in relation to broad institutional and social-structural shifts, and we welcome normative political reflection."

10. "Grip," also spelled "grippe," is an archaic word for influenza or the flu.

11. John Kingdon, *Agendas, Alternatives, and Public Policies* (New York: Harper Collins [1984] 1995); Kyle Whyte, "Against Crisis Epistemology" in *The Routledge Handbook of Critical Indigenous Studies*, ed. Brendan Hokowhitu, Aileen Moreton-Robinson, Linda Tuhiwai-Smith, Chris Andersen, and Steve Larkin (New York: Routledge, 2020), 55. Elizabeth Cohen offers a related but different discussion about the ways in which understandings about time shape understandings of issues. Elizabeth Cohen, *The Political Value of Time: Citizenship, Duration, and Democratic Justice* (New York: Cambridge University Press, 2018).

12. Rodgers, *Contested Truths*, 3.

13. Justin Grimmer and Brandon Stewart, "Text as Data: The Promise and Pitfalls of Automatic Content Analysis Methods for Political Texts," *Political Analysis* 21, no. 3 (2011): 267. As I explain in greater detail in appendices A and B, while most of the analyses in this book rely on "textual data," and although I draw on and am indebted to ideas and methods associated with "text-as-data" approaches, I do not treat text as data in the sense that methodologists use this term. As Kenneth Benoit explains, textual data is "text that has undergone selection and refinement for the purpose of more analysis." Treating text as data, however "means converting it into features of data and analysing or mining these features for patterns, rather than making sense of a text directly." Kenneth Benoit, "Text as Data: An Overview," in *Handbook of Research Methods in Political Science and International Relations*, ed. Luigi Curini and Robert Franzese (Thousand Oaks, CA: Sage, 2020), 467, 491. See appendices A and B for more detail.

14. Grimmer and Stewart, "Text as Data," 267.

15. Rodgers continues, "If the words work. For the making of words is indeed an act, not a business distinct from the hard, behavioural part of politics thing people do. So by the same token, are the acts of repeating other people's words, rallying to them, being moved by them, believing them. The old dichotomy between behavior and ideas, intellectual history and the history of politics, shopworn with use, never in truth made much sense. Political talk is political action of a particular, often powerful, sort." Rodgers, *Contested Truths*, 5.

16. Shanto Iyengar, *Is Anyone Responsible? How Television Frames Political Issues* (Chicago: University of Chicago Press, 1991); Michael McCann, "Causal versus Constitutive Explanations (or, On the Difficulty of Being so Positive . . .)," *Law & Social Inquiry* 21 (1996): 457–82; Teun van Dijk, "What Is Political Discourse Analysis?," *Belgian Journal of Linguistics* 11, no. 1 (1997): 11–52. See appendices A and B for more detail about keyword analysis, critical discourse analysis, and my approach to textual analysis more generally.

17. Robert Entman, "Framing: Toward Clarification of a Fractured Paradigm," *Journal of Communication* 43, no. 4 (1993): 51–58. See also Erving Goffman, *Frame Analysis: An Essay on the Organization of Experience* (Cambridge, MA: Harvard University Press, 1974); Dennis Chong and James Druckman, "Framing Theory," *Annual Review of Political Science* 10 (2007): 103–26. Note, too, that many scholars argue and demonstrate that frames can and, under some conditions, do effect public attitudes and policy outcomes. See, for example, Frank R. Baumgartner, Suzanna L. De Boef, and Amber E. Boydstun, *The Decline of the Death Penalty and the Discovery of Innocence* (New York: Cambridge University Press, 2008); Leslie McCall, *The Undeserving Rich: American Beliefs about Inequality, Opportunity, and Redistribution* (New York: Cambridge University Press, 2013).

18. Murray Edelman, "Political Language and Political Reality," *PS: Political Science and Politics* 18, no. 1 (1985): 11.

19. Anne Larason Schneider and Helen Ingram, *Policy Design for Democracy* (Lawrence: University Press of Kansas 1997); Deborah Stone, "Causal Stories and the Formation of Policy Agendas," *Political Science Quarterly* 104, no. 2 (1989): 281–300; Ange-Marie Hancock, *The Politics of Disgust* (New York: New York University Press, 2004).

20. Lisa Wedeen, "Conceptualizing Culture: Possibilities for Political Action," *American Political Science Review* 94, no. 4 (2002): 714.

21. Lisa Wedeen argues that rhetoric and symbols "not only exemplify but also can produce political compliance," and that it is important to understand what terms such as *democracy* and *religion* mean to the political actors "who invoke or consume them and how these perceptions might affect political outcomes." Lisa Wedeen, "Conceptualizing Culture: Possibilities for Political Science," *American Political Science Review* 94, no. 4 (2002): 714.

22. Fraser and Gordon, "Genealogy of Dependency," 310.

23. Fraser and Gordon, "Genealogy of Dependency," 310.

24. Fraser and Gordon, "Genealogy of Dependency," 310.

25. Raymond Williams, *Keywords: A Vocabulary of Culture and Society*, new ed. (New York: Oxford University Press, [1976] 2015).

26. Williams, *Keywords*, xxvi; Tony Bennett et al., *New Keywords: A Revised Vocabulary of Culture and Society* (Malden, MA: Blackwell, 2005), xvii–xix.

27. Williams, *Keywords*, xxvi; Bruce Burgett and Glenn Hendler, *Keywords for American Cultural Studies* (New York: New York University Press, 2007), 2. In addition to shifting and adding meanings, Tony Bennett, Lawrence Grossberg, and Meaghan Morris argue that keywords also change "in relationship to changing political, social, and economic situations and needs," giving "expression to new experiences of reality." See Bennett et al., *New Keywords*, xvii.

28. Williams, *Keywords*, xxvii.

29. Williams, *Keywords*, xxvii.

30. Williams, *Keywords*, xxvii.

31. Bennett et al., *New Keywords*, xvii.

32. Bennett et al., *New Keywords*, xviii.

33. Bennett et al., *New Keywords*, xviii.

34. Bennett et al., *New Keywords*, xvii–xvix.

35. "Crisis," OED Online, https://www.oed.com/view/Entry/44539.

36. The exact wording in the online *Oxford English Dictionary* reads: "3. transf. and fig. A vitally important or decisive stage in the progress of anything; a turning-point; also, a state of affairs in which a decisive change for better or worse is imminent; now applied esp. to times of difficulty, insecurity, and suspense in politics or commerce (note especially the "now" in last clause).

37. Bennett et al., *New Keywords*, xix.

38. Williams, *Keywords*, xxxvi.

39. Bennett et al., *New Keywords*, xvii–xix.

40. This meaning is similar to the more general ways in which many scholars have defined crisis. For example, Uriel Rosenthal, Michael Charles, and Paul Hart define it as "a serious threat to the basic structures or the fundamental values and norms of a social system, which—under time pressure and highly uncertain circumstances—necessitates making critical decisions." Uriel Rosenthal, Michael Charles, and Paul Hart, *Coping with Crises: The Management of Disasters, Riots and Terrorism* (Springfield, MA: Charles C. Thomas, 1989), 10. Arjen Boin writes similarly that the term *crisis* is typically used as a "catch-all concept, which encompasses all types of 'un-ness' events" and "applies to situations that are unwanted, unexpected, unprecedented, and almost unmanageable, causing widespread disbelief and uncertainty." Arjen Boin, "From Crisis to Disaster," in *What Is a Disaster: New Answers to Old Questions*, edited by Ronald W. Perry and E. L. Quarantelli (Philadelphia: Xlibris), 161.

41. Arjen Boin gestures toward this idea when he writes that the "crisis concept . . . helps to remedy at least one problem inherent to the classic disaster definition: it not

only covers clear-cut disasters, but also a wide variety of events, processes and time periods that may not meet the disaster definition but certainly merit the attention of disaster students." Boin, "From Crisis to Disaster," 161.

42. Desmond King, "The American State and the Obama Presidency: A Preliminary Discussion," *DMS: Der Modern Staat* 5 (2011): 269–81; Desmond King, "The American State as an Agent of Race Equity: The Systemic Limits of Shock and Awe in Domestic Policy," in *Beyond Discrimination: Racial Inequality in a Post-Racial Era* (New York: Russell Sage Foundation 2013); Frances Fox Piven and Richard Cloward, *Poor People's Movements* (New York: Vintage Books, 1977).

43. Martin Luther King, Jr., "Letter from Birmingham Jail," *Liberation: An Independent Monthly* 8, no. 4 (1963): 10–16, 23.

44. Giorgio Agamben, *State of Exception* (Chicago: University of Chicago Press, 2005). See also Bonnie Honig, *Emergency Politics: Paradox, Law, Democracy* (Princeton, NJ: Princeton University Press, 2009); and Whyte, "Against Crisis Epistemology."

45. Frank Baumgartner and Bryan Jones, *Agendas and Instability in American Politics* (Chicago: University of Chicago Press, 1993); Kingdon, *Agendas*.

46. See, for example, Joseph Gusfield, *Contested Meanings: The Construction of Alcohol Problems* (Madison: University of Wisconsin Press, 1996); Stone, "Causal Stories"; Schneider and Ingram, *Policy Design for Democracy*.

47. Fraser and Gordon, "'Dependency' Demystified," 11. In these ways, crisis construction echoes some aspects of the "disaster narratives" that, Michele Dauber argues, policymakers used to justify welfare state expansion during the New Deal. She shows that President Franklin Roosevelt, for example, would often compare the Depression to floods or hurricanes. In this "compelling moral narrative of fault and blame," she writes, the Depression "was narrated as a 'disaster' whose victims were entitled to federal relief" because they suffered harm "through no fault of their own." But while disaster narratives emphasize deservingness and innocence as the basis for welfare state redistribution, crisis construction is concerned primarily with transforming understandings of ongoing conditions from ones that are natural, inevitable, and unresolvable into problems that can and should be solved through state intervention and resources. Michele Dauber, *The Sympathetic State: Disaster Relief and the Origins of the American Welfare State* (Chicago: University of Chicago Press, 2013), 14.

48. Janet Roitman, *Anti-Crisis* (Durham, NC: Duke University Press, 2013). Although Roitman does not use the term *keyword*, as I suggest in the text, her framework treats crisis in the spirit of one and offers some hints about how she views the rhetorical work that *crisis* does.

49. Fraser and Gordon, "Genealogy of Dependency," 324.

50. Lani Guinier and Gerald Torres, *The Miner's Canary: Enlisting Race, Resisting Power, Transforming Democracy* (Cambridge, MA: Harvard University Press, 2002), 11. As Guinier and Torres write,

Miners often carried a canary into the mine alongside them. The canary's more fragile respiratory system would cause it to collapse from noxious gases long before humans were affected, thus alerting the miners to danger. The canary's distress signaled that it was time to get out of the mine because the air was becoming too poisonous to breathe. Those who are racially marginalized are like the miner's canary: Their distress is the first sign of a danger that threatens us all. It is easy enough to think that when we sacrifice this canary, the only harm is to communities of color. Yet others ignore problems that converge around racial minorities at their own peril, for these problems are symptoms warning us that we are all at risk.... Starting with the experience of people of color we can begin to identify the crucial missing elements of American democracy—missing elements that make the system fail not just for blacks or Latinos but for other groups that are similarly situated. (11, 171)

51. Dara Strolovitch, *Affirmative Advocacy* (Chicago: University of Chicago Press, 2007), 31–32.

52. Desmond King, "Against the State" (unpublished manuscript, n.d.), 11. My argument about the ways in which crisis can be endogenous to politics encompasses King's argument that political actors designate events and problems as crises "for political and electoral reasons," but is also broader.

53. Edgar Morin, "Pour une Crisologie," *Communications* 25 (1976): 160.

54. Peter Schuck analyses the related concept of catastrophe, arguing that six features are present "in varying degrees in different cases": "magnitude, pervasiveness, uncertainty, preventability and responsibility, irreversibility, and crisis." Peter Schuck, "Crisis and Catastrophe in Science, Law, and Politics: Mapping the Terrain," in *Catastrophe: Law, Politics, and the Humanitarian Impulse*, ed. Austin Sarat and Javier Lezaun (Amherst: University of Massachusetts Press, 2009), 21–22. Richard Posner classifies four categories of the related concept of catastrophe: natural, scientific accidents, unintentional but man-made, and deliberate. See Richard Posner, *Catastrophe* (New York: Oxford University Press, 2004), 21–89.

55. Roitman, *Anti-Crisis*, 3.

56. Whyte, "Against Crisis Epistemology," 53.

57. Claus Offe, "'Crisis of Crisis Management': Elements of a Political Crisis Theory," *International Journal of Politics* 6, no. 3 (1976): 77–98.

58. Antonio Vázquez-Arroyo, "How Not to Learn from Catastrophe: Critical Theory and the Catastrophization of Political Life," *Political Theory* 41 (2013): 738; E. L. Quarantelli, *What Is a Disaster? Perspectives on the Question* (London: Routledge, 1998).

59. Quarantelli, *What Is a Disaster?*; Arjen Boin, Paul 't Hart, and Sanneke Kuipers, "The Crisis Approach," in *Handbook of Disaster Research*, ed. Havidán Rodríguez, William Donner, and Joseph E. Trainor (New York: Springer International, 2017); Boin, "From Crisis to Disaster."

60. Koselleck, "Crisis"; Morin, "Crisologie"; Schuck, "Crisis and Catastrophe"; J. B. Shank, "Crisis: A Useful Category of Post-Social Scientific Historical Analysis?," *American Historical Review* 113, no. 4 (2008): 1090–99; Vázquez-Arroyo, "How Not to Learn."

61. For examples of work that catalogues many definitions of crisis and offers a definitive one, see Boin, "From Crisis to Disaster." Boin also provides a particularly helpful approach to distinguishing between crisis and disaster, as well as some persuasive ways in these two concepts are related to one another.

62. Dauber, *Sympathetic State*, 14.

63. Amber Boydstun and Rebecca Glazier, "The Crisis Framing Cycle" (unpublished manuscript, n.d.); Rebecca A. Glazier and Amber E. Boydstun, "The President, the Press, and the War: A Tale of Two Framing Agendas," *Political Communication* 29 (2012): 428–46.

64. James Scott, *Domination and the Arts of Resistance: Hidden Transcripts* (New Haven, CT: Yale University Press, 1992); Laura Ann Stoler, "Colonial Archives and the Arts of Governance," *Archival Science* 2 (2002): 87–109.

65. As Williams writes in the introduction to *Keywords*, keywords are "the record of an inquiry into a vocabulary: a shared body of words and meanings in our most general discussions, in English, of the practices and institutions which we group as *culture* and *society*" (15).

66. Roitman, *Anti-Crisis*, 2. Or, as Iain White and Gauri Nandedkar write, how it is that "crises have become less of a one-off event and more of a modern lived condition that may never be 'solved' but rather redistributed politically." Iain White and Gauri Nandedkar, "The Housing Crisis as an Ideological Artefact: Analysing How Political Discourse Defines, Diagnoses, and Responds," *Housing Studies* 36 (2019): 215.

67. Ian Haney-Lopez, *Dog Whistle Politics: How Coded Racial Appeals Have Reinvented Racism and Wrecked the Middle Class* (New York: Oxford University Press, 2013); Eduardo Bonilla-Silva, *Racism without Racists* (New York: Rowman and Littlefield, 2013); LaFleur Stephens-Dougan, *Race to the Bottom: How Racial Appeals Work in American Politics* (Chicago: University of Chicago Press, 2020).

68. Burgett and Hendler, *Keywords for American Cultural Studies*, 3.

69. George Orwell, "Politics and the English Language," *Horizon* 13 (1946): 265; see also Morin, "Crisologie."

70. At the same time, although we often take as given that the reason we hear so much about crisis is because things are pretty bad, and although part of what crisis tries to do as a keyword is to raise the urgency of issues, it has also come to be tossed about more casually.

71. Rodgers, *Contested Truths*, 3.

72. Rodgers, *Contested Truths*, 5.

73. Barbara Melosh, *Gender and American History since 1890* (New York: Routledge, 1993).

74. Melosh, *Gender and American History*, 2.

75. Jacob A. C. Remes and Andy Horowitz, "Introducing Critical Disaster Studies," in *Critical Disaster Studies: New Perspectives on Disaster, Risk, Vulnerability, and Resilience*, ed. Jacob A. C. Remes and Andy Horowitz (Philadelphia: University of Pennsylvania Press, 2021), 4.

Chapter Two

1. Thomas Paine, *The American Crisis* (London: R. Carlile, [1776] 1819).
2. Figure 2.1 depicts data from Google Books (American), an interface that allows users to download and manipulate Google Ngram data. As Junyan Jiang, Tianyang Xi, and Haojun Xie explain,

> Google Ngram is a massive linguistic database that provides yearly counts for billions of words and short phrases (up to five words in length) from 28 million publications in Google Books' digital catalogue. The publications are drawn from the collections of Google's partner libraries . . . [and] are roughly evenly divided between (a) regular academic and popular books and (b) a diverse set of "non-book" items such as policy memos and reports, pamphlets, manuals, government documents, yearbooks, magazines, journals, and newspapers. . . . The Ngram database was initially developed to study the evolution of language and culture over time, but has turned out to be a valuable tool for exploring other important socioeconomic trends and assessing public reactions to major natural or social events. . . . Ngram has become a widely used tool in the current "computational turn" in many social sciences and humanities disciplines, such as history, linguistics, anthropology, sociology, communication, and cultural studies. However, it is still relatively under-used in political science.

Junyan Jiang, Tianyang Xi, and Haojun Xie, "In the Shadows of Great Men: Leadership Turnovers and Power Dynamics in Autocracies," *SSRN* (2020), 15–16, https://ssrn.com/abstract=3586255.

As I discuss at greater length in the appendices, scholars have raised concerns about the reliability and validity of Google Ngram data. Alexander Koplenig, for example, has raised concerns about the lack of metadata about the books included the corpus (including information about the authors and titles that are included in it); about the overrepresentation of scientific texts and, therefore, of academic language; about the unevenness of the sampling of works spanning two centuries and the consequent over-representation of more recent texts; and about the unknown implications of scanning only books that have "high optical character recognition scores." Alexander Koplenig, "The Impact of Lacking Metadata for the Measurement of Cultural and Linguistic Change using the Google Ngram Data Sets—Reconstructing the Composition of the German Corpus in Times of WWII," *Digital Scholarship in the Humanities* 32 (2017): 169–88.

Jiang, Xi, and Xie acknowledge these concerns, but based on their own analyses and their review of several others, they contend that Google Ngram counts track closely with and are reliable indicia of real-world events. Sean Richey and J. Benjamin Taylor, too, conducted a range of validity tests and argue that Ngram data have "content validity and can be used as a proxy measure for previously difficult-to-research phenomena and questions" and are "effective proxies for novel, difficult-to-measure variables." Sean Richey and J. Benjamin Taylor, "Google Books Ngrams and Political Science: Two Validity Tests for a Novel Data Source," *PS: Political Science & Politics* 53 (2020): 72. See also Eitan Adam Pechenick, Christopher M. Danforth, and Peter Sheridan Dodds, "Characterizing the Google Books Corpus: Strong Limits to Inferences of Socio-Cultural and Linguistic Evolution" in *PLoS ONE* 10, no. 10 (2015): e0137041.

Rather than using Google's own "Ngram" interface, I accessed the data through Brigham Young University's Corpora Project (corpus.byu.edu). BYU Corpora allow users to download and manipulate a wide range of textual data, including Google Books data. The data were compiled by searching the database for the following terms: "crisis OR crises", "accident", and "poverty". I chose to compare the incidence of the word *crisis* to other words to provide some visual context for its variation over time. Like *crisis*, *poverty* and *accident* are both nouns and have long been part of the English language: The *Oxford English Dictionary* records *poverty* as having entered English in 1225 and *accident* as having entered in 1395 (*crisis* entered a bit later, in 1545). The key point here, however, is that the differences among the levels of use of these three words provide strong evidence that the changes observed when it comes to *crisis* are likely not a function of general increases in the use of all words.

3. I used ProQuest Historical Newspapers database to compile the *New York Times* data. The data in figure 2.2 were compiled by searching for the following terms in the titles of editorials or in articles appearing on the front page: "crisis OR crises", "accident", and "poverty". Note that it proved prohibitive to tabulate the total number of editorials and front page stories in the *New York Times*. As a consequence, unlike the data depicted in other figures, figure 2.2 depicts only the number of observations of the terms *crisis* and *crises* in these pieces and not the proportion of the total that they comprise. I draw heavily on evidence from the *New York Times* here and in chapter 5, in part because its status as the "paper of record" makes it an important and appropriate part of the transcript of dominant politics. I say more about my decisions to use the *New York Times* and other sources in appendices A and B. See also Frank R. Baumgartner, Suzanna L. De Boef, and Amber E. Boydstun. *The Decline of the Death Penalty and the Discovery of Innocence* (New York: Cambridge University Press, 2008); Nikki Usher, *Making News at The*

New York Times (Ann Arbor: University of Michigan Press, 2014). Note that each data source covers a somewhat different time period, and that their periodization varies as well. For example, the Google Books data in figure 2.1 begin in 1810 and are classified by decade—"1810s," "1820s," and so forth. The *New York Times* data in figure 2.2 begin in 1851 and are classified as "1851–59," "1860–69," etc.).

4. I downloaded the full text of all major party platforms available from the University of California, Santa Barbara's American Presidency Project, compiled by Gerhard Peters and John T. Woolley. The first available platforms are from the 1840 presidential election. After cleaning the text, I used the software Linguistic Inquiry and Word Count (LIWC) to search each platform for the words *crisis* and *crises*, creating a spreadsheet with the contextualizing text for each observation (see table 2.1); figure 2.3 summarizes the number of observations by year. In addition to coding the full text, I also used party platform data compiled by Christina Wolbrecht and made available through the University of Texas's US Policy Agendas Project (USPAP). USPAP collects data from archived sources to trace changes in the national policy agenda and public policy outcomes, classifying policy activities into 20 major topics and over 200 subtopics, allowing scholars to track and compare them over time. In the case of bills and hearings, USPAP codes each document in its entirety. In the case of party platforms and State of the Union addresses, USPAP codes each "quasi-sentence" in each document. I describe USPAP at further length in the appendices and in notes 17–18 and 22 below. Figures 2.4 and 2.5 summarize data that I compiled using ProQuest Congressional to track the use of *crisis/es* in the full text and titles of bills and hearings. The data depicted in figure 2.6 were compiled by downloading the full text of all State of the Union addresses from State of the Union, stateoftheunion.onetwothree.net, created by Brad Borevitz.

5. Although neither party uses the word *crisis* again until 1916, the Republicans use the word *calamity* in their 1896 platform, in a section in which they condemn the tariffs imposed by Democratic administrations and Democrats' repeal of reciprocity arrangements "negotiated by the last Republican Administration" as constituting a "National calamity."

6. Jeffrey Berry and Sarah Sobieraj, *The Outrage Industry: Political Opinion Media and the New Incivility* (New York: Oxford University Press, 2014); Kenneth Cmiel, *Democratic Eloquence: The Fight over Popular Speech in Nineteenth-Century America* (Berkeley: University of California Press, 1990); Zoltan Kovecses, *Metaphor and Emotion: Language, Culture, and Body in Human Feeling* (New York: Cambridge University Press, 2000).

7. Susan Herbst, *Rude Democracy: Civility and Incivility in American Politics* (Philadelphia: Temple University Press, 2010); Kovecses, *Metaphor and Emotion*, 260–61. See also Daniel M. Shea and Alex Sproveri, "The Rise and Fall of Nasty Politics in America," *PS: Political Science & Politics* 45 (2012): 416–21.

8. Cmiel, *Democratic Eloquence*, 63.

9. Cmiel, *Democratic Eloquence*, 63–65.

10. From the definition of *evil* in the 1989 edition of the *Oxford English Dictionary*.

11. The 1900 Democratic platform similarly uses the word *evil* to decry monopolies and trusts. Even if political actors used the term *evil* in some contexts in which their late-twentieth century analogues might have used the term *crisis*, however, it is not used so frequently that it can said to constitute a replacement for *crisis*. Although presidents quite regularly used it in their State of the Union addresses, it did not appear in the title of a congressional hearing until 2002, for example, after which it was used only once more (in 2003) through 2016. It appeared in only twenty-four bill titles and summaries between 1789 and 1959, and only fourteen times in the text of party platforms from 1840 through 1956 (once in a Whig platform, four times in Democratic platforms, and nine times in Republican platforms).

12. In his history of disaster management, historian Scott Knowles shows that the terms *catastrophe, calamity, emergency,* and *crisis* are "often used interchangeably in the historical record" with disaster. I add *critical juncture, panic,* and *turning point* as other alternatives to crisis. Scott Knowles, *The Disaster Experts: Mastering Risk in Modern America* (Philadelphia: University of Pennsylvania Press, 2011), 18.

13. Like figure 2.1, figure 2.7 depicts data compiled using the Google Books (American) database supported by Brigham Young University's Corpora Project (corpus.byu.edu).

14. As Duane A. Gill and Liesel A. Ritchie explain,

> Under the dominant disaster paradigm in the U.S., federal government responses to natural disasters are the purview of the Federal Emergency Management Agency (FEMA) and guided by the Stafford Act. States have similar emergency management agencies and most local governments and communities have some form of emergency management.

Duane A. Gill and Liesel A. Ritchie, "Contributions of Technological and Natech Disaster Research to the Social Science Disaster Paradigm," in Rodríguez, Donner, and Trainor, *Handbook of Disaster Research*, 51. More generally, as Horowitz and Remes remind us,

> In many polities, a legal disaster declaration can authorize emergency action and facilitate funding. Denying that legal definition effectively inhibits government action or funding. The anticipation of disaster alone can give license for state and nonstate actions that might otherwise be absent, inform new modes of discourse and governance, and create new logics understood both by governors and the governed. To understand "disaster" as a discursive and political construction with material consequences

thus heightens the need to study how the category is constructed and understood, as well as how it is instantiated by law, politics, and society.

Jacob A. C. Remes and Andy Horowitz, "Introducing Critical Disaster Studies," in *Critical Disaster Studies: New Perspectives on Disaster, Risk, Vulnerability, and Resilience*, ed. Jacob A. C. Remes and Andy Horowitz (Philadelphia: University of Pennsylvania Press, 2021), 4.

15. Democratic Party Platforms, 1916 Democratic Party Platform Online by Gerhard Peters and John T. Woolley, The American Presidency Project, https://www.presidency.ucsb.edu/node/273203.

16. The Suez crisis was the Cold War battle in which Israeli, French, and British forces invaded Egypt, following Egyptian president Gamal Abdel Nasser's 1956 nationalization of the Suez Canal. The invasion prompted Soviet leader Nikita Khrushchev to threaten a nuclear attack on Western Europe. The Berlin crisis was another Cold War battle, this one over the occupation of that city that had begun in 1958 when Khrushchev demanded that Western powers withdraw in exchange for which the Soviets would cede control to East Germany.

17. For more information about the University of Texas–based US Policy Agendas Project (USPAP), see comparativeagendas.net.

18. In the case of bills and hearings, USPAP codes each document in its entirety. In the case of party platforms and State of the Union addresses, USPAP codes each "quasi-sentence" in each document. A quasi-sentence is "an argument which is the verbal expression of one political idea or issue." Thomas Daubler et al., "Natural Sentences as Valid Units for Coded Political Texts," *British Journal of Political Science* 42 (2012): 940.

The comprehensiveness of USPAP's coding of party platforms and State of the Union addresses made it possible for me to analyse the subject of every observation of the word *crisis* or *crises* in the full text of each plank (in the case of platforms) or sentence (in the case of State of the Unions addresses) (beginning in 1952 in the case of the former and 1946 in the case of the latter), to track how these have changed over time and to gauge their relative incidence as a proportion of the planks and quasi-sentences that address these topics as well. Conducting analogous analyses of the use of *crisis* and *crises* in the full text of congressional hearings and bills proved prohibitive (although I do conduct full-text searches in the case of some of the more narrowly tailored searches in chapter 5). The documents in these two sources are not only far more numerous and much longer, but at the time that I conducted this research, the full text of congressional bills and hearings was also available mainly through scanned PDFs. Although scholars could purchase text files and metadata derived from these PDFs, those data were prohibitively expensive and also require extensive processing before they are usable. After consulting with several colleagues who employ text analysis (including several data scientists), I was convinced that the costs of the additional time and resources necessary to conduct full-text analyses of the use of *crisis* would outweigh the additional benefits possible by analyzing its use in the *titles* of hearings and bills. A full-text analysis would no doubt be revealing, and since ProQuest has recently made the full text of these and other government sources more usable through TDM Studio, I hope eventually to replicate the analyses of hearing and bill titles and summaries for the full text of these sources in the future.

19. A "quasi-sentence" is "an argument which is the verbal expression of one political idea or issue." Daubler et al., "Natural Sentences as Valid Units," 940.

As comprehensive and indispensable as the USPAP data are, the congressional hearings and bills datasets do not include the titles of those documents. To compile the congressional hearings data in figure 2.8 and the bills data in figure 2.10, I therefore first used ProQuest to search for the terms *crisis* and *crises* in hearing and bill titles. I then used the Legacy CIS numbers (the only record identifier variable common to both ProQuest and USPAP) to match each result from the ProQuest hearing and bill title searches with its coded USPAP entry, using a Python script to aggregate those to the year level. In the case of party platforms and State of the Union addresses, I created an indicator variable to identify instances of all possible variations of the word *crisis* and *crises* (*CRISIS, CRISES, Crises, Crisis, crises, crisis,* and so on) in USPAP party platforms and State of the Union data, and then aggregated those up to the year level as well. I then used these year-level data to calculate the percent of the bill titles and summaries, hearing titles, platform statements, and State of the Union statements containing *crisis/es* by topic for all available years (which varied by data source), repeating this calculation first for the period up to 1967 and then for the post-1967 period.

In addition, although USPAP hearings, Democratic Party platform, and State of the Union data are available through 2020, at the time of publication, data for congressional bills were reliable through only 2014 and were available for Republican Party platforms only through 2016. To keep the analyses relatively comparable, figures 2.8, 2.9, and 2.11 depict data through 2016 while figure 2.10 depicts data through 2014.

20. Carmen Reinhardt and Kenneth Rogoff, *This Time Is Different: Eight Centuries of Financial Folly* (Princeton, NJ: Princeton University Press, 2010).

21. These five USPAP topics were Government Operations; International Affairs and Foreign Aid; Law, Crime, and Family Issues; Public Lands and Water Management; and Transportation.

22. The congressional hearings data in figure 2.8 and the State of the Union data in figure 2.10 were collected by the Policy Agendas Project at the University of Texas at Austin. The party platform data in figure 2.9 were collected by Christina Wolbrecht and are made possible in part by support from the Institute for Scholarship in the Liberal Arts (ISLA), College of Arts & Letters, University of Notre Dame. Neither ISLA nor the original collectors of the data bear any responsibility

for the analysis reported here. The congressional bill data in figure 2.10 were collected by E. Scott Adler and John Wilkerson, Congressional Bills Project: (1947–
2015), NSF 00880066 and 00880061. The views expressed are those of the authors
and not the National Science Foundation.

23. Murray Edelman, *Political Language: Words That Succeed and Policies That
Fail* (New York: Academic Press, 1977), 43–44.

24. Desmond King, "Against the State" (unpublished manuscript, n.d.), 11.

25. Michele Dauber, *The Sympathetic State: Disaster Relief and the Origins of
the American Welfare State* (Chicago: University of Chicago Press, 2013), 14.

26. Paul Pierson, *Politics in Time* (Princeton, NJ: Princeton University Press,
2004).

27. Antonio Vázquez-Arroyo, "How not to Learn from Catastrophe: Critical Theory and the Catastrophization of Political Life," *Political Theory* 41, no. 5
(2013): 738–65. As Henry Waxman (D-CA) argued in the case of HIV/AIDS, for
example, "What society judged was not the severity of the disease but the social acceptability of the individuals affected with it." Randy Shilts, *And the Band Played
on: Politics, People, and the AIDS Epidemic* (London: Souvenir Press, 2011), 143-4.

28. Colin Hay, "Crisis and the Structural Transformation of the State: Interrogating the Process of Change," *British Journal of Politics and International Relations* 1, no. 3 (1999): 254.

29. King, "Against the State."

30. John Kingdon, *Agendas, Alternatives, and Public Policies* (New York: Harper
Collins, [1984] 1995); Frank Baumgartner and Bryan Jones, *Agendas and Instability
in American Politics* (Chicago: University of Chicago Press, 1993); E. E. Schattschneider, *The Semisovereign People* (New York: Holt, Rinehart and Winston,
1960).

31. As elaborated below, this meaning is related to but distinct from Janet Roitman's observation that crisis has come to be "construed as a protracted historical
and experiential condition." Janet Roitman, *Anti-Crisis* (Durham, NC: Duke University Press, 2013), 2.

32. As Roitman writes, "Crisis engenders certain forms of critique, which polit-
icize interest groups." Roitman, *Anti-Crisis*, 12.

33. Ruth Wilson Gilmore, *Golden Gulag: Prisons, Surplus, Crisis and Opposition in Globalizing California* (Berkeley: University of California Press, 2007);
Leah Bassel and Akwugo Emejulu, *Minority Women and Austerity: Survival and
Resistance in France and Britain* (Bristol, UK: Bristol University Press, 2017); Robert Nixon, *Slow Violence and the Environmentalism of the Poor* (Cambridge, MA:
Harvard University Press, 2011). As Anne McClintock explains in her discussion of
the BP oil disaster in the Gulf of Mexico, "We are accustomed to think of violence
as immediate and spectacular, bounded by space and time." Slow violence, in contrast, is characterized by what she calls "attritional devastation" that "takes place
gradually over time and space." Although slow violence "may be less visible and
less media-sensational," she explains, "it enacts a toll no less lethal and lasting for

being slow and out of sight." "On what abacus can we count the slowly dying, the invisibly hurt, the already poisoned but not yet dead?" Anne Mcclintock, "Slow Violence and the BP Oil Crisis in the Gulf of Mexico: Militarizing Environmental Catastrophe," *E-misférica* 9, no. 1 (2012): 19, 26. Susan Sterett makes a related point about "the problem of understanding when we might demarcate" the end of disaster. "If we were to think about long-term poverty as we think about disaster victimization," she argues, disaster relief would, indeed, have no end, "and the catastrophic state would become the welfare state." Susan Sterett, "New Orleans Everywhere: Bureaucratic Accountability and Housing Policy after Katrina," in *Catastrophe: Law, Politics, and the Humanitarian Impulse*, ed. Austin Sarat and Javier Lezaun (Amherst: University of Massachusetts Press, 2009), 88.

34. Ariella Azoulay and Adi Ophir, "The Order of Violence," in *The Power of Inclusive Exclusion*, ed. Adi Ophir, Michal Giovoni, and Sari Hanfi (New York: Zone Books 2009), 99–140; Bassel and Emejulu, *Minority Women and Austerity*; Annie Menzel, "Crisis and Epistemologies of Ignorance" (paper presented at the American Political Science Association conference, Washington, DC, 2–5 September 2010); Pierson, *Politics in Time*; Shannon Sullivan, "White Ignorance and Colonial Oppression: Or, Why I Know so Little about Puerto Rico," in *Race and Epistemologies of Ignorance*, ed. Shannon Sullivan and Nancy Tuana (Albany: SUNY Press, 2007), 153–71; Vázquez-Arroyo, "How Not to Learn"; Antonio Vázquez-Arroyo, "The Orders of Violence: Structures, Catastrophes, and Agents," *New Political Science* 34, no. 2 (2012): 211–21.

35. Mary White Ovington, "How the National Association for the Advancement of Colored People Began," *Crisis* 8, no. 4 (1914): 187. For more detailed accounts of the founding and early years of *The Crisis*, see, inter alia, Lamia Dzanouni, Hélène Le Dantec-Lowry, and Claire Parfait, "From One Crisis to the Other: History and Literature in *The Crisis* from 1910 to the Early 1920s," *European Journal of American Studies* 11 (2016): 1–26; Amy Helene Kirschke and Phillip Luke Sinitiere, eds., *Protest and Propaganda: W E B Du Bois, the* Crisis*, and American History* (Columbia: University of Missouri Press, 2019); Amy Helene Kirschke, "Dubois and 'The Crisis' Magazine: Imaging Women and Family," *Source: Notes in the History of Art* 24 (2005): 35–45; Amy Helene Kirschke, *Art in Crisis. W. E. B. Du Bois and the Struggle for African American Identity and Memory* (Bloomington: Indiana University Press, 2007); Brian Johnson, ed., *DuBois on Reform: Periodical-Based Leadership for African Americans* (New York: AltaMira Press, 2005); David Levering Lewis, *W. E. B. Du Bois: Biography of a Race, 1868–1919* (New York: Henry Holt, 1993); David Levering Lewis, *W. E. B. Du Bois: The Fight for Equality and the American Century, 1919–1963* (New York: Henry Holt, 2000); Martina Mallocci, "'All Art Is Propaganda': W. E. B Du Bois's *The Crisis* and the Construction of a Black Public Image," *USAbroad–Journal of American History and Politics* 1 (2018); Sondra Wilson, The Crisis *Reader: Stories, Poetry, and Essays from the N.A.A.C.P.'s* Crisis *Magazine* (New York: Modern Library Harlem Renaissance 1999).

36. Ovington, "How the National Association for the Advancement of Colored

People Began," 188. Many of the sources in this book use archaic language, including but not limited to the use of the term "Negro" in historical documents, spelling "black" using a lowercase "b," using "blacks" as a noun, using "man" and "male" as universals, and the casual use of terms such as "rapacious" as a synonym for "extractive" or "greedy," which might seem to normalize sexual violence.

37. Nancy Fraser and Linda Gordon, "A Genealogy of Dependency: Tracing a Keyword of the U.S. Welfare State," *Signs: Journal of Women in Culture and Society* 19, no. 2 (1994): 310.

38. W. E. B. Du Bois, "Editorial: The Crisis," *Crisis* 1, no. 1 (1910): 10.

39. On archaic language in sources, see note 36.

40. Du Bois, "Editorial."

41. Megan Ming Francis, *Civil Rights and the Making of the Modern American State* (New York: Cambridge University Press, 2014), 4.

42. Megan Ming Francis, "The Battle for the Hearts and Minds of America," *Souls* 13 (2011): 57. Francis argues further that while this "publicity strategy was greatly influenced by Ida B. Wells," her role has been insufficiently appreciated, in part because the NAACP "sidelined Wells in the early years of the organization's development," believing that she "was more of a threat and a liability than a resource and would ultimately undermine the organization." As a result," Francis argues, "the NAACP was without the counsel of the most courageous crusader against lynching in the United States"(66).

43. It is more challenging than one might expect to find downloadable and searchable copies of *The Crisis*. They are available from 1910–1922 in PDF form via the Modernist Journal Project and from the Internet Archive through 1923. Later issues are available through Google Books, but that platform does not make it possible to download or scrape the issues, so searches must therefore be done online using the (not very flexible) Google Books interface and search engine. With these limitations, I determined how *Crisis* magazine writers used the term *crisis* or *crises* by searching for each instance of those terms (which was not an eponymous reference to the magazine itself) in all issues from 1910–1959, coding each valid observation for the type of article in which the term was used, type of issue to which it referred (domestic or international), whether the issue pertained to race/racial inequality, whether it was being used to describe a clear-cut crisis and/or in a way that suggests that the issue in question faced some kind of turning point, and if so, whether there is a call for government action or resources to address it. See the appendices, particularly appendix B, for further details about the coding rubric.

44. An additional four instances of the term *crisis* appear in passages from works of fiction and are out of scope for these purposes.

45. "The Truth," *Crisis* 1, no. 6 (April 1911): 21–22.

46. Ansel may also have helped save Franklin from being attacked by a lynch mob.

47. On archaic language in sources, see note 36.

48. "The Truth," *Crisis*.

49. Patricia Strach, *Hiding Politics in Plain Sight: Cause Marketing, Corporate Influence, and Breast Cancer Policymaking* (New York: Oxford University Press, 2016).

50. Roitman, *Anti-Crisis*, 2.

51. Nancy Fraser and Linda Gordon, "'Dependency' Demystified: Inscriptions of Power in a Keyword of the Welfare State," *Social Politics: International Studies in Gender, State, and Society* 1, no. 1 (1994): 4–31. In this sense, condition-as-crisis is similar to what Desmond King calls "designated crises," which he defines as endogenous events or continuing problems "deemed a crisis for political and electoral reasons." See King, "Against the State," 11.

52. The "first observations" in table 2.3 were compiled by Andrew Proctor using the "kwic" command (key words in context) in the R quanteda package. Doing so produces an output file that identifies the year, row in data, context before the word, and context after the word, from which bi-gram and tri-grams were identified. This list was then sorted alphabetically and by source and year to identify the earliest observation for each bi-gram and tri-gram.

53. Raymond Williams, *Keywords* (New York: Oxford University Press, 1976).

54. Frank Baumgartner and Bryan Jones, *The Politics of Information* (Chicago: University of Chicago Press, 2015).

55. Stephanie J. Nawyn, "Refugees in the United States and the Politics of Crisis," in *The Oxford Handbook of Migration Crises*, ed. Cecilia Menjívar, Marie Ruiz, and Immanuel Ness (New York: Oxford University Press, 2019), 163–80.

56. Reinhart Koselleck, "Crisis," *Journal of the History of Ideas* 67, no. 2 (2006): 399.

57. Although the proliferation of calamity-as-crisis diluted some of the specificity of condition-as-crisis as a way to reframe longer-term conditions as problems facing critical junctures, it did not replace it, nor did it end the use of crisis as a way to argue that issues warranted state intervention and resources. In addition to the references to the crises in the previous paragraph, for example, the 1984 Democratic Party platform also included a plank stating that the "crises devastating many of our nation's youth is nowhere more dramatically evidenced than in the alarming rate of increase in teenage suicide." The statement did not invoke crisis in a way that framed teen suicide as a problem that suddenly faced a critical juncture or as a problem related to longer-term ones (such as a lack of access to mental health services). But the platform did go on to argue for "a national policy of prevention," "guidance to our state and local governments," and "the creation of a national panel on teenage suicide to respond to this challenge."

Similarly, in 1992, the Republican platform called HIV/AIDS "a crisis of tragic proportions" and argued that it required "a massive commitment of resources" and the "personal determination on the part of the President." Although the Republicans were suggesting that HIV/AIDS was a problem that could be addressed by the state, they made no attempt to link it to—much less to use it to denaturalize the inevitability of—longer-term problems such as homophobia or the lack of universal health care.

58. Dauber, *Sympathetic State*.

59. Marc Bacharach, "War Metaphors: How Presidents Use the Language of War to Sell Policy" (PhD diss., Miami University, 2006), http://rave.ohiolink.edu/etdc /view?acc_num=miami1154105266; Peter Andreas and Richard Price, "From War Fighting to Crime Fighting: Transforming the American National Security State," *International Studies Review* 3, no. 3 (2001): 31–52; Mary Dudziak, *War Time: An Idea, Its History, Its Consequences* (New York: Oxford University Press, 2012).

60. Roitman, *Anti-Crisis*, 2.

Chapter Three

1. Frank Baumgartner and Bryan Jones, *The Politics of Information: Problem Definition and the Course of Public Policy in America* (Princeton, NJ: Princeton University Press, 2015).

2. Nancy Fraser and Linda Gordon, "'Dependency' Demystified: Inscriptions of Power in a Keyword of the Welfare State," *Social Politics* 1, no. 1 (1994): 4–31; Nancy Fraser and Linda Gordon, "A Genealogy of Dependency: Tracing a Keyword of the U.S. Welfare State," *Signs: Journal of Women in Culture and Society* 19 (1994): 309–36.

3. The data in table 3.1 are subsets of those depicted in figure 2.8 and table A.5. As I explain at greater length in chapter 2 and the appendices, the hearings data were collected by using the Legacy CIS numbers to match each result from the ProQuest hearing title search with its coded USPAP entry. I then used USPAP topic codes to determine whether the issue being addressed in each hearing was primarily domestic. The party platform and State of the Union data were collected using ProQuest Congressional and the US Policy Agendas Project. I used ProQuest Congressional to search for the terms *crisis* and *crises* in bill and hearing titles and used a Python script to calculate counts for each year. I next created an indicator variable to identify instances of all possible variations of the word *crisis/es* (*CRISIS, CRISES, Crises, Crisis, crises, crisis*, and so on) in USPAP party platforms and State of the Union data, and then aggregated those up to the year level as well. I then used these year-level data to calculate the percent of the bill titles and summaries, hearing titles, platform statements, and State of the Union statements containing *crisis/es* by topic, in this case for the period 1965–79. See appendices for additional details.

4. Stuart Hall et al., *Policing the Crisis: Mugging, the State, and Law and Order* (London: Macmillan, 1978).

5. Keeanga-Yamahtta Taylor, *Race for Profit: How Banks and the Real Estate Industry Undermined Black Homeownership* (Chapel Hill: University of North Carolina Press, 2019).

6. Democratic Party Platforms, 1960 Democratic Party Platform Online by Gerhard Peters and John T. Woolley, The American Presidency Project, https://www.presidency.ucsb.edu/node/273234.

7. Gary Orfield and Susan Eaton, *Dismantling Desegregation: The Quiet Reversal of* Brown v. Board of Education (New York: New Press, 1996); Kathryn McDermott, *Controlling Public Education: Localism versus Equity* (Lawrence: University Press of Kansas, 1999).

8. That they did not link crisis language to these facets of their discussion of education is all the more salient in light of the fact that the section of the platform addressing education follows directly those addressing topics, including "A Program for the Aging," "Welfare," "Equality for Women," and "Intergroup Relations," none of which they labeled or framed as crises either.

9. *Population Crisis: Hearings before the Subcommittee on Foreign Aid Expenditures of the Senate Committee on Government Operations*, 89th Cong. (1965).

10. Elaine Tyler May, *America and the Pill: A History of Promise, Peril, and Liberation* (New York: Basic Books 2011). These invited witnesses included three from Planned Parenthood (two of whom were physicians), one from the UN Commission on the Status of Women, and one from the Women's International League for Peace and Freedom.

11. Laura Kaplan, *The Story of Jane: The Legendary Underground Feminist Abortion Service* (New York: Knopf Doubleday, 1995).

12. Angela Davis, *Women, Race, and Class* (New York: Random House, 1982); Betsy Hartmann, *Reproductive Rights and Wrongs: The Global Politics of Population Control*, rev. ed. (Boston: South End Press, 1995); Monica Bahati Kuumba, "Perpetuating Neo-Colonialism through Population Control: South Africa and the United States," *Africa Today* 40 (1993): 79–85; Dorothy Roberts, *Killing the Black Body* (New York: Vintage, 1997); Helen Simons, "Cairo: Repackaging Population Control," *International Journal of Health Services* 25 (1995): 559–66.

13. *Population Crisis: Hearings*, 1058.

14. *Population Crisis: Hearings*, 1058.

15. *Population Crisis: Hearings*, 1155.

16. Davis, *Women, Race, and Class*, 215; italics in original.

17. This framing of the crisis stands in contrast to two papers entered as exhibits into the record by Naomi Thomas Gray, a Black social worker who served at the time as field director of Planned Parenthood-World Population. Among the things that Gray did in these papers was to summarize the results of research by sociologist Alice Day showing that it was "couples in the upper income, well-educated groups" who were "now having large families." *Population Crisis: Hearings*, 977.

18. Meg Jacobs, *Panic at the Pump: The Energy Crisis and the Transformation of American Politics in the 1970s* (New York: Macmillan, 2016).

19. *Part 12: Narcotics-Crime Crisis in the Washington Area: Hearings before the Senate Committee on the District of Columbia*, 91st Cong. (1970). A growing body

of scholarship has explored the racial implications of the "wars on" crime and drugs. See, for example, Michelle Alexander, *The New Jim Crow: Mass Incarceration in the Age of Colorblindness* (New York: New Press, 2010); James Foreman, *Locking Up Our Own: Crime and Punishment in Black America* (New York: Farrar, Straus, and Giroux, 2017); Elizabeth Hinton, *From the War on Poverty to the War on Crime: The Making of Mass Incarceration in America* (Cambridge, MA: Harvard University Press, 2017); Naomi Murakawa, *The First Civil Right: How Liberals Built Prison America* (New York: Oxford University Press, 2014).

20. *Part 12: Narcotics-Crime Crisis: Hearings*, 2655.

21. *Part 12: Narcotics-Crime Crisis: Hearings*, 2655.

22. *Part 12: Narcotics-Crime Crisis: Hearings*, 2803.

23. *Part 12: Narcotics-Crime Crisis: Hearings*, 2661.

24. *Part 12: Narcotics-Crime Crisis: Hearings*, 2661.

25. *Part 12: Narcotics-Crime Crisis: Hearings*, 2742.

26. *Financial Institutions and the Urban Crisis: Hearings before the Subcommittee on Financial Institutions of the Senate Committee on Banking and Currency*, 90th Congress (1968).

27. National Advisory Commission on Civil Disorders and Otto Kerner, *Report of the National Advisory Commission on Civil Disorders* (Washington, DC: GPO, 1968).

28. National Advisory Commission on Civil Disorders and Otto Kerner, *Commission on Civil Disorders*, 1.

29. Julian Zelizer, ed., *The Kerner Report: The National Advisory Commission on Civil Disorders* (Princeton, NJ: Princeton University Press, 2016).

30. Sidney M. Milkis, ed., *The Great Society and the High Tide of Liberalism* (Amherst: University of Massachusetts Press, 2005), 240; Keeanga-Yamahtta Taylor, *Race for Profit: How Banks and the Real Estate Industry Undermined Black Homeownership* (Chapel Hill: University of North Carolina Press, 2019).

31. *Financial Institutions and the Urban Crisis: Hearings*, 1.

32. Milkis, *Great Society*; Taylor, *Race for Profit*.

33. *Financial Institutions and the Urban Crisis: Hearings*, 233.

34. On archaic language in sources, see chap. 2, note 36.

35. *Financial Institutions and the Urban Crisis: Hearings*, 233.

36. *Financial Institutions and the Urban Crisis: Hearings*, 5.

37. *Financial Institutions and the Urban Crisis: Hearings*, 5.

38. Mehrsa Baradaran, *The Color of Money: Black Banks and the Racial Wealth Gap* (Cambridge, MA: Belknap Press of Harvard University Press, 2017); Chester Hartman and Gregory Squires, *From Foreclosure to Fair Lending: Advocacy Organizing, Occupy, and the Pursuit of Equitable Credit* (New York: New Village Press, 2013); Louis Hyman, *Debtor Nation: A History of American in Red Ink* (Princeton, NJ: Princeton University Press, 2011); Mallory E. SoRelle, *Democracy Declined: The Failed Politics of Consumer Financial Protection* (Chicago: University of Chicago Press, 2020); Chloe Thurston, *At the Boundaries of Homeownership* (New York: Cambridge University Press, 2018).

39. Monica Prasad, *The Land of Too Much: American Abundance and the Paradox of Poverty* (Cambridge, MA: Harvard University Press, 2012); Greta Krippner, *Capitalizing on Crisis: The Political Origins of the Rise of Finance* (Cambridge, MA: Harvard University Press, 2011); Greta Krippner, "Democracy of Credit: Ownership and the Politics of Credit Access in Late Twentieth-Century America," *American Journal of Sociology* 123 (2017): 1–47; Abbye Atkinson, "Borrowing Equality," *Columbia Law Review* 120 (2020): 1403–70.

40. Moreover, as Taylor demonstrates (and as I discuss at greater length in chapters 4 and 5), "the transition from the exclusionary policies of HUD and the FHA to inclusion into the world of urban real estate sales was fraught with problems," in part because "'public-private partnership[s]' obscured the ways that the federal government became complicit with private sector practices that promoted residential segregation and racial discrimination.... Racially informed real estate practices were not the actions of an industry impervious to change and old in its ways; instead, racial discrimination persisted in the new market because it was good business." Taylor, *Race for Profit*, 3–7.

41. Hartman and Squires, *From Foreclosure to Fair Lending*; Michael Klarman, *From Jim Crow to Civil Rights: The Supreme Court and the Struggle for Racial Equality* (New York: Oxford University Press, 2004); Taylor, *Race for Profit*.

42. As Taylor writes, "'Urban crisis,' as a description of infrastructural and complex policy problems in the built environment in the early 1960s, was absorbed into a pattern of coded speech used to describe those who lived in distressed urban communities. Coded speech was, of course, invoked to communicate ideas that could no longer be spoken of freely on their own terms. The new uses of 'urban crisis' were a means of articulating the perception of crisis in American cities without using race as its catalyst." Taylor, *Race for Profit*, 20. See also Stuart Hall et al., *Policing the Crisis: Mugging, the State, and Law and Order* (London: Macmillan 1978); Tom Sugrue, *The Origins of the Urban Crisis: Race and Inequality in Postwar Detroit* (Princeton, NJ: Princeton University Press, 1996).

43. Republican Party Platforms, Republican Party Platform of 1980 Online by Gerhard Peters and John Woolley, The American Presidency Project, https://www.presidency.ucsb.edu/node/273420.

44. Taylor, *Race for Profit*, 231–32.

45. Taylor, *Race for Profit*, 231.

46. US Department of Labor, *The Negro Family: The Case for National Action* (Washington, DC: US Department of Labor, 1965). The archaic term "Negro" is used in the original.

47. Susan D. Greenbaum, *Blaming the Poor: The Long Shadow of the Moynihan Report on Cruel Images about Poverty* (New Brunswick, NJ: Rutgers University Press, 2015), 2.

48. Department of Labor, *Negro Family*, ii.

49. Department of Labor, *Negro Family*, ii.

50. Department of Labor, *Negro Family*, ii.

51. Department of Labor, *Negro Family*, ii.

52. Department of Labor, *Negro Family*, 19.

53. Department of Labor, *Negro Family*, 1.

54. Department of Labor, *Negro Family*, 1. For example, Douglas Massey and Robert Sampson argue that the purpose of the report "was to make an impassioned moral case for a massive federal intervention to break the cycle of black poverty and put African Americans on the road to socioeconomic achievement and integration into American society." Douglas S. Massey and Robert Sampson. "Moynihan Redux: Legacies and Lessons," *Annals of the American Academy of Political and Social Science* 621 (2009): 6. See also James T. Patterson, *Freedom Is Not Enough: The Moynihan Report and America's Struggle over Black Family Life—from LBJ to Obama* (New York: Basic Books 2010).

55. Department of Labor, *Negro Family*, 1.

56. Department of Labor, *Negro Family*, 1.

57. Department of Labor, *Negro Family*, 1.

58. Many of the initial critiques of the report, including several that made this point about blaming African American values and behaviors rather than white racism as the source of the "crisis" in question, were compiled by Lee Rainwater and William C. Yancey in *The Moynihan Report and the Politics of Controversy* (Cambridge, MA: MIT Press, 1967). Of those published there, among the most germane to this point were those by James Farmer, Martin Luther King Jr., Bayard Rustin, Herbert Gans, and William Ryan. Ryan subsequently expanded on the arguments documented in the Rainwater and Yancey volume in *Blaming the Victim*, the title of which captures the core of his critique (New York: Vintage, [1971] 1976). For detailed accounts of these controversies, see Daniel Geary, *Beyond Civil Rights: The Moynihan Report and Its Legacy* (Philadelphia: University of Pennsylvania Press, 2015); Herbert Gans, "The Moynihan Report and Its Aftermaths: A Critical Analysis," *Du Bois Review* 8 (2011): 315–27; Greenbaum, *Blaming the Poor*; Alice O'Connor, *Poverty Knowledge: Social Science, Social Policy, and the Poor in Twentieth-Century U.S. History* (Princeton, NJ: Princeton University Press, 2001); Touré Reed, *Toward Freedom: The Case against Race Reductionism* (New York: Verso, 2020).

59. These aspects of the report's argument, which Paul Butler characterizes as "patriarchy masquerading as social justice," have been the subject of much critique, both at the time of the report's publication and in subsequent decades. Paul Butler, "Black Male Exceptionalism? The Problems and Potential of Black Male-Focused Interventions," *Du Bois Review* 10 (2013): 485–511. Among the report's earliest feminist and Black feminist critics were Frances Bearle, Jean Carey Bond and Patricia Perry, Mary Merrillee Dolan, Brenda Eichelberger, Aileen Hernandez, Eleanor Holmes Norton, June Jordan, Dublin Keyserling, Joyce Ladner, Pauli Murray, and Michelle Wallace; see Geary, *Beyond Civil Rights*, chap. 5. See also Frances Beale, "Double Jeopardy: To Be Black and Female," in *The*

Black Woman: An Anthology, ed. Toni Cade (New York: New American Library 1970), 109–22; Merrillee Dolan, "Moynihan, Poverty Programs, and Women—A Female Viewpoint," reprinted in *Welfare in the United States: A History with Documents, 1935–1996*, ed. Premilla Nadasen, Jennifer Mittelstadt, and Marisa Chappell (New York: Routledge, [1972] 2009), 180–83; June Jordan, "Memo to Daniel Pretty Moynihan," in *New Days: Poems of Exile and Return* (New York: Emerson Hall, [1970] 1974), 6; Carol B. Stack, *All Our Kin: Strategies for Survival in a Black Community* (New York: Basic Books 1975); Michelle Wallace, *Black Macho and the Myth of the Superwoman* (New York: Verso Press, [1978] 1994); Jean Carey Bond and Patricia Perry, "Is the Black Male Castrated?" in Cade, *Black Woman*; Eleanor Holmes Norton, "For Sadie and Maude," in *Sister-hood Is Powerful: An Anthology of Writings from the Women's Liberation Movement*, ed. Robin Morgan (New York: Random House, 1970), 357; Joyce A. Ladner, *Tomorrow's Tomorrow: The Black Woman* (Garden City, NY: Doubleday 1971). More recent critiques and analyses of the ways in which racism, misogyny, and heterosexism intersect in the report include Patricia Hill Collins, "A Comparison of Two Works on Black Family Life," *Signs: Journal of Women in Culture and Society* 14, no. 4 (1989): 875–84; Roderick Ferguson, *Aberrations in Black: Toward a Queer of Color Critique* (Minneapolis: University of Minnesota Press, 2004); Nikol Alexander-Floyd, "We Shall Have Our Manhood: Black Macho, Black Nationalism, and the Million Man March," *Meridians: Feminism, Race and Transnationalism* 3, no. 2 (2003): 171–203; Willie Legette, "The Crisis of the Black Male: A New Ideology of Black Politics," in *Without Justice for All: New Liberalism and Our Retreat from Racial Equality*, ed. Adolph Reed (Boulder, CO: Westview Press, 1999); Kevin Mumford, "Untangling Pathology: The Moynihan Report and Homosexual Damage, 1965–1975," *Journal of Policy History* 24 (2012): 53–73; Adolph Reed, "The Election in Perspective: The Myth of the 'Cultural Divide' and the Triumph of Neoliberal Ideology," *American Quarterly* 57 (2005): 1–15; Dorothy Roberts, *Killing the Black Body* (New York: Vintage, 1997). See also Johnnie Tillmon, "Welfare Is a Women's Issue," *Ms.*, Spring 1972; Premilla Nadasen, *Welfare Warriors: The Welfare Rights Movement in the United States* (New York: Routledge, 2005); Felicia Kornbluh, *The Battle for Welfare Rights: Politics and Poverty in Modern America* (Philadelphia: University of Pennsylvania Press, 2007).

  60. Greenbaum, *Blaming the Poor*, 2, 12.

  61. Ferguson, *Aberrations in Black*, 111, 124.

  62. Hall et al., *Policing the Crisis*.

  63. See, inter alia, Alexander, *New Jim Crow*; Fraser and Gordon "'Dependency' Demystified"; Hall et al., *Policing the Crisis*; Hinton, *From the War on Poverty to the War on Crime*; Greenbaum, *Blaming the Poor*; Murakawa, *First Civil Right*; O'Connor, *Poverty Knowledge*; Orfield and Eaton, *Dismantling Desegregation*; Reed, *Toward Freedom*; and Taylor, *Race for Profit*.

  64. Eduardo Bonilla-Silva, *Racism without Racists* (New York: Rowman and

Littlefield, 2013); Leslie Carr, *"Colorblind" Racism* (Thousand Oaks, CA: Sage 1997); Klarman, *From Jim Crow to Civil Rights*.

65. See, inter alia, Andrea Louise Campbell, *How Policies Make Citizens: Senior Political Activism and the American Welfare State* (Princeton, NJ: Princeton University Press, 2003); Katherine J. Cramer, *The Politics of Resentment: Rural Consciousness in Wisconsin and the Rise of Scott Walker* (Chicago: University of Chicago Press, 2016); Michael Dawson, *Behind the Mule* (Princeton, NJ: Princeton University Press, 1995); Martin Gilens, *Why Americans Hate Welfare* (Chicago: University of Chicago Press, 1999); Jane Gingrich, "Visibility, Values, and Voters: The Informational Role of the Welfare State," *Journal of Politics* 76 (2014): 565–80; Jacob S. Hacker, *The Divided Welfare State: The Battle over Public and Private Social Benefits in the United States* (New York: Cambridge University Press, 2002); Jacob Hacker, "Privatizing Risk without Privatizing the Welfare State: The Hidden Politics of Social Policy Retrenchment in the United States," *American Political Science Review* 98 (2004): 243–60; John R. Hibbing and Elizabeth Theiss-Morse, eds., *What Is It about Government That Americans Dislike?* (New York: Cambridge University 2001); Lawrence R. Jacobs and Suzanne Mettler, "When and How New Policy Creates New Politics: Examining the Feedback Effects of the Affordable Care Act on Public Opinion," *Perspectives on Politics* 16 (2018): 345–63; Jane Junn and Natalie Masuoka, "Asian American Identity: Shared Racial Status and Political Context," *Perspectives on Politics* 6 (2008): 729–40; Ira Katznelson, *When Affirmative Action Was White* (New York: W. W. Norton, 2005); Katherine Krimmel and Kelly Rader, "The Federal Spending Paradox: Economic Self-Interest and Symbolic Racism in Contemporary Fiscal Politics," *American Politics Research* 45 (2017): 727–54; Amy E. Lerman and Katherine T. McCabe, "Personal Experience and Public Opinion: A Theory and Test of Conditional Policy Feedback," *Journal of Politics* 79 (2017): 624–41; Leslie McCall, *The Undeserving Rich: American Beliefs about Inequality, Opportunity, and Redistribution* (New York: Cambridge University Press, 2013); Suzanne Mettler, *The Submerged State* (Chicago: University of Chicago Press, 2011); Suzanne Mettler, *The Government-Citizen Disconnect* (New York: Russell Sage Foundation, 2018); Jamila Michener, *Fragmented Democracy: Medicaid, Federalism, and Unequal Politics* (New York: Cambridge University Press, 2018); Kimberly J. Morgan and Andrea Louise Campbell, *The Delegated Welfare State: Medicare, Markets, and the Governance of Social Policy* (New York: Oxford University Press, 2011); Tatishe Nteta, "United We Stand? African Americans, Self-Interest, and Immigration Reform," *American Politics Research* 41 (2013): 147–72; Christopher Parker and Matt Barreto, *Change They Can't Believe In: The Tea Party and Reactionary Politics in America* (Princeton, NJ: Princeton University Press, 2011); Jill Quadagno, *The Color of Welfare: How Racism Undermined the War on Poverty* (New York: Oxford University Press, 1996); SoRelle, *Democracy Declined*; Dara Z. Strolovitch, "Playing Favorites: Public Attitudes toward Race- and Gender-Targeted Anti-discrimination Policy," *National*

Women's Studies Association Journal 10 (1998): 27–53; Christopher J. Williams and Gregory Shufeldt, "How Identity Influences Public Attitudes Towards the US Federal Government: Lessons from the European Union," *Acta Politica*, 11 June 2020.

66. Daniel Rodgers, *Contested Truths: Keywords in Politics* (Cambridge, MA: Harvard University Press, 1987), 13.

67. Murray Edelman, *Political Language: Words That Succeed and Policies That Fail* (New York: Academic Press, 1977), 43–44.

68. Edelman, *Political Language*, 43–44.

69. Roitman, *Anti-Crisis*, 2.

70. Koselleck, "Crisis," 399.

71. Roitman, *Anti-Crisis*, 2.

72. Mary Dudziak, *War Time: An Idea, Its History, Its Consequences* (New York: Oxford University Press, 2012).

73. Marc Raboy and Bernard Degenais, *Media, Crisis, and Democracy* (Thousand Oaks, CA: Sage, 1992).

74. Colin Hay, "Crisis and the Structural Transformation of the State: Interrogating the Process of Change," *British Journal of Politics and International Relations* 1, no. 3 (1999): 254.

75. See also Ariella Azoulay and Adi Ophir on "withheld" versus "eruptive" violence, as well as Michel Foucault and Lauren Berlant on "endemics," Lauren Berlant on "slow death," Ruth Wilson Gilmore on "premature death," Robert Nixon on "slow violence," Frederick Frey and John Gaventa on "non-issues," Matthew Crenson on "un-politics," and Murray Edelman on "semantically masked crises." See Ariella Azoulay and Adi Ophir, "The Order of Violence," in *The Power of Inclusive Exclusion*, ed. Adi Ophir, Michal Givoni, and Sari Hanfi (New York: Zone Books, 2009), 99–140; Lauren Berlant, *Cruel Optimism* (Durham, NC: Duke University Press, 2011); Michel Foucault, *Society Must Be Defended* (New York: Picador, 2003), 243; Ruth Gilmore Wilson, *Golden Gulag: Prisons, Surplus, Crisis and Opposition in Globalizing California* (Berkeley: University of California Press, 2007); Robert Nixon, *Slow Violence and the Environmentalism of the Poor* (Cambridge, MA: Harvard University Press, 2011); Frederick Frey, "Comment: On Issues and Nonissues in the Study of Power," *American Political Science Review* 65, no. 4 (1971): 1081–1101; John Gaventa, *Power and Powerlessness* (Champagne: University of Illinois Press, 1980); Matthew Crenson, *The Un-politics of Air Pollution* (Baltimore: Johns Hopkins University Press, 1971); Edelman, *Political Language*, 47.

Chapter Four

1. National Bureau of Economic Research, "Business Cycle Dating Committee," 2010, http://www.nber.org/cycles/sept2010.pdf.

2. Una Prudie, "90% of Jobs Created in US Last Year Went to Men," *Women's Views on News*, 22 March 2011, http://www.womensviewsonnews.org/2011/03/90-of -jobs-created-in-us-last-year-went-to-men/.

3. Steven Pitts, "Research Brief: Black Workers and the Public Sector," University of California, Berkeley, Center for Labor Research and Education, 2011; Dara Strolovitch, "Of Mancessions and Hecoveries: Race, Gender, and the Political Construction of Economic Crises and Recoveries," *Perspectives on Politics* 13 (2013): 167–76.

4. For more on the term *semantically masked*, see Murray Edelman, *Political Language: Words That Succeed and Policies That Fail* (New York: Academic Press, 1977), 47.

5. Louis Althusser, "Ideology and Ideological State Apparatuses," *La Pensee* 151 (1970).

6. Daniel Immergluck, "Too Little, Too Late, and Too Timid: The Federal Response to the Foreclosure Crisis at the Five-Year Mark," *Housing Policy Debate* 23 (2013): 202–4.

7. US Department of Housing and Urban Development (HUD), Office of Policy Development and Research, *Report to Congress on the Root Causes of the Foreclosure Crisis* (2010).

8. Immergluck, "Too Little, Too Late," 202; US House-Senate Joint Economic Committee, "Momentum Builds for Schumer's Call for Additional Federal Funds to Avert Subprime Foreclosure Crisis," press release, 5 June 2007, https://www.jec .senate.gov/public/index.cfm/democrats/media?page=129.

9. Immergluck, "Too Little, Too Late," 202–4.

10. Jeff Crump et al., "Cities Destroyed (Again) for Cash: Forum on the Foreclosure Crisis," *Urban Geography* 29 (2008): 756. See also Adalberto Aguirre Jr. and Rubén Martinez, "The Foreclosure Crisis, the American Dream, and Minority Households in the United States: A Descriptive Profile," *Social Justice* 40, no. 3 (2014): 6–15.

11. Crump et al., "Cities Destroyed," 756.

12. Debbie Gruenstein Bocian, Wei Li, and Keith Ernst, *Foreclosures by Race and Ethnicity*, CRL Research Report (Durham, NC: Center for Responsible Lending, 2010), https://www.responsiblelending.org/mortgage-lending/research-analysis /foreclosures-by-race-and-ethnicity.pdf.

13. Following McCoy and Renuart, I use the term *subprime* to refer to the mortgages, not to the borrowers themselves: that is, I use it to refer, as they do, to "home mortgage loans that carry higher interest rates, points, or fees when compared with loans extended to the best-qualified borrowers (also known as 'prime' borrowers)." As they explain, "although the subprime market was designed for borrowers with impaired credit, lenders also frequently made subprime loans to unsuspecting borrowers who could have qualified for the best-rate prime mortgages." Accordingly, their definition of subprime loans "turns on the high-cost nature of those loans,

not on the borrowers' credit profiles." See Patricia McCoy and Elizabeth Renuart, "The Legal Infrastructure of Subprime and Nontraditional Home Mortgages,"
in *Borrowing to Live: Consumer and Mortgage Credit Revisited*, ed. Nicolas Retsinas and Eric Belsky (Washington: Brookings Institute Press, 2008), 110. While
subprime has come to be understood as a designator for a kind of loan or credit,
however, Keeanga-Yamahtta Taylor explains that the term itself originated as way
to circumvent prohibitions against redlining by providing an ostensibly "racially
neutral" description of African American neighborhoods. As Taylor writes, it was a
way for the Federal Housing Administration to dismiss its own practices of redlining "as a problem of location and not of race," by claiming that it excluded urban
areas from its insurance "because of the age and condition of the structures in those
areas. FHA officials, of course, failed to take into account their own references to
race as part of the underwriting criteria used to determine eligibility for mortgage
insurance." By pretending to ignore race and by dismissing these and other "racially inscribed policies" as outdated practices of an earlier era, however, "new
practices that were intended to facilitate inclusion reinforced existing patterns of
inequality and discrimination." Among these practices was that the poor housing
and neighborhood conditions that resulted from "earlier FHA policies became the
basis on which new lenders . . . could still continue to treat potential Black homeowners differently." To this end, "African American neighborhoods were given the
racially neutral descriptor 'subprime,' " which "allowed for certain kinds of lenders
while justifying the continued inactivity of other lenders." In other words, although
race was apparently no longer a factor, "its cumulative effect had already marked
Black neighborhoods in such ways that still made them distinguishable and vulnerable to new forms of financial manipulation." Inclusion was possible, Taylor
concludes, "but on predatory and exploitative terms." Keeanga-Yamahtta Taylor,
*Race for Profit: How Banks and the Real Estate Industry Undermined Black Home-
ownership* (Chapel Hill: University of North Carolina Press Book, 2020), 17–18. As
Laura Gottesdiener writes, "who was allowed to buy what type of mortgage was
so stark that the word 'subprime' . . . became a demographic category as much as a
financial definition." Laura Gottesdiener, *A Dream Foreclosed: Black America and
the Fight for a Place to Call Home* (New York Zuccotti Park Press, 2013), 63. Paula
Chakravartty and Denise Ferreira da Silva argue similarly that *subprime* became
a category of people "construed as intellectually (illiterate) and morally (greedy),
unfit if measured against any existing descriptors of the modern economic subject."
Paula Chakravartty and Denise Ferreira da Silva, "Accumulation, Dispossession,
and Debt: The Racial Logic of Global Capitalism—An Introduction," *American
Quarterly* 64 (2012): 362.

    14. Consumer Financial Protection Bureau, *2013 Home Ownership and Equity
Protection Act (HOEPA) Rule: Small Entity Compliance Guide*, 2 May 2013, tinyurl
.com/ya2ma5c6.

    15. I discuss some of these policies and practices at greater length later in this

chapter. Chloe Thurston summarizes some of the most common ones, explaining that "although racial exclusion in local real estate predated the [Federal Housing Act]," through the development

> [of the] field of real estate valuation and appraisal, and the incorporation of their methods and theories into the FHA's own underwriting guidelines, exclusion became routinized, nationalized, and concretely tied to beliefs that the future value of a house was related to its neighborhood's racial homogeneity and the likelihood of changing racial (or "user group") characteristics over time.

This belief in segregation, Thurston explains further, was codified into real estate practices and "contributed to the movement of capital out of black neighborhoods." She argues that for women, the sources of exclusion had less to do with ideas about the determinants of property values and more to do with ideas about the borrower. Among other factors, Thurston explains, "women's exclusion from mortgage credit was built out of beliefs about what constituted stable employment and income over time and credit bureau reporting practices that generated just one report per household, eliminating a married woman's individual economic standing." For low-income households, Thurston writes, "the barriers to access were more straightforward, in that those people tended to lack the cash for a down payment and to have incomes too low and unstable to meet underwriting guidelines." Chloe Thurston, *At the Boundaries of Homeownership* (New York: Cambridge University Press, 2018), 26–27. To these exclusions, Margot Canaday adds the less-well-understood one in which, because the Veterans Administration "denied G.I. Bill benefits to any soldier with an undesirable discharge 'issued because of homosexual acts or tendencies,'" LGBTQ people were essentially denied access to the housing loans that made homeownership accessible to other (white, male) veterans. Margot Canaday, "Building a Straight State: Sexuality and Social Citizenship under the 1944 GI Bill," *Journal of American History* 90 (2003): 935.

K-Sue Park argues that foreclosures are an innovation of settler colonialism. She traces the racialized history of mortgage foreclosure in the United States and what she describes as the "powerful feedback loop between migration, occupation, and profit" to the colonial period, when colonists "introduced novel practices of foreclosure in the seventeenth century in order to expropriate lands held by Native nations." This racial practice, she argues, served to both normalize mortgage foreclosure among the colonists while also helping to "inaugurate a two-track local economy, one based on different treatment for different, racially demarcated groups," thereby transforming "the instrument of foreclosure from a rarely used option of last resort to a quotidian practice and a central part of the machinery ensuring the liquidity of real estate." K-Sue Park, "Race, Innovation, and Financial Growth: The Example of Foreclosure," in *Histories of Racial Capitalism*, ed. Destin Jenkins and Justin Leroy (New York: Columbia University Press, 2021), 27–28, 34,

NOTES TO CHAPTER FOUR

43. See also Jean M. O'Brien, *Dispossession by Degrees: Indian Land and Identity in Natick, Massachusetts, 1650–1790* (New York: Cambridge University Press, 1997).

For more comprehensive accounts and histories of the many exclusionary, extractive, and usurious policies and practices authorized, implemented, and used by local, state, and federal government entities as well as "private" actors such as banks, appraisers, and lenders, see, for example, Mehrsa Baradaran, *The Color of Money: Black Banks and the Racial Wealth Gap* (Cambridge, MA: Belknap Press of Harvard University Press, 2017); Christopher Bonastia, *Knocking on the Door: The Federal Government's Attempt to Desegregate the Suburbs* (Princeton, NJ: Princeton University Press, 2006); Emily Card, *Staying Solvent: A Comprehensive Guide to Equal Credit for Women* (New York: Holt, Rinehart and Winston, 1985); Dalton Conley, *Being Black, Living in the Red: Race, Wealth, and Social Policy in America* (Berkeley: University of California Press, 1999); N. D. B. Connolly, *A World More Concrete: Real Estate and the Remaking of Jim Crow South Florida* (University of Chicago Press, 2014); Matthew Desmond, *Evicted: Poverty and Profit in the American City* (New York: Penguin Random House, 2017); Mitchell Duneier, *Ghetto: The Invention of a Place, the History of an Idea* (New York: Farrar, Straus and Giroux, 2017); David M. P. Freund, *Colored Property: State Policy and White Racial Politics in Suburban America* (Chicago: University of Chicago Press, 2007); Edward G. Goetz, *New Deal Ruins: Race, Economic Justice, and Public Housing Policy* (Ithaca, NY: Cornell University Press, 2013); James Greer, "The Better Homes Movement and the Origins of Mortgage Redlining in the United States," in *Statebuilding from the Margins: Between Reconstruction and the New Deal*, ed. Julie Novkov and Carol Nackenoff (Philadelphia: University of Pennsylvania Press, 2014), 203–36; Cheryl I. Harris, "Whiteness as Property," in *Critical Race Theory: The Key Writings That Formed the Movement*, ed. Kimberlé Crenshaw, Neil Gotanda, Gary Peller, and Kendall Thomas (New York: New Press, 1995), 276–91; Chester Hartman and Gregory Squires, *From Foreclosure to Fair Lending: Advocacy, Organizing, Occupy, and the Pursuit of Equitable Credit* (New York: New Village Press, 2013); Rose Helper, *Racial Policies and Practices of Real Estate Brokers* (Minneapolis: University of Minnesota Press, 1969); Louis Hyman, *Debtor's Nation: The History of America in Red Ink* (Princeton, NJ: Princeton University Press, 2011); Louis Hyman, *Borrow: The American Way of Debt* (New York: Vintage, 2012); Kenneth T. Jackson, *Crabgrass Frontier: The Suburbanization of America* (New York: Oxford University Press, 1985); Ira Katznelson, *When Affirmative Action Was White: An Untold Story of Racial Inequality in Twentieth Century America* (New York: W. W. Norton, 2006); Charles M. Lamb, *Housing Segregation in Suburban America since 1960: Presidential and Judicial Politics* (New York: Cambridge University Press, 2005); Serena Laws, "What Kind of Relief? Consumer Bankruptcy and Private Administration in the Neoliberal American Welfare State," *New Political Science* 42 (2020): 333–56; John R. Logan and Harvey L. Molotch, *Urban Fortunes: The*

Political Economy of Place (Berkeley: University of California Press, 1987); Douglas S. Massey and Nancy A. Denton, *American Apartheid: Segregation and the Making of the Underclass* (Cambridge, MA: Harvard University Press, 1993); John H. Mollenkopf, *The Contested City* (Princeton, NJ: Princeton University Press, 1983); Mary Pattillo, *Black on the Block: The Politics of Race and Class in the City* (Chicago: University of Chicago Press, 2010); Patricia Posey, "Lessons of Financial Institutions: Racialized Resource Provision, Regulatory Design, and Political Learning" (paper presented at the Workshop on the Politics of Credit and Debt, Trinity College, Hartford, CT, November 2020); Gail Radford, *Modern Housing for America: Policy Struggles in the New Deal Era* (Chicago: University of Chicago Press, 1996); Richard Rothstein, *The Color of Law: A Forgotten History of How Our Government Segregated America* (New York: Liveright, 2017); Beryl Satter, *Family Properties: Race, Real Estate, and the Exploitation of Black Urban America* (New York: St. Martin's Press, 2009); Mallory E. SoRelle, *Democracy Declined: The Failed Politics of Consumer Financial Protection* (Chicago: University of Chicago Press, 2020); Gregory D. Squires, *Capital and Communities in Black and White: The Intersections of Race, Class, and Uneven Development* (Albany: SUNY Press, 1994); Chloe N. Thurston, *At the Boundaries of Homeownership: Credit, Discrimination, and the American State* (Cambridge: Cambridge University Press, 2018); US Department of Housing and Urban Development, Office of Policy Development and Research, *Women and Mortgage Credit: An Annotated Bibliography* (Washington, DC: US Department of Housing and Urban Development, 1979); Rhonda Y. Williams, *The Politics of Public Housing: Black Women's Struggles against Urban Inequality* (New York: Oxford University Press, 2004).

16. As Thurston explains, "US homeownership rates saw their fastest growth between 1940 and 1960," and that while it is true that "no single factor can explain this rise," scholars have estimated that the availability of FHA mortgage insurance "likely accounted for 12 percent of the overall increase in homeownership between 1940 and 1960," with additional, but harder to estimate, spillover effects. Thurston, *Boundaries of Homeownership*, 60.

17. Thurston, *Boundaries of Homeownership*, 26–27.

18. Thurston, *Boundaries of Homeownership*, 41, 49. The period during which foreclosures dropped was 1926–1933.

19. Thurston, *Boundaries of Homeownership*, 41.

20. Thurston, *Boundaries of Homeownership*, 41.

21. Bruce Mitchell and Juan Franco, "HOLC 'Redlining' Maps: The Persistent Structure of Segregation and Economic Inequality." National Community Reinvestment Coalition, 20 March 2018, 5, https://ncrc.org/wp-content/uploads/dlm_uploads/2018/02/NCRC-Research-HOLC-10.pdf.

22. Rothstein, *Color of Law*, 52.

23. Mitchell and Franco, "HOLC 'Redlining' Maps," 5.

24. Rothstein, *Color of Law*, 64–65. On archaic language in sources, see chap. 2, note 36.

25. HOLC also did not refuse all requests to refinance properties in these "redlined" neighborhoods. It also did not share its maps outside of "select government circles." LaDale C. Winling and Todd M. Michney, "The Roots of Redlining: Academic, Governmental, and Professional Networks in the Making of the New Deal Lending Regime," *Journal of American History* 108 (2021): 63.

26. Thurston, *Boundaries of Homeownership*, 50.

27. Thurston, *Boundaries of Homeownership*, 56–57.

28. Thurston, *Boundaries of Homeownership*, 71.

29. Thurston, *Boundaries of Homeownership*, 71–72.

30. Thurston, *Boundaries of Homeownership*, 77–81.

31. Thurston, *Boundaries of Homeownership*, 81.

32. Thurston, *Boundaries of Homeownership*, 82; Canaday, "Building a Straight State," 935.

33. Federal Housing Administration, *Underwriting Manual* (Washington, DC: GPO, 1936), pt. 2, sec. 304 e.

34. The archaic term "Negro" is used in the original.

35. Guy Stuart, *Discriminating Risk: The U.S. Mortgage Lending Industry in the Twentieth Century* (Ithaca, NY: Cornell University Press, 2003), 92–93.

36. Thurston, *Boundaries of Homeownership*, 77.

37. Katharine Johnson, "'Why Is This the Only Place in Portland I See Black People?' Teaching Young Children about Redlining," *Rethinking Schools* 27 (2012): 19–24.

38. Keeanga-Yamahtta Taylor, *Race for Profit: How Banks and the Real Estate Industry Undermined Black Homeownership* (Chapel Hill: University of North Carolina Press, 2019), 257; Rachel E. Dwyer, "Credit, Debt, and Inequality," *Annual Review of Sociology* 44 (2018): 241. For some illustrative and detailed examples of the myriad ways in which the policies and practices of the FHA and private lenders "aided and abetted the growth and development of increased segregation in U.S. residential neighborhoods," see George Lipsitz, "The Possessive Investment in Whiteness: Racialized Social Democracy and the 'White' Problem in American Studies," *American Quarterly* 47 (1995): 376–77.

39. Thurston, *Boundaries of Homeownership*, 147. Thurston explains while the FHA "left some discretion to the lender," the Department of Veterans' Affairs (VA) "continued to categorically refuse to count any of a wife's income toward loan amounts" through the 1950s, "even for the few female veterans eligible for GI Bill benefits." That is, even when it was "the wife's" military service that made a married couple eligible for VA housing assistance, it counted only her husband's income in determining loan eligibility. In February 1973, the same year that the Equal Credit Opportunity Act was introduced in Congress, a VA bulletin "cryptically suggest[ed] that baby letters, if 'voluntarily submitted by the veteran to the lender . . . cannot very well be refused upon receipt in the VA." Thurston, *Boundaries of Homeownership*, 147–49.

40. Thurston, *Boundaries of Homeownership*, 147.

41. Dwyer, "Credit, Debt, and Inequality," 243.

42. Thurston, *Boundaries of Homeownership*, 161–63.

43. Thurston, *Boundaries of Homeownership*, 157.

44. Dwyer, "Credit, Debt, and Inequality," 243.

45. Thurston, *Boundaries of Homeownership*, 152–54.

46. Here, too, there is some evidence that the VA's practices were even worse than those of the FHA. Thurston recounts a particularly vivid complaint from a magazine editor named Carole Lewicke. Although she earned twice as much as her husband, the VA "loan officer only agreed to the loan after she and her husband produced signed affidavits that she would have an immediate abortion if she were to become pregnant, and that her husband would undergo a vasectomy if she ever quit using birth control." Thurston, *Boundaries of Homeownership*, 157.

47. Thurston, *Boundaries of Homeownership*, 144–45.

48. Thurston, *Boundaries of Homeownership*, 144–45.

49. Taylor, *Race for Profit*, 191–92.

50. Thurston, *Boundaries of Homeownership*, 154.

51. Thurston, *Boundaries of Homeownership*, 126, 162. Thurston explains that "while it was clear that lenders regularly treated women differently in matters of lending," many professed that they were simply "acting according to a sound economic rationale." Witnesses testifying on behalf of banks and other lenders at hearings about what became the 1974 Equal Credit Opportunity Act, for example, dismissed what seemed clearly to be irrefutable evidence of discrimination against would-be women borrowers claiming, among other things, that although "some practices might appear discriminatory" they actually reflected the sound business practices "necessary for a savings and loan association to come out in the black at the end of the year or it wouldn't be in existence.'" Thurston, *Boundaries of Homeownership*, 154–55.

52. Thurston, *Boundaries of Homeownership*, 81–82.

53. Thurston, *Boundaries of Homeownership*, 163.

54. Thurston, *Boundaries of Homeownership*, 162.

55. Thurston, *Boundaries of Homeownership*, 162.

56. Thurston continues, "Another study, conducted by two researchers from CWPS [the Center for Women Policy Studies], examined only banks that had a history of lending to women and men on similar terms, and found no evidence that women were a worse credit risk than men. Finally, casting doubt on the assertion that women were more prone to quitting their jobs than men, advocates presented evidence from the Department of Labor that labor turnover was influenced less by sex and more by characteristics of the job itself, the age of the worker, and the worker's length of service." Thurston, *Boundaries of Homeownership*, 162–63.

57. Dwyer, "Credit, Debt, and Inequality," 240.

58. "Nearly two decades after the FHA removed explicit racial criteria from

its own Underwriting Manual," Thurston explains, training materials continued to emphasize "the same basic elements of mortgage risk: a combination of the soundness of the security (real estate), the borrower's credit and personal characteristics, and the terms of the loan." The American Savings and Loan Institute textbook continued to emphasize "the changing racial and ethnic makeup of a neighborhood as a relevant factor to consider when determining a property's likelihood to hold value," while surveys of mortgage lenders in the 1970s "found that many were basing their policy of discounting a working wife's income on federal guidelines that had since been updated, the news of which had not reached many lenders." Similarly, the 1971 American Savings and Loan Institute textbook advised lenders to use "personal references" to look for information "on the applicant's nonfinancial background and habits." It may turn out, the guide counseled, "that the applicant is Joe Average in his personal life, that he has managed major medical or other bills with a degree of responsibility that doesn't show up in the coded facts and figures on a credit report." But they may also learn "that he drinks heavily and has serious marital difficulties." Thurston, *Boundaries of Homeownership*, 83–84.

59. This decision was based, in part, on the majority decision in the 2020 case *Bostock v. Clayton County*, in which the Supreme Court "held that workplace prohibitions on sex discrimination include discrimination because of sexual orientation and gender identity." U.S. Department of Housing and Urban Development, "HUD to Enforce Fair Housing Act to Prohibit Discrimination on the Basis of Sexual Orientation and Gender Identity," press release no. HUD 21-021, 11 February 2011, https://www.hud.gov/press/press_releases_media_advisories /hud_no_21_021. At the time of the decision, twenty US states provided no explicit protections against housing discrimination based on sexual orientation or gender identity, and only twenty-two explicitly prohibited discrimination based on both. "Nondiscrimination Laws," Movement Advancement Project, data current as of 12 August 2022, http://www.lgbtmap.org/equality-maps/non_discrimination_laws /housing. For many years, data limitations have made it almost impossible for researchers to track discrimination against LGBTQ people and same-sex couples in the sale, rental, and financing of housing. Recent research, however, suggests that this discrimination is widespread. A 2013 HUD matched-pair study of fifty metropolitan areas found that same-sex couples were significantly less likely to received responses to email inquiries about rental properties. M. Davis and Co. et al., *An Estimate of Housing Discrimination Against Same-Sex Couples*, Office of Policy Development and Research, June 2013, https://www.huduser.gov/portal /publications/fairhsg/discrim_samesex.html. A 2017 study found that 22 percent of LGBT-identified adults reported experiencing discrimination while attempting to buy or rent housing. National Public Radio, Robert Wood Johnson Foundation, and Harvard T. H. Chan School of Public Health, *Discrimination in America: Experiences and Views of LGBTQ Americans*, November 2017, https://legacy.npr.org /documents/2017/nov/npr-discrimination-lgbtq-final.pdf. Several studies suggest

that housing discrimination is even more pronounced when it comes to trans people, gay men, and gay Black men in particular. For example, almost one-quarter of the 27,715 participants in the 2015 U.S. Transgender Survey reported experiencing some form of housing discrimination in the previous year, including substantially higher rates of being denied an apartment, being evicted, and being harassed by neighbors and landlords, with substantially higher rates for transgender women of color and undocumented respondents. S. E. James et al., *The Report of the 2015 U.S. Transgender Survey* (Washington, DC: National Center for Transgender Equality, 2016), https://transequality.org/sites/default/files/docs/usts/USTS-Full -Report-Dec17.pdf. In a matched-pair study of the Boston area, legal scholar Jamie Langowski and her colleagues found that transgender and gender-nonconforming people "received discriminatory differential treatment 61% of the time," that they "were 27% less likely to be shown additional areas of the apartment complex" and "21% less likely to be offered a financial incentive to rent." They were also "12% more likely to be told negative comments about the apartment and the neighborhood, and 9% more likely to be quoted a higher rental price than people who were not transgender and conformed to gender stereotypes." Jamie Langowski, William L. Berman, Regina Holloway, and Cameron McGinn, "Transcending Prejudice: Gender Identity and Expression- Based Discrimination in the Metro Boston Rental Housing Market," *Yale Journal of Law & Feminism* 29 (2018), 322–71.

The combined effects of such practices alongside family rejection also mean that disproportionately high rates of LGBTQ people, particularly LGBTQ youth, lack stable housing or are unhoused. So although queer and trans youth account for only about 7 percent of the total youth population, they comprise an estimated 40 percent of the homeless youth population. Soon Kyu Choi et al., *Serving Our Youth 2015: The Needs and Experiences of Lesbian, Gay, Bisexual, Transgender, and Questioning Youth Experiencing Homelessness* (Los Angeles: Williams Institute, UCLA School of Law, 2015), https://williamsinstitute.law.ucla.edu/publica tions/serving-our-youth-lgbtq/. See also Amy Hillier and Devin Michelle Bunten, "A Queer and Intersectional Approach to Fair Housing," in *Perspectives on Fair Housing*, ed. Vincent J. Reina, Wendell E. Pritchett, and Susan M. Wachter (Philadelphia: University of Pennsylvania Press, 2021), 154–85.

60. This last extension also followed *Bostock v. Clayton County*, and includes "actual or perceived nonconformity with traditional sex- or gender-based stereotypes, and discrimination based on an applicant's social or other associations." Consumer Financial Protection Bureau, "CFPB Clarifies That Discrimination by Lenders on the Basis of Sexual Orientation and Gender Identity Is Illegal," news release, 9 March 2021, https://www.consumerfinance.gov/about-us/news room/cfpb-clarifies-discrimination-by-lenders-on-basis-of-sexual-orientation-and -gender-identity-is-illegal/. At the time of the decision, thirty-five US states, along with five territories and the District of Columbia, provided no explicit protections against credit discrimination based on sexual orientation or gender identity, and

only fifteen explicitly prohibited discrimination based on both. https://www.lgbt
map.org/equality-maps/non_discrimination_laws/credit. As in the case of housing
discrimination, data limitations have made it difficult to track mortgage lending
discrimination against LGBTQ people and same-sex couples. However, as I noted
above, the VA explicitly denied G.I. Bill benefits—including housing loans—to
soldiers with undesirable discharges "because of homosexual acts or tendencies."
Canaday, "Building a Straight State," 935. More recently, Hua Sun and Lei Gao
analyzed HMDA data from 1990–2015 and found that mortgage loan applications
from same-sex couples were approximately 73 percent more likely to be denied
than those submitted by different-sex applicants with similar characteristics, leading to mortgage approval rates for same-sex applicants that are 3–8 percent lower
that they are for their ostensibly heterosexual counterparts with similar profiles.
Same-sex borrowers are also charged interest rates between 0.02 and 0.2 percent higher than ostensibly heterosexual couples, leading to between $8.6 million
and $86 million more in interest and fees over time. They also found that as the
proportion of same-sex households in a neighborhood increases, both same-sex
and different-sex borrowers experienced lower approval rates and higher interest rates and fees. Hua Sun and Lei Gao, "Lending Practices to Same-Sex Borrowers," *Proceedings of the National Academy of Sciences* 116 (2019): 9293–9302.
Shahar Dillbary and Griffin Edwards find similar patterns. In addition to finding
that, holding all else equal, same-sex male couples of every racial configuration
were significantly less likely than their white heterosexual counterparts to have
their mortgage applications approved, Dillbary and Edwards's analysis also reveals evidence that sexuality-based discrimination is exacerbated by the intersecting effects of race and sexuality, as applications from Black same-sex and inter-
racial couples were significantly less likely to be approved than those of white
same-sex couples, though all were less likely to be approved than their heterosexual
counterparts. J. Shahar Dillbary and Griffin Edwards, "An Empirical Analysis of
Sexual Orientation Discrimination," *University of Chicago Law Review* 86 (2019):
1–76. As a consequence of these and other factors (such as the fact that LGBTQ
people are more likely to live in cities, where rates of homeownership are typically lower), LGBTQ people are far less likely to own their homes than their heterosexual counterparts (49.8 percent of LGBTQ adults and 70.1 percent of non-
LGBTQ adults), with even lower rates among trans people and LGBTQ people
of color. Adam P. Romero, Shoshana K. Goldberg, and Luis A. Vasquez, *LGBT
People and Housing Affordability, Discrimination, and Homelessness* (Los Angeles:
Williams Institute, UCLA School of Law, 2020), https://williamsinstitute.law.ucla
.edu/publications/lgbt-housing-instability/.

61. Prasad argues further that "understanding credit as an alternative form of
redistribution" makes sense of what she characterizes as "an otherwise puzzling
feature of the politics of deregulation: why the American Left was so supportive of
financial deregulation in the 1970s." She argues that deregulation of the American

financial sector "resulted at least partly because groups from across political lines joined together to argue in favor of it." The Depository Institutions Deregulation and Monetary Control Act of 1980, she explains, "was passed when Democrats were in control of the White House and both houses of Congress," and even had the support of consumer advocate Ralph Nader, who testified to Congress in 1973 "that Depression-era regulations were less relevant" because the United States had become, in his view "truly a credit-oriented installment payment economy." Prasad, *Land of Too Much*, 239–40.

62. Krippner, *Capitalizing on Crisis*. For a discussion about the broader move to privatization and their implications for "risk," see Jacob S. Hacker, *The Great Risk Shift: The New Economic Insecurity and the Decline of the American Dream* (New York: Oxford University Press, 2019).

63. Dwyer, "Credit, Debt, and Inequality," 239.

64. Souphala Chomsisengphet and Anthony Pennington-Cross, "The Evolution of the Subprime Mortgage Market," *Federal Reserve Bank of St. Louis Review* 88 (2006): 38.

65. As a result of this holding, which came to be known as the "exportation doctrine," McCoy and Renuart explain, "national banks could establish their head-quarters in states with high usury limits—or none at all—and charge the high in-terest rates permitted by the bank's home state to borrowers located in any other state." See McCoy and Renuart, "Legal Infrastructure," 113.

66. Contrasting the United States with other countries, Prasad explains that while

> European countries focused on top-down efforts at reconstruct-ing their economies by focusing on production and restraining consumption, the United States pioneered a form of "mortgage Keynesianism" in which mortgage finance was a primary mecha-nism for sustaining economic growth. These developments in turn yielded a political economy that undermined the public welfare state and established dependence on the development of credit-financed private consumption for economic growth, in contrast to the production-oriented economies of Europe.

Prasad, *Land of Too Much*, 93.

67. Atkinson, "Borrowing Equality," 1408. See also Baradaran, *Color of Money*; Hartman and Squires, *From Foreclosure to Fair Lending*; Hyman, *Debtor Nation*; Thurston, *Boundaries of Homeownership*.

68. Atkinson, "Borrowing Equality," 1408. Atkinson argues further that in valo-rizing "borrowing money as a catalyst for equality," Congress has evinced what she calls a "borrowing-as-equality" policy that has "proffered credit as a means of equality without expressly accounting for the countervailing force of debt relative to social subordination." But debt, she argues, functions "as a mechanism of the

very subordination that Congress's invocation of 'credit' aspires to address," and is "central to the project of discrimination and the reproduction of social hierarchy." "In this light," she concludes, "the notion that marginalized groups in the grips of historical and entrenched subordination can borrow their way into greater socio-economic equality and social position seems unworkable." Atkinson, "Borrowing Equality," 1402, 1468.

69. Baker, "Eroding the Wealth of Women," 75–77.

70. For a full discussion of specific legislative steps taken by the state to promote financialization, see Katherine Newman, "The Perfect Storm: Contextualizing the Foreclosure Crisis," *Urban Geography* 29 (2008): 750–54; Jamie Peck and Adam Tickell, "Neoliberalizing Space," *Antipode* 34 (2002): 380–404; and Mary Poovey, *Genres of the Credit Economy: Mediating Value in Eighteenth- and Nineteenth-Century Britain* (Chicago: University of Chicago Press, 2008).

71. Virginia Eubanks, *Automating Inequality: How High-Tech Tools Profile, Police, and Punish the Poor* (New York: St. Martin's Press, 2018). See also Ruha Benjamin, *Race after Technology: Abolitionist Tools for the New Jim Code* (Medford, MA: Polity Press, 2019); Catherine D'Ignazio and Lauren F. Klein, *Data Feminism* (Cambridge, MA: MIT Press, 2020); Safiya Umoja Noble, *Algorithms of Oppression: How Search Engines Reinforce Racism* (New York: New York University Press, 2018); Cathy O'Neil, *Weapons of Math Destruction: How Big Data Increases Inequality and Threatens Democracy* (New York: Crown, 2016).

72. Krippner, *Capitalizing on Crisis*; Krippner, "Democracy of Credit"; Atkinson, "Borrowing Equality"; Eubanks, *Automating Inequality*; Benjamin, *Race after Technology*; D'Ignazio and Klein, *Data Feminism*; O'Neil, *Weapons of Math Destruction*.

73. Krippner, "Democracy of Credit," 21.

74. Dwyer, "Credit, Debt, and Inequality," 243.

75. These arguments—which Taylor characterizes as "racism and exclusion . . . articulated as risk"—had been made to justify the earlier wave of legislation, including the 1968 Housing and Urban Development Act. As Taylor writes,

> The private market had largely ignored the regular refrain for more safe, sound, and affordable housing, but the advent of low-interest mortgage loans with the full backing of the federal government piqued the interest of the real estate industry. For decades, the FHA maintained that the deteriorating housing stock and "inharmonious" racial groups within American cities made them too risky for the risk-averse real estate and banking industries. The new legislation induced private sector involvement by removing said risk. . . . In an earlier era, risk had been the pretext for excluding potential Black homeowners; by the late 1960s, risk had made Black buyers attractive.

Taylor, *Race for Profit*, 8, 18, 257. See also Baker, "Eroding the Wealth of Women"; James Greer, "The Better Homes Movement and the Origins of Mortgage Redlining in the United States," in *Statebuilding from the Margins: Between Reconstruction and the New Deal*, ed. Julie Novkov and Carol Nackenoff (Philadelphia: University of Pennsylvania Press, 2014), 203–36; Dan Immergluck, *Foreclosed: High-Risk Lending, Deregulation, and the Undermining of America's Mortgage Market* (Ithaca, NY: Cornell University Press, [2009] 2011); Immergluck, "Too Little, Too Late"; Daniel Immergluck, *Preventing the Next Mortgage Crisis: The Meltdown, the Federal Response, and the Future of Housing in America* (New York: Rowman and Littlefield, 2015); Thurston, *Boundaries of Homeownership*.

76. Elvin Wyly and C. S. Ponder argue that they took these measures because "the scale of the disaster was so vast that it was impossible to cling to the ideology of individual, personal responsibility." Elvin Wyly and C. S. Ponder, "Gender, Age, and Race in Subprime America," *Housing Policy Debate* 21 (2011): 560.

77. Baker, "Eroding the Wealth of Women," 77. See also Taylor, *Race for Profit*.

78. Sarah L. Quinn, *American Bonds: How Credit Markets Shaped a Nation* (Princeton, NJ: Princeton University Press, 2020), 209.

79. Louise Seamster and Raphaël Charron-Chénier, "Predatory Inclusion and Education Debt: A New Approach to the Growing Racial Wealth Gap,. *Social Currents* 4 (2017), 199–207; Taylor, *Race for Profit*, 5. See also Baker, "Eroding the Wealth of Women"; Dan Immergluck, *Credit to the Community: Community Reinvestment and Fair Lending Policy in the United States* (New York: Routledge 2004); William Apgar, Amal Bendimerad, and Ren Essene, *Mortgage Market Channels and Fair Lending: An Analysis of HMDA Data* (Cambridge, MA: Joint Center for Housing Studies of Harvard University, 2007).

80. McCoy and Renuart, "Legal Infrastructure," 119. HOEPA is title I, subtitle B, of the Riegle Community Development and Regulatory Improvement Act of 1994, which "amends the Truth in Lending Act to prohibit certain terms and require additional disclosures of the terms of home equity loans and second mortgages with certain interest rates or origination fees."

81. CFPB, *2013 HOEPA Rule*. HOEPA restricted or banned the following for "high-cost" mortgages: "balloon clauses, loans without regard to the borrowers' ability to pay, negative amortization, increased interest rates after default, prepayment penalties, due-on-demand clauses, payments to home improvement contractors, and early refinancings. In addition, lenders who make HOEPA loans must provide special truth in lending disclosures to loan applicants in advance of closing. Lenders that violate HOEPA and their assignees are liable to borrowers for violations of the act." See McCoy and Renuart, "Legal Infrastructure," 119.

82. *Adding Injury to Injury: Credit on the Fringe: Hearings before the House Committee on Banking, Housing, and Urban Affairs*, 103rd Cong. 2–5 (1993).

83. *Adding Injury to Injury: Hearings*.

84. *Adding Injury to Injury: Hearings*.

85. *Adding Injury to Injury: Hearings*, 1.

86. *Adding Injury to Injury: Hearings*, 1. Archaic use of "ghetto" and "barrio" in the original.

87. *The Homeownership and Equity Protection Act of 1993 - S. 924: Hearings before the Senate Committee on Banking, Housing, and Urban Affairs*, 103rd Cong. 5 (1993).

88. *Homeownership and Equity Protection Act: Hearings*, 5.

89. *Homeownership and Equity Protection Act: Hearings*, 5.

90. *Homeownership and Equity Protection Act: Hearings*, 29.

91. *Homeownership and Equity Protection Act: Hearings*, 30.

92. Elinore Longobardi, "How 'Subprime' Killed 'Predatory,'" *Columbia Journalism Review* (2009) 48.

93. Immergluck, *Foreclosed*, 11.

94. Wyly and Ponder, "Subprime America," 533.

95. *Homeownership and Equity Protection Act: Hearings*, 2.

96. McCoy and Renuart, "Legal Infrastructure," 119.

97. Congressional hearings are a particularly rich source of information about the policy agenda and about how issues are taken up by policymakers. In addition to collecting information about potential legislation, hearings also, as Bryan Jones and Michelle Whyman note, assess and examine problems of implementation and explore "situations in the future that may require legislative action." Jones and Whyman go as far as to argue that congressional hearings are the *most* reliable indicator of the formal institutional policy agenda. If they are correct, it seems that the racialized and gendered patterns in exploitative mortgages and in the rising rates of foreclosure during this period were of little concern to the setters of the formal political agenda in the 1980s, 1990s, and first years of the twenty-first century. See Bryan Jones and Michelle Whyman, "The Great Broadening: Agenda Politics and the Transformation of the American Political System" (working paper of the US Policy Agendas Project, 2014). See also Roger Cobb and Charles Elder, *Participation in American Politics: The Dynamics of Agenda-Building* (Boston: Allyn and Bacon 1972); Frank Baumgartner and Bryan Jones, *Agendas and Instability in American Politics*, 2nd ed. (Chicago: University of Chicago Press, 2009).

98. *H.R. 3153, The Home Equity Protection Act of 1993: Hearings before the Subcommittee on Consumer Credit and Insurance of the House Committee on Banking, Housing, and Urban Affairs*, 103rd Cong. 42 (1994).

99. *H.R. 3153: Hearings*, 50. See also Vanesa Estrada Correa, "Blueprint for the American Dream? A Critical Discourse Analysis of Presidential Remarks on Minority Home Ownership," *Social Justice* 40 (2014): 16–27; Wyly and Ponder, "Subprime America." Whereas the scheduled payments for self-amortizing loans consist of both interest and principal and ensure that the principal decreases over time and the full amount will be paid off at the end of the loan's term, negatively amortized loans are characterized by initial monthly payments that do not cover

the interest, with the difference added to the principal, which therefore increases rather than decreases over time.

100. *Homeownership and Equity Protection Act: Hearings*, 25–26.

101. *Homeownership and Equity Protection Act: Hearings*, 5.

102. *Homeownership and Equity Protection Act: Hearings*, 5.

103. US Congress, Senate, Committee on Banking, Housing, and Urban Affairs, *The Homeownership and Equity Protection Act of 1993 - S. 924*, 19.

104. *H.R. 3153: Hearings.* Or, as Wyly and Ponder put it,

> Disclosure requirements are not enough: for a generation, con-
> sumers have been ever more overwhelmed by lengthening
> microscopic-font legal disclosures of precisely how they may be
> deceived and exploited. If scholars and policy makers suggest that
> Beatrice, Veronica, Anna Mae, and Addie should have read things
> carefully before they signed, consider the exponential expansion
> of digital legal disclosures that now bury us all: have you read ev-
> ery line of every End-User License Agreement (EULA) for every
> piece of software that has required you to check off that 'I've read
> the terms and conditions' during installation?

Wyly and Ponder, "Subprime America," 559.

105. *Homeownership and Equity Protection Act: Hearings* 19 (statement of Margot Saunders, Managing Attorney, National Consumer Law Center, Washington, DC).

106. McCoy and Renuart, "Legal Infrastructure."

107. US Department of Housing and Urban Development, *Root Causes of Foreclosure Crisis* ix. For more extensive discussions of the inadequacy of the mortgage lending disclosure system, see E. M. Gramlich, "Booms and Busts: The Case of Subprime Mortgages," *Economic Review* 92 (2007): 105–13; Ren S. Essene and William C. Apgar, *Understanding Mortgage Market Behavior: Creating Good Mortgage Options for All Americans* (Cambridge, MA: Joint Center for Housing Studies of Harvard University 2007); McCoy and Renuart, "Legal Infrastructure."

108. Immergluck, *Foreclosed*, 11.

109. Chomsisengphet and Pennington-Cross, "Subprime Mortgage Market," 37.

110. National Training and Information Center, *Preying on Neighborhoods: Subprime Mortgage Lenders and Chicago Land Foreclosures* (Chicago: National Training and Information Center, 1999). See also Jacob Faber, "Racial Dynamics of Subprime Mortgage Lending at the Peak," *Housing Policy Debate* 23 (2013): 328–49.

111. US Department of Housing and Development (HUD), and US Department of Treasury, *Curbing Predatory Home Mortgage Lending: A Joint Report* (June 2000), 47.

112. Association of Community Organizations for Reform Now, *Separate and*

Unequal: Predatory Lending in America (Washington, DC: Association of Community Organizations for Reform Now, 2000), 24.

113. Association of Community Organizations for Reform Now, *Separate and Unequal*, 24.

114. National Training and Information Center, *Preying on Neighborhoods*. See also Faber, "Racial Dynamics."

115. HUD and US Department of Treasury, *Curbing*, 48.

116. HUD and US Department of Treasury, *Curbing*, 48.

117. Jacob Rugh, Len Albright, and Douglas Massey, "Race, Space, and Cumulative Disadvantage: A Case Study of the Subprime Lending Collapse," *Social Problems* 62 (2015): 186–218.

118. Baker, "Eroding the Wealth of Women," 77. See also Kathe Newman and Elvin Wyly, "Geographies of Mortgage Market Segmentation: The Case of Essex County, New Jersey," *Housing Studies* 19 (2004): 53–83; David Kaplan, "Foreclosures, Predatory Lending, and Reverse Redlining," *Urban Geography* 29 (2008): 762–66.

119. As Maya Sen notes in a working paper, although evidence of race and gender disparities in rates of subprime mortgage lending is long standing and well established, it has proven difficult to establish that the overrepresentation of women and people of color among subprime borrowers is caused by discrimination because "many important personal data—including credit scores, employment histories, savings, and debt obligations—are highly proprietary and are not collected by the federal government via the HMDA." Maya Sen, "Quantifying Discrimination: Exploring the Role of Race and Gender in the Subprime Lending Crisis" (working paper, Harvard University, Cambridge, MA, 2012), 3.

120. The 1999 report from the National Training and Information Center cited above provides an example of the elision of gender. Part 3 of the report profiled five former homeowners "who may lose or have lost their properties in foreclosure subsequent to taking out one or more subprime loans." The profiles list the race of all five of them as African American; the profiles do not specify their sex, but all five are referred to as "Ms." Neither race nor gender is ever thematized in the report, however. National Training and Information Center, "Preying on Neighborhoods."

As Wyly and Ponder write,

On the matter of racial and ethnic disparities in credit markets, there is a vast body of rigorous research—internal disagreements notwithstanding—that acknowledges the significance of systemic inequalities in observed outcomes. Gender, however, has received very little attention in the research literature. Models of lending decisions sometimes include controls for borrower sex, but there is little explicit consideration of gender disparities. . . . Research, therefore, has been distorted by a partial and disjointed view of social inequalities, while public policy has been impoverished by the small research infrastructure.

Wyly and Ponder, "Subprime America," 534. As in the case of racial discrimination in lending, these elisions reflected long-standing—but also long-refuted—stereotypes and assumptions about women's creditworthiness and labor force participation.

121. Allen Fishbein and Patrick Woodall, *Women Are Prime Targets for Subprime Lending: Women are Disproportionately in High-Cost Mortgage Market* (Washington, DC: Consumer Federation of America, 2006), 10–11. See also Amy Castro Baker, "Eroding the Wealth of Women: Gender and the Subprime Foreclosure Crisis," *Social Science Review* 88, no. 1 (2014): 59–91; Gary Dymski, Jesus Hernandez, and Lisa Mohanty, "Race, Gender, Power, and the US Subprime Mortgage and Foreclosure Crisis: A Meso Analysis," *Feminist Economics* 19, no. 3 (2013): 124–51; Sandra Phillips, "The Subprime Mortgage Calamity and the African American Woman," *Review of Black Political Economy* 39 (2012): 227–37; Wyley and Ponder, "Subprime America;" Sen, "Quantifying Discrimination."

122. Bronwen Lichtenstein and Joe Weber, "Women Foreclosed: A Gender Analysis of Housing Loss in the US Deep South," *Social & Cultural Geography* 16 (2015), 4. Reporter Molly Ginty reported about one mortgage broker who was on record declaring that "it's time to go granny hunting!" Molly Ginty, "In Subprime Fallout, Women Take a Heavy Hit," *Women's e-News*, 13 January 2010, http://womensenews.org/story/economyeconomic-policy/100113/in-subprime fallout-women-take-heavy-hit.

123. Fishbein and Woodall, *Women Are Prime Targets*, 3. See also Jacob Rugh and Douglas Massey, "Racial Segregation and the American Foreclosure Crisis," *American Sociological Review* 75 (2010): 629–51; Wyly and Ponder, "Subprime America."

124. Fishbein and Woodall, *Women Are Prime Targets*, 3.

125. Wyly and Ponder, "Subprime America."

126. Fishbein and Woodall, *Women Are Prime Targets*, 15.

127. Fishbein and Woodall, *Women Are Prime Targets*; Phillips, "Subprime Mortgage Calamity." Sun and Gao find some evidence that LGBTQ borrowers experience related discrimination, showing that although same-sex borrower couples exhibit similar default risk but lower prepayment risk than opposite-sex couples, their applications are denied at higher rates and they received less favorable loan terms. Sun and Gao, "Lending Practices," 9300.

128. Fishbein and Woodall, *Women Are Prime Targets*, 12–13.

129. Baker, "Eroding the Wealth of Women," 81.

130. Baker, "Eroding the Wealth of Women," 77; Rick Brooks and Ruth Simon, "Subprime Debacle Traps Even Very Credit-Worthy as Housing Boomed,

Industry Pushed Loans to Broader Market," *Wall Street Journal*, 4 December 2007, 3; Fishbein and Woodall, *Women Are Prime Targets*; Kathleen Keest, "The Way Ahead: A Framework for Policy Responses" (paper presented at the Subprime Housing Crisis Symposium, University of Iowa, 10–11 October 2008).

131. Debbie Gruenstein Bocian, Wei Li, Carolina Reid, and Roberto G. Quercia, "Lost Ground, 2011: Disparities in Mortgage Lending and Foreclosures" (Durham, NC: Center for Responsible Lending, 2011), https://www.responsiblelending .org/mortgage-lending/research-analysis/Lost-Ground-2011.pdf.

132. US Department of Housing and Urban Development, Office of Policy Development and Research, *"Subprime Lending Report: Unequal Burden in Baltimore: Income and Racial Disparities in Subprime Lending,"* (Washington, DC: US Department of Housing and Urban Development, 2000), https://www.huduser .gov/Publications/pdf/baltimore.pdf.

133. Bocian et al., *Foreclosures*, 3.

134. Bocian et al., *Foreclosures*, 3.

135. Crump et al., "Cities Destroyed."

136. Joint Center for Housing Studies of Harvard University, *The State of the Nation's Housing 2009* (Cambridge, MA: Joint Center for Housing Studies of Harvard University, 2009), 29. http://www.jchs.harvard.edu/sites/jchs.harvard.edu/files /son2009.pdf.

137. Immergluck, *Preventing the Next Mortgage Crisis*, 11.

138. Baker, "Eroding the Wealth of Women." See also Jeff Crump, "Subprime Lending and Foreclosure in Hennepin and Ramsey Counties," *CURA Reporter* 37 (2007): 14–18.

139. David Harvey, *The Enigma of Capital and the Crises of Capitalism* (New York: Oxford University Press, 2010), 1.

140. Robert Cotterman, *New Evidence on the Relationship Race and Mortgage Default: The Importance of Credit History Data*, Unicon Research Corp., 23 May 2002, https://www.huduser.gov/Publications/PDF/crhistory.pdf.

141. National Training and Information Center, "Preying on Neighborhoods."

142. Immergluck, *Foreclosed*, xi.

143. Immergluck, *Foreclosed*, xi–xii.

144. Baker, "Eroding the Wealth of Women," 77; Immergluck, *Foreclosed*; Immergluck, *Credit to the Community*. For discussions about activist organizing around foreclosures and subprime and predatory lending, see Heidi J. Swarts, *Organizing Urban America: Secular and Faith-Based Progressive Movements* (Minneapolis: University of Minnesota Press, 2008); and M. David Forrest, *Giving Voice without Power? Organizing for Social Justice in Minneapolis* (Minneapolis: University of Minnesota Press, 2022).

145. Baker, "Eroding the Wealth of Women," 77; Immergluck, *Foreclosed*; Immergluck, *Credit to the Community*; Rhea Myerscough, "Regulating the Predatory Economy: Inequality, Policy, and the Power of Organized Interests" (paper

presented at the American Political Science Association conference, Boston, MA, 30 August–2 September 2018); Chloe Thurston and Emily Zackin, "The Missing Movement: Consumer Debtors and Their Advocates in the Twentieth Century" (paper presented at the Workshop on the Politics of Credit and Debt, Trinity College, Hartford, CT, November 2020). McCoy and Renuart explain that by the beginning of 2007,

> twenty-nine states and the District of Columbia had "mini-HOEPA" laws. Some of these states—along with other states—also had older provisions on their books restricting prepayment penalties and sometimes balloon terms. In addition, other states that eschewed mini-HOEPA laws implemented alternative approaches to predatory lending, such as broker certification, licensing statutes, disclosure laws, or state banking regulations. State antipredatory lending laws of one type or another became so widespread that by the start of 2007, only six states—Arizona, Delaware, Montana, North Dakota, Oregon, and South Dakota—did not regulate any of the subprime loan terms generating the greatest concern, namely prepayment penalties, balloon clauses, or mandatory arbitration clauses.

McCoy and Renuart, "Legal Infrastructure," 119.

146. Amy Borrus, "Congress Draws a Bead on Predatory Lending," *Business Week*, 4 April 2005, http://search.ebscohost.com.ezproxy.princeton.edu/login.aspx?direct=true&db=rgm&AN=504030887&site=ehost-live.

147. Baker, "Eroding the Wealth of Women," 77. See also Immergluck, *Foreclosed*; Immergluck, *Credit to the Community*.

148. Baker, "Eroding the Wealth of Women," 77; Immergluck, *Foreclosed*; Immergluck, *Credit to the Community*.

149. McCoy and Renuart, "Legal Infrastructure," 120. McCoy and Renuart make clear that while some of the OTS regulations predated the passage of state anti-predatory lending laws, the OCC's were issued mainly in response to these laws. As they write: "Starting in 1999, as more and more states adopted those laws, national banks and their mortgage-lending subsidiaries lobbied their federal regulator, the Office of the Comptroller of the Currency (OCC), to afford them the same relief as federal thrifts. Eager to accommodate its regulated entities and to encourage state banks to convert their charters to federal charters, the OCC issued its now-famous 2004 regulation that was virtually identical to the preemption regulation adopted by the OTS. . . . Collectively, these pronouncements permit national banks and federal saving associations to ignore a whole host of state credit protection laws. . . . In addition, state agencies have no right to enforce even applicable state laws, such as state lending discrimination laws, against these institutions." McCoy and Renuart, "Legal Infrastructure," 120–21.

150. HUD, *Root Causes*, ix.

151. HUD, *Root Causes*, ix.

152. Crump et al., "Cities Destroyed," 753.

153. Apgar et al., "Mortgage Market Channels," iv.

154. Baker, "Eroding the Wealth of Women," 83–84.

Chapter Five

1. Robert Entman, "Images of Blacks and Racism in Local Television News," *Critical Studies in Media Communication* 7 (2019): 332–45.

2. As I explain at greater length in appendices A and B, I focus the analyses on economic reporting in the *New York Times* and the *Wall Street Journal* because their status as "papers of record" makes them particularly important parts of the transcript of dominant politics. While some scholarship relies exclusively on the *New York Times*, including evidence from the more conservative but still relatively mainstream *Wall Street Journal*—often considered the "financial newspaper of record"— provides some ideological variation. And although the *Wall Street Journal* engaged in less overtly racist vilification of subprime borrowers than was typical of more extreme-right news outlets, its relative moderation means that it is a harder test for the presence of racialized (and gendered) frames than would be true of analyses of coverage in outlets such as Fox News or the *New York Post*. In addition, I replicated several key searches and analyses using the *Readers' Guide to Periodical Literature*. I report these results in tables A.1 and A.2 and appendix B, which show that the patterns in this source are highly correlated with those in the *New York Times* and the *Wall Street Journal*. Searches of executive orders turned up no attention to subprime lending and foreclosure, so while I mention them in passing when relevant, they do not appear in any tables or figures.

3. I recognize that the periods 1995–2006 and 2007–8 are uneven and aesthetically odd, but as historian Ludmilla Jordanova writes, "there are a number of criteria according to which the past can be divided up, in order to produce manageable chunks, organize our thoughts, and offer readings and historical accounts." The accounts in chapter 4 and in the analyses that follow make clear that it makes sense substantively to begin the non-crisis period a year after the passage of the 1994 Home Ownership and Equity Protection Act (HOEPA) and to put the needle of the record of the crisis period in 2007. Ludmilla Jordanova, *History in Practice* (London: Bloomsbury, 2019), 150.

4. Vanesa Estrada Correa, "Blueprint for the American Dream? A Critical Discourse Analysis of Presidential Remarks on Minority Homeownership," *Social Justice* 40 (2014): 16–27; Dean Starkman, *The Watchdog that Didn't Bark: The Financial Crisis and the Disappearance of Investigative Journalism* (New York: Columbia Journalism Review Press, 2014).

5. Timothy O'Brien, "Lowering the Credit Fence; Big Players Are Jumping into the Risky Loan Business," *New York Times*, 13 December 1997, D1.

6. I used ProQuest US Newsstream to compile the data for all *New York Times* and *Wall Street Journal* searches. The data in table 5.1 were compiled by searching these sources using the search strings "subprime NEAR mortgage" and "rising NEAR foreclosure" or "increasing NEAR foreclosure" (in the full text and titles of documents for all available years, which begin in 1980 for the *Times* and in 1982 for the *Wall Street Journal*). The NEAR command returns documents that contain the two search terms, in any order, within four words apart. In the case of the *Wall Street Journal*, I further specified that the search ignore items in several regular features: "New Securities Issues," "New Stock Listings," and "Bids and Offers," as these are not substantive articles but rather, as their names suggest, simply listings of securities and stocks for sale and offers made to purchase companies. I downloaded all the resulting data and metadata into a spreadsheet and downloaded and cleaned the full text of all articles, using Nvivo and LIWC to conduct keyword searches that generated analyzable data. Pablo Barbera, Amber Boydstun, Suzanna Linn, Ryan McMahon, and Jonathan Nagler explain in a 2021 article that searching by keyword returns more comprehensive results than subject searching. In this case, for example, a subject search for *subprime mortgage* in the *New York Times* from 1980 through 2006 returned only 17 results compared with 72 using the keyword search. Although the items returned through this approach are generally germane, they are also likely to include more "false positives" than a subject search. Before analyzing the data, I therefore removed irrelevant observations and duplicate entries before conducting any analyses. In the case of this search, for example, I determined that 4 of the original 72 hits returned for the *New York Times* from the period 1980 to 2006 and 21 of the original 210 for the *Wall Street Journal* were not relevant and were therefore excluded. See appendices A and B for more detail. Pablo Barbera, Amber E. Boydstun, Suzanna Linn, Ryan McMahon, and Jonathan Nagler, "Automated Text Classification of News Articles: A Practical Guide," *Political Analysis* 29 (2021): 19–42. See also Laura Nelson et al., "The Future of Coding: A Comparison of Hand-Coding and Three Types of Computer Assisted Text Analysis Methods," *Sociological Methods and Research*, 27 May 2018.

7. I used Nvivo to identify and compile a list of all descriptors accompanying "credit" in these articles and calculated the proportion of articles that contained any of these (mostly) bi-grams. I replicated this search using the *Readers' Guide to Periodical Literature* and found that an almost identical proportion (62.5 percent, or fifteen out of twenty-four) of stories about subprime mortgage lending during this period used these kinds of descriptors to characterize the credit of people who took out such loans. Similarly, of the sixty-nine articles addressing subprime mortgages in the Ethnic NewsWatch database from 1995 through 2006, forty-four (63.8 percent) used damning descriptors to characterize the credit of people who took out such loans. See tables A.1, A.2, and A.3 and appendix B for more detail.

8. "Tell Citibank" (www.tellcitibank.org) was a website created in 2001 by the Social Investment Forum Foundation and Co-op America, and was intended to provide a forum for people "to speak out about abusive lending practices." Jake Lewis, "Predatory Associates," *Multinational Monitor* 23, no. 4 (April 2002): 15–18. Ulrich Beck, *Risk Society: Towards a New Modernity*, vol. 17 (Newberry Park, CA: Sage, 1992); Anthony Giddens, "Risk and Responsibility," *Modern Law Review* 62 (1999): 1–10; Paula Chakravartty and Denise Ferreira da Silva, "Accumulation, Dispossession, and Debt: The Racial Logic of Global Capitalism — An Introduction," *American Quarterly* 64 (2011): 361–85.

9. O'Brien, "Lowering the Credit Fence," D1.

10. Paula Treichler, *How to Have Theory in an Epidemic* (Durham, NC: Duke Univeristy Press, 1999), 316. As the reports I described in chapter 4 make clear, not only were these frames not new, they were also not uncontested. See tables A.1, A.2, and A.3 and appendix B, for example, for evidence that economic reporters from progressive magazines and Black-, Latino-, and Indigenous-serving news outlets also presented an alternative set of perspectives in the case of race but not when it came to gender.

11. Keeanga-Yamahtta Taylor explains that this was particularly true of the mostly low-income and working-class Black women, many of whom also received public assistance, who bought homes under HUD-FHA-assisted programs in the late 1960s and early 1970s. As Taylor explains, "Black women who purchased homes through HUD's programs became the focal point of congressional and media inquiries. These women were portrayed as unsophisticated and domestically dysfunctional, evidenced by alleged difficulty with the simple maintenance of their homes." In one particularly telling example, Taylor recounts a 1970 hearing at which President Richard Nixon's Housing Secretary George Romney appeared:

> [T]he congressmen at the hearing, and the men of the MBA . . . looked to tap into existing ideas that categorically blamed African Americans for the condition of their housing and their neighborhoods. . . . The idea that Black renters and owners were destructive and careless was so deeply ingrained in the popular consciousness that it was almost effortless to make the charge. HUD even went so far as to produce a fifteen-cent pamphlet, called *Simplified Housekeeping Directions for Homemakers*, for women in subsidized housing on how to clean one's home. The pamphlet included visual instructions on "how to dust furniture" and "how to keep trash cans clean," among other instructions.

See Keeanga-Yamahtta Taylor, *Race for Profit* (Chapel Hill: University of North Carolina Press, 2019), 191–92. See also Chloe Thurston, *At the Boundaries of Homeownership* (New York: Cambridge University Press, 2018).

12. Here too, see tables A.1, A.2, and A.3 and appendix B for evidence that

economic reporters from progressive magazines and Black-, Latino-, and Indigenous-serving news outlets also presented an alternative set of perspectives in the case of race but not when it came to gender.

13. These elisions are also related to the "episodic" news frames that, as Shanto Iyengar describes, are typical of much reporting having to with issues of race and the economy. Episodic frames, Iyengar explains, typically depict issues in terms of "concrete instances," in part by highlighting particular individuals or event-centered information. Thematic frames, in contrast, place "public issues in some more general or abstract context," often taking the form of reports directed at explaining "general outcomes or conditions." Shanto Iyengar, *Is Anyone Responsible? How Television Frames Political Issues* (Chicago: University of Chicago Press, 1991), 13. Before 2006, for example, only five *Wall Street Journal* articles and only thirteen in the *New York Times* mentioned DIDMCA (which overrode state usury laws and interest rate caps in mortgage lending). This was true as well of several of its alternative appellations, with the exception of the "Monetary Control Act," which was discussed in nineteen *Wall Street Journal* articles and in thirty-seven pieces in the *New York Times*. Searches for other names by which the bill was known yielded little more—neither the *New York Times* nor the *Wall Street Journal* ever referenced the "Consumer Checking Account Equity Act," "Financial Regulation Simplification Act," or "Truth in Lending Simplification and Reform Act." The "Depository Institutions Deregulation Act" produced four observations in the *Times* and one in the *Wall Street Journal*: one each in 1980, 1982 (which is about Italy), 1984, and 1990. However, only about a quarter (27 percent) of these articles in the *Times* and only 16 percent of those in the *Wall Street Journal* addressed the implications of this law for mortgage lending, and none of the articles that did so referenced subprime lending in particular. Even less attention was devoted to AMTPA (which permitted the use of variable interest rates and balloon payments); it was never referenced in the *Times* and was referred to only twice in the *Wall Street Journal* over the course of this period (2001 and 2002).

Attention to the 1986 Tax Reform Act (which allowed interest deductions on mortgages for up to two homes but prohibited the deduction of interest on consumer loans) seems, at first, to deviate from this pattern. Each paper published just over 400 stories that referenced this law, and approximately 56 percent of those in the *Wall Street Journal* stories and 62 percent of those in the *New York Times* stories addressed mortgage lending. None of these stories, however, contained any discussion of subprime mortgages, and only a tiny number contemplated the law's possible effects for mortgage lending to marginalized groups in particular.

The transcript of dominant politics similarly evinces very little interest in the federal government's role in creating the subprime lending that precipitated rising foreclosures. Although the 1980 Democratic platform commits itself to "vigorous enforcement of truth-in-lending, anti-redlining, and fair credit reporting laws," it never referenced the role of subsequent legislation such as AMTPA in undermining the force of such laws. In fact, AMTPA was never mentioned (either directly or descriptively) in party platforms or State of the Union addresses during this period. The Republicans made one mention of the 1986 TRA in their 1988 platforms, but it was not its implications for subprime lending that they noted. Instead, they claimed, it had led to "the largest income transfer to lower-income Americans since the early 1970s" by removing "six million poor . . . from the tax rolls." No platform ever mentioned DIDMCA or any of its alternative names, although in his last State of the Union address in 1981, Jimmy Carter noted it as one of two "major pieces of financial reform legislation . . . which has provided the basis for the most far-reaching changes in the financial services industry since the 1930's," arguing that it "provide[d] for the phased elimination of a variety of anti-competitive barriers to financial institutions and freedom to offer services to and attract the savings of consumers, especially small savers" (https://www.jimmycarterlibrary.gov /assets/documents/speeches/su81jec.phtml). DIDMCA is mentioned in two relevant hearings (1981, 1984), the TRA in four (1986, 1987, 1988, 1990), and AMTPA never. References to particular laws in these contexts is not super common, nor is it necessary to establish that economic reporters and political actors recognized the federal government's role in creating subprime lending. Nonetheless, their absence reinforces the sense that this role was not recognized.

14. Allen Fishbein and Patrick Woodall, *Women Are Prime Targets for Subprime Lending: Women are Disproportionately in High-Cost Mortgage Market* (Washington, DC: Consumer Federation of America, 2006). Once again, see tables A.1, A.2, and A.3 and appendix B for evidence that alternative news sources did little to correct these distorted portrayals. As Chloe Thurston makes clear, both the use of "zombie facts" about women's alleged lack of creditworthiness as well as outright lender discrimination against them have long histories:

> Unlike in the case of African Americans, where discrimination was subtle and often concealed, lenders openly conceded that they used separate procedures to evaluate the creditworthiness of men and women. A 1972 NOW audit of New York area lending institutions found that, of 180 applications from women across three lending institutions, only five of their mortgages were approved. One woman who was turned down was a widower with children and a guaranteed income. She reported that the loan officer had said to her, "What does a woman need a house for?" ... [A]dvocates [also] underscored that there was very little evidence at all that women were a worse credit risk than men. Instead, the limited evidence available suggested that women posed a similar, or in some cases lower, risk than men. For example, a 1964 study found that women were more likely than men with the same marital status to keep their credit accounts in good standing. An even earlier study, from 1941, looked specifically at mortgages and found that women were a better risk than men, and that two-earner families

defaulted at lower rates than families with only one breadwinner. Sensitive to the problem that earlier studies only examined
the outcomes of borrowers who made it through the application
process (and not those filtered out along the way), activists also
pointed to two studies that could apply to women more broadly.
The first was conducted by an organization that provided home
improvement loans to elderly and low-income households, many
of which were headed by single women. A study of the program
found that female-headed households had a delinquency rate of
2 percent, while the overall delinquency rate was 4 percent. Another study, conducted by two researchers from CWPS [the Center for Women Policy Studies], examined only banks that had a
history of lending to women and men on similar terms, and found
no evidence that women were a worse credit risk than men. Instead, the evidence pointed to key explanatory variables for
risk that had to do with the "characteristics of the loan itself"
(i.e., the terms of the financing, particularly the loan to value ratio,
the presence of junior financing and loan purpose), rather than
the characteristics of the borrower."

Chloe Thurston, *At the Boundaries of Homeownership* (New York: Cambridge
University Press, 2018), 161–63.

15. Amy Castro Baker, "Eroding the Wealth of Women: Gender and the Subprime Foreclosure Crisis," *Social Science Review* 88, no. 1 (2014): 59–91.

16. Iyengar, *Is Anyone Responsible?*

17. The data upon which these numbers are based were compiled by searching
each paper for "'rising NEAR foreclosure' OR 'increasing NEAR foreclosure'",
which returns documents that contain the two search terms, in any order, within
four words apart. As with the search for subprime mortgages, in the case of the
Wall Street Journal, I further specified that the search ignore items in "New Securities Issues," "New Stock Listings," and "Bids and Offers." I downloaded the resulting data and metadata into a spreadsheet and downloaded and cleaned the full text
of all articles. As with previous searches, although the items returned through this
approach are generally germane, they are also likely to include more "false positives" than a subject search. I therefore went through them and removed irrelevant
observations and duplicate entries before conducting analyses.

18. Alan Oser, "Foreclosures Spur a Volume Business in Refurbishing and Selling Homes; Buyers Get Benefit of Easier Terms, but Some Charge Deception,"
New York Times, 27 June 1999, 1.

19. Peter Kilborn, "Easy Credit and Hard Times Bring Foreclosures," *New York
Times*, 24 November 2002, 1.30.

20. Iyengar, *Is Anyone Responsible?*

21. To determine whether articles addressed people of color or race and whether
these issues could be said to be their focus, I searched each article and coded them

as "1" if they included (and "0" if they did not include) *African American, American Indian, Asian American, Black, Hispanic, "inner city," Latino, minority/minorities, Native American*. Similarly, to determine whether articles addressed women or gender and whether such issues were the focus the story, I searched each article and coded them as "1" if they included (and "0" if they did not include): *female, gender, lady/ladies, and woman/women*. I also searched for the terms *discriminate* and *discrimination*. I then read each story in which these terms were present to determine whether they did, in fact, address these issues. An example of a story that was coded as focusing on race is a 14 November 1999 article in the *New York Times* titled "Study Discerns Disadvantage for Blacks in Home Mortgages." An example of a story that was coded as addressing race in a secondary way is one published on 29 June 2000 in the *New York Times* titled, "New State Rules Aim to Curb Loan Abuses." Though the story does not *focus on* people of color, it notes that "predatory lenders typically use high-pressure tactics to talk home-owners into exorbitant loans that often force them into bankruptcy or foreclosure. The most frequent victims are the elderly, women, and residents of minority neighborhoods." See appendix B for more detail.

22. See tables A.1, A.2, and A.3 and appendix B for evidence that economic reporters from Black-, Latino-, and Indigenous-serving news outlets paid more attention than their mainstream counterparts to the implications of subprime loans and foreclosures for people of color during the non-crisis period.

23. Once again, see tables A.1, A.2, and A.3 and appendix B, in this case for evidence that economic reporters from progressive magazines, feminist media, and Black-, Latino-, and Indigenous-serving news were no different than their mainstream counterparts when it comes to gender. Aleksandra Cislak, Magdalena Formanowicz, and Tamar Saguy find that research on gender bias gains far less traction than research about racial discrimination. See Aleksandra Cislak, Magdalena Formanowicz, and Tamar Saguy, "Bias Against Research on Gender Bias," *Scientometrics* 115 (2018): 189.

24. Oser, "Foreclosures Spur."

25. Baker, "Eroding the Wealth of Women"; Leslie McCall, "Increasing Class Disparities among Women and the Poitics of Gender Equity," in *The Sex of Class: Women Transforming American Labor*, ed. Sue Cobble (Ithaca, NY: Cornell University Press, 2007), 15–34; Jane Junn, "Square Pegs and Round Holes: Challenges of Fitting Individual-Level Analysis to a Theory of Politicized Context of Gender," *Politics & Gender* 3 (2007): 123–34; Jane Junn, "Dynamic Categories and the Context of Power," in *The Future of Political Science: 100 Perspectives*, ed. Gary King, Kay Schlozman and Norman Nie (New York: Routledge 2009), 25–27.

26. Iyengar, *Is Anyone Responsible?*

27. Thurston, *Boundaries of Homeownership*, 163; Baker, "Eroding the Wealth of Women," 77; Rick Brooks and Ruth Simon, "Subprime Debacle Traps Even Very Credit-Worthy as Housing Boomed, Industry Pushed Loans to Broader Market," *Wall Street Journal*, 4 December 2007, 3; Fishbein and Woodall, *Women Are Prime*

Targets; Kathleen Keest, "The Way Ahead: A Framework for Policy Responses" (paper presented at the Subprime Housing Crisis Symposium, University of Iowa, 10–11 October 2008).

28. Iyengar, *Is Anyone Responsible?*

29. Douglas Massey, Jacob Rugh, Justin Steil, and Len Albright, "Riding the Stagecoach to Hell: A Qualitative Analysis of Racial Discrimination in Mortgage Lending," *City & Community* 15 (2016): 118–36. Patricia Hill Collins defines controlling images as ones that "are designed to make racism, sexism, poverty, and other forms of social injustice appear to be natural, normal, and inevitable parts of everyday life." Patricia Hill Collins, *Black Sexual Politics: African Americans, Gender, and the New Racism* (New York: Routledge, 2005), 69.

30. Though not quite as relevant, it is also worth noting that not one story about subprime mortgage lending published in either the *New York Times* or the *Wall Street Journal* during this period referenced the Supreme Court ruling in *Shelley v. Kraemer*, which held that racially restrictive housing covenants were unenforceable under the Equal Protection Clause of the Fourteenth Amendment. As a rough point of comparison, reporting about issues such as segregation in education and abortion regularly referenced landmark legal and legislative developments; almost none of the coverage of subprime lending and rising rates of foreclosures referred to analogous touchstones. From 1980–2016, for example, 27 percent of articles in the *New York Times* addressing school segregation (348/1,279—"segregation NEAR school") contained references to *Brown v. Board of Education* and 7 percent (2,630/36,502) of articles about abortion referenced *Roe v. Wade*.

31. Iyengar, *Is Anyone Responsible?*, 59.

32. Catherine Squires, "Bursting the Bubble: A Case Study of Counterframing in the Editorial Pages," *Critical Studies in Media Communication* 28 (2011): 32.

33. Martin Gilens, *Why Americans Hate Welfare* (Chicago: University of Chicago Press, 1999). As I have noted previously, we would likely observe more overtly racist demonization in more extreme new outlets such as Fox News or the *New York Post*.

34. John Wilke, "Justice, FTC Probe Lenders, Allege Abuses," *Wall Street Journal*, 30 January 1998, A3.

35. On archaic language in sources, see chap. 2, note 36.

36. James Hagerty and Joseph T. Hallinan, "Blacks Are Much More Likely to Get Subprime Mortgages; Weaker Lender Competition in Some Low-Income Areas Is Cited as Part of Problem," *Wall Street Journal*, 11 April 2005, A.2.

37. See also Correa, "Blueprint for the American Dream?"; Massey et al., "Riding the Stagecoach."

38. Robert Shiller, *Irrational Exuberance*, 2nd ed. (Princeton, NJ: Princeton University Press, 2005).

39. While neither the film nor the book version of *The Big Short* addresses the race or gender implications of the mortgage crisis, the 2015 film adaption of the

book (directed by Adam McKay) features the titillation of a presumptively na-
ked Margot Robbie drinking champagne in a bubble bath to explain how Michael
Burry was able to profit from his bet against the mortgage-backed securities comprised of subprime loans. Later in the film, we are also introduced to "Dr. Richard
Thaler, father of behavioral economics, and Selena Gomez"—the former shown
wearing a blazer, the latter wearing a cocktail dress—who explain synthetic collat-
eralized debt obligations (CDOs) to the audience. Along with "world famous chef
Anthony Bourdain," who is featured in a restaurant kitchen wearing chef gear,
and who uses an analogy about fish purchasing—something about which he has
professional expertise—to explain CDOs, Thaler is featured fully clothed and in
his professional capacity. Robbie and Gomez, on the other hand, are essentially
two gendered "sight gags" aimed at the heterosexual male gaze: two scantily clad
women simultaneously defying and reinforcing gender tropes and stereotypes by
explaining complicated economic concepts and financial instruments. The film also
exploits racial stereotypes about Asian Americans: In a scene in which Ryan Gos-
ling's character is challenged by his colleagues about the soundness of his calcula-
tions regarding an investment idea he has proposed, he establishes its credibility
by introducing the Asian American man sitting silently at the table: "Jiang is my
quant," he says. "Look at him, he doesn't even speak English. He won a national
math competition in China. China. Yeah I'm sure of the math." "Jiang" (played by
Asian American actor Stanley Wong) then turns to the camera and says, "Actually
I do speak English. Jared likes to say I don't because he thinks it makes me seem
more authentic. And I finished second in the national math competition. Some
people at work think Jared's a dick but he's great at his job." *The Big Short*, directed by Adam McKay (Paramount Pictures, 2015); Michael Lewis, *The Big Short:
Inside the Doomsday Machine* (New York: W. W. Norton, 2010).

40. Starkman, *Watchdog That Didn't Bark.*

41. I used ProQuest US Newsstream to search each paper for "'mortgage crisis'
OR 'foreclosure crisis' OR 'subprime crisis'" to collect the data for figure 5.1. As
with previous searches, although the items returned through this approach are generally germane, they are also likely than a subject search to include more "false
positives." I therefore removed irrelevant observations.

42. I replicated this search using the *Readers' Guide to Periodical Literature.*
I report these results in tables A.1 and A.2, which show that the patterns in this
source are highly correlated with those in the *New York Times* and the *Wall Street
Journal.*

43. Ron Nixon, "Study Predicts Foreclosure for 1 in 5 Subprime Loans," *New
York Times*, 20 December 2006.

44. Nixon, "Study Predicts Foreclosure."

45. To compile these data, I downloaded the full text of all party platforms
and executive orders from the University of California, Santa Barbara's American
Presidency Project and the full text of all State of the Union addresses from Brad

Borevitz's State of the Union website. I then used Nvivo to search for the terms "mortgage crisis", "foreclosure crisis", and "subprime crisis", which also allowed me to compile and code the results. Note, however, that searching executive orders turned up no attention to subprime lending and foreclosure, so they are not included in tables or figures.

46. To compile the data depicted in figure 5.2, I used ProQuest Congressional to search the full text of hearings for the terms "'mortgage crisis' OR 'foreclosure crisis' OR 'subprime crisis'". See appendices A and B for more detail.

47. *Problems Surrounding the Mortgage Origination Process: Hearings before the Subcommittee on Financial Institutions and Regulatory Relief and the Subcommittee on Housing Opportunity and Community Development of the Senate Committee on Banking, Housing, and Urban Affairs*, 105th Cong. 77–79 (1997).

48. *Predatory Mortgage Lending: The Problem, Impact, and Responses: Hearings before the Senate Committee on Banking, Housing, and Urban Affairs*, 107th Cong. 252–55 (2001).

49. *Community Solutions for the Prevention and Management of Foreclosures: Hearings before the Subcommittee on Housing and Community Opportunity of the House Committee on Financial Services*, 109th Cong. 51 (2006).

50. Shiller, *Irrational Exuberance*.

51. Edmund Andrews and Gretchen Morgenson, "Fed and Regulators Shrugged as the Subprime Crisis Spread," *New York Times*, 18 December 2007.

52. Jonathan McCarthy and Richard Peach, "Are Home Prices the Next 'Bubble?,'" *FRBNY Economic Policy Review* 10, no. 3 (2004): 2.

53. Collins, *Black Sexual Politics*.

54. Elinore Longobardi makes a related but somewhat different argument. Finding that the term *predatory lending* had been in wide use in business journalism in the late 1990s before being replaced by the term *subprime* in the post-2007 period, she argues that this change shifted the focus from lenders to borrowers, making a slightly different claim—namely that there had been momentum building against the lenders in the late 1990s. Longobardi, "How 'Subprime' Killed 'Predatory,'" 48. The data in table 5.3 and figures 5.3–5.5 were compiled using ProQuest US Newsstream to search the *New York Times* and the *Wall Street Journal* for the following search strings: "subprime NEAR mortgage", "nonconforming NEAR mortgage", and "predatory NEAR mortgage". The NEAR command returns documents that contain the two search terms, in any order, within four words apart. As I did with the previously described searches of the *Wall Street Journal*, I further specified that the search ignore items in several regular features: "New Securities Issues," "New Stock Listings," and "Bids and Offers." I downloaded the resulting data and metadata into a spreadsheet and downloaded the full text of all articles. As with previous searches, although the items returned through this approach are generally germane, they are also more likely than a subject search to include "false positives." I therefore removed irrelevant observations before conducting any analyses.

55. Although it precedes the period of interest, it is worth noting that neither *subprime* nor *nonconforming* appears more frequently in the years leading up to or immediately following the passage of HOEPA. In 1993, as that law was being crafted and debated, I found no stories using the term *subprime mortgage* in either paper, which was true as well in 1994, the year that HOEPA was passed.

56. "subprime, adj. and n." *OED Online*, June 2020, Oxford University Press. https://www-oed-com.ezproxy.princeton.edu/view/Entry/272160?redirectedFrom =subprime (accessed 19 August 2020).

57. Coverage was similarly modest in the early 1990s as Congress debated HOEPA. Economic reporters likewise devoted very little attention to HOEPA itself: The bill was never referenced directly in the *Wall Street Journal* when it was being considered by Congress, nor was the law as passed mentioned before 2000, after which it was referenced only five times before 2007 and three times after that point. The *New York Times* did not reference HOEPA itself until 2002, after which it referred to it only three times before 2007. Its parent bill, the Community Development and Regulatory Improvement Act of 1994, was never referenced by name in either newspaper.

58. The data upon which these numbers are based were compiled by searching each paper for "'rising NEAR foreclosure' OR 'increasing NEAR foreclosure'", which returns documents that contain the two search terms, in any order, within four words apart. As with the previous searches, in the case of the *Wall Street Journal*, I further specified that the search ignore items in "New Securities Issues," "New Stock Listings," and "Bids and Offers." I downloaded the resulting data and metadata into a spreadsheet and downloaded and cleaned the full text of all articles. As with previous searches, although the items returned through this approach are generally germane, they are also more likely to include "false positives" than a subject search. I therefore removed irrelevant observations before conducting analyses. See appendices A and B for more detail.

59. These systematic searches combined inductive and deductive approaches and a combination of keyword searches, coding, close reading, and data from the US Policy Agendas Project to determine how much attention was paid to these issues by dominant political actors. As I did in the case of the *New York Times* and *Wall Street Journal*, I began by searching the full text of all party platforms, State of the Union addresses, hearings, and bills for the terms *subprime mortgage, nonconforming mortgage*, and *predatory mortgage*. Having uncovered little evidence of any attention to these issues in any of these sources before 2007, I next searched the full text of all party platforms and State of the Union addresses for any instances of the words *mortgage* and *foreclosure*. Because of their limited numbers and manageable length, I was also able to read each platform and SOTU address to search for *any* discussion related to homeownership, coding those that address subprime mortgages and foreclosure.

I combined these full-text searches with data from the US Policy Agendas Project with the help of (then) University of Texas graduate student and Policy Agendas

Project Graduate Research Fellow Maraam Dwidar. We began by first searching USPAP data for bills, hearings, public laws, executive orders, and State of the Union address and party platform quasi-sentences for those categorized by the USPAP's coding scheme as falling under 1400 (General Community Development and Housing Issues), 1401 (Housing and Community Development), 1403 (Urban Economic Development and General Urban Issues), 1404 (Rural Housing and FmHA Housing Assistance Programs), 1405 (Rural Economic Development), 1406 (Low and Middle Income Housing Programs and Needs), 1407 (Veterans Housing Assistance and Military Housing Programs), 1408 (Elderly and Handicapped Housing), 1409 (Housing Assistance for Homeless and Homeless Issues), 1410 (Secondary Mortgage Market), 1501 (US banking System and Financial Institution Regulation), 1504 (Consumer Finance, Mortgages, and Credit Cards), and 1525 (Consumer Safety and Consumer Fraud). We dropped all observations outside of the timeframe of interest (1980–2014) and then conducted keyword searches of each file for a set of search terms intended to identify whether each observation in each file discussed mortgage lending, subprime lending, predatory mortgages, homeownership and/or home buying, and/or rising rates of foreclosure, creating binary variables for each of these five categories, spot-checking every tenth observation for accuracy (see the appendices for more detail, including a list of search terms).

We next ran cross-tabulations in Stata that returned a raw count of the total number of observations in each file pertaining to each topic by year (mortgage lending, subprime lending, predatory mortgages, and/or rising rates of foreclosure, and homeownership/buying). We then used these counts to calculate two percentages: (1) the percentage of observations addressing mortgage lending, subprime lending, predatory mortgage lending, rising rates of foreclosure, and home buying/homeownership in a given year as a percentage of *all* hearings, bills, laws, executive orders, and platform and State of the Union quasi-sentences in a given year (so, e.g., the total number of congressional hearings addressing subprime mortgages in 1998/total number of hearings conducted in 1998, and so on, for each year, each topic, and each source); and (2) the percentage of observations addressing mortgage lending, subprime lending, predatory mortgage lending, rising rates of foreclosure, and home buying/homeownership in a given year as a percentage of hearings in each subtopic category (so, e.g., the total number of congressional hearings addressing subprime mortgages in 1998/total number of all hearings on all the USPAP topics listed above; see appendices for further detail, including a robustness check we conducted to be sure that our search parameters yielded accurate results). See appendices A and B for more detail.

60. There is only one reference to foreclosure itself as a problem in the platforms of either party at any point before 2007, in a 1992 Republican plank that "urge[d] federal departments and agencies to work with the private sector to bring foreclosed housing stock back into service as soon as possible." As this passage makes clear, the concern being addressed in this plank had nothing to do with

people losing their homes to foreclosure but was rather about rehabilitating foreclosed properties.

61. As I explained previously, using keyword searches for substantive analyses of the full text of congressional hearings and bills remains unwieldy, and while it was feasible to do so for the narrower terms *subprime crisis, mortgage crisis*, and *foreclosure*, my initial attempts to do so for the unmodified terms *mortgage* and *foreclosure* proved prohibitive. I also found that ProQuest's subject terms do not include ones that would be necessary to use that feature to search the full text of these documents in an effective way. Happily, the subject coding done by the US Policy Agendas Project provides an effective way to assess how much and what kind of attention dominant political actors devoted to these issues and how this has varied over time. See previous note 56 and appendices A and B for a full description.

62. Monica Prasad, *The Land of Too Much: American Abundance and the Paradox of Poverty* (Cambridge, MA: Harvard University Press, 2012); Abbye Atkinson, "Borrowing Equality," *Columbia Law Review* 120 (2020): 1403–70.

63. Julie Creswell and Vikas Bajaj, "A Mortgage Crisis Begins to Spiral, and the Casualties Mount," *New York Times*, 5 March 2007, https://www.nytimes.com/2007/03/05/business/05lender.html.

64. *Mortgage Market Turmoil: Causes and Consequences: Hearings before the Senate Committee on Banking, Housing, and Urban Affairs*, 110th Cong. 1 (2007).

65. It is worth nothing that, even as presidents began to make increasing use of executive orders to address a growing array of issues, never during either phase of increasing subprime lending and foreclosure did President Clinton, Bush, or Obama use this power to address or call for action on either issue, nor did any of them address these issues or predatory lending in a State of the Union address during this first period. See William Howell, *Power without Persuasion: The Politics of Direct Political Action* (Princeton, NJ: Princeton University Press, 2003).

66. Gretchen Morgenson, "Beware of Exploding Mortgages," *New York Times*, 10 June 2007, https://www.nytimes.com/2007/06/10/business/yourmoney/10gret.html.

67. Rick Brooks and Ruth Simon, "Subprime Debacle Traps Even Very Credit-Worthy," *Wall Street Journal*, 3 December 2007, A1.

68. Jonathan Karp, "How the Mortgage Bar Keeps Moving Higher; Home Buyers with Good Credit Confront Increased Scrutiny and Fewer Choices as Lenders React to Subprime Debacle," *Wall Street Journal*, 14 August 2007, D.1.

69. Reuters, "Pimco Foresees Widening Subprime Harm," *New York Times*, 27 June 2007, https://www.nytimes.com/2007/06/27/business/27pimco.html.

70. Vikas Bajaj, "Senate Questioning on Mortgages Puts Regulators on the Defensive," *New York Times*, 23 March 2007, https://www.nytimes.com/2007/03/23/business/23lend.html; *Mortgage Market Turmoil: Hearings*, 1.

71. Vikas Bajaj, "Bad Loans Put Wall St. in a Swoon," *New York Times*, 14 March 2007, C1; Vikas Bajaj, "For Some Subprime Borrowers, Few Good Choices," *New York Times*, 22 March 2007, C1.

72. I retrieved all *New York Times* and *Wall Street Journal* editorials and op-ed pieces addressing rising or increasing rates of foreclosure and, with the help of (then) graduate student Andrew Proctor, coded each observation for whether it mentioned federal, state, or local intervention or the possibility for it and, for each positive observation, for whether these mentions are supportive, unsupportive, or neutral with regard to said intervention. See appendices for additional details.

73. Editorial, "After the Fed," *New York Times*, 31 January 2008.

74. David Wessel, "Why Some Mortgage Bailouts Make Sense," *Wall Street Journal*, 15 November 2007. It is worth noting that although Wessel's suggestions are relatively generous and forgiving, they also reinforce distinctions between—and the presumption that we can easily distinguish between—those who deserve assistance and those who do not, either because they were dishonest (ignoring evidence that it was often realtors and mortgage lenders or brokers who neglected or fabricated information about borrowers) or because they are a lost cause who should not be helped because they cannot really afford these homes in the first place.

75. American Presidency Project, https://www.presidency.ucsb.edu/documents /2008-democratic-party-platform.

76. American Presidency Project, https://www.presidency.ucsb.edu/documents /2008-republican-party-platform. HOPE NOW described itself as "a non-profit alliance between counselors, mortgage companies, investors, regulators and other mortgage market participants. The alliance was encouraged by The Department of the Treasury and the US Department of Housing and Urban Development to bring together diverse stakeholders to address challenges in the mortgage market and create collaborations to solve problems. Membership works towards creating a unified, coordinated plan to assist homeowners, communities and government partners to repair the mortgage market. The HOPE NOW servicers represent a commitment to improving the customer experience and industry excellence. The HOPE NOW members have achieved trust and support through sharing best practices, collaborating with regulators and supporting non-profit partners. HOPE NOW servicers reported almost two million solutions in 2014." https://web.archive.org /web/20200115011626/http://www.hopenow.com/about-us.php.

The organization announced in June 2020 that it would suspend operations "due in part to the fact that events it staged to bring borrowers and servicers together are . . . 'an approach that is incompatible with the health risks posed by COVID-19.'" Bonnie Sinnock, "Hope Now to Suspend Operations, Citing Coronavirus Restrictions," *National Mortgage News*, 1 July 2020, https://www.nationalmortgage news.com/news/hope-now-to-suspend-operations-citing-coronavirus-restrictions.

77. Barack Obama, Inaugural Address, 20 January 2009, transcript, CBS News, https://www.cbsnews.com/news/barack-obama-inaugural-address-2009/.

78. Julie Creswell and Vikas Bajaj, "A Mortgage Crisis Begins to Spiral, and the Casualties Mount," *New York Times*, 5 March 2007, https://www.nytimes.com /2007/03/05/business/05lender.html.

79. Edmund L. Andrews, "Fed Shrugged as Subprime Crisis Spread," *New York Times*, 18 December 2007, https://www.nytimes.com/2007/12/18/business /18subprime.html.

80. Bob Herbert, "A Swarm of Swindlers," *New York Times*, 20 November 2007. Ancestry.com, *US Social Security Applications and Claims Index, 1936–2007* (online database), 2015. Original data: Social Security Applications and Claims, 1936–2007, US Bureau of the Census; *Seventeenth Census of the United States, 1950*, record group 29 (Chicago, Cook, Illinois; roll 3930; sheet number 73; enumeration district 103–295).

81. Herbert, "A Swarm of Swindlers."

82. *New York Times* Editors, "Mortgages and Minorities," *New York Times*, 9 December 2008. It is also striking that two of the three pieces that attend to issues of gender are op-eds; Squires argues that in the case of race, the editorial pages of mainstream newspapers "supply moments of self-reflexivity and even arguably a counter-discourse that trouble dominant narratives, giving readers a chance to reconsider 'common sense' renderings of race, wealth production, and housing," providing a space "for counter discourses on race and policy to emerge and take root." The lack of detail and the recapitulation of gender stereotypes evident in these examples, however, suggests that while editorial pages might play a similar role in drawing attention to gender, they may also be less likely to disrupt "common sense renderings" when it comes to discourses about gender and economics. Squires, "Bursting the Bubble," 30–32.

83. Bob Tedeschi, "Why Women Pay Higher Interest," *New York Times*, 21 January 2007, https://www.nytimes.com/2007/01/21/realestate/21mort.html. Such stereotypes smack of paternalism and "old fashioned sexism." Other gendered tropes deployed during and about the crisis, though less prevalent, were no less malign.

84. Commenting on the subprime crisis in his June 2007 "Investment Outlook," for example, Pimco analyst Bill Gross wrote: "Well prudence and rating agency standards change with the times, I suppose. What was chaste and AAA years ago may no longer be the case today. Our prim remembrance of Gidget going to Hawaii and hanging out with the beach boys [*sic*] seems to have been replaced in this case with an image of Heidi Fleiss setting up a floating brothel in Beverly Hills. AAA? You were wooed Mr. Moody's and Mr. Poor's by the makeup, those six-inch hooker heels, and a 'tramp stamp.' Many of these good looking girls are not high-class assets worth 100 cents on the dollar." Bill Gross, "Looking for Contagion in All the Wrong Places," *PIMCO* (2007), https://www.pimco.com/en-us/insights/economic -and-market-commentary/investment-outlook/looking-for-contagion-in-all-the -wrong-places/. Gross's comments echo, in some ways, the examples from the film adaptation of *The Big Short* that I describe in note 39 above.

85. Louis Althusser, "Ideology and Ideological State Apparatuses," *La Pensée* 151 (1970).

86. Eleanor Flexner, *Century of Struggle: The Women's Rights Movement in the United States* (Cambridge, MA: Harvard University Press, 1959); Eleanor Flexner

and Ellen Fitzpatrick, *Century of Struggle: The Women's Rights Movement in the United States* (Cambridge, MA: Harvard University Press, 1996); David Mayhew, "Wars and American Politics," *Perspectives on Politics* 3 (2005): 473–93; Frances Fox Piven and Richard Cloward, *Poor People's Movement* (New York: Vintage Books 1977); Michael Goldfield, "Worker Insurgency, Radical Organization, and New Deal Labor Legislation," *American Political Science Review* 83 (1989): 1257–82; Michele Dauber, *The Sympathetic State: Disaster Relief and the Origins of the American Welfare State* (Chicago: University of Chicago Press, 2013); Gretchen Ritter, "Gender and Politics over Time," *Politics & Gender* 3 (2007): 386–97; Theda Skocpol, *Protecting Soldiers and Mothers* (Cambridge, MA: Harvard University Press, 1992); Mary Dudziak, *Cold War Civil Rights* (Princeton, NJ: Princeton University Press, 2000); Philip Klinkner and Rogers Smith, *The Unsteady March* (Chicago: University of Chicago Press, 1999); Julie Novkov, "Sacrifice and Civic Membership: Race, Gender, Sexuality and the Acquisition of Rights in Times of Crisis" (paper presented at the annual meeting of the Midwest Political Science Association, Chicago, IL, 22–25 April 2010); Christopher Parker, "When Politics Becomes Protest," *Journal of Politics* 71 (2009): 113–31.

87. Lee Ann Banaszak, *Why Movements Succeed or Fail: Opportunity, Culture and the Struggle for Woman Suffrage* (Princeton, NJ: Princeton University Press, 1996); Ronald Ingelhart, "The Silent Revolution in Europe: Intergenerational Change in Post-Industrial Societies," *American Political Science Review* 65 (1971): 991–1017; Ronald Ingelhart, *The Silent Revolution. Changing Values and Political Styles in Advanced Industrial Society* (Princeton, NJ: Princeton University Press, 1977); Ronald Ingelhart, "Changing Values among Western Publics from 1970 to 2006," *West European Politics* 31 (2008): 130–46; Jeffrey Berry, *The New Liberalism* (Washington, DC: Brookings Institution Press, 1999); Elizabeth Zechmeister and Jennifer Merolla, *Democracy at Risk: How Terrorist Threats Affect the Public* (Chicago: University of Chicago Press, 2009); David Sanger, *The Inheritance: The World Obama Confronts and the Challenges to American Power* (New York: Broadway Books, 2009); Dara Strolovitch, "Advocacy in Hard Times," in *Nonprofit Advocacy*, ed. Steven Smith, Yutaka Tsujinaka, and Robert Pekkanen (Baltimore: Johns Hopkins University Press, 2014), 137–69.

88. Andy Horowitz and Jacob A. C. Remes make a similar point about the concept of "restoring order" after a disaster, which, they argue, seems like "common sense until one recognizes that the existing order served some people much better than it served others, and its restoration therefore represents a power play par excellence." Jacob A. C. Remes and Andy Horowitz, "Introducing Critical Disaster Studies," in *Critical Disaster Studies: New Perspectives on Disaster, Risk, Vulnerability, and Resilience*, ed. Jacob A. C. Remes and Andy Horowitz (Philadelphia: University of Pennsylvania Press, 2021), 3. Jonathon Catlin writes similarly that "the history of the AIDS epidemic in the United States reveals how the end of a deadly crisis for one group was the beginning of an ignored non-crisis for another." Jonathon Catlin, "When Does an Epidemic Become a 'Crisis'? Analogies between

Covid-19 and HIV/AIDS in American Public Memory," *Memory Studies* 14 (2021): 1460.

89. Baker, "Eroding the Wealth of Women"; Correa, "Blueprint for the American Dream?"; Immergluck, *Preventing the Next Mortgage Crisis*; Elvin Wyly and C. S. Ponder, "Gender, Age, and Race in Subprime America," *Housing Policy Debate* 21 (2011): 529–64.

90. Immergluck, "Too Little, Too Late."

91. Immergluck, "Too Little, Too Late," 204; Taylor, *Race for Profit*; Thurston *At the Boundaries of Homeownership*.

92. US House-Senate Joint Economic Committee, "Momentum Builds for Schumer's Call for Additional Federal Funds to Avert Subprime Foreclosure Crisis," press release, 5 June 2007, https://www.jec.senate.gov/public/index.cfm/democrats/media?page=129.

93. House-Senate Joint Economic Committee, "Momentum Builds."

94. Baker, "Eroding the Wealth of Women."

95. Baker, "Eroding the Wealth of Women."

96. Julie Schmit, "Foreclosures Hit a Five-Year Low," *USA Today*, 11 October 2012.

97. Nomi Prins and Krisztina Ugrin, *It Takes a Pillage: Behind the Bailouts, Bonuses, and Backroom Deals from Washington to Wall Street* (Hoboken: Wiley, 2010); Ellen Reese, "Defending Homes and Making Banks Pay: California's Home Defenders League," *Social Justice* 40, no. 3 (2014): 85–86.

98. Brad Heath, "Mortgage Complaints Raised Red Flags," *USA Today*, 12 April 2011, https://search.proquest.com/docview/861734359?accountid=13314. See also Laura Briggs, *How All Politics Became Reproductive Politics: From Welfare Reform to Foreclosure to Trump* (Berkeley: University of California Press, 2017).

99. Immergluck, "Too Little, Too Late," 207.

100. Baker, "Eroding the Wealth of Women," 85.

101. Adalberto Aguirre, *State of Exception* (Chicago: University of Chicago Press, 2005).

102. Peter Dreier et al., *Underwater America: How the So-Called Housing "Recovery" Is Bypassing Many American Communities* (Berkeley: Haas Institute for a Fair and Inclusive Society, 2014); Baker, "Eroding the Wealth of Women"; Immergluck, *Preventing the Next Mortgage Crisis*.

103. Immergluck, *Preventing the Next Mortgage Crisis*, 60. Also telling is that the US Department of Housing and Urban Development Office of Policy Development and Research January 2010 *Report to Congress on the Root Causes of the Foreclosure Crisis* pays only very passing attention to issues of race and says absolutely nothing about gender. US Department of Housing and Urban Development (HUD), Office of Policy Development and Research, *Report to Congress on the Root Causes of the Foreclosure Crisis* (Washington, DC: US Department of Housing and Urban Development, 2010).

104. Immergluck, *Preventing the Next Mortgage Crisis*, 60.

105. Dara Strolovitch, "Of Mancessions and Hecoveries: Race, Gender, and the Political Construction of Economic Crises and Recoveries," *Perspectives in Politics* 13 (2013): 167–76; Dreier et al., *Underwater America*; Baker, "Eroding the Wealth of Women."

106. The same was true among Latinos, for whom rates of homeownership saw a net gain from 41.2 percent in 1994 to 47 in 2016, although this rate was still lower than it was at its peak of 49.7 percent in 2007. See Richard Fry and Anna Brown, *In a Recovering Market, Homeownership Rates Are Down Sharply for Blacks, Young Adults*, Pew Research Center, 15 December 2016.

107. Elizabeth Korver Glenn, "Compounding Inequalities: How Racial Stereotypes and Discrimination Accumulate Across the Stages of Housing Exchange," *American Sociological Review* 83 (2018): 627–56 ; Massey et al., "Riding the Stagecoach to Hell"; Jacob Faber, "Segregation and the Geography of Creditworthiness: Racial Inequality in a Recovered Mortgage Market," *Housing Policy Debate* 28 (2018): 215–47.

108. Faber, "Segregation and Creditworthiness."

109. Melanie G. Long, "Pushed into the Red? Female-Headed Households and the Pre-Crisis Credit Expansion," *Forum for Social Economics* 47 (2018): 224–36.

110. See Maureen R. St. Cyr, "Gender, Maternity Leave, and Home Financing: A Critical Analysis of Mortgage Lending Discrimination Against Pregnant Women," *University of Pennsylvania Journal of Law and Social Change* 15 (2011): 109–41. See also Tara Siegel Bernard, "Need a Mortgage? Don't Get Pregnant," *New York Times*, 19 July 2010, https://www.nytimes.com/2010/07/20/your-money/mortgages/20mortgage.html.

111. St. Cyr, "Gender, Maternity Leave, and Home Financing," 119. See the article for additional practices.

112. *H.R. 3153, The Home Equity Protection Act of 1993: Hearings before the Subcommittee on Consumer Credit and Insurance of the House Committee on Banking, Housing, and Urban Affairs*, 103rd Cong. (1993). For an overview and history of such practices, see Beryl Satter, *Family Properties: Race, Real Estate, and the Exploitation of Black Urban America* (New York: St. Martin's Press, 2009).

113. Dan Immergluck, "Old Wine in Private Equity Bottles? The Resurgence of Contract-for-Deed Home Sales in US Urban Neighborhoods," *International Journal of Urban and Regional Research* 42 (2018): 651–65.

114. As Nicola Smith sums it up, "the consequences of, and very constitution of, neoliberal crisis are reproductive of heteronormative gender logics and power relations, which in turn serve to naturalize and normalize structural inequality and disadvantage." Smith, "Queer Political Economy of Crisis," 246.

115. Dan Immergluck, *Foreclosed: High-Risk Lending, Deregulation, and the Undermining of America's Mortgage Market* (Ithaca, NY: Cornell University Press [2009] 2011), 11.

116. Immergluck, *Foreclosed*, 11.

117. As Baker explains, the policy response mainly created "slightly stronger consumer protections designed to inform prospective buyers." Baker, "Eroding the Wealth of Women," 84.

118. For in-depth accounts of the response to the crisis, see, inter alia, Dan Immergluck, "Too Little, Too Late, and Too Timid: The Federal Response to the Foreclosure Crisis at the Five-Year Mark," *Housing Policy Debate* 23 (2013): 199–232; Dan Immergluck, *Preventing the Next Mortgage Crisis: The Meltdown, the Federal Response, and the Future of Housing in America* (Lanham, MD: Rowman and Littlefield, 2015); Baker, "Eroding the Wealth of Women"; Gary Dymski, Jesus Hernandez, and Lisa Mohanty, "Race, Gender, Power, and the US Subprime Mortgage and Foreclosure Crisis: A Meso Analysis," *Feminist Economics* 19, no. 3 (2013): 124–51; HUD , *Root Causes*.

119. Sarah Haley, *No Mercy Here: Gender, Punishment, and the Making of Jim Crow Modernity* (Chapel Hill: University of North Carolina Press, 2016); Elvin Wyly and C. S. Ponder, "Gender, Age, and Race in Subprime America," *Housing Policy Debate* 21 (2011): 529–64.

120. Lani Guinier and Gerald Torres, *The Miner's Canary: Enlisting Race, Resisting Power, Transforming Democracy* (Cambridge, MA: Harvard University Press, 2002).

121. Dara Strolovitch, *Affirmative Advocacy: Race, Class, and Gender in Interest Group Politics* (Chicago: University of Chicago Press, 2007).

122. Strolovitch, *Affirmative Advocacy*, 94–95.

123. Iyengar, *Is Anyone Responsible?*

124. Wyly and Ponder, "Gender, Age, and Race," 530.

Conclusions and Epilogue

1. Randy Shilts, *And the Band Played on: Politics, People, and the AIDS Epidemic* (London: Souvenir Press, 2011).

2. Paul Butler, "Black Male Exceptionalism? The Problems and Potential of Black Male-Focused Interventions," *Du Bois Review* 10 (2013): 485–511; Andrew Grant-Thomas, "Representing the Race: The Black Male Crisis and the Politics of Neglect" (PhD thesis, University of Chicago, 2000), available from ProQuest Dissertations & Theses Global; Willie Legette, "The Crisis of the Black Male: A New Ideology of Black Politics," in *Without Justice for All: New Liberalism and Our Retreat from Racial Equality*, ed. Adolph Reed (Bolder, CO: Westview Press, 1999); Pedro A. Noguera, "Reconsidering the "Crisis" of the Black Male in America," *Social Justice* 24 (1997): 147–64.

3. Jonathon Catlin, "When Does an Epidemic Become a 'Crisis'? Analogies between Covid-19 and HIV/AIDS in American Public Memory," *Memory Studies* 14 (2021): 1460. Steven Thrasher explains that "the white rate [of AIDS cases] peaked

at 15.4 [per 100,000] in 1995" and was just 2.4 by 2015, while it was 21.8 for Black Americans." Steven Thrasher, *The Viral Underclass: The Human Toll When Inequality and Disease Collide* (New York: Caledon Books, 2022), 167. See also Cathy Cohen, *The Boundaries of Blackness* (Chicago: University of Chicago Press, 1999).

4. As Stephanie J. Nawyn writes, "Labeling a refugee migration as a 'crisis' is not an inevitable action to large-scale forced migration. It is a choice that is steeped in racial, gender, and colonialist politics." Stephanie J. Nawyn, "Refugees in the United States and the Politics of Crisis," in *The Oxford Handbook of Migration Crises*, ed. Cecilia Menjívar, Marie Ruiz, and Immanuel Ness (New York: Oxford University Press, 2019), 163. See also Lisa Sun-Hee Park, *Entitled to Nothing: The Struggle for Immigrant Health Care in the Age of Welfare Reform* (New York: New York University Press, 2011).

5. Catlin, "When Does an Epidemic Become a 'Crisis'?," 1460.

6. M. Brielle Harbin, "The Contingency of Compassion: Media Depictions of Drug Addiction" (unpublished manuscript, n.d.); Sonia Mendoza, Allyssa Stephanie Rivera, and Helena Bjerring Hansen, "Re-racialization of Addiction and the Redistribution of Blame in the White Opioid Epidemic," *Medical Anthropology Quarterly* 33 (2019): 242–62; E. Summerson Carr, "The Work of 'Crisis' in the 'Opioid Crisis,'" *Journal of Extreme Anthropology* 3 (2019): 161–66; Miriam J. Laugesen and Eric M. Patashnik, "Framing, Governance, and Partisanship: Putting Politics Front and Center in the Opioid Epidemic," *Journal of Health Politics, Policy and Law* 45 (2020): 365–72; Jin Woo Kim, Evan Morgan, and Brendan Nyhan, "Treatment versus Punishment: Understanding Racial Inequalities in Drug Policy," *Journal of Health Politics, Policy and Law* 45 (2020): 177–209; Carmel Shachar et al., "Criminal Justice or Public Health: A Comparison of the Representation of the Crack Cocaine and Opioid Epidemics in the Media," *Journal of Health Politics, Policy and Law* 45 (2020): 211–39. This framing is cross-cut by classism too, however. In her research about what she calls the "opiate panic" in Vermont, for example, Rebecca Tiger shows that although treatment is framed as the appropriate response for middle-class white people, punishment remains the modal response for addiction among poor white people: "the 'crisis' of opiate use is framed as a 'scourge' in quaint Bennington and in Rutland, a 'blue-collar' town filled with addicts and drug dealers. . . . The notion that this is a 'gentler drug war' conflicts with the punitive response I see in practice, in which poor White drug users are caught at the intersection of the criminal justice, drug treatment, and child protection systems." Rebecca Tiger, "Race, Class, and the Framing of Drug Epidemics," *Contexts* 16 (2017): 47–48.

7. Ginia Bellafante, "In the Bronx, Heroin Woes Never Went Away," *New York Times*, 23 March 2017, https://www.nytimes.com/2017/03/23/nyregion/bronx-heroin-opioid-crisis.html.

8. URLs for COVID-19-related advertisements and campaigns: Coke, https://co cacolaunited.com/home/billboard-banner/; Gucci, https://mobile.twitter.com/gucci

/status/1243216709605097472?lang=en; Seattle and King County, WA, https://king county.gov/depts/health/communicable-diseases/disease-control/novel-coronavirus /~/media/depts/health/communicable-diseases/documents/viruses-dont-discrim inate.ashx; Mastercard, https://www.mastercard.com/news/latin-america/en/news room/digital-press-kits/dpk-en/2020/april/apart-but-united-coming-together-to -overcome-covid-19/; PCI Security Standards Council, https://blog.pcisecuritystand ards.org/we-are-all-in-this-together-responding-to-the-covid-19-pandemic.

9. Safia Samee Ali, "'Not by Accident': False 'Thug' Narratives Have Long Been Used to Discredit Civil Rights Movements," NBC News, 27 September 2020. https://www.nbcnews.com/news/us-news/not-accident-false-thug-narratives-have -long-been-used-discredit-n1240509.

10. Antonio Vázquez-Arroyo, "In the Shadows of Coronavirus," *Critical Times* 3 (2020): 1, https://ctjournal.org/2020/04/29/in-the-shadows-of-coronavirus/.

11. Megan Ming Francis, *Civil Rights and the Making of the Modern American State* (New York: Cambridge University Press, 2014), 4; Megan Ming Francis, "The Battle for the Hearts and Minds of America," *Souls* 13 (2011): 46–71.

12. Chester Hartman and Gregory Squires, *There Is No Such Thing as a Natural Disaster: Race, Class, and Hurricane Katrina* (New York: Routledge, 2006); Phil O'Keefe, Ken Westgate, and Ben Wisner, "Taking the Naturalness out of Natural Disasters," *Nature* 260 (1976): 566–67; Andy Horowitz, *Katrina: A History, 1915– 2015* (Cambridge, MA: Harvard University Press, 2020); Anthony Oliver-Smith, "What is a Disaster? Anthropological Perspectives on a Persistent Question," in *The Angry Earth: Disasters in Anthropological Context*, ed. Anthony Oliver-Smith and Susanna M. Hoffman (New York: Routledge, 1999), 18–34; Ted Steinberg, *Acts of God: the Unnatural History of Natural Disasters in America*, 2nd ed. (Oxford: Oxford University Press, 2006).

13. Jacob A. C. Remes and Andy Horowitz, "Introducing Critical Disaster Stud- ies," in *Critical Disaster Studies: New Perspectives on Disaster, Risk, Vulnerability, and Resilience*, ed. Jacob A. C. Remes and Andy Horowitz (Philadelphia: Univer- sity of Pennsylvania Press, 2021), 1.

14. Ayesha Rascoe and Colin Dwyer, "Trump Received Intelligence Briefings on Coronavirus Twice in January," National Public Radio, 2 May 2020, https://www .npr.org/sections/coronavirus-live-updates/2020/05/02/849619486/trump-received -intelligence-briefings-on-coronavirus-twice-in-january.

15. Katherine Eban, "How Jared Kushner's Secret Testing Plan 'Went Poof into Thin Air,'" *Vanity Fair*, 30 July 2020, https://www.vanityfair.com/news/2020/07/how -jared-kushners-secret-testing-plan-went-poof-into-thin-air.

16. Jeffrey Mays and Joseph Goldstein, "Mayor Resisted Drastic Steps on Virus. Then Came a Backlash from His Aides," *New York Times*, 16 March 2020, https:// www.nytimes.com/2020/03/16/nyregion/coronavirus-bill-de-blasio.html.

17. Zack Budryk, "Obama Officials Walked Trump Aides through Global Pandemic Exercise in 2017: Report," *Hill*, 17 March 2020, https://thehill.com

/policy/healthcare/488069-obama-officials-walked-trump-aides-through-global-pan demic-exercise-in-2017.

18. Jane Timm, "Fact Check: Trump Falsely Claims Obama Left him 'Nothing' in the National Stockpile," *NBC News*, 6 May 2020, https://www.nbcnews .com/politics/donald-trump/fact-check-trump-falsely-claims-obama-left-him -nothing-national-n1201406; Glenn Kessler and Meg Kelly, "Was the White House Office for Global Pandemics Eliminated?" *Washington Post*, 20 March 2020, https://www.washingtonpost.com/politics/2020/03/20/was-white-house-office-glo bal-pandemics-eliminated/; Tim Morrison, "No, the White House Didn't 'Dissolve' Its Pandemic Response Office. I Was There," *Washington Post*, 16 March 2020, https://www.washingtonpost.com/opinions/2020/03/16/no-white-house-didnt -dissolve-its-pandemic-response-office/.

19. Paul Constant, "Coronavirus Didn't Bring the Economy Down—40 Years of Greed and Corporate Malfeasance Did," *Business Insider*, 10 April 2020, https://www.businessinsider.com/pitchfork-economics-coronavirus-not-hurt ing-economy-corporate-greed-is-2020-4?fbclid=IwAR3gM9TB9QfZY-c03u3 XKgoBZj-DRnjPkMEXl_asOfeRH6DbuW44NVBO_NE.

20. See, for example, Michelle Alexander, *The New Jim Crow: Mass Incarceration in the Age of Colorblindness* (New York: New Press, 2010); James Foreman, *Locking Up Our Own: Crime and Punishment in Black America* (New York: Farrar, Straus, and Giroux, 2017); Elizabeth Hinton, *From the War on Poverty to the War on Crime: The Making of Mass Incarceration in America* (Cambridge, MA: Harvard University Press, 2017); Naomi Murakawa, *The First Civil Right: How Liberals Built Prison America* (New York: Oxford University Press, 2014); Francis, *Civil Rights*, 4; Francis, "Battle."

21. amfAR, "amfAR Study Shows Disproportionate Impact of COVID-19 on Black Americans," press release, 5 May 2020, https://www.amfar.org/amfAR -Study-Shows-Disproportionate-Impact-of-COVID-19-on-Black-Americans/.

22. Kimberlé Williams Crenshaw, "When Blackness is a Preexisting Condition," *New Republic*, 4 May 2020, https://newrepublic.com/article/157537/blackness-pre existing-condition-coronavirus-katrina-disaster-relief?fbclid=IwAR1G-s0JnTOn XbCW40--WroteI0C3TMB7kT-GgAQ8W9rlPlggw5UWslkxoU.

23. Richard E. Besser and Rebecca Cokley, "Disabled Americans Can't Be a Covid-19 Afterthought," *CNN*, 23 April 2020, https://www.cnn.com/2020/04/23 /opinions/disabled-americans-need-help-covid-19-cokley-besser/index.html?fb clid=IwAR0IFmCZUfdcMxjHYBHsgnsDBmc4Dwt-_vrW9v_zwgxa1v_CoZq7 -Np9VJk; Petruce Jean-Charles, "LGBTQ Americans Are Getting Coronavirus, Losing Jobs; Anti-gay Bias Is Making It Worse for Them," *USA Today*, 9 May 2020, https://www.usatoday.com/story/news/nation/2020/05/09/discrimination-racism -fuel-covid-19-woes-lgbtq-americans/3070036001/; Sabrina Tavernise and Richard A. Oppel Jr., "Spit On, Yelled At, Attacked: Chinese-Americans Fear for Their Safety," *New York Times*, 23 March 2020, https://www.nytimes.com/2020/03/23/us /chinese-coronavirus-racist-attacks.html.

24. Jamila Michener and Margaret Teresa Brower, "What's Policy Got to Do with It? Race, Gender & Economic Inequality in the United States," *Daedalus* 149 (2020): 100–118.

25. Tiffany D. Barnes and Mirya Holman, "Essential Work Is Gender Segregated: This Shapes the Gendered Representation of Essential Workers in Political Office," *Social Science Quarterly*, 30 July 2020.

26. Several studies suggest that the pandemic also increased the risks of domestic and family violence again women, children, and LGBTQ people. There were also death threats and misogyny-laden attacks against Michigan governor Gretchen Whitmer.

27. Adam Serwer, "The Coronavirus Was an Emergency Until Trump Found Out Who Was Dying," *Atlantic*, 8 May 2020, https://www.theatlantic.com/ideas/archive/2020/05/americas-racial-contract-showing/611389/.

28. Keeanga-Yamahtta Taylor, "The Black Plague," *New Yorker*, 16 April 2020.

29. Susan Sterett and Laura Mateczun, Disaster Cascades in Court: Governance Gaps and Familiar Pathways" (unpublished paper, n.d.).

30. Judith Butler, *Frames of War: When Is Life Grievable?* (New York: Verso, 2009).

31. As Adam Serwer wrote in the *Atlantic*,

> To restrict the freedom of white Americans, just because nonwhite Americans are dying, is an egregious violation of the racial contract . . . This is a very old and recognizable story—political and financial elites displaying a callous disregard for the workers of any race who make their lives of comfort possible. But in America, where labor and race are so often intertwined, the racial contract has enabled the wealthy to dismiss workers as both undeserving and expendable. White Americans are also suffering, but the perception that the coronavirus is largely a black and brown problem licenses elites to dismiss its impact. In America, the racial contract has shaped the terms of class war for centuries; the COVID contract shapes it here.

Serwer, "Coronavirus Was an Emergency." Research by LaFleur Stephens-Dougan find evidence for Serwer's arguments among members of the mass public as well, showing that racially prejudiced white Americans who were told that COVID-19 had a disproportionate impact on African Americans became less supportive of masking and more supportive of "outdoor activities without social distancing guidelines, more likely to perceive shelter-in-place orders as a threat to their individual rights and freedoms, and less likely to perceive African Americans as following social distancing guidelines." These effects were not evident among white Americans who did not endorse anti-Black stereotypes, who were instead *less* likely "to perceive shelter-in-place orders as a threat to their individual rights and more likely to perceive African Americans as following social distancing guidelines."

LaFleur Stephens-Dougan, "White Americans' Reactions to Racial Disparities in COVID-19," *American Political Science Review* FirstView (2022): 1.

32. Hartman and Squires, *No Such Thing*, 2.

33. Remarks by President Trump, Vice President Pence, and Members of the Coronavirus Task Force in Press Briefing, 7 April 2020, https://www.whitehouse.gov/briefings-statements/remarks-president-trump-vice-president-pence-members-coronavirus-task-force-press-briefing-april-7-2020/.

34. Michel Foucault, *Society Must Be Defended* (New York: Picador, 2003). In an analysis of analogies between Covid-19 and HIV/AIDS, Jonathon Catlin reminds readers that "while Fauci became a hero among American liberals for representing science, expertise, and reason in the face of denialism and xenophobia" in the case of COVID-19,

> his reputation regarding HIV/AIDS was far more ambivalent. On the one hand, at the height of the AIDS crisis, he called upon the public to avoid "uncalled for discrimination" against those with AIDS. He ultimately befriended ACT UP organizers such as Peter Staley and praised Larry Kramer for his courage. On the other hand, he represented the status quo of the United States's failing and unresponsive healthcare system. At the ACT UP demonstration that 'stormed' the National Institutes of Health (NIH) in May, 1990, protestors carried an effigy of his head on a stick and held signs proclaiming, "DR. FAUCI, YOU ARE KILLING US."

Catlin, "When Does an Epidemic Become a 'Crisis'?," 1448.

35. Mark Leibovich, "For A.O.C., 'Existential Crises' as Her District Becomes the Coronavirus Epicenter," *New York Times*, 4 May 2020, https://www.nytimes.com/2020/05/04/us/politics/coronavirus-alexandria-ocasio-cortez.html.

36. Crenshaw, "Blackness is a Preexisting Condition." Saidiya Hartman made a similar point about the relationship between COVID-19 and what she characterized as "the everyday character of catastrophe, the uneventfulness of black and indigenous death":

> Many of us live the uneventful catastrophe, the everyday state of emergency, the social distribution of death that targets the ones deemed fungible, disposable, remaindered, and surplus. For those usually privileged and protected, the terror of COVID-19 is its violation of and indifference to the usual distributions of death. Yet, even in this case the apportionment of risk and the burden of exposure maintains a fidelity to the given distributions of value. It appears that even a pathogen discriminates and the vulnerable are more vulnerable. The health and service workers, the home aides, delivery guys, porters and janitors, construction and factory workers, nannies, warehouse clerks, cashiers—the essential low-

> wage workers bear the weight of social reproduction, of tending to and meeting our needs and wants. There are the risks of living while poor, while abandoned and corralled in the large blocks of public housing, while trapped in the slums, while confined in prisons and detention centers.

Saidiya Hartman, "The Death Toll," *Los Angeles Review of Books*, 14 April 2020.

37. Alex Doherty, "Why the Neoliberals Won't Let This Crisis Go to Waste," *Jacobin Magazine*, 16 May 2020, jacobinmag.com/2020/05/neoliberals-response -pandemic-crisis.

38. Rahm Emanuel, "Let's Make Sure This Crisis Doesn't Go to Waste," *Washington Post*, 25 March 2020, https://www.washingtonpost.com/opinions/2020/03/25 /lets-make-sure-this-crisis-doesnt-go-waste/.

39. Christine Vestal, "Racism Is a Public Health Crisis, Say Cities and Counties," *Stateline*, 15 June 2020, https://www.pewtrusts.org/en/research-and-analysis/blogs /stateline/2020/06/15/racism-is-a-public-health-crisis-say-cities-and-counties.

40. Memorandum, "Resolution Condemning Police Brutality and Declaring Racism a Public Health Emergency," 8 June 2020, http://goleta.granicus.com/Doc umentViewer.php?file=goleta_0103c1aad9602b7efc226e5202abf942.pdf.

41. The seven measures were: (1) Working to progress as an equity and justice-oriented organization, by continuing to identify specific activities to enhance diversity and to ensure antiracism principles across our leadership, staffing and contracting; (2) Promoting equity through policies approved by the Town and enhance educational efforts aimed at understanding, addressing and dismantling racism and how it affects the delivery of human and social services, economic development and public safety; (3) Improving the quality of the data our town collects and the analysis of that data, as it is not enough to assume that an initiative is producing its intended outcome, qualitative and quantitative data should be used to assess inequities in impact and continuously improve; (4) Advocating locally for relevant policies that improve health in communities of color, and support local, state, regional, and federal initiatives that advance efforts to dismantle systemic racism; (5) Working further to solidify alliances and partnerships with other organizations that are confronting racism and encourage other local, state, regional, and national entities to recognize racism as a public health crisis; (6) Supporting community efforts to amplify issues of racism and engage actively and authentically with communities of color wherever they live; and (7) Identify clear goals and objectives, including periodic reports to the Mayor, Legislative Council, Community and Human Rights and Relations Commission, to assess progress and capitalize on opportunities to further advance racial equity. http://www.hamden .com/DocumentCenter/View/2655/07202020_Resolution-Declaring-Racism-as-a -Public-Health-Crisis-in-Hamden.

42. Amanda Holpuch, "The 'Shecession': Why Economic Crisis Is Affecting Women More Than Men," *Guardian*, 4 August 2020, https://www.theguardian

.com/business/2020/aug/04/shecession-coronavirus-pandemic-economic-fallout
-women?fbclid=IwAR2oyP2SE9DoikXKWI_HYpcWPHvgaUkGLkIP_ZKFPqM
Frxblzeoy93g2rBY; Chabeli Carrazana, "America's First Female Recession," *The
19th*, 2 August 2020, https://19thnews.org/2020/08/americas-first-female-recession
/?fbclid=IwAR3Gq06QvBo4KMRUsGbiQ13FgzgfgNxi8uGKgxv52snAFCl6pQ
VfKj8o6-0. As Aida Hozić and Jacqui True observe in the introductory essay to
their 2016 edited volume about gender and the politics of financial crises, "the
media, especially in the United States, promptly declared a 'gender role reversal.'
The 2009 headlines were quite telling: 'Will the Recession Change Gender Roles?'
(*Business Week*); 'Recession Prompts Gender Role Reversal' (ABC News); 'The
Gender-Bending Recession' (*The Nation*); and 'They Call It the Reverse Gender
Gap' (*The New York Times*)." Aida Hozić and Jacqui True, eds. *Scandalous Eco-
nomics: Gender and the Politics of Financial Crises* (New York: Oxford University
Press, 2016), 7.

43. Holpuch, "'Shecession.'"

44. Penny Griffin summarizes the response thusly:

> From around 2007 to 2009, a particular panic about male unem-
> ployment . . . led to an outbreak of descriptions of the financial
> crisis as a so-called "mancession" or "he-cession." A discourse of
> crisis emerged based on repetitions of a 1950s, male-breadwinner
> style of gender relations and, despite existing research showing
> the disproportionate job losses faced by women during the Asian
> financial crisis, . . . reports continued to claim that the crisis was
> disproportionately hurting men. . . . Subsequent, and more accu-
> rate, reporting suggests that women . . . continue to suffer dispro-
> portionately during times of slowed economic growth, precarious
> employment, and increased food prices. . . . Evidence has also sug-
> gested that men actually experienced job losses during the global
> financial crisis at a lower rate than in earlier recessions. . . . The
> assertion, across a number of popular newsmedia, protest, and
> policy channels that men were being hardest hit by the crisis and
> that a "he-cession" was imminent, and imminently catastrophic,
> reflected widely held assumptions of men's central role in local
> and global economic systems.

Penny Griffin, "Gender, Finance, and Embodiments of Crisis," in Hozic and True,
Scandalous Economics, 196–97.

45. Mark J. Perry, "The Great Mancession of 2008–2009," *Testimony before the
House Ways and Means Committee Subcommittee on Income Security and Family
Support on "Responsible Fatherhood Programs,"* 17 June 2010.

46. In 2011, 32 percent of women and 24.3 percent of men were earning poverty-
level wages; Lawrence Mishel et al., *The State of Working America* (Ithaca, NY:
Cornell University Press, 2012).

47. Mishel et al., *State of Working America*.

48. In spite of this, jobs held by women came to account for close to 50 percent of employment during the Great Recession, in part because women constituted more than 50 percent of the population, but also suggesting that more women than men held more than one paid job. See Joan Williams and Allison Anna Tait, "'Mancession' or 'Momcession?': Good Providers, a Bad Economy, and Gender Discrimination," *Chicago Kent Law Review* 86 (2011): 857.

49. Austin Sarat and Javier Lezaun, eds., *Catastrophe: Law, Politics, and the Humanitarian Impulse* (Amherst: University of Massachusetts Press, 2009), 1. Commenting on the relationship between sexual scandals and financial crises, Aida Hozić observes similarly that although "contention over gender roles . . . stands at the heart of scandals in societies experiencing crisis, the relevance of gender itself can be obscured by the noise that scandals generate." She concludes that, perhaps ironically, "scandals have powerful stabilizing effects on social norms and gender relations. Despite all the huffing and puffing, they ultimately deliver power back to the powerful." Aida A. Hozić, "We, Neoliberals," in Hozic and True, *Scandalous Economics*, 165.

50. Holpuch, "'Shecession.'"

51. Drew D. Hansen, *The Dream* (New York: HarperCollins, 2003), 67; Diallo Brooks, "We Don't Need to Return to Normal—We Need a New Normal," *Color Lines*, 15 May 2020, https://www.colorlines.com/articles/we-dont-need-return-normal -we-need-new-normal-op-ed; Peter Baker, "'We Can't Go Back to Normal': How Will Coronavirus Change the World?" *Guardian*, 31 March 2020, https://www.the guardian.com/world/2020/mar/31/how-will-the-world-emerge-from-the-corona virus-crisis. As Jack Halberstam summed it up, "If we think we want normal to return, we deserve all the injustice upon which it relies." Jack Halberstam, "Frantic," *Los Angeles Review of Books*, 14 April 2020.

52. Daniel Carpenter and Darrick Hamilton, "A Federal Job Guarantee: Anti-Poverty and Infrastructure Policy for a Better Future," 30 April 2020, https://schol ars.org/contribution/federal-job-guarantee.

53. "'Normal Wasn't Working'—John Kerry, Phillip Atiba Goff and Others on the New Social Contract Post-COVID," World Economic Forum, 24 June 2020, https://www.weforum.org/agenda/2020/06/great-reset-social-contract-john-kerry -phillip-goff/.

54. "To Move Forward, We Need to Redefine 'Normal.'" *Marie Claire*, 22 January 2021, https://www.marieclaire.com/politics/a35281127/alicia-garza-normal-is -complacent/.

55. Rebecca Solnit, "Who Will Win the Fight for a Post-Coronavirus America?" *New York Times*, 29 March 2020, https://www.nytimes.com/2020/03/29/opinion /coronavirus-revolution.html. See also "Call for a Feminist COVID-19 Policy," which was "endorsed by more than 1600 individuals and women's networks and organizations from more than 100 countries" and which called on governments "to recall and act in accordance with human rights standards in their response to

COVID-19 and uphold the principles of equality and non-discrimination, centering the most marginalized people, including but not limited to women, children, elderly, people with disabilities, people with compromised health, rural people, unhoused people, institutionalized people, LGBT+ people, refugees, migrants, indigenous peoples, stateless people, human rights defenders, and people in conflict and war zones." "Call for a Feminist COVID Policy," Feminist Alliance for Rights, updated on 28 May 2020, http://feministallianceforrights.org/blog/2020/03/20/action-call-for-a-feminist-covid-19-policy/.

Appendix A

1. Justin Grimmer, Margaret E. Roberts, and Brandon M. Stewart, "Machine Learning for Social Science: An Agnostic Approach," *Annual Review of Political Science* 24 (2021): 396.

2. See Laura Nelson et al., "The Future of Coding: A Comparison of Hand-Coding and Three Types of Computer Assisted Text Analysis Methods," *Sociological Methods and Research*, 27 May 2018.

3. See, for example, Grimmer et al., "Machine Learning"; Nelson et al., "Future of Coding"; Pablo Barbera, Amber E. Boydstun, Suzanna Linn, Ryan McMahon, and Jonathan Nagler, "Automated Text Classification of News Articles: A Practical Guide," *Political Analysis* 29 (2021): 19–42. See also Nelson et al., "Future of Coding."

4. Kenneth Benoit, "Text as Data: An Overview," in *Handbook of Research Methods in Political Science and International Relations*, ed. Luigi Curini and Robert Franzese (Thousand Oaks, CA: Sage, 2020), 467, 491.

5. Nelson et al., "Future of Coding," 3.

6. Nelson et al., "Future of Coding," 18.

7. Nelson et al., "Future of Coding," 27–28.

8. Nelson et al., "Future of Coding," 6.

9. Nelson et al., "Future of Coding," 17–20.

10. Nikki Usher, *Making News at the New York Times* (Ann Arbor: University of Michigan Press, 2014), 6–8. As the joke goes, the *Wall Street Journal* is read by the people who run the country, the *New York Times* by those who think they run the country, the *Washington Post* by those who think they ought to run the country, and the *Boston Globe* by people whose parents used to run the country.

11. Frank R. Baumgartner, Suzanna L. De Boef, and Amber E. Boydstun, *The Decline of the Death Penalty and the Discovery of Innocence* (New York: Cambridge University Press, 2008), 103.

12. On the idea that the *Wall Street Journal* is the "financial newspaper of record," see, for example, "Newspapers," Georgetown University Library, last updated 1 July 2022, https://guides.library.georgetown.edu/c.php?g=76038&p=488969.

13. As Noelle Stout writes:

> As mortgage markets collapsed and property values plummeted after 2008, TV shows like *60 Minutes* described homeowners who defaulted on their mortgages as moral hazards, while Fox News pundits declared them deadbeats and losers, likening them to those who handed Europe to the Nazis. Talking heads claimed that mortgage assistance programs like HAMP misused taxpayer money to benefit homeowners living beyond their means. The most famous attack was leveled by CNBC correspondent Rick Santelli, who in February 2009 launched into a rant against the newly established mortgage modification programs on the floor of the Chicago stock exchange. Santelli compared the programs to Cuban socialism, and his tirade culminated when he invited viewers to throw tea into the harbor in protest, a moment credited as having birthed the libertarian Tea Party movement.

Noelle Stout, *Dispossessed: How Predatory Bureaucracy Foreclosed on the American Middle Class* (Berkeley: University of California Press, 2019), 13.

14. Eitan Adam Pechenick, Christopher M. Danforth, and Peter Sheridan Dodds, "Characterizing the Google Books Corpus: Strong Limits to Inferences of Socio-Cultural and Linguistic Evolution," *PloSNE* 10, no. 10 (2015): e0137041.

15. "What Does the Ngram Viewer Do?," Google Books, accessed 12 November 2020, https://books.google.com/ngrams/info.

16. Burgett and Hendler explain further that the term *keyword* is itself an example of the dynamic they describe, and they use it to briefly illustrate what can be revealed through a brief keyword analysis:

> In contemporary usage, "keyword" generally refers to a type of information. The OED's primary definition is "a word serving as a key to a cipher or code," one that provides "a solution or explanation" or one that is "of particular importance or significance." Dating from the mid-eighteenth century, these usages represent keywords as data that unlock mysteries. The OED's second definition is a term "chosen to indicate or represent the content of a larger text or record" in an "index, catalogue, or database." Dating from the early nineteenth century, this usage represents keywords as tools for information retrieval within various archiving systems. This second meaning points toward the most familiar usage of the term today. Keywords are forms of metadata that authors, librarians, book indexers, concordance makers, web designers, and database builders add to a print or digital text to guide users to significant clusters of meaning. The interactive information ecologies of "Web 2.0" extend this usage in interesting ways. They

enable consumers of information to produce their own metadata,
which can then be visualized as word clouds or tag clouds. Metadata becomes a user-centered and interactive means of organizing, customizing, and sharing data.

Bruce Burgett and Glenn Hendler, "Keywords: An Introduction," in *Keywords for American Cultural Studies*, 3rd edition, ed. Bruce Burgett and Glenn Hendler (New York: New York University Press, 2020), vii.

17. Burgett and Hendler, "Keywords: An Introduction," vii

18. Pablo Barbera, Amber E. Boydstun, Suzanna Linn, Ryan McMahon, and Jonathan Nagler, "Automated Text Classification of News Articles: A Practical Guide," *Political Analysis* 29 (2021): 19–42. See also Nelson et al., "Future of Coding."

19. Nadja Younes and Ulf-Dietrich Reips, "Guideline for Improving the Reliability of Google Ngram Studies: Evidence from Religious Terms," *PloS ONE* 14 (2019): e0213554.

20. Junyan Jiang, Tianyang Xi, and Haojun Xie, "In the Shadows of Great Men: Leadership Turnovers and Power Dynamics in Autocracies," *SSRN* (2020), https://ssrn.com/abstract=3586255.

21. Jiang, Xi, and Xie, "In the Shadows of Great Men."

22. Alexander Koplenig, "The Impact of Lacking Metadata for the Measurement of Cultural and Linguistic Change using the Google Ngram Data Sets–Reconstructing the Composition of the German Corpus in Times of WWII," *Digital Scholarship in the Humanities* 32 (2017): 169–88.

23. Eitan Adam Pechenick, Christopher M. Danforth, and Peter Sheridan Dodds, "Characterizing the Google Books Corpus: Strong Limits to Inferences of Socio-Cultural and Linguistic Evolution," *PloS ONE* 10 (2015): e0137041, 1.

24. Jiang, Xi, and Xie, "In the Shadows of Great Men."

25. Sean Richey and J. Benjamin Taylor, "Google Books Ngrams and Political Science: Two Validity Tests for a Novel Data Source," *PS: Political Science & Politics* 53 (2020): 72. Richey and Taylor note that Google Ngram is still "a nascent tool in the published literature" in political science, but is has yielded some interested findings. "[Daniel] Shea and [Alex] Sproveri . . . showed how the debate about 'nasty' politics in the United States is not, in fact, a new discussion. Additionally, [Navid] Hassanpour, using arguments from normative theories about political speech, made the case for understanding the changes in political semantics in several political contexts through Google Ngrams. Finally, [Alexander] Bentley [and his co-authors] showed how changes in the use of language around climate-change–related information can become more diffused in society, which should make people more aware of understanding this important political issue."

26. Koplenig, "Impact of Lacking Metadata," 184.

Appendix B

1. ProQuest lists the following "ethnic communities" in its Ethnic NewsWatch: African American/Caribbean/African; Arab/Middle Eastern; Asian/Pacific Islander; European/Eastern European; Hispanic; Jewish; and Native People.

2. Alyssa Katz, "Prime Suspect," *Mother Jones*, September/October 2006, https://www.motherjones.com/politics/2006/09/prime-suspect/.

3. "Lending Traps!" *Essence*, August 2001, 88.

4. A quasi-sentence is "an argument which is the verbal expression of one political idea or issue." Thomas Daubler et al., "Natural Sentences as Valid Units for Coded Political Texts," *British Journal of Political Science* 42 (2012): 940.

Bibliography

Adams, Rachel, Benjamin Reiss, and David Serlin. 2015. *Keywords for Disability Studies*. New York: New York University Press.

Adamson, Joni, William Gleason, and David Pellow. 2016. *Keywords for Environmental Studies*. New York: New York University Press.

Adler, E. Scott, and John Wilkerson. *Congressional Bills Project* (1947–2015), NSF 00880066 and 00880061.

Agamben, Giorgio. 2005. *State of Exception*. Chicago: University of Chicago Press.

Aguirre, Adalberto, Jr., and Rubén O. Martinez. 2014. "The Foreclosure Crisis, the American Dream, and Minority Households in the United States: A Descriptive Profile." *Social Justice* 40 (3): 6–15.

Aguirre, Adalberto, Jr., and Ellen Reese. 2014. "Introduction—Foreclosure Crisis in the United States: Families and Communities at Risk." *Social Justice* 40 (3): 1–5.

Aldrich, Daniel. 2010. "Fixing Recovery: Social Capital in Post-Crisis Resilience." *Journal of Homeland Security* 6:1–10.

———. 2011a. "The Externalities of Social Capital: Post-Tsunami Recovery in Southeast India." *Journal of Civil Society* 8:81–99.

———. 2011b. "The Power of the People: Social Capital's Role in Recovery from the 1995 Kobe Earthquake." *Natural Hazards* 56:595–611.

———. 2012a. "Social, Not Physical, Infrastructure: The Critical Role of Civil Society in Disaster Recovery." *Disasters: The Journal of Disaster Studies, Policy and Management* 36:398–419.

———. 2012b. *Building Resilience: Social Capital in Post-Disaster Recovery*. Chicago: University of Chicago Press.

Aldrich, Daniel, and Kevin Crook. 2008. "Strong Civil Society as a Double-Edged Sword: Siting Trailers in Post-Katrina New Orleans." *Political Research Quarterly* 61:279–389.

Alexander, Jeffrey C. 2019. *What Makes a Social Crisis? The Societalization of Social Problems*. Medford, MA: Polity Press.

Alexander, Michelle. 2010. *The New Jim Crow: Mass Incarceration in the Age of Colorblindness*. New York: New Press.

Alexander-Floyd, Nikol. 2003. "We Shall Have Our Manhood: Black Macho, Black Nationalism, and the Million Man March." *Meridians: Feminism, Race and Transnationalism* 3:171–203.

Althusser, Louis. 1970. "Ideology and Ideological State Apparatuses." *La Pensee* (151).

Andreas, Peter, and Richard Price. 2001. "From War Fighting to Crime Fighting: Transforming the American National Security State." *International Studies Review* 3 (3): 31–52.

Andrews, Edmund L., and Gretchen Morgenson. 2007. "Fed and Regulators Shrugged as the Subprime Crisis Spread." *New York Times*, late ed. (East Coast), 18 December 2007, A1.

Apgar, William, Amal Bendimerad, and Ren S. Essene. 2007. *Mortgage Market Channels and Fair Lending: An Analysis of HMDA Data*. Cambridge, MA: Joint Center for Housing Studies of Harvard University.

Arendt, Hannah. 1963. *Eichmann in Jerusalem*. New York: Viking Press. Atkinson, Abbye. 2020. "Borrowing Equality." *Columbia Law Review* 120:1403–70.

Association of Community Organizations for Reform Now. 2000. *Separate and Unequal: Predatory Lending in America*. Washington, DC: Association of Community Organizations for Reform Now.

Austin, Algernon. 2010. *Uneven Pain*. Washington, DC: Economic Policy Institute.

Azoulay, Ariella, and Adi Ophir. 2009. "The Order of Violence." in *The Power of Inclusive Exclusion*, edited by Adi Ophir, Michal Givoni, and Sari Hanfi, 99–140. New York: Zone Books.

Bacharach, Marc. 2006. "War Metaphors: How Presidents Use the Language of War to Sell Policy." PhD diss., Miami University, 2006. https://etd.ohiolink.edu/.

Báez, Jillian, and Mari Castañeda. 2014. "Two Sides of the Same Story: Media Narratives of Latinos and the Subprime Mortgage Crisis." *Critical Studies in Media Communication* 31:27–41.

Baker, Amy Castro. 2014. "Eroding the Wealth of Women: Gender and the Subprime Foreclosure Crisis." *Social Science Review* 88 (1): 59–91.

Banaszak, Lee Ann. 1996. *Why Movements Succeed or Fail: Opportunity, Culture and the Struggle for Woman Suffrage*. Princeton, NJ: Princeton University Press.

Baradaran, Mehrsa. 2017. *The Color of Money: Black Banks and the Racial Wealth Gap*. Cambridge, MA: Belknap Press of Harvard University Press.

Barbera, Pablo, Amber E. Boydstun, Suzanna Linn, Ryan McMahon, and Jonathan Nagler. 2021. "Automated Text Classification of News Articles: A Practical Guide." *Political Analysis* 29:19–42.

Barnes, Tiffany D., and Mirya Holman. 2020. "Essential Work Is Gender Segregated: This Shapes the Gendered Representation of Essential Workers in Political Office." *Social Science Quarterly*, 30 July 2020.

Bartels, Larry. 2008. *Unequal Democracy*. Princeton, NJ: Princeton University Press.

Bassel, Leah, and Akwugo Emejulu. 2017. *Minority Women and Austerity: Survival and Resistance in France and Britain*. Bristol, UK: Bristol University Press.

Baumgartner, Frank R., Suzanna L. De Boef, and Amber E. Boydstun. 2008. *The Decline of the Death Penalty and the Discovery of Innocence*. New York: Cambridge University Press.

Baumgartner, Frank R., and Bryan D. Jones. 1993. *Agendas and Instability in American Politics*. Chicago: University of Chicago Press.

———. 2009. *Agendas and Instability in American Politics*. 2nd ed. Chicago: University of Chicago Press.

———. 2015. *The Politics of Information: Problem Definition and the Course of Public Policy in America*. Chicago: University of Chicago Press.

Beale, Frances. 1970. "Double Jeopardy: To Be Black and Female." In *The Black Woman: An Anthology*, edited by Toni Cade, 109–22. New York: New American Library.

Beck, Ulrich. 1992. *Risk Society: Towards a New Modernity*. Vol. 17. Thousand Oaks, CA: Sage.

Benjamin, Ruha. 2019. *Race after Technology: Abolitionist Tools for the New Jim Code*. Medford, MA: Polity Press.

Benjamin, Walter. 1985. "Central Park." *New German Critique* 34:32–58.

Bennett, Tony, Lawrence Grossberg, and Meaghan Morris. 2005. *New Keywords: A Revised Vocabulary of Culture and Society*. Malden, MA: Blackwell.

Benoit, Kenneth. 2020. "Text as Data: An Overview." In *Handbook of Research Methods in Political Science and International Relations*, edited by Luigi Curini and Robert Franzese, 461–97. Thousand Oaks, CA: Sage.

Berinsky, Adam. 2009. *In a Time of War*. Chicago: University of Chicago Press.

Berlant, Lauren G. 2011. *Cruel Optimism*. Durham, NC: Duke University Press.

Berry, Jeffrey. 1999. *The New Liberalism*. Washington, DC: Brookings Institution Press.

Berry, Jeffrey M., and Sarah Sobieraj. 2014. *The Outrage Industry: Political Opinion Media and the New Incivility*. New York: Oxford University Press.

Birkland, Thomas. 1997. *After Disaster*. Washington, DC: Georgetown University Press.

———. 2006. *Lessons of Disaster*. Washington, DC: Georgetown University Press.

Bocian, Debbie Gruenstein, Wei Li, and Keith S. Ernst. 2010. Foreclosures by Race and Ethnicity. CRL Research Report. Durham, NC: Center for Responsible Lending. https://www.responsiblelending.org/mortgage-lending/research -analysis/foreclosures-by-race-and-ethnicity.pdf.

Bocian, Debbie Gruenstein, Wei Li, Carolina Reid, and Roberto G. Quercia. 2011. "Lost Ground, 2011: Disparities in Mortgage Lending and Foreclosures." Durham, NC: Center for Responsible Lending. https://www.responsiblelending.org /mortgage-lending/research-analysis/Lost-Ground-2011.pdf.

354 BIBLIOGRAPHY

Boin, Arjen. "From Crisis to Disaster." 2005. In *What Is a Disaster: New Answers to Old Questions*, edited by Ronald W. Perry and E. L. Quarantelli, 153–72. Philadelphia: Xlibris.

Boin, Arjen, Paul 't Hart, and Sanneke Kuipers. 2017. "The Crisis Approach." In *Handbook of Disaster Research*, edited by Havidán Rodríguez, William Donner, and Joseph E. Trainor, 23–38. New York: Springer International.

Boin, Arjen, Allan McConnell, and Paul 't Hart. 2008. *Governing after Crisis: The Politics of Investigation, Accountability and Learning*. London: Cambridge University Press.

Bolin, Bob, and Liza Kurtz. 2017. "Race, Class, Ethnicity, and Disaster Vulnerability." In *Handbook of Disaster Research*, edited by Havidán Rodríguez, William Donner, and Joseph E. Trainor, 181–204. New York: Springer International.

Bonastia, Christopher. 2006. *Knocking on the Door: The Federal Government's Attempt to Desegregate the Suburbs*. Princeton, NJ: Princeton University Press.

Bond, Jean Carey, and Patricia Perry. 1970. "Is the Black Male Castrated?" In *The Black Woman: An Anthology*, edited by Toni Cade, 113–18. New York: New American Library.

Bonilla-Silva, Eduardo. 2013. *Racism without Racists*. New York: Rowman and Littlefield.

Borevitz, Brad. State of the Union. http://stateoftheunion.onetwothree.net.

Bourdieu, Pierre. 1977. *Outline of a Theory of Practice*. Cambridge: Cambridge University Press.

Boydstun, Amber, and Rebecca Glazier. n.d. "The Crisis Framing Cycle." Unpublished manuscript.

Bremmer, Ian. 2022. *The Power of Crisis: How Three Threats—and Our Response—Will Change the World*. New York: Simon and Schuster.

Briggs, Laura. 2017. *How All Politics Became Reproductive Politics: From Welfare Reform to Foreclosure to Trump*. Berkeley: University of California Press.

Brooks, Rick, and Ruth Simon. 2007. "Subprime Debacle Traps Even Very Credit-Worthy as Housing Boomed, Industry Pushed Loans to a Broader Market." *Wall Street Journal*, 4 December 2007, 3.

Brown, Wendy. 2007. *Edgework*. Princeton, NJ: Princeton University Press.

Brown-Dean, Khalilah L. 2010. "From Exclusion to Inclusion: Negotiating Civic Engagement When Times are Always Hard." Paper delivered at the 2010 Annual Meeting of the American Political Science Association, Washington, DC, 2–5 September 2010.

Burgett, Bruce, and Glenn Hendler. 2007. *Keywords for American Cultural Studies*. New York: New York University Press.

———. 2020. "Keywords: An Introduction." In *Keywords for American Cultural Studies*. 3rd ed., edited by Bruce Burgett and Glenn Hendler, vii–xiii. New York: New York University Press.

Butler, Judith. 2009. *Frames of War: When Is Life Grievable?* New York: Verso.

Butler, Paul. 2013. "Black Male Exceptionalism? The Problems and Potential of Black Male-Focused Interventions." *Du Bois Review* 10:485–511.

Bystydzienski, Jill M., Jennifer Suchland, and Rebecca Wanzo, eds. 2013. "Introduction to Feminists Interrogate States of Emergency." Special issue, *Feminist Formations* 25:vii–xiii.

Campbell, Andrea Louise. 2003. *How Policies Make Citizens: Senior Political Activism and the American Welfare State.* Princeton, NJ: Princeton University Press.

Canaday, Margot. 2003. "Building a Straight State: Sexuality and Social Citizenship under the 1944 GI Bill." *Journal of American History* 90:935–57.

———. 2009. *The Straight State.* Princeton, NJ: Princeton University Press.

Card, Emily. 1985. *Staying Solvent: A Comprehensive Guide to Equal Credit for Women.* New York: Holt, Rinehart and Winston.

Carr, E. Summerson. 2019. "The Work of 'Crisis' in the 'Opioid Crisis.'" *Journal of Extreme Anthropology* 3:161–66.

Carr, Leslie G. 1997. *"Colorblind" Racism.* Thousand Oaks, CA: Sage.

Catlin, Jonathon. 2018. "Catastrophe Now," *History and Theory* 60: 573–584.

———. "When Does an epidemic Become a 'Crisis'? Analogies between Covid-19 and HIV/AIDS in American Public Memory." *Memory Studies* 14:1445–74.

Chakravartty, Paula, and Denise Ferreira da Silva. 2012. "Accumulation, Dispossession, and Debt: The Racial Logic of Global Capitalism—An Introduction." *American Quarterly* 64:361–85.

Cherry, Elyse, "Where the Housing Crisis Continues." *New York Times,* 3 June 2015. http://www.nytimes.com/2015/06/03/opinion/where-the-housing-crisis-continues.html.

Choi, Kyu, Bianca D. M. Wilson, Jama Shelton, and Gary Gates. 2015. *Serving Our Youth 2015: The Needs and Experiences of Lesbian, Gay, Bisexual, Transgender, and Questioning Youth Experiencing Homelessness.* Williams Institute, UCLA School of Law. https://williamsinstitute.law.ucla.edu/publications/serving-our-youth-lgbtq/.

Chomsisengphet, Souphala, and Anthony Pennington-Cross. 2006. "The Evolution of the Subprime Mortgage Market." *Federal Reserve Bank of St. Louis Review* 88 (2006): 31–56.

Chong, Dennis, and James Druckman. 2007. "Framing Theory." *Annual Review of Political Science* 10 (1): 103–26.

Churchwell, Sarah. 2018. *Behold, America: The Entangled History of "America First" and "the American Dream."* New York: Basic Books.

Cislak, Aleksandra, Magdalena Formanowicz, and Tamar Saguy. 2018. "Bias Against Research on Gender Bias." *Scientometrics* 115:189.

Cmiel, Kenneth. 1990. *Democratic Eloquence: The Fight over Popular Speech in Nineteenth-Century America.* Berkeley: University of California Press.

Cobb, Rogers, and Charles D. Elder. 1972. *Participation in American Politics: The Dynamics of Agenda-Building.* Boston: Allyn and Bacon.

Cohen, Cathy J. 1999. *The Boundaries of Blackness*. Chicago: University of Chicago Press.

Cohen, Elizabeth F. 2018. *The Political Value of Time: Citizenship, Duration, and Democratic Justice*. New York: Cambridge University Press.

Collins, Jane L., and Victoria Mayer. 2010. *Both Hands Tied: Welfare Reform and the Race to the Bottom in the Low-Wage Labor Market*. Chicago: University of Chicago Press.

Collins, Patricia Hill. 1989. "A Comparison of Two Works on Black Family Life." *Signs: Journal of Women in Culture and Society* 14:875–84.

———. 2005. *Black Sexual Politics: African Americans, Gender, and the New Racism*. New York: Routledge.

Conley, Dalton. 1999. *Being Black, Living in the Red: Race, Wealth, and Social Policy in America*. Berkeley: University of California Press.

Connolly, N. D. B. 2014. *A World More Concrete: Real Estate and the Remaking of Jim Crow South Florida*. University of Chicago Press.

Consumer Financial Protection Bureau (CFPB). 2013. *2013 Home Ownership and Equity Protection Act (HOEPA) Rule: Small Entity Compliance Guide*. tinyurl .com/ya2ma5c6.

———. 2017. "What is a Subprime Mortgage?" https://www.consumerfinance.gov /ask-cfpb/what-is-a-subprime-mortgage-en-110/.

Correa, Vanesa Estrada. 2014. "Blueprint for the American Dream? A Critical Discourse Analysis of Presidential Remarks on Minority Homeownership." *Social Justice* 40:16–27.

Costain, Anne N. 1992. *Inviting Women's Rebellion*. Baltimore: Johns Hopkins University Press.

Cotterman, Robert F. 2002. "New Evidence on the Relationship between Race and Mortgage Default: The Importance of Credit History Data." Unicon Research Corp., 23 May 2002. https://www.huduser.gov/portal/Publications/PDF /crhistory.pdf.

Cramer, Katherine J. 2016. *The Politics of Resentment: Rural Consciousness in Wisconsin and the Rise of Scott Walker*. Chicago: University of Chicago Press.

Crenshaw, Kimberlé. 1989. "Demarginalizing the Intersection of Race and Sex." *University of Chicago Legal Forum* 39:139–67.

Crenson, Matthew. 1971. *The Un-politics of Air Pollution*. Baltimore: John Hopkins University Press.

Crump, Jeff. 2007. "Subprime Lending and Foreclosure in Hennepin and Ramsey Counties." *CURA Reporter* 37:14–18.

Crump, Jeff, et al. 2008. "Cities Destroyed (Again) for Cash: Forum on the US Foreclosure Crisis." *Urban Geography* 29:745–84.

Cvetkovich, Ann. 2003. *An Archive of Feelings*. Durham, NC: Duke University Press.

Dauber, Michele. 2013. *The Sympathetic State: Disaster Relief and the Origins of the American Welfare State*. Chicago: University of Chicago Press.

Daubler, Thomas, Kenneth Benoit, Slava Mikhaylov, and Michael Laver. 2012. "Natural Sentences as Valid Units for Coded Political Texts." *British Journal of Political Science* 42:937–51.

Davies, Mark. 2011–. *Google Books Corpus* (based on Google Books n-grams). Available at http://googlebooks.byu.edu/.

Davis, Angela. 1982. *Women, Race, and Class*. New York: Random House.

Davis, Darren W., and Brian D. Silver. 2004. "Civil Liberties vs. Security: Public Opinion in the Context of the Terrorist Attacks on America." *American Journal of Political Science* 48 (1): 28–46.

Dawson, Michael. 1995. *Behind the Mule*. Princeton, NJ: Princeton University Press.

deMause, Neil. 2009. "The Recession and the 'Deserving Poor': Poverty Finally on Media Radar—but Only When It Hits the Middle Class." *FAIR*. https://fair.org /extra/the-recession-and-the-deserving-poor/.

Desmond, Matthew. 2017. *Evicted: Poverty and Profit in the American City*. New York: Penguin Random House.

D'Ignazio, Catherine, and Lauren F. Klein. 2020. *Data Feminism*. Cambridge, MA: MIT Press.

Dillbary, J. Shahar, and Griffin Edwards. 2019. "An Empirical Analysis of Sexual Orientation Discrimination." *University of Chicago Law Review* 86:1–76.

Dolan, Merrillee. [1974] 2009. "Moynihan, Poverty Programs, and Women—A Female Viewpoint." Reprinted in *Welfare in the United States: A History with Documents, 1935–1996*, edited by Premilla Nadasen, Jennifer Mittelstadt, and Marisa Chappell, 180–83. New York: Routledge.

Dreier, Peter, Saqib Bhatti, Rob Call, Alex Schwartz, and Gregory Squires. 2014. *Underwater America: How the So-Called Housing "Recovery" Is Bypassing Many American Communities*. Berkeley: Haas Institute for a Fair and Inclusive Society.

DuBois, W. E. B. 1910. "Editorial: The Crisis." *Crisis* 1 (1): 10.

Dudziak, Mary. 2000. *Cold War Civil Rights*. Princeton, NJ: Princeton University Press.

———. 2012. *War Time: An Idea, Its History, Its Consequences*. New York: Oxford University Press.

Duneier, Mitchell. 2017. *Ghetto: The Invention of a Place, the History of an Idea*. New York: Farrar, Straus and Giroux.

Dwyer, Rachel E. 2018. "Credit, Debt, and Inequality." *Annual Review of Sociology* 44:237–61.

Dymski, Gary, Jesus Hernandez, and Lisa Mohanty. 2013. "Race, Gender, Power, and the US Subprime Mortgage and Foreclosure Crisis: A Meso Analysis." *Feminist Economics* 19:3.

Dzanouni, Lamia, Hélène Le Dantec-Lowry, and Claire Parfait. 2016. "From One Crisis to the Other: History and Literature in *The Crisis* from 1910 to the Early 1920s." *European Journal of American Studies* 11:1–26.

Eagleton, Terry. 2002. *Sweet Violence: The Idea of the Tragic*. Oxford: Blackwell.

Edelman, Murray. 1964. *The Symbolic Uses of Politics*. Urbana: University of Illinois Press.

———. 1977. *Political Language: Words that Succeed and Policies that Fail*. New York: Academic Press.

———. 1985. "Political Language and Political Reality." *PS: Political Science and Politics*, 18 (1): 10–19.

Edwards, Erica, Roderick Ferguson, and Jeffrey Ogbar. 2018. *Keywords for African American Studies*. New York: New York University Press.

Emejulu, Akwugo, and Leah Bassel. 2017. "Whose Crisis Counts? Minority Women, Austerity and Activism in France and Britain." In *Gender and the Economic Crisis in Europe*, edited by Johanna Kantola and Emanuela Lombardo, 185–208. London: Palgrave Macmillan.

Enarson, Elaine, Alice Fothergill, and Lori Peek. 2017. "Gender and Disaster: Foundations and New Directions for Research and Practice." In *Handbook of Disaster Research*, edited by Havidán Rodríguez, William Donner, and Joseph E. Trainor, 205–24. New York: Springer International.

Engel, Sascha. 2014. "A Crisis of Crisis Narratives?" *New Political Science* 36:266–71.

Enloe, Cynthia. 2000. *Maneuvers*. Berkeley: University of California Press.

Entman, Robert. 1990. "Images of Blacks and Racism in Local Television News." *Critical Studies in Media Communication* 7:332–45.

———. 1993. "Framing: Toward Clarification of a Fractured Paradigm." *Journal of Communication* 4:51–58.

Entman, Robert, and Andrew Rojecki. 2000. *The Black Image in the White Mind*. Chicago: University of Chicago Press.

Essene, Ren S., and William C. Apgar. 2007. *Understanding Mortgage Market Behavior: Creating Good Mortgage Options for All Americans*. Cambridge, MA: Joint Center for Housing Studies of Harvard University.

Eubanks, Virginia. 2018. *Automating Inequality: How High-Tech Tools Profile, Police, and Punish the Poor*. New York: St. Martin's Press.

Faber, Jacob. 2013. "Racial Dynamics of Subprime Mortgage Lending at the Peak." *Housing Policy Debate* 23:328–49.

———. 2018. "Segregation and the Geography of Creditworthiness: Racial Inequality in a Recovered Mortgage Market." *Housing Policy Debate* 28:215–47.

Federal Home Loan Mortgage Corporation (Freddie Mac). 2007. "Freddie Mac Announces Tougher Subprime Lending Standards to Help Reduce the Risk of Future Borrower Default." Press Releases Relating to the Financial Crisis of 2007–2009 (27 February 2007). https://fraser.stlouisfed.org/title/5132/item/518857.

Federal Housing Administration. 1936. *Underwriting Manual*. Washington, DC: GPO.

Ferguson, Roderick. 2004. *Aberrations in Black: Toward a Queer of Color Critique.* Minneapolis: University of Minnesota Press.

Fishbein, Allen, and Patrick Woodall. 2006. *Women Are Prime Targets for Subprime Lending: Women Are Disproportionately in High-Cost Mortgage Market.* Washington, DC: Consumer Federation of America.

Flexner, Eleanor. 1959. *Century of Struggle: The Woman's Rights Movement in the United States.* Cambridge, MA: Harvard University Press.

Flexner, Eleanor, and Ellen F. Fitzpatrick. 1996. *Century of Struggle: The Woman's Rights Movement in the United States.* Cambridge, MA: Harvard University Press.

Foreman, James. 2017. *Locking Up Our Own: Crime and Punishment in Black America.* New York: Farrar, Straus, and Giroux.

Forrest, M. David. 2022. *Giving Voice without Power? Organizing for Social Justice in Minneapolis.* Minneapolis: University of Minnesota Press.

Foucault, Michel. 1984. "Nietzsche, Genealogy, History." In *The Foucault Reader,* edited by Paul Rabinow, 76–100. New York: Pantheon.

———. 2003. *Society Must Be Defended.* New York: Picador

Francis, Megan Ming. 2011. "The Battle for the Hearts and Minds of America." *Souls* 13:46–71.

———. 2014. *Civil Rights and the Making of the Modern American State.* New York: Cambridge University Press.

Fraser, Nancy, and Linda Gordon. 1994. "'Dependency' Demystified: Inscriptions of Power in a Keyword of the Welfare State." *Social Politics: International Studies in Gender, State & Society* 1 (1): 4–31.

———. 1994. "A Genealogy of Dependency: Tracing a Keyword of the US Welfare State." *Signs: Journal of Women in Culture and Society* 19:309–36.

Freund, David M. P. 2007. *Colored Property: State Policy and White Racial Politics in Suburban America.* Chicago: University of Chicago Press.

Frey, Frederick. 1971. "Comment: On Issues and Nonissues in the Study of Power." *American Political Science Review* 65 (4): 1081–1101.

Friedman, Milton. [1962] 1982. *Capitalism and Freedom.* Chicago: University of Chicago Press.

Fritsch, Kelly, Clare O'Connor, and AK Thompson, eds. 2016. *Keywords for Radicals: The Contested Vocabulary of Late-Capitalist Struggle.* Chico: AK Press.

Fry, Richard, and Anna Brown. 2016. *In a Recovering Market, Homeownership Rates Are Down Sharply for Blacks, Young Adults.* Pew Research Center. https://www.pewsocialtrends.org/2016/12/15/in-a-recovering-market-homeownership-rates-are-down-sharply-for-blacks-young-adults/.

Frymer, Paul, Dara Z. Strolovitch, and Dorian Warren. 2006. "New Orleans Is Not the Exception." *Du Bois Review* 3:37–57.

Gans, Herbert. 1965. "The Negro Family: Reflections on the 'Moynihan Report.'" *Commonweal* 83:47–51.

————. 1979. *Deciding What's News: A Study of CBS Evening News, NBC Nightly News, Newsweek, and Time*. New York: Random House.

————. 2011. "The Moynihan Report and Its Aftermaths: A Critical Analysis." *Du Bois Review* 8:315–27.

Gaventa, John. 1980. *Power and Powerlessness*. Champagne: University of Illinois Press.

Geary, Daniel. 2015. *Beyond Civil Rights: The Moynihan Report and Its Legacy*. Philadelphia: University of Pennsylvania Press.

Giddens, Anthony. 1999. "Risk and Responsibility." *Modern Law Review* 62:1–10.

Gilens, Martin. 1999. *Why Americans Hate Welfare*. Chicago: University of Chicago Press.

Gill, Duane A., and Liesel A. Ritchie. 2017. "Contributions of Technological and Natech Disaster Research to the Social Science Disaster Paradigm." In *Handbook of Disaster Research*, edited by Havidán Rodríguez, William Donner, and Joseph E. Trainor, 39–62. New York: Springer International.

Gilmore, Ruth Wilson. 2007. *Golden Gulag: Prisons, Surplus, Crisis, and Opposition in Globalizing California*. Berkeley: University of California Press.

Gingrich, Jane. 2014. "Visibility, Values, and Voters: The Informational Role of the Welfare State." *Journal of Politics* 76:565–80.

Glazier, Rebecca, and Amber Boydstun. 2012. "The President, the Press, and the War: A Tale of Two Framing Agendas." *Political Communication* 29:428–46.

Goetz, Edward G. 2013. *New Deal Ruins: Race, Economic Justice, and Public Housing Policy*. Ithaca, NY: Cornell University Press.

Goffman, Erving. 1974. *Frame Analysis: An Essay on the Organization of Experience*. Cambridge, MA: Harvard University Press.

Goldfield, Michael. 1989. "Worker Insurgency, Radical Organization, and New Deal Labor Legislation." *American Political Science Review* 83:1257–82.

Gottesdiener, Laura. 2013. *A Dream Foreclosed: Black America and the Fight for a Place to Call Home*. New York Zuccotti Park Press.

Gouldner, Alvin. 1970. *The Coming Crisis of Western Sociology*. New York: Basic Books.

Graber, Robert. 1995. *A Scientific Model of Social and Cultural Evolution*. Kirksville, MO: Thomas Jefferson University Press.

Gramlich, Edward M. 2007. "Booms and Busts: The Case of Subprime Mortgages." *Economic Review* 92:105–13.

Gramsci, Antonio. 1971. *Selections from the Prison Notebooks*. New York: International.

Grant-Thomas, Andrew. 2000. "Representing the Race: The Black Male Crisis and Politics of Neglect." PhD thesis, University of Chicago. ProQuest Dissertations & Theses Global.

Greenbaum, Susan D. 2015. *Blaming the Poor: The Long Shadow of the Moynihan Report on Cruel Images about Poverty*. New Brunswick, NJ: Rutgers University Press.

Greer, James. 2014. "The Better Homes Movement and the Origins of Mortgage Redlining in the United States." In *Statebuilding from the Margins: Between Reconstruction and the New Deal*, edited by Julie Novkov and Carol Nackenoff, 203–36. Philadelphia: University of Pennsylvania Press.

Griffin, Penny. 2016. "Gender, Finance, and Embodiments of Crisis." In *Scandalous Economics: Gender and the Politics of Financial Crises*, edited by Aida A. Hozić and Jacqui True, 196–97. New York: Oxford University Press.

Grimmer, Justin, Margaret E. Roberts, and Brandon M. Stewart. 2021. "Machine Learning for Social Science: An Agnostic Approach." *Annual Review of Political Science* 24:395–419.

Grimmer, Justin, and Brandon Stewart. 2011. "Text as Data: The Promise and Pitfalls of Automatic Content Analysis Methods for Political Texts." *Political Analysis* 21:267–97.

Guinier, Lani, and Gerald Torres. 2002. *The Miner's Canary: Enlisting Race, Resisting Power, Transforming Democracy*. Cambridge, MA: Harvard University Press.

Gusfield, Joseph R. 1996. *Contested Meanings: The Construction of Alcohol Problems*. Madison: University of Wisconsin Press.

Gutenberg Project., ed. 2013. *The American Crisis*, gutenberg.org/files/3741/3741-h/3741-h.htm.

———. *The Federalist Papers*. gutenberg.org/files/1404/1404-h/1404-h.htm.

Hacker, Jacob S. 2002. *The Divided Welfare State: The Battle over Public and Private Social Benefits in the United States*. New York: Cambridge University Press.

———. 2004. "Privatizing Risk without Privatizing the Welfare State: The Hidden Politics of Social Policy Retrenchment in the United States." *American Political Science Review* 98:243–60.

———. 2019. *The Great Risk Shift: The New Economic Insecurity and the Decline of the American Dream*. New York: Oxford University Press.

Hacker, Jacob, and Paul Pierson. 2010. *Winner-Take-All Politics*. New York: Simon and Schuster.

Halberstam, Jack. 2020. "Frantic." *Los Angeles Review of Books*, 14 April 2020.

Haley, Sarah. 2016. *No Mercy Here: Gender, Punishment, and the Making of Jim Crow Modernity*. Chapel Hill: University of North Carolina Press.

Hall, Stuart, Chas Critcher, Tony Jefferson, John Clarke, and Brian Roberts. 1978. *Policing the Crisis: Mugging, the State, and Law and Order*. London: Macmillan.

Hamilton, Donna, and Charles Hamilton. 1992. "The Dual Agenda of African American Organizations since the New Deal." *Political Science Quarterly* 107:435–53.

Hancock, Ange-Marie. 2004. *The Politics of Disgust*. New York: New York University Press.

Haney-Lopez, Ian. 2013. *Dog Whistle Politics: How Coded Racial Appeals Have Reinvented Racism and Wrecked the Middle Class*. New York: Oxford University Press.

Hansen, Drew D. 2003. *The Dream: Martin Luther King, Jr., and the Speech That Inspired a Nation.* New York: HarperCollins.

Harbin, M. Brielle. 2018. "The Contingency of Compassion: Media Depictions of Drug Addiction." Unpublished manuscript.

Harris, Cheryl I. 1995. "Whiteness as Property." In *Critical Race Theory: The Key Writings That Formed the Movement,* edited by Kimberlé Crenshaw, Neil Gotanda, Gary Peller, and Kendall Thomas, 276–91. New York: New Press.

Hartman, Chester, and Gregory Squires, eds. 2006. *There Is No Such Thing as a Natural Disaster: Race, Class, and Hurricane Katrina.* New York: Routledge.

———, eds. 2013. *From Foreclosure to Fair Lending: Advocacy, Organizing, Occupy, and the Pursuit of Equitable Credit.* New York: New Village Press.

Hartman, Saidiya. 2020. "The Death Toll." *Los Angeles Review of Books,* 14 April 2020.

Hartmann, Betsy. 1995. *Reproductive Rights and Wrongs: The Global Politics of Population Control.* Rev. ed. Boston: South End Press.

Harvey, David. 2010. *The Enigma of Capital and the Crises of Capitalism.* New York: Oxford University Press.

Hay, Colin. 1999. "Crisis and the Structural Transformation of the State: Interrogating the Process of Change." *British Journal of Politics and International Relations* 1:317–44.

Heath, Brad. 2011. "Mortgage Complaints Raised Red Flags." Retrieved from https://search.proquest.com/docview/861734359?accountid=1331.

Helper, Rose. 1969. *Racial Policies and Practices of Real Estate Brokers.* Minneapolis: University of Minnesota Press.

Herbst, Susan. 2010. *Rude Democracy: Civility and Incivility in American Politics.* Philadelphia: Temple University Press.

Hibbing, John R., and Elizabeth Theiss-Morse, eds. 2001. *What Is It about Government That Americans Dislike?* New York: Cambridge University Press.

Hillier, Amy, and Devin Michelle Bunten. 2020. "A Queer and Intersectional Approach to Fair Housing." In *Perspectives on Fair Housing,* edited by Vincent J. Reina, Wendell E. Pritchett, and Susan M. Wachter, 154–85. Philadelphia: University of Pennsylvania Press.

Hinton, Elizabeth. 2017. *War on Poverty to War on Crime: The Making of Mass Incarceration in America.* Cambridge, MA: Harvard University Press.

Homer-Dixon, Thomas. 2010. *The Upside of Down: Catastrophe, Creativity, and the Renewal of Civilization.* Washington, DC: Island Press.

Honig, Bonnie. 2009. *Emergency Politics: Paradox, Law, Democracy.* Princeton, NJ: Princeton University Press.

Horn, Eva. 2018. *The Future as Catastrophe: Imagining Disaster in the Modern Age.* Translated by Valentine Pakis. New York: Columbia University Press.

Horowitz, Andy. 2020. *Katrina: A History, 1915–2015.* Cambridge, MA: Harvard University Press.

Howell, William G. 2003. *Power without Persuasion: The Politics of Direct Presidential Action*. Princeton, NJ: Princeton University Press.

Howell, William G., and Faisal Z. Ahmed. 2014. "Voting for the President: The Supreme Court during War." *Journal of Law, Economics, & Organization* 30:39–71.

Howell, William G., Saul P. Jackman, and Jon C. Rogowski. 2013. *The Wartime President: Executive Influence and the Nationalizing Politics of Threat*. Chicago: University of Chicago Press.

Hozić, Aida A. 2016. "We, Neoliberals." In *Scandalous Economics: Gender and the Politics of Financial Crises*, edited by Aida A. Hozić and Jacqui True, 165–78. New York: Oxford University Press.

Hozić, Aida A., and Jacqui True, eds. 2016. *Scandalous Economics: Gender and the Politics of Financial Crises*. New York: Oxford University Press.

Huddy, Leonie, and Stanley Feldman. 2011. "Americans Respond Politically to 9/11: Understanding the Impact of the Terrorist Attacks and Their Aftermath." *American Psychologist* 66:455–67.

Huddy, Leonie, Stanley Feldman, Charles Taber, and Gallya Lahav. 2005. "Threat, Anxiety, and Support of Antiterrorism Policies." *American Journal of Political Science* 49:593–608.

Huddy, Leonie, Stanley Feldman, and Christopher Weber. 2007. "The Political Consequences of Perceived Threat and Felt Insecurity." *Annals of the American Academy of Political and Social Science* 614:131–53.

Hunter, Tera W. 2017. *Bound in Wedlock*. Cambridge, MA: Harvard University Press.

Hyman, Louis. 2011. *Debtor Nation: A History of American in Red Ink*. Princeton, NJ: Princeton University Press.

———. 2012. *Borrow: The American Way of Debt*. New York: Vintage.

Immergluck, Dan. 2004. *Credit to the Community: Community Reinvestment and Fair Lending Policy in the United States: Community Reinvestment and Fair Lending Policy in the United States*. New York: Routledge.

———. [2009] 2011. *Foreclosed: High-Risk Lending, Deregulation, and the Undermining of America's Mortgage Market*. Ithaca, NY: Cornell University Press.

———. 2013. "Too Little, Too Late, and Too Timid: The Federal Response to the Foreclosure Crisis at the Five-Year Mark." *Housing Policy Debate* 23:199–232.

———. 2015. *Preventing the Next Mortgage Crisis: The Meltdown, the Federal Response, and the Future of Housing in America*. New York: Rowman and Littlefield.

———. 2018. "Old Wine in Private Equity Bottles? The Resurgence of Contract-for-Deed Home Sales in US Urban Neighborhoods." *International Journal of Urban and Regional Research* 42:651–65.

Ingelhart, Ronald. 1971. "The Silent Revolution in Europe: Intergenerational Change in Post-Industrial Societies." *American Political Science Review* 65:991–1017.

———. 1977. *The Silent Revolution. Changing Values and Political Styles in Advanced Industrial Society*. Princeton, NJ: Princeton University Press.

———. 2008. "Changing Values among Western Publics from 1970 to 2006." *West European Politics* 31:130–46.

Iyengar, Shanto. 1991. *Is Anyone Responsible? How Television Frames Political Issues*. Chicago: University of Chicago Press.

Iyengar, Shanto, and Donald Kinder. 1987. *News That Matters*. Chicago: University of Chicago Press.

Jackson, Kenneth T. 1985. *Crabgrass Frontier: The Suburbanization of America*. New York: Oxford University Press.

Jacobs, Lawrence, and Desmond King. 2009. "America's Political Crisis: The Unsustainable State in a Time of Unraveling." *PS: Political Science & Politics* 42:277–85.

Jacobs, Lawrence R., and Suzanne Mettler. 2018. "When and How New Policy Creates New Politics: Examining the Feedback Effects of the Affordable Care Act on Public Opinion." *Perspectives on Politics* 16:345–63.

Jacobs, Meg. 2016. *Panic at the Pump: The Energy Crisis and the Transformation of American Politics in the 1970s*. New York: Macmillan.

Jacobson, Gary C. 2003. "Terror, Terrain, and Turnout." *Political Science Quarterly* 118:1–22.

James, S. E., J. L. Herman, S. Rankin, M. Keisling, L. Mottet, and M. Anafi. 2016. *The Report of the 2015 U.S. Transgender Survey*. Washington, DC: National Center for Transgender Equality. https://transequality.org/sites/default/files/docs/usts/USTS-Full-Report-Dec17.pdf.

Jameson, Fredric. 2002. "The Dialectics of Disaster." *South Atlantic Quarterly* 101:297–304.

Jeffrey, Craig, and John Harriss. 2014. *Keywords for Modern India*. New York: Oxford University Press.

Johnson, Brian, ed. 2005. *DuBois on Reform: Periodical-Based Leadership for African Americans*. New York: AltaMira Press.

Johnson, Katharine. 2012. "'Why Is This the Only Place in Portland I See Black People?' Teaching Young Children about Redlining." *Rethinking Schools* 27:19–24.

Joint Center for Housing Studies of Harvard University. 2009. *The State of the Nation's Housing 2009*. Cambridge, MA: Joint Center for Housing Studies of Harvard University. http://www.jchs.harvard.edu/sites/jchs.harvard.edu/files/son2009.pdf.

Jones, Bryan, and Michelle Whyman. 2014. "The Great Broadening: Agenda Politics and the Transformation of the American Political System." Working paper of the US Policy Agendas Project.

Jones, Marian Moser. 2013. *The American Red Cross from Clara Barton to the New Deal*. Baltimore: Johns Hopkins University Press.

Jordan, June. [1970] 1974. "Memo to Daniel Pretty Moynihan." In *New Days: Poems of Exile and Return*, 6. New York: Emerson Hall.

Jordan-Young, Rebecca M., and Katrina Karkazis. 2019. *Testosterone: An Unauthorized Biography*. Cambridge, MA: Harvard University Press.

Jordanova, Ludmilla. 2019. *History in Practice*. London: Bloomsbury.

Junn, Jane. 2007. "Square Pegs and Round Holes: Challenges of Fitting Individual-Level Analysis to a Theory of Politicized Context of Gender." *Politics & Gender* 3:124–34.

———. 2009. "Dynamic Categories and the Context of Power." In *The Future of Political Science: 100 Perspectives*, edited by Gary King, Kay L. Schlozman, and Norman Nie, 25–27. New York: Routledge.

Junn, Jane, and Natalie Masuoka. 2008. "Asian American Identity: Shared Racial Status and Political Context." *Perspectives on Politics* 6:729–40.

Kaplan, David. 2008. "Foreclosures, Predatory Lending, and Reverse Redlining." *Urban Geography* 29:762–66.

Kaplan, Laura. 1995. *The Story of Jane: The Legendary Underground Feminist Abortion Service*. New York: Knopf Doubleday

Katznelson, Ira. 2005. *When Affirmative Action Was White*. New York: W. W. Norton.

———. 2013. *Fear Itself: The New Deal and the Origins of Our Time*. New York: Liveright.

Keest, Kathleen. 2008. "The Way Ahead: A Framework for Policy Responses." Paper presented at the Subprime Housing Crisis Symposium, University of Iowa, 10–11 October 2008. https://www.responsiblelending.org/sites/default/files/nodes/files/research-publication/Iowa-Subprime-Symposium.pdf.

Kennedy, Tony and David Phelps. 2001. "NWA Will Lay Off 10,000; $15 Billion Airline Aid OK'd." *Minneapolis Star Tribune*, 22 September 2001.

Kenney, Sally J. 2003. "Where Is Gender in Agenda Setting?" *Women & Politics* 25:179–207.

Kim, Jin Woo, Evan Morgan, and Brendan Nyhan 2020. "Treatment versus Punishment: Understanding Racial Inequalities in Drug Policy." *Journal of Health Politics, Policy and Law* 45:177–209.

King, Desmond. 2011. "The American State and the Obama Presidency: A Preliminary Discussion." *der modern staat-dms: Zeitschrift fur Public Policy, Recht und Management*. 4(2): 269–81.

———. 2013. "The American State as an Agent of Race Equity: The Systemic Limits of Shock and Awe in Domestic Policy." In *Beyond Discrimination: Racial Inequality in a Post-Racial Era*, edited by Fredrick Harris and Robert Lieberman, 73–104. New York: Russell Sage Foundation.

———. n.d. "Against the State." Unpublished manuscript.

King, Martin Luther, Jr. 1963. "Letter from Birmingham Jail." *Liberation: An Independent Monthly* 8 (4): 10–16, 23.

Kingdon, John W. [1984] 1995. *Agendas, Alternatives, and Public Policies*. New York: HarperCollins.

Kirschke, Amy Helene. 2005. "Dubois and '*The Crisis*' Magazine: Imaging Women and Family." *Source: Notes in the History of Art* 24:35–45.

———. 2007. *Art in Crisis: W. E. B. Du Bois and the Struggle for African American Identity and Memory*. Bloomington: Indiana University Press.

Kirschke, Amy Helene, and Phillip Luke Sinitiere, eds. 2019. *Protest and Propaganda: WEB Du Bois, the Crisis, and American History*. Columbia: University of Missouri Press.

Klarman, Michael J. 2004. *From Jim Crow to Civil Rights: The Supreme Court and the Struggle for Racial Equality*. New York: Oxford University Press.

Klein, Naomi. 2007. *The Shock Doctrine: The Rise of Disaster Capitalism*. New York: Metropolitan Books.

Klinenberg, Eric. 2003. *Heat Wave*. Chicago: University of Chicago Press.

Klinkner, Philip A., and Rogers M. Smith. 1999. *The Unsteady March*. Chicago: University of Chicago Press.

Knowles, Scott. 2011. *The Disaster Experts: Mastering Risk in Modern America*. Philadelphia: University of Pennsylvania Press.

———. 2020. "Slow Disaster in the Anthropocene: A Historian Witnesses Climate Change on the Korean Peninsula." *Daedalus* 149: 192–206.

Koplenig, Alexander. 2017 "The Impact of Lacking Metadata for the Measurement of Cultural and Linguistic Change using the Google Ngram Data Sets—Reconstructing the Composition of the German Corpus in Times of WWII." *Digital Scholarship in the Humanities* 32:169–88.

Kornbluh, Felicia. 2007. *The Battle for Welfare Rights: Politics and Poverty in Modern America*. Philadelphia: University of Pennsylvania Press.

Korver Glenn, Elizabeth. 2018. "Compounding Inequalities: How Racial Stereotypes and Discrimination Accumulate Across the Stages of Housing Exchange." *American Sociological Review* 83:627–56.

Koselleck, Reinhart. 2006. "Crisis." *Journal of the History of Ideas* 67:357–400.

Kovecses, Zoltan. 2000. *Metaphor and Emotion: Language, Culture, and Body in Human Feeling*. New York: Cambridge University Press.

Krebs, Ron. 2006. "The Father of All Things? Hypotheses on the Effects of War on Democracy." Paper read at International Studies Association Annual Convention, San Diego, CA, 22–25 March.

Krimmel, Katherine, and Kelly Rader. 2017. "The Federal Spending Paradox: Economic Self-Interest and Symbolic Racism in Contemporary Fiscal Politics." *American Politics Research* 45:727–54.

Krippner, Greta. 2011. *Capitalizing on Crisis: The Political Origins of the Rise of Finance*. Cambridge, MA: Harvard University Press.

———. 2017. "Democracy of Credit: Ownership and the Politics of Credit Access in Late Twentieth-Century America." *American Journal of Sociology* 123:1–47.

Kryder, Daniel. 2001. *Divided Arsenal*. New York: Cambridge University Press.

Kuipers, Sanneke. 2006. *The Crisis Imperative: Crisis Rhetoric and Welfare State Reform in Belgium and the Netherlands in the Early 1990s*. Amsterdam: Amsterdam University Press.

Kushner, Rabbi Harold. 1981. *When Bad Things Happen to Good People*. New York: Schocken Books.

Kuumba, Monica Bahati. 1993. "Perpetuating Neo-Colonialism through Population Control: South Africa and the United States." *Africa Today* 40:79–85.

Ladner, Joyce A. 1971. *Tomorrow's Tomorrow: The Black Woman.* Garden City, NY: Doubleday.

Lakoff, George P. 1996. *Moral Politics.* Chicago: University of Chicago Press.

———. 2006. *Whose Freedom?* New York: Farrar, Straus, and Giroux.

———. 2008. *The Political Mind: Why You Can't Understand 21st Century American Politics with an 18th Century Brain.* New York: Penguin Group.

Lamb, Charles M. 2005. *Housing Segregation in Suburban America since 1960: Presidential and Judicial Politics.* New York: Cambridge University Press.

Langowski, Jamie, William L. Berman, Regina Holloway, and Cameron McGinn. 2018. "Transcending Prejudice: Gender Identity and Expression- Based Discrimination in the Metro Boston Rental Housing Market." *Yale Journal of Law & Feminism* 29:322–71.

Laugesen, Miriam J., and Eric M. Patashnik. 2020. "Framing, Governance, and Partisanship: Putting Politics Front and Center in the Opioid Epidemic." *Journal of Health Politics, Policy and Law* 45:365–72.

Laws, Serena. 2020. "What Kind of Relief? Consumer Bankruptcy and Private Administration in the Neoliberal American Welfare State." *New Political Science* 42:333–56.

Legette, Willie. 1999. "The Crisis of the Black Male: A New Ideology of Black Politics." In *Without Justice for All: New Liberalism and Our Retreat from Racial Equality*, edited by Adolph Reed, 291–326. Boulder, CO: Westview Press.

Lerman, Amy E., and Katherine T. McCabe. 2017. "Personal Experience and Public Opinion: A Theory and Test of Conditional Policy Feedback." *Journal of Politics* 79:624–41.

Levitsky, Steven, and Daniel Ziblatt. 2018. *How Democracies Die.* New York: Broadway Books.

Lewis, David Levering. 1993. *W. E. B. Du Bois: Biography of a Race, 1868–1919.* New York: Henry Holt.

———. 2000. *W. E. B. Du Bois: The Fight for Equality and the American Century, 1919–1963.* New York: Henry Holt.

Lewis, Michael. 2010. *The Big Short: Inside the Doomsday Machine.* New York: W. W. Norton.

Lichtenstein, Bronwen, and Joe Weber. 2015. "Women Foreclosed: A Gender Analysis of Housing Loss in the US Deep South." *Social & Cultural Geography* 16:1–21.

Lipsitz, George. 1995. "The Possessive Investment in Whiteness: Racialized Social Democracy and the 'White' Problem in American Studies." *American Quarterly* 47:369–87.

Logan, John R., and Harvey L. Molotch. 1987. *Urban Fortunes: The Political Economy of Place.* Berkeley: University of California Press.

Long, Melanie G. 2018. "Pushed into the Red? Female-Headed Households and the Pre-Crisis Credit Expansion," *Forum for Social Economics* 47:224–36.

Longobardi, Elinore. 2009. "How 'Subprime' Killed 'Predatory.' " *Columbia Journalism Review* 48:45–49.

Lowande, Kenneth, and Jon C. Rogowski. 2021. "Executive Power in Crisis." *American Political Science Review* 115:1406–23.

Luft, Rachel E. 2016. "Racialized Disaster Patriarchy: An Intersectional Model for Understanding Disaster Ten Years After Hurricane Katrina." *Feminist Formations* 28:1–26.

MacCabe, Colin, and Holly Yanacek. 2018. *Keywords for Today: A 21st Century Vocabulary*. New York: Oxford University Press.

MacDougald, James. 2010. *Unsustainable*. Abingdon, UK: Marsden House.

Mallocci, Martina. 2018. " 'All Art is Propaganda': WEB Du Bois's The Crisis and the Construction of a Black Public Image." *USAbroad: Journal of American History and Politics* 1.

Marcuse, Herbert. 2006. *One-Dimensional Man: Studies in the Ideology of Advanced Industrial Society*. London: Routledge.

Massey, Douglas S., and Nancy A. Denton. 1993. *American Apartheid: Segregation and the Making of the Underclass*. Cambridge, MA: Harvard University Press.

Massey, Douglas S., Jacob S. Rugh, Justin P. Steil, and Len Albright. 2016. "Riding the Stagecoach to Hell: A Qualitative Analysis of Racial Discrimination in Mortgage Lending." *City & Community* 15:118–36.

Massey, Douglas S., and Robert Sampson. 2009. "Moynihan Redux: Legacies and Lessons." *Annals of the American Academy of Political and Social Science* 621:6–27.

Masur, Kate. 2007. " 'A Rare Phenomenon of Philological Vegetation': The Word 'Contraband' and the Meanings of Emancipation in the United States." *Journal of American History* 93 (4): 1050–84.

May, Elaine Tyler. 2011. *America and the Pill: A History of Promise, Peril, and Liberation*. New York: Basic Books.

Mayhew, David. 2005. *Divided We Govern: Party Control, Lawmaking, and Investigations, 1946–2002*. New Haven, CT: Yale University Press.

———. 2005. "Wars and American Politics." *Perspectives on Politics* 3:473–93.

McAdam, Doug. 1982. *Political Process and the Development of Black Insurgency, 1930–1970*. Chicago: University of Chicago Press.

McCall, Leslie. 2007. "Increasing Class Disparities among Women and the Politics of Gender Equity." In *The Sex of Class: Women Transforming American Labor*, edited by Sue Cobble, 15–34. Ithaca, NY: Cornell University Press.

———. 2013. *The Undeserving Rich: American Beliefs about Inequality, Opportunity, and Redistribution*. New York: Cambridge University Press.

McCann, Michael. 1996. "Causal versus Constitutive Explanations (or, On the Difficulty of Being so Positive . . .)." *Law & Social Inquiry* 21:457–82.

McCarthy, Jonathan, and Richard W. Peach. 2004. "Are Home Prices the Next 'Bubble'?" *FRBNY Economic Policy Review* 10 (3): 1–17.

McCarty, Nolan, Keith Poole, and Howard Rosenthal. 2013. *Polarized America: The Dance of Ideology and Unequal Riches*. Cambridge, MA: MIT Press.

McClintock, Anne. 2012. "Slow Violence and the BP Oil Crisis in the Gulf of Mexico: Militarizing Environmental Catastrophe." *E-misférica* 9, nos. 1–2.

———. 2012. "Soft-Soaping Empire: Commodity Racism and Imperial Advertising." In *The Media Studies Reader*, edited by Laurie Ouellette, 227–40. New York: Routledge.

McCoy, Patricia, and Elizabeth Renuart. 2008. "The Legal Infrastructure of Subprime and Nontraditional Home Mortgages." In *Borrowing to Live: Consumer and Mortgage Credit Revisited*, edited by Nicolas Retsinas and Eric Belsky, 110–37. Washington, DC: Brookings Institute Press.

McDermott, Kathryn A. 1999. *Controlling Public Education: Localism versus Equity*. Lawrence: University Press of Kansas.

McKay, Adam, director. 2015. *The Big Short*. Paramount Pictures.

M. Davis and Co., Samantha Friedman, Angela Reynolds, Susan Scovill, Florence R. Brassier, Ron Campbell, and McKenzie Ballou. 2013. *An Estimate of Housing Discrimination Against Same-Sex Couples*. Office of Policy Development and Research. https://www.huduser.gov/portal/publications/fairhsg/discrim_samesex.html.

Melosh, Barbara. 1993. *Gender and American History Since 1890*. New York: Routledge.

Mendoza, Sonia, Allyssa Stephanie Rivera, and Helena Bjerring Hansen. 2019. "Re-racialization of Addiction and the Redistribution of Blame in the White Opioid Epidemic." *Medical Anthropology Quarterly* 33:242–62.

Menzel, Annie. 2010. "Crisis and Epistemologies of Ignorance." Paper presented at the American Political Science Association conference, Washington, DC, 2–5 September 2010.

Mettler, Suzanne. 2007. *Soldiers to Citizens*. New York: Oxford University Press.

———. 2011. *The Submerged State*. Chicago: University of Chicago Press.

———. 2018. *The Government-Citizen Disconnect*. New York: Russell Sage Foundation Press.

Meyer, David S. 1993. "Peace Protest and Policy." *Policy Studies Journal* 21:35–51.

———. 1993. "Protest Cycles and Political Process." *Political Research Quarterly* 46:451–79.

Meyer, David S., and Debra Minkoff. 2004. "Conceptualizing Political Opportunity." *Social Forces* 82:1457–92.

Michel, Jean-Baptiste, Yuan Kui Shen, Aviva Presser Aiden, Adrian Veres, Matthew K. Gray, Google Books Team, Joseph P. Pickett, Dale Hoiberg, Dan Clancy, Peter Norvig, Jon Orwant, Steven Pinker, Martin A. Nowak, and Erez Lieberman Aiden. 2011. "Quantitative Analysis of Culture Using Millions of Digitized Books." *Science* 331:176–82.

Michener, Jamila. 2018. *Fragmented Democracy: Medicaid, Federalism, and Unequal Politics*. New York: Cambridge University Press.

Michener, Jamila, and Margaret Teresa Brower. 2020. "What's Policy Got to Do with It? Race, Gender & Economic Inequality in the United States." *Daedalus* 149:100–18.

Milkis, Sidney M., ed. 2005. *The Great Society and the High Tide of Liberalism*. Amherst: University of Massachusetts Press.

Miller, Joanne, and Jon A. Krosnick. 2004. "Threat as a Motivator of Political Activism: A Field Experiment." *Political Psychology* 25:507–24.

Mink, Gwendolyn. 1990. "The Lady and the Tramp." In *Women, the State, and Welfare*, edited by Linda Gordon, 92–122. Madison: University of Wisconsin Press.

Mishel, Lawrence, Josh Bivens, Elise Gould, and Heidi Shierholz. 2012. *The State of Working America*. Ithaca, NY: Cornell University Press.

Mitchell, Bruce, and Juan Franco. 2018. "HOLC 'Redlining' Maps: The Persistent Structure of Segregation and Economic Inequality." National Community Reinvestment Coalition. https://ncrc.org/wp-content/uploads/dlm_uploads/2018/02/NCRC-Research-HOLC-10.pdf.

Mollenkopf, John H. 1983. *The Contested City*. Princeton, NJ: Princeton University Press.

Monahan, Brian A. 2010. *The Shock of the News*. New York: New York University Press.

Morgan, Kimberly J., and Andrea Louise Campbell. 2011. *The Delegated Welfare State: Medicare, Markets, and the Governance of Social Policy*. New York: Oxford University Press.

Morin, Edgar. 1976. "Pour une crisologie." *Communications* 25:149–63.

Mumford, Kevin. 2012. "Untangling Pathology: The Moynihan Report and Homosexual Damage, 1965–1975." *Journal of Policy History* 24:53–73.

Murakawa, Naomi. 2006. "The Racial Antecedents to Federal Sentencing Guidelines." *Roger Williams University Law Review: Symposium on Sentencing Rhetoric* 1:473–94.

———. 2014. *The First Civil Right*. New York: Oxford University Press.

Myerscough, Rhea. 2018. "Regulating the Predatory Economy: Inequality, Policy, and the Power of Organized Interests." Paper presented at the American Political Science Association conference, Boston, MA, 30 August–2 September 2018.

Nadasen, Premilla. 2005. *Welfare Warriors: The Welfare Rights Movement in the United States*. New York: Routledge.

Nair, Rukmini Bhaya, and Peter Ronald deSouza. 2020. *Keywords for India: A Conceptual Lexicon for the 21st Century*. New York: Bloomsbury Academic.

National Bureau of Economic Research. 2010. "Business Cycle Dating Committee." http://www.nber.org/cycles/sept2010.pdf.

National Public Radio, Robert Wood Johnson Foundation, and Harvard T. H. Chan School of Public Health. 2017. *Discrimination in America: Experiences*

and Views of LGBTQ Americans. https://legacy.npr.org/documents/2017/nov
/npr-discrimination-lgbtq-final.pdf.

National Training and Information Center. 1999. "Preying on Neighborhoods: Sub-prime Mortgage Lenders and Chicago Land Foreclosures." Chicago: National Training and Information Center.

Nawyn, Stephanie J. 2019. "Refugees in the United States and the Politics of Cri-sis." In *The Oxford Handbook of Migration Crises*, edited by Cecilia Menjívar, Marie Ruiz, and Immanuel Ness, 163–80. New York: Oxford University Press.

Nel, Philip, Lissa Paul, and Nina Christensen. 2021. *Keywords for Children's Litera-ture*. 2nd ed. New York: New York University Press.

Nelson, Barbara J. 1984. *Making an Issue of Child Abuse: Political Agenda Setting for Social Problems*. Chicago: University of Chicago Press.

Nelson, Laura K., Derek Burk, Marcel Knudsen, and Leslie McCall. 2018. "The Fu-ture of Coding: A Comparison of Hand-Coding and Three Types of Computer-Assisted Text Analysis Methods." *Sociological Methods & Research*, 27 May 2018.

Newman, Kathe. 2008. "The Perfect Storm: Contextualizing the Foreclosure Cri-sis." *Urban Geography* 29:750–54.

Newman, Kathe, and Elvin K. Wyly. 2004. "Geographies of Mortgage Market Seg-mentation: The Case of Essex County, New Jersey." *Housing Studies* 19 (1): 53–83.

Nixon, Robert. 2011. *Slow Violence and the Environmentalism of the Poor*. Cam-bridge, MA: Harvard University Press.

Noble, Safiya Umoja. 2018. *Algorithms of Oppression: How Search Engines Rein-force Racism*. New York: New York University Press.

Noguera, Pedro A. 1997. "Reconsidering the 'Crisis' of the Black Male in Amer-ica." *Social Justice* 24:147–64.

Norton, Bruce. 2013. "Economic Crises." *Rethinking Marxism* 25 (1): 10–22.

Norton, Eleanor Holmes. 1970. "For Sadie and Maude." In *Sisterhood Is Powerful: An Anthology of Writings from the Women's Liberation Movement*, edited by Robin Morgan, 397–404. New York: Random House.

Novkov, Julie. 2009. "Rights, Race, and Manhood." http://works.bepress.com/julie_novkov/6/

———. 2010. "Sacrifice and Civic Membership: Race, Gender, Sexuality and the Acquisition of Rights in Times of Crisis." Paper presented at the annual meet-ing of the Midwest Political Science Association, Chicago, IL, 22–25 April.

NRC (Nonprofit Research Collaborative). 2010. "November 2010 Fundraising Survey." http://foundationcenter.org/gainknowledge/research/pdf/nrc_survey 2010.pdf.

Nteta, Tatishe. 2013. "United We Stand? African Americans, Self-Interest, and Im-migration Reform." *American Politics Research* 41:147–72.

Obama, Barack. 2016. "Guns Are Our Shared Responsibility." *New York Times*, 8 January 2016. https://www.nytimes.com/2016/01/08/opinion/president-barack -obama-guns-are-our-shared-responsibility.html.

O'Brien, Jean M. 1997. *Dispossession by Degrees: Indian Land and Identity in Natick, Massachusetts, 1650–1790*. New York: Cambridge University Press.

O'Connor, Alice. 2001. *Poverty Knowledge: Social Science, Social Policy, and the Poor in Twentieth-Century U.S. History*. Princeton, NJ: Princeton University Press.

OED Online. n.d. "subprime, adj. and n." Oxford University Press, accessed 20 June 2018. https://www.oed.com/view/Entry/272160?redirectedFrom=subprime&.

Offe, Claus. 1976. "'Crisis of Crisis Management': Elements of a Political Crisis Theory." *International Journal of Politics* 6:29–67.

O'Keefe, Phil, Ken Westgate, and Ben Wisner. 1976. "Taking the Naturalness Out of Natural Disasters." *Nature* 260:566–67.

Oliver-Smith, Anthony. 1999. "What Is a Disaster? Anthropological Perspectives on a Persistent Question." In *The Angry Earth: Disasters in Anthropological Context*, edited by Anthony Oliver-Smith and Susanna M. Hoffman, 18–34. New York: Routledge.

Omoto, Allen M., Mark Snyder, and Justin D. Hackett. 2011. "Everyday Helping and Responses to Crises: A Model for Understanding Volunteerism." Working paper.

O'Neil, Cathy. 2016. *Weapons of Math Destruction: How Big Data Increases Inequality and Threatens Democracy*. New York: Crown.

Orfield, Gary, and Susan Eaton. 1996. *Dismantling Desegregation: The Quiet Reversal of* Brown v. Board of Education. New York: New Press.

Orwell, George. 1946. "Politics and the English Language." *Horizon* 13:252–65.

Ouellette, Laurie, and Jonathan Gray. 2017. *Keywords for Media Studies*. New York: New York University Press.

Paine, Thomas. [1776] 1819. *The American Crisis*. London: R. Carlisle.

Park, K-Sue. 2021. "Race, Innovation, and Financial Growth: The Example of Foreclosure." In *Histories of Racial Capitalism*, edited by Destin Jenkins and Justin Leroy, 27–51. New York: Columbia University Press.

Park, Lisa Sun-Hee. 2011. *Entitled to Nothing: The Struggle for Immigrant Health Care in the Age of Welfare Reform*. New York: New York University Press.

Parker, Christopher S. 2009. *Fighting for Democracy*. Princeton, NJ: Princeton University Press.

———. 2009. "When Politics Becomes Protest." *Journal of Politics* 71:113–31.

Parker, Christopher, and Matt Barreto. 2013. *Change They Can't Believe In: The Tea Party and Reactionary Politics in America*. Princeton, NJ: Princeton University Press.

Patterson, James T. 2010. *Freedom Is Not Enough: The Moynihan Report and America's Struggle over Black Family Life—from LBJ to Obama*. New York: Basic Books.

Pattillo, Mary. 2010. *Black on the Block: The Politics of Race and Class in the City*. Chicago: University of Chicago Press.

Pechenick, Eitan Adam, Christopher M. Danforth, and Peter Sheridan Dodds. 2015. "Characterizing the Google Books Corpus: Strong Limits to Inferences of Socio-Cultural and Linguistic Evolution." *Plos ONE* 10 (10): e0137041. doi .org/10.1371/journal.pone.0137041.

Peck, Jamie, and Adam Tickell. 2002. "Neoliberalizing Space." *Antipode* 34:380–404.

Pellow, David Naguib. 2009. "'We Didn't Get the First 500 Years Right, So Let's Work on the Next 500 Years': A Call for Transformative Analysis and Action." *Environmental Justice* 2:3–6.

Perrow, Charles. 1999. *Normal Accidents: Living with High-Risk Technologies.* Princeton, NJ: Princeton University Press.

Perry, Mark J. 2010. "The Great Mancession of 2008–2009." *Testimony before the House Ways and Means Committee Subcommittee on Income Security and Family Support on "Responsible Fatherhood Programs,"* 17 June 2010. http://www .aei.org/files/2010/06/17/GreatMancessionTestimony.pdf

Perry, Ronald W., and E. L. Quarantelli. 2005. *What Is a Disaster? New Answers to Old Questions.* Philadelphia: Xlibris.

Phillips, Sandra. 2012. "The Subprime Mortgage Calamity and the African American Woman." *Review of Black Political Economy* 39:227–37.

Pierson, Paul. 2004. *Politics in Time.* Princeton, NJ: Princeton University Press.

Pitts, Steven. 2011. "Research Brief: Black Workers and the Public Sector." University of California, Berkeley, Center for Labor Research and Education.

Piven, Frances Fox, and Richard Cloward. 1977. *Poor People's Movements.* New York: Vintage Books.

Poovey, Mary. 2008. *Genres of the Credit Economy: Mediating Value in Eighteenth- and Nineteenth-Century Britain.* Chicago: University of Chicago Press.

Posey, Patricia. 2020. "Lessons of Financial Institutions: Racialized Resource Provision, Regulatory Design, and Political Learning." Paper presented at the Workshop on the Politics of Credit and Debt, Trinity College, Hartford, CT, November 2020.

Posner, Richard. 2004. *Catastrophe.* New York: Oxford University Press.

Prasad, Monica. 2012. *The Land of Too Much: American Abundance and the Paradox of Poverty.* Cambridge, MA: Harvard University Press.

Prins, Nomi. 2010. *It Takes a Pillage: Behind the Bailouts, Bonuses, and Backroom Deals from Washington to Wall Street.* Hoboken: Wiley.

PRNewswire. 2007. "Department of Defense Issues Revised Statement About 'Don't Ask, Don't Tell.'" 26 June 2007.

Prowse, Gwen. 2022. "Three Essays on Racialized Disaster and Grassroots Resistance in U.S. Politics." PhD diss., Yale University.

Puar, Jasbir K. 2007. *Terrorist Assemblages.* Durham, NC: Duke University Press.

Purdie, Una. 2011. "90% of Jobs Created in US Last Year Went to Men." *Women's View on News.* http://www.womensviewsonnews.org/2011/03/90-of-jobs-created -in-us-last-year-went-to-men/.

Quadagno, Jill. 1996. *The Color of Welfare: How Racism Undermined the War on Poverty*. New York: Oxford University Press.

Quarantelli, E. L. 1998. *What Is a Disaster? Perspectives on the Question*. London: Routledge.

Quinn, Sarah L. 2020. *American Bonds: How Credit Markets Shaped a Nation*. Princeton, NJ: Princeton University Press.

Raboy, Marc, and Bernard Degenais. 1992. *Media, Crisis, and Democracy*. Thousand Oaks, CA: Sage.

Radford, Gail. 1996. *Modern Housing for America: Policy Struggles in the New Deal Era*. Chicago: University of Chicago Press.

Rainwater, Lee, and William C. Yancey. 1967. *The Moynihan Report and the Politics of Controversy*. Cambridge, MA: MIT Press.

Reed, Adolph. 2005. "The 2004 Election in Perspective: The Myth of 'Cultural Divide' and the Triumph of Neoliberal Ideology." *American Quarterly* 57:1–15.

Reed, Touré. 2020. *Toward Freedom: The Case against Race Reductionism*. New York: Verso.

Reese, Ellen. 2014. "Defending Homes and Making Banks Pay: California's Home Defenders League." *Social Justice* 40 (3): 81–98.

Reinhardt, Carmen, and Kenneth Rogoff. 2010. *This Time Is Different: Eight Centuries of Financial Folly*. Princeton, NJ: Princeton University Press.

Remes, Jacob A. C., and Andy Horowitz, eds. 2021. "Introducing Critical Disaster Studies." In *Critical Disaster Studies: New Perspectives on Disaster, Risk, Vulnerability, and Resilience*, 1–8. Philadelphia: University of Pennsylvania Press.

Richey, Sean, and J. Benjamin Taylor. 2020. "Google Books Ngrams and Political Science: Two Validity Tests for a Novel Data Source." *PS: Political Science & Politics* 53:72–77.

Ritter, Gretchen. 2007. "Gender and Politics over Time." *Politics & Gender* 3:386–97.

Roberts, Dorothy. 1997. *Killing the Black Body*. New York: Vintage.

Robin, Corey. 2004. *Fear: The History of a Political Idea*. New York: Oxford University Press.

Rodgers, Daniel. 1987. *Contested Truths: Keywords in Politics*. New York: Basic Books.

Rodríguez, Havidán, William Donner, and Joseph E. Trainor, eds. 2017. *Handbook of Disaster Research*. New York: Springer International.

Roitman, Janet. 2013. *Anti-Crisis*. Durham, NC: Duke University Press.

Romero, Adam P., Shoshana K. Goldberg, and Luis A. Vasquez. 2020. *LGBT People and Housing Affordability, Discrimination, and Homelessness*. Los Angeles: Williams Institute, UCLA School of Law. https://williamsinstitute.law.ucla.edu/publications/lgbt-housing-instability/.

Romine, Scott, and Jennifer Rae Greeson. 2016. *Keywords for Southern Studies*. Athens: University of Georgia Press.

Rosenthal, Uriel, Michael Charles, and Paul Hart. 1989. *Coping with Crises: The Management of Disasters, Riots and Terrorism*. Springfield, MA: Charles C. Thomas.

Rossiter, Clinton. [1948] 2005. *Constitutional Dictatorship: Crisis Government in the Modern Democracies*. New York: Transaction.

Rothstein, Richard. 2017. *The Color of Law: A Forgotten History of How Our Government Segregated America*. New York: Liveright.

Rozario, Kevin. 2007. *The Culture of Calamity: Disaster and the Making of Modern America*. Chicago: University of Chicago Press.

Rugh, Jacob S., Len Albright, and Douglas S. Massey. 2015. "Race, Space, and Cumulative Disadvantage: A Case Study of the Subprime Lending Collapse." *Social Problems* 62:186–218.

Rugh, Jacob, and Douglas Massey. 2010. "Racial Segregation and the American Foreclosure Crisis." *American Sociological Review* 75:629–51.

Runciman, David. 2013. *The Confidence Trap: A History of Democracy in Crisis from World War I to the Present*. Princeton, NJ: Princeton University Press.

Ryan, William. [1971] 1979. *Blaming the Victim*. New York: Vintage.

Saldin, Robert P. 2004. "Executive Power and the Constitution in Times of Crisis." *White House Studies* 4:489–504.

Sales, Stephen M. 1973. "Threat as a Factor in Authoritarianism: An Analysis of Archival Data." *Journal of Personality and Social Psychology* 28:44–57.

Sanger, David. 2009. *The Inheritance: The World Obama Confronts and the Challenges to American Power*. New York: Broadway Books.

Sarat, Austin, and Lezaun, Javier, eds. 2009. *Catastrophe: Law, Politics, and the Humanitarian Impulse*. Amherst: University of Massachusetts Press.

Satter, Beryl. 2009. *Family Properties: Race, Real Estate, and the Exploitation of Black Urban America*. New York: St. Martin's Press.

Schattschneider, E. E. 1960. *The Semisovereign People*. New York: Holt, Rinehart and Winston.

Schlund-Vilas, Cathy, Linda Trinh Võ, and K. Scott Wang. 2015. *Keywords for Asian American Studies*. New York: New York University Press.

Schmit, Julie. 2012. "Foreclosures Hit a Five-Year Low." *USA Today*, 11 October 2012. https://www.usatoday.com/story/money/business/2012/10/11 /foreclosures -five-year-low/1624719/.

Schneider, Anne Larason, and Helen Ingram. 1997. *Policy Design for Democracy*. Lawrence: University Press of Kansas.

Schnell, Karen, and Frauke Callaghan. 2001. "Assessing the Democratic Debate: How the News Media Frame Elite Policy Discourse." *Political Communication* 18:183–212.

Schuck, Peter. 2009. "Crisis and Catastrophe in Science, Law, and Politics: Mapping the Terrain." In *Catastrophe: Law, Politics, and the Humanitarian Impulse*, edited by Austin Sarat and Javier Lezaun, 19–59. Amherst: University of Massachusetts Press.

Scott, James C. 1992. *Domination and the Arts of Resistance: Hidden Transcripts.* New Haven, CT: Yale University Press.

Seamster, Louise and Raphaël Charron-Chénier. 2017. "Predatory Inclusion and Education Debt: A New Approach to the Growing Racial Wealth Gap." *Social Currents* 4:199–207.

Sen, Maya. 2012. "Quantifying Discrimination: Exploring the Role of Race and Gender in the Subprime Lending Crisis." Working paper, Harvard University, Cambridge, MA. https://j.mp/2ozMiIP.

Serres, Michel. 2014. *Times of Crisis: What the Financial Crisis Revealed and How to Reinvent Our Lives and Future.* New York: Bloomsbury.

Sewell, William H. 1996. "Historical Events as Transformations of Structures: Inventing Revolution at the Bastille." *Theory and Society* 25:841–81.

Shachar, Carmel, Tess Wise, Gali Katznelson, and Andrea Louise Campbell. 2020. "Criminal Justice or Public Health: A Comparison of the Representation of the Crack Cocaine and Opioid Epidemics in the Media." *Journal of Health Politics, Policy and Law* 45:211–39.

Shank, J. B. 2008. "Crisis: A Useful Category of Post-Social Scientific Historical Analysis?" *American Historical Review* 113 (4): 1090–99.

Shea, Daniel M., and Alex Sproveri. 2012. "The Rise and Fall of Nasty Politics in America." *PS: Political Science & Politics* 45:416–21.

Shiller, Robert. 2005. *Irrational Exuberance.* 2nd ed. Princeton, NJ: Princeton University Press.

Shilts, Randy. 1987. *And the Band Played On.* New York: St. Martin's Press.

Simons, Helen. 1995. "Cairo: Repackaging Population Control." *International Journal of Health Services* 25:559–566.

Sinnock, Bonnie. "Hope Now to Suspend Operations, Citing Coronavirus Restrictions." *National Mortgage News*, 1 July 2020. https://www.nationalmortgagenews.com/news/hope-now-to-suspend-operations-citing-coronavirus-restrictions.

Skocpol, Theda. 1992. *Protecting Soldiers and Mothers.* Cambridge, MA: Harvard University Press.

———. 2002. "Will 9/11 and the War on Terror Revitalize American Civic Democracy?" *PS: Political Science and Politics* 35:537–40.

Skocpol, Theda, Kenneth Finegold, and Michael Goldfield. 1990. "Explaining New Deal Labour Policy." *American Political Science Review* 84:1297–1315.

Smith, Nicola. 2016. "Toward a Queer Political Economy of Crisis." In *Scandalous Economics: Gender and the Politics of Financial Crises,* edited by Aida A. Hozić and Jacqui True, 231–47. New York: Oxford University Press.

Solnit, Rebecca. 2009. *A Paradise Built in Hell.* New York: Viking.

SoRelle, Mallory E. 2020. *Democracy Declined: The Failed Politics of Consumer Financial Protection.* Chicago: University of Chicago Press.

Squires, Catherine. 2011. "Bursting the Bubble: A Case Study of Counterframing in the Editorial Pages." *Critical Studies in Media Communication* 28:30–49.

Squires, Gregory D. 1994. *Capital and Communities in Black and White: The Intersections of Race, Class, and Uneven Development.* Albany: State University of New York Press.

Stack, Carol B. 1975. *All Our Kin: Strategies for Survival in a Black Community.* New York: Basic Books.

Starkman, Dean. 2014. *The Watchdog That Didn't Bark: The Financial Crisis and the Disappearance of Investigative Journalism.* New York: Columbia University Press.

Starn, Randolph. 1971. "Historians and 'Crisis.'" *Past and Present* 52:3–22.

St. Cyr, Maureen R. 2011. "Gender, Maternity Leave, and Home Financing: A Critical Analysis of Mortgage Lending Discrimination Against Pregnant Women." *University of Pennsylvania Journal of Law and Social Change* 15:109–41.

Stebbins, Phillip E. 1971. "Truman and the Seizure of Steel: A Failure in Communication." *Historian* 34:1–21.

Steinberg, Ted. 2006. *Acts of God: The Unnatural History of Natural Disasters in America.* 2nd ed. Oxford: Oxford University Press.

Stephens-Dougan, LaFleur. 2020. *Race to the Bottom: How Racial Appeals Work in American Politics.* Chicago: University of Chicago Press.

———. 2022. "White Americans' Reactions to Racial Disparities in COVID-19." *American Political Science Review* FirstView: 1–8.

Sterett, Susan. 2009. "New Orleans Everywhere: Bureaucratic Accountability and Housing Policy after Katrina." In *Catastrophe: Law, Politics, and the Humanitarian Impulse,* edited by Austin Sarat and Javier Lezaun, 83–115. Amherst: University of Massachusetts Press.

Sterett, Susan, and Laura Mateczun. n.d. "Disaster Cascades in Court: Governance Gaps and Familiar Pathways." Unpublished manuscript.

Stoler, Ann Laura. 2002. "Colonial Archives and the Arts of Governance." *Archival Science* 2:87–109.

Stone, Deborah A. 1989. "Causal Stories and the Formation of Policy Agendas." *Political Science Quarterly* 104:281–300.

Stout, Noelle. 2019. *Dispossessed: How Predatory Bureaucracy Foreclosed on the American Middle Class.* Berkeley: University of California Press.

Strach, Patricia. 2007. *All in the Family.* Palo Alto, CA: Stanford University Press.

———. 2016. *Hiding Politics in Plain Sight: Cause Marketing, Corporate Influence, and Breast Cancer Policymaking.* New York: Oxford University Press.

Strach, Patricia, and Virginia Sapiro. 2011. "Campaigning for Congress in the '9/11' Era." *American Politics Research* 39:264–90.

Strolovitch, Dara Z. 1998. "Playing Favorites: Public Attitudes toward Race- and Gender-Targeted Anti-discrimination Policy." *National Women's Studies Association Journal* 10:27–53.

———. 2004. "Politics and Federal Policy." In *The Encyclopedia of Poverty and Social Welfare,* edited by Gwendolyn Mink and Alice O'Connor, 548–52. Santa Barbara: ABC-Clio.

———. 2006. "Do Interest Groups Represent the Disadvantaged? Advocacy at the Intersections of Race, Class, and Gender." *Journal of Politics* 68:894–910.

———. 2007. *Affirmative Advocacy: Race, Class, and Gender in Interest Group Politics.* Chicago: University of Chicago Press.

———. 2013. "Of Mancessions and Hecoveries: Race, Gender, and the Political Construction of Economic Crises and Recoveries." *Perspectives on Politics* 13:167–76.

———. 2014. "Advocacy in Hard Times." In *Nonprofit Advocacy*, edited by Steven R. Smith, Yutaka Tsujinaka, and Robert Pekkanen, 137–69. Baltimore: Johns Hopkins University Press.

Stuart, Guy. 2003. *Discriminating Risk: The US Mortgage Lending Industry in the Twentieth Century.* Ithaca, NY: Cornell University Press.

Sturm, Albert L. 1949. "Emergencies and the Presidency." *Journal of Politics* 11:121–44.

Sugrue, Tom. 1996. *The Origins of the Urban Crisis: Race and Inequality in Postwar Detroit.* Princeton, NJ: Princeton University Press.

Sulkin, Tracy. 2005. *Issue Politics in Congress.* New York: Cambridge University Press.

Sullivan, Shannon. 2007. "White Ignorance and Colonial Oppression: Or, Why I Know So Little about Puerto Rico." In *Race and Epistemologies of Ignorance*, edited by Shannon Sullivan and Nancy Tuana, 153–71. Albany: SUNY Press.

Sun, Hua, and Lei Gao. 2019. "Lending Practices to Same-Sex Borrowers." *Proceedings of the National Academy of Sciences* 116:9293–9302.

Sundstrom, William. 1992. "Last Hired, First Fired? Unemployment and Urban Black Workers during the Great Depression." *Journal of Economic History* 52:415–29.

Swarts, Heidi J. 2008. *Organizing Urban America: Secular and Faith-Based Progressive Movements.* Minneapolis: University of Minnesota Press.

Taylor, Keeanga-Yamahtta. 2019. *Race for Profit: How Banks and the Real Estate Industry Undermined Black Homeownership.* Chapel Hill: University of North Carolina Press.

Temkin, Kenneth, Jennifer E. H. Johnson, and Diane Levy. 2002. *Subprime Markets, the Role of GSEs, and Risk-Based Pricing.* Prepared for US Department of Housing and Urban Development Office of Policy Development and Research.

Thrasher, Steven. 2022. *The Viral Underclass: the Human Toll when Inequality and Disease Collide.* New York: Caledon Books.

Thurston, Chloe. 2018. *At the Boundaries of Homeownership: Credit, Discrimination, and the American State.* New York: Cambridge University Press.

Thurston, Chloe, and Emily Zackin. 2020. "The Missing Movement: Consumer Debtors and Their Advocates in the Twentieth Century." Paper presented at the Workshop on the Politics of Credit and Debt, Trinity College, Hartford, CT, November 2020.

Thylstrup, Nanna Bonde, Daniela Agostinho, and Annie Ring. 2021. *Uncertain Archives: Critical Keywords for Big Data*. Cambridge, MA: MIT Press.

Tierney, Kathleen. 2019. *Disasters: A Sociological Approach*. Medford, MA: John Wiley and Sons.

Tiger, Rebecca. 2017. "Race, Class, and the Framing of Drug Epidemics." *Contexts* 16:46–51.

Tillmon, Johnnie. 1972. "Welfare Is a Women's Issue," *Ms.*, Spring 1972.

Treichler, Paula. 1999. *How to Have Theory in an Epidemic*. Durham, NC: Duke University Press.

Tuchman, Gaye. 1978. *Making the News: A Study in the Construction of Reality*. Ann Arbor: University of Michigan Press.

UN Women and David Snyder. 2020. "COVID-19 and the Care Economy: Immediate Action and Structural Transformation for a Gender-Responsive Recovery." https://www.unwomen.org/en/digital-library/publications/2020/06/policy-brief -covid-19-and-the-care-economy#view.

US Congress. House Committee on Banking, Housing, and Urban Affairs. 1993. Hearing on "Adding Injury to Injury: Credit on the Fringe." 4 February 1993.

———. Subcommittee on Consumer Credit and Insurance. 1994. Hearing on "H.R. 3153, the Home Equity Protection Act of 1993." 103rd Congress. 22 March 1994.

US Congress. House Committee on Financial Services. Subcommittee on Housing and Community Opportunity. 2006. Field Hearing on "Community Solutions for the Prevention and Management of Foreclosures." 23 August 2006.

US Congress. House-Senate Joint Economic Committee. 2007. "Momentum Builds for Schumer's Call for Additional Federal Funds to Avert Subprime Foreclosure Crisis."

US Congress. Senate Committee on Banking and Currency. Subcommittee on Financial Institutions. 1968. Hearing on "Financial Institutions and the Urban Crisis." 30 September and 1–4 October 1968.

US Congress. Senate Committee on Banking, Housing, and Urban Affairs. 1993. Hearing on "The Home Ownership and Equity Protection Act of 1993—S. 924." 19 May 1993.

———. Subcommittee on Financial Institutions and Regulatory Relief and the Subcommittee on Housing Opportunity and Community Development. 1997. Hearing on "Problem Surrounding the Mortgage Origination Process." 15 July 1997.

———. 2001. Hearing on "Predatory Mortgage Lending: The Problem, Impact, and Responses." 26 and 27 July 2001.

———. 2007. Hearing on "Mortgage Market Turmoil: Causes and Consequences." 22 March 2007.

US Congress. Senate Committee on the District of Columbia. 1970. Hearing on "Crime in the National Capital Part 12: Narcotics—Crime Crisis in the Washington Area." 13 February; 11 June; 6 and 22 October 1970.

US Congress. Senate Committee on Foreign Aid Expenditures. 1965. Hearing on "Population Crisis." 29 June; 9, 21, and 28 July; 10, 11, 17, 18, and 24 August 1965.

US Department of Housing and Urban Development, Office of Policy Development and Research. 1979. *Women and Mortgage Credit: An Annotated Bibliography*.

———. 2000. *Subprime Lending Report: Unequal Burden in Baltimore: Income and Racial Disparities in Subprime Lending*. https://www.huduser.gov/Publica tions/pdf/baltimore.pdf.

———. 2010. *Report to Congress on the Root Causes of the Foreclosure Crisis*.

US Department of Housing and Urban Development, and US Department of Treasury. 2000. *Curbing Predatory Home Mortgage Lending: A Joint Report*.

US Department of Labor. 1965. *The Negro Family: The Case for National Action*.

US National Advisory Commission on Civil Disorders, and Otto Kerner. 1968. *Report of the National Advisory Commission on Civil Disorders*. Washington, DC: GPO.

US Policy Agendas Project at the University of Texas at Austin. 2017. www.com parativeagendas.net.

Usher, Nikki. 2014. *Making News at the* New York Times. Ann Arbor: University of Michigan Press.

Valentino, Nick, Vince Hutchings, and Ismail White. 2002. "Cues that Matter: How Political Ads Prime Racial Attitudes during Campaigns." *American Political Science Review* 96:75–90.

van Dijk, Teun. 1997. "What Is Political Discourse Analysis?" *Belgian Journal of Linguistics* 11:11–52.

Vázquez-Arroyo, Antonio. 2012. "The Antinomies of Violence and Catastrophe: Structures, Orders, and Agents." *New Political Science* 34 (2): 211–21.

———. 2013. "How Not to Learn from Catastrophe: Critical Theory and the Catastrophization of Political Life." *Political Theory* 41:738–65.

———. 2020. "In the Shadows of Coronavirus." *Critical Times* 3. https://ctjournal .org/2020/04/29/in-the-shadows-of-coronavirus/.

Wallace, Michele. [1978] 1994. *Black Macho and the Myth of the Superwoman*. New York: Verso Press.

Warren, Elizabeth, and Amelia Warren Tyagi. 2003. *The Two-Income Trap: Why Middle-Class Parents Are Going Broke*. New York: Basic Books.

Wedeen, Lisa. 2002. "Conceptualizing Culture: Possibilities for Political Science." *American Political Science Review* 94:713–28.

White, Iain, and Gauri Nandedkar. 2021. "The Housing Crisis as an Ideological Artefact: Analysing How Political Discourse Defines, Diagnoses, and Responds." *Housing Studies* 36:213–34.

Whyte, Kyle. 2020. "Against Crisis Epistemology." In *The Routledge Handbook of Critical Indigenous Studies*, edited by Brendan Hokowhitu, Aileen Moreton-Robinson, Linda Tuhiwai-Smith, Chris Andersen, and Steve Larkin, 52–62. New York: Routledge.

Williams, Christopher J., and Gregory Shufeldt. 2020. "How Identity Influences Public Attitudes Towards the US Federal Government: Lessons from the European Union." *Acta Politica*, 11 June 2020.

Williams, Joan, and Allison Anna Tait. 2011. "'Mancession' or 'Momcession?': Good Providers, a Bad Economy, and Gender Discrimination." *Chicago Kent Law Review* 86 (2): 857.

Williams, Raymond. [1976] 2015. *Keywords: A Vocabulary of Culture and Society.* New ed. New York: Oxford University Press.

Williams, Rhonda Y. 2004. *The Politics of Public Housing: Black Women's Struggles against Urban Inequality.* New York: Oxford University Press.

Wilson, Sondra. 1999. *The Crisis Reader: Stories, Poetry, and Essays from the N.A.A.C.P.'s Crisis Magazine.* New York: Modern Library Harlem Renaissance.

Winling, LaDale C., and Todd M. Michney. 2021. "The Roots of Redlining: Academic, Governmental, and Professional Networks in the Making of the New Deal Lending Regime." *Journal of American History* 108:42–69.

Wise, Tess. 2020. "Social Meanings of Credit/Debt for America's Precarious Middle Class." Paper presented at the Workshop on the Politics of Credit and Debt, Trinity College, Hartford, CT, November 2020.

Wisner, Ben, Piers Blaikie, Piers M. Blaikie, Terry Cannon, and Ian Davis. 2004. *At Risk: Natural Hazards, People's Vulnerability and Disasters.* New York: Routledge.

Wolbrecht, Christina. *American Political Party Platforms: 1948–2008.*

Wyly, Elvin, and C. S. Ponder. 2011. "Gender, Age, and Race in Subprime America." *Housing Policy Debate* 21:529–64.

Younes, Nadja, and Ulf-Dietrich Reips. 2019. "Guideline for Improving the Reliability of Google Ngram Studies: Evidence from Religious Terms." *PLoS ONE* 14 (3): e0213554.

Zechmeister, Elizabeth J., and Jennifer L. Merolla. 2009. *Democracy at Risk: How Terrorist Threats Affect the Public.* Chicago: University of Chicago Press.

Zelizer, Julian E., ed. 2016. *The Kerner Report: The National Advisory Commission on Civil Disorders.* Princeton, NJ: Princeton University Press.

Index